STRANGE FIRE

AN OCCAM'S EDGE NOVEL

With much love to my parents, family, and G-d.
I hope I honor you with this work.
You taught me to reach beyond...

First published in Israel, 2025
by Rishona Studios

ISBN: 978-965-93234-1-8
Second Edition
© T/R Ellison 2025

The moral right of T/R Ellison to be identified as the author of this work has been asserted in accordance with the Copyright, Designs, and Patents Act of 1988.

All rights reserved Except for brief quotations in critical articles or reviews, no part of this book may be reproduced in any manner without prior written permission from the publisher.

Unless otherwise indicated, all the names, characters, businesses, places, events and incidents in this book are either the product of the author's imagination or used in a fictitious manner. Any resemblance to actual persons, living or dead, or actual events is purely coincidental.

Although the publisher and the author have made every effort to ensure that the information in this book was correct at press time and while this publication is designed to provide accurate information in regard to the subject matter covered, the publisher and the author assume no responsibility for errors, inaccuracies, omissions, or any other inconsistencies herein and hereby disclaim any liability to any party for any loss, damage, or disruption caused by errors or omissions, whether such errors or omissions result from negligence, accident, or any other cause.

Design by: BenHerskowitz.com

Tree of Life/Flower of Life Graphic by Fred the Oyster, CC BY-SA 4.0
https://commons.wikimedia.org/wiki/File:Tree-of-Life_Flower-of-Life_Stage.svg

https://TamiEllison.com

Reality is merely an illusion, albeit a very persistent one.
— Albert Einstein

It is never too late to be what you might have been.
— George Eliot

The limits of the possible can only be defined by going beyond them into the impossible.
— Arthur C. Clarke

I don't speak because I have the power to speak;
I speak because I don't have the power to remain silent.
— Rabbi A.Y. Kook

> I have set watchmen upon thy walls, O Jerusalem, they shall never hold their peace day nor night: Ye that are the LORD'S remembrancers, take ye no rest, And give Him no rest, till He will establish, and till He make Jerusalem a praise in the earth.
> – Isaiah 62:6-7

PROLOGUE

Dead? Not dead? Twenty-eight-year-old Joshua E. Katz wondered whether there might be a better middle-ground alternative between the absolutes. One minute, he was underground in the bowels of Zedekiah's Cave trying to wrestle the Deadman's switch out of the suicide bomber's hand, and in the next he found himself standing on the eastern ramparts of *Har HaBayit* — the Temple Mount.

And he wasn't alone.

If there was indeed safety in numbers, then Joshua took comfort in the sheer number of "others" with him. Setting aside the obvious question of "What in the hell was going on?" he thought of asking those "standing" with him, but they seemed oblivious to his sudden appearance amongst their ranks. Instead, their attention was focused on the eastern horizon, at the figure standing at the top of the 3,000-year-old Mount of Olives Cemetery.

While a firm believer in empirical data, checking to see if his head was still attached to his body, fell into the TMI category... *way* Too Much Information. While Joshua had the sensation of a body, it could, nonetheless, be a red herring, a phantom limb phenomenon only on a grander scale. If his proprioceptors were fooling him as part of some god-awful cosmic joke with the punchline, "Look ma, no hands!" or anything else then the *shahid* had succeeded in blowing himself up and taking Joshua along with him. Not quite ready to confront that particular misery, Joshua cautiously looked around him, to his left, right, and then upward at a row of "others" manning the Temple Mount's upper ramparts' tier. Logic dictated, that if he perceived them, then he *could* also perceive himself. Was he the same as them, or different? Curiosity is the devil's tool and apparently, he wasn't immune. Cautiously, he looked down to where he perceived his body should be, only there wasn't one. Instead, he was confronted with a shimmer that distorted his former self-space and his ability to discern who or what he was. Joshua thought of asking those around him, but they still seemed intent on watching the figure on the horizon.

If you can't beat them, you might as well join them, he thought, and then turned his attention to the figure who paradoxically seemed to be standing still, while simultaneously moving closer. That, or they were moving closer to him in yet another Twilight Zone anomaly requiring explanation. Interestingly, no one else seemed disturbed by their state of being, or non-being, but were intently focused on the figure on a straight-line approach through *Har HaZei'tim* — the final resting place for over 150,000 people.

The Mount of Olives cemetery easily ranked among the hottest properties in all of Jerusalem at an average cost of $30,000 for a standard 7' by 2.5' plot of land, a bargain price for securing front-row seats to the Redemption. Jewish tradition held that these souls would be among the first to be resurrected with the coming of the long-awaited Messiah, while the rest of the world would be tunneling through bedrock to join the *Techiyat HaMei'tim* party, the Resurrection of the Dead *sans* the Zombie Apocalypse or Walking Dead nightmare scenarios. Joshua's parents and grandparents were nestled into adjoining plots on the middle tier, near the "Path of the *Kohanim*" with a scenic view of the Old City walls. With his current proximity to his own final resting place, plot number 520, next to his mom Shoshana "Shosh" Katz, maybe, *this* was a waiting room, an antechamber for souls, before being granted entry through the pearly gates. Joshua was fast reconciling himself to being on the "dead" side of the equation but if *this* was the queue shouldn't he have been given a number or ticket to effect an orderly entry into the afterlife.

Cautiously, he ventured another look at those around him. While he couldn't place his finger, or any other body part, on it, there was something oddly familiar about the others, all of them. The intangible something defied explanation as their individual, semi-incorporeal markers became confluent with one another, and with him, flowing together, conjoined into a single entity. He was reminded of the uber-large organisms on the planet, an 8 square kilometer grove of Aspen trees in Utah known as Pando; its biomass outranked an 8.9 square kilometer mushroom "patch" in Oregon, to earn its status in the Guinness Book of World Records. Joshua figured that the energetic convergence of human souls would easily outrank the gargantuan fungi and plants, or at least give them a run for their money for the World Record title.

While there was still an abundance of confounding variables all factoring into his trying to understand his new state of being, Joshua's anxiety was checkmated by an overwhelming Spidey sense of home. It would seem that these connected souls co-existed with him, in life and death, transcending all boundaries. There, emerging from the shimmer was a familiar pattern, a ball and stick construction arranged in the classic *Kabbalistic* Tree of Life symbol. While the hierarchical Tree of Life structure was recognizable, depicting the ten *Sefirot* — the ethereal emanations through which G-d is revealed — it was nonetheless different. This conformation dynamically pulsed with soul sparks in a vibrational dance across the paired attributes, nodes, and bridges, lighting up the Tree of Life like a Christmas tree.

In completing the thought, understanding dawned as Joshua realized he wasn't seeing just one Tree of Life, but rather he, and the others, were part of multiple interconnected Trees of Life. Their multidimensional confluences of conjoined soul sparks linked through the various nodes and branches, connecting the different *Sefirot* in a swirling continuum of rainbow-colored hues. Each of the ten Divine Attributes was individually represented within the electromagnetic spectrum of visible light frequencies; the energetic pulses, however, were interwoven, emitting the breath of light and life. Alive, even in this interspace. But while his soul might have survived the *shahid's* death wish, apparently he had not.

He wasn't surprised that the Tree of Life figured prominently in this other-worldly experience. For as long as Joshua could remember, he'd been fascinated by the Tree of Life. At age six, he'd first seen a colorful Tree of Life on a needlepoint pillow his *Oma* Rachel made… her last needlepoint. Even in the two-dimensional design, the arrangement of colorful threads hinted at the structure's hidden dimensionality. Compelled by a borderline obsessive-compulsive drive, he first tried building a replica with marshmallows and spaghetti pasta before moving on to popsicle sticks, then to a 3-D model using Zome® tools to add dimensionality to the structure, before finally graduating at age eleven to wireframes using a Computer-Assisted Design (CAD) program. But none of his representations compared to this multi-dimensional reality, and none had ever captured the shimmering manifestation he now recognized as *his* own soul root. In their pure essence, he knew them all. But considering the "others" hadn't bothered to acknowledge his presence, Joshua couldn't help but wonder if he knew them, then why didn't they know him as well, or at least say something to welcome the new guy?

The visual display was enough to occupy his thoughts, wondering if he'd ever seen anything resembling this depiction. In developing *HaMikdash3.0*, Hazon Labs' premier virtual reality mecca built around the Third Jewish Temple, the *Beit HaMikdash*, he'd researched every variation on the *Kabbalistic* Tree of Life theme or so he thought. More recently, Joshua had delved into the unity of relationships between the "Seed of Life," "Flower of Life," and "Tree of Life" trying to uncover their co-related mysteries. Not surprisingly, this new version of the Tree of Life pulsed among the flowers and seeds.

He theorized that if a life's cycle could be expressed within the context of seed, flower, and tree, the age-old chicken and egg conundrum could be applied; namely, which came first the seed, the flower, or the tree? In a transcendent algorithm infused with mystical, spiritual, and religious symbolism, the Flower of Life was seen in elaborated repeating patterns in nature, art, architecture, and science, and which embedded both the Seeds and Trees of Life. In his mind's eye, Joshua could see a different kind of confluence, a composite image where seeds, flowers, and trees were extant as a single unit. While each was singular and self-sustaining, it was also part of a greater whole. The circular structure could be joined with others in an ever-expanding array of Flowers of Life. The incomplete flowers' edges hinted at their becoming… of being part of something other than, greater than, the sum of the individual parts and extending beyond any one circumscribed Flower of Life. The Tree of Life could be placed along the central axis, and others could be rotated around the flower's six-fold symmetry, interweaving the *Sefirot* of one soul life with another… a continuum of interconnected *Sefirot*. The pattern could be repeated, connecting seeds, flowers, and trees, and where there was no sum to its completion except, if possible, wherever Infinity might be found.

The Gestalt of each Flower of Life could be considered complete, in and of itself, but the construct was also incomplete as the parts of one belonged to, and with, another. Within the infinitely connected circles there was a continuum of interlocking Flowers of Life within an array of multiplexed, multi-dimensional Trees of Life in all its resplendent plurality; a dynamic structure reflecting the ultimate G-d reference as the *Ain Sof*. Without end. Unfathomable. Despite the unknowns surrounding his present condition and his "if alive" status, Joshua couldn't help but wonder if he had time to update the Tree of Life depictions in HaMikdash3.0 to reflect this new multi-dimensional vision. *If he had time*, the phrase made him smile. *What was he thinking?*

Only one question remained, was he still alive or dead? He tried to recall the last moments when he fought with the *shahid* devil. The suicide bomber, who had been dressed in the Border Police uniform, spewed venomous oxymoronic, antithetical *Alla-hu Akbars* enough times to wake the proverbial dead, and which apparently he had, at least on some level. The diatribe left little doubt about the *shahid's* intentions or his affiliation. But what role the *shahid* played in this particular drama remained a critical unknown; or, for that matter, his role in *this*, whatever *this* was. Ironically, the question of his role in the so-called bigger picture, the "why" of his being had consumed him, driving Joshua to create manifest the third *Beit HaMikdash* as HaMikdash3.0, albeit a virtual Holy Temple.

He believed HaMikdash3.0 would be heralded for its novel, peaceful resolution to the ongoing Temple Mount rights and ownership disputes. In Joshua's mind by virtually incarnating the Third Temple, the current Temple Mount fixtures, namely the *al-Aqsa Mosque* and Dome of the Rock, could remain intact. HaMikdash3.0 could achieve a means-to-an-end solution without needing to invoke any non-compete clauses. Joshua, or rather HaMikdasah3.0, found champions among religious and secular leaders from the Jewish, Muslim, and Christian communities — leaders who not only believed that the Abrahamic religions could coexist but that to truly fulfill G-d's purpose in creating mankind, they *must* coexist. He found initial support among those driven by a shared belief in one G-d; a belief that triumphed over the hate-filled rhetoric of the extremists desperate to keep the long-prophesized union mired in war and politics. Rabbi Dr. Yakov Nagen of the Ohr Torah Interfaith Center, sees an opportunity to develop a narrative founded on the Oneness of G-d, freed from self-interest and the distortions of identity-centered politics, as the springboard for a "renewed paradigm for a shared future," a shared narrative that even made space for an actual *Beit HaMikdash* to be built on the Temple Mount. But it would take a miracle to challenge the bedrock of hate and mistrust nurtured by fundamentalists and which by their rhetoric denied a key fundamental, a foundational principle of the Abrahamic religions… a belief in one G-d.

While heralded on one hand, Joshua also found himself reviled by an odd-bedfellow mix of Jewish, Christian, and Muslim clerics from across extremist camps, united in labeling 3.0 an abomination, blasphemous, the work of the Devil, with a capital D. Ironically, in being the object of their contempt and Hellfire damnations, he also became a great unifier. Maybe one day, they, too, would gratefully acknowledge his contributions even if they were offered in epitaphs written about him.

At times though, even he wondered whether they were justified in challenging his motives and driving ambition… his need to bring HaMikdash3.0 to the world. Was it only a self-centered, self-serving mission that cast G-d into a secondary role, relegating Him to the backseat of a semi-autonomous vehicle fueled by Joshua's own hubris and arrogance? Had he ever sought guidance, even permission? Had he lost sight of the One?

When asked about the genesis and mission of HaMikdash3.0, Joshua offered only well-rehearsed responses, ones suitable for public consumption but in reality far from the truth. Real estate disputes aside, he cited the popularity of vegetarianism and veganism. As such, he highly doubted that actual animal sacrifices would ever be part of *any* rebuilt Jewish Temple, giving his detractors another accusing finger-pointing opportunity citing his unmitigated arrogance. Throughout the millennia countless questions and opinions had been proffered about the Third Temple… who would build it; how would it be built; would it start tangibly but be finished miraculously? Or would the Temple drop down from the Heavens onto the

Temple Mount landing a direct hit on the Dome of the Rock, reclaiming the Foundation Stone's place within the Holy of Holies, the *Kadosh HaKadoshim*? Or would it rise from a hidden warren beneath the Temple Mount restored intact and ready for use? What role would the *Moshiach*, the Messiah, the Anointed One, play in the drama of the day?

But any infringement of a Temple on the Temple Mount would spark an all-out war. Muslims considered *al-Aqsa* to include the entire 35-acre Temple Mount area and not just the mosque at the southern end. With the ongoing questions on the "how" of the *Beit HaMikdash*, Joshua was free to consider his virtual version of the Third Temple without constraints. But now that the moment seemed closer than ever, he realized there was yet another scenario of how the Third Temple could come into being... one which he hadn't previously considered.

Joshua perceived a smile spreading across his face as he recognized the now-obvious presentation of a magnificent, explanation-defying hovering structure that would enthrall the world. He imagined the close encounters of the fifth-kind folks would abandon Area 51 and instead sign up for special pilgrimage packages to Jerusalem offered by the folks from MUFON (Mutual Unidentified Flying Object Network). The Third Temple would engage a new audience of alien lovers, eagerly waiting for the hovering Temple to transform into a spaceship like the shape-shifting pyramid on the fictitious planet of *Abydos* in the original Stargate film.

Logically, the Temple's appearance could never only be a one-time event, amazing and spectacular as that might be. In an era of deepfakes, no matter how many videos and images of the event were posted across social media, a one-time event was too easy for fact-checking skeptics to dismiss as hokum and a far cry from a miracle. An actual miracle would be buried under an avalanche of criticism and claims of AI-generated fakery before canceling the offender be it a country, company, or individual, and generating a new conspiracy legend almost impossible to delete. More importantly, a one-time event would be too easily displaced by the next "big thing" ready to captivate the collective's ever-shortening attention span. But a hovering Third Temple would meet all the criteria needed to compel a disbelieving world into believing... a tiny step for some, but a giant leap of faith for others. With a hovering Third Temple, the question of animal sacrifices would also be moot, unless, or perhaps until, *Kohanim* and *Levi'im* learned to fly, or were willing to strap on a jetpack. There would be no sacrifices, except maybe the token kind bought and brought digitally to the Temple just as Joshua had envisioned for HaMikdash3.0. Ironically, or fortuitously, Joshua could easily incorporate this new/not-so-new vision version into HaMikdash3.0 almost as if it were always meant to be that way.

Strange, he wondered, why hadn't he considered a hovering structure, framing the *Beit HaMikdash* in the purest of possibilities, beyond the limitations of 21st-century technology or human engineering? But even within that suspended scenario, the Dome of the Rock would, nonetheless, also meet its end as the Foundation Stone would need to be raised or revealed beyond the confines of the gold-domed structure and gone in either case. At least no one, save for G-d, could be blamed or attacked. The ongoing miracle of a suspended Third Temple would be proof enough for all to see with their own eyes, refuting any deepfake claims, silencing the conspiracists, and be extolled with non-stop *Ameins*, *Hallelujahs*, *Praise Be*, and redefining *Allu-ah Akbar* without the blood-curdling scream.

WOW, in all caps, Joshua thought. THE actual *Beit HaMikdash* would be a "seeing is believing" ongoing, first-person experience. Joshua was reminded of the song *Ve'Haviotim*, the Hebrew verse of *Isaiah 56:7* put to music. "Even them will I bring to My Holy mountain and make them joyful in My house of prayer; their burnt offerings and their sacrifices shall be acceptable upon Mine altar; for My house shall be called a house of prayer for <u>all</u> peoples." While Judaism didn't proselytize for new converts, the song proclaimed the universality of G-d and a time when all would be welcome. The inspirational song kept him going during the long nights working on HaMikdash3.0, especially after his grandfather, his *Opa Jacob*, was no longer there to cheer him on. The version from the husband-and-wife duo of Yoni and Nina, known simply as YONINA, could always bring him to tears in an instantaneous rewind in time to *Yom Kippur* 2021 when his *Opa* passed away.

Their group of thirty-six ascended the Temple Mount, singing *Ve'Haviotim* in full voice. It surprised Joshua at first, since he'd been warned that praying, let alone singing, might be "challenging," disallowed by the *Wakf*, the *Islamic Authority*, and enforced by *Magav*, Israel's Border Police. A Temple Mount regular from *Beyadenu*, an organization dedicated to restoring Jewish sovereignty and open prayer on the Temple Mount, explained that for the first time in recent memory, *Har HaBayit* had been closed to Muslims to honor the Jewish holiday. Generally, hours for all non-Muslims was restricted to two shifts, four hours in the morning and then one hour in the afternoon; a total of five hours per day, Sunday through Thursday, with access often denied entirely on Fridays, other Muslim Holy days and during *Ramadan*, for all thirty days.

But in a rare moment of parity and clarity, the Temple Mount was closed to Muslims on *Yom Kippur 2021*, the holiest day on the Jewish calendar. Their group along with hundreds of other groups ascended throughout the day as Jews, openly prayed and praised the Almighty without offending anyone in the process. The follow-up reports of the events of the day, however, claimed the SETTLER JEWS, a double pejorative, had once again stormed *al-Aqsa* in an oft-repeated libelous claim designed to incite violence. It was no accident that *Hamas* used the Temple Mount as a flashpoint, calling the October 7, 2023, rampage: *Operation al-Aqsa Flood*.

While hushed, the sudden murmuring among the souls drew Joshua's attention back to the moment and to the silhouetted figure now standing at the *Ha'Masuot* lookout, at the top of the Mount of Olives. He appeared closer, but still distant. Joshua couldn't help but wonder what he was waiting for, and how much longer they, he, would have to wait. The answer to his unspoken question was given voice… a deep rumble that began slowly, building in force until the entire Temple Mount began to tremble. Yet, he and the other watchers on the wall remained steady, unshaken by the happenings in the physical world. That dimensional separation came with another realization as Joshua understood that the Western Wall, the *Kotel HaMa'aravi*, would also likely fall victim to a Third Temple reality.

All of the "old" symbols that had fortified the faithful throughout the generations would be relegated to History to make way for the new and invoking an airtight, non-compete clause that yielded supremacy and service only to the Third Temple. Then as if the realization somehow raised his soul's status, Joshua and his soul group saw the thousands of thousands — 599,999 other soul groups — gathered in the *Kidron Valley* at the base of *Har HaZei'tim*. Whatever sense of self he'd managed to build while being a watcher on the rampart walls disappeared in a flash as the scene was laid bare before him. But then another question entered his thoughts, why was *his* soul group still on the Eastern ramparts? Why hadn't they been joined with and to the others in the *Kidron Valley*? Once again, he tried to figure out the "why" of it all, or how in this liminal space he could still be consciously aware, formulating questions … all of which was beyond his genius-level IQ to comprehend. What he did understand was that these other soul groups had been granted front-row seats, or at least a primo vantage point, to witness the Final Redemption and the actualization of Joshua's Truth… the real reason behind his obsession with the *Beit HaMikdash*. How could G-d deny them… deny him still?

* * *

> On that day, his feet shall stand on the Mount of Olives, which lies before Jerusalem on the east; and the Mount of Olives shall be split in two from east to west by a wide valley, so that one-half of the Mount shall move northward, and the other half southward.
>
> – Zechariah 14:4

The deep rumbling continued. Only this time it wasn't coming from the ground, but from a powerful, angel-summoning *shofar* blast echoing from the Heavens. The air trembled, a quivering, shimmering mirage rearranging and reforming parts of itself like an Impressionistic water scene, and where he became part of the "Redemption" canvas. Unfettered by human breath, each phrasing of the *shofar's* mighty sounds, the *tekiah, teruah,* and *shevarim-teruah* heard on the Jewish New Year, were punctuated by an angelic choir, voicing the refrain, "Today, the world stands as it once was at its birth." But the second Hebrew word, *haras,* in the phrase *HaYom Haras HaOlam,* could be re-framed to mean, "Today the world stands as it was conceived to be" with all its potential and birthed anew. The rebirth would wipe the slate clean of poor judgments, misuse of the Earth's bounty, and a lack of appreciation for her precious gifts which had been squandered casually and callously for nearly 6,000 years. A new beginning that would usher in an ethical, faithful, contemplative era of gratitude, at peace, and thankful for the bounty of G-d's gifts and justice.

Instinctively, Joshua knew the *shofar* blasts would continue until all one hundred sounds (*kolot*) were voiced. In his ambiguous awareness of Space and Time, he couldn't help but wonder what would come next. Was this how death felt, or was he still alive, perhaps awakened for the first time? Or was this quasi-state between life and death an antechamber for the World to Come, or, at least in his case, a waiting room to Hell to give his soul another round of fire and brimstone rectification? Or was it possible that he would finally be reunited with his family? He had so many questions about the next steps, the next world, but then once again the past intruded on the present and his first thoughts became his last… did he prevent the suicide bomber from blowing himself up or did he fail? Did the explosion trigger a cataclysmic seismic event, priming the Earth to release her dead?

And with that thought, Joshua E. Katz found himself back in Zedekiah's Cave, back in Time, with only seconds left before the countdown clock of his life reached zero.

FRIDAY

Chapter 1

**Six days before Rosh Hashanah,
Jewish New Year 5785
Jerusalem, Israel**

The Hazon Labs' offices were blissfully quiet, save for the occasional foosball cheers from the company's skeleton crew of two White Hats. The counter-hacking squad had 24/7 responsibilities for tracking and monitoring any possible intrusions into HaMikdash3.0; a challenge on any day but further complicated because HaMikdash3.0 used a publicly distributed computing network. The strategy leveraged player-members' personal computers, phones, tablets, and other devices, for distributing the virtual community's petabyte processing load across a co-opted network. Unfortunately, the virtual space's unprecedented computing power came at a price, creating multiple vulnerable access points for black-hat hackers to exploit.

Tzion Beru Mengistu didn't envy the White Hat team. Their successes or failures in keeping HaMikdash3.0 up and running were on display 24/7. *All* he had to worry about was nailing HaMikdash3.0's initial baker's dozen of intersecting storylines for the long-awaited post-*Sukkot* product launch. He shut the door to the editing suite and settled in, hoping to work on HaMikdash3.0's introductory sequence for the next few hours. The delicious aroma from the freshly brewed cup of *shahee* filled the room. He sipped the Ethiopian spiced tea made of cardamom, cinnamon, nutmeg, cloves, and ginger, then promptly burned his tongue when he heard the three quick raps on the door jamb. The signature knock belonged to Joshua E. Katz, the CEO and visionary founder of Hazon Labs.

"Mind if I come in?" Joshua asked, then apologetically added, "sorry to bother you."

"No bother, just getting started. It's quieter here most Fridays."

"I wanted to apologize for bumping you off the presentation schedule yesterday. The uptick in attempted intrusions is concerning and, unfortunately, all-consuming."

"No worries," Tzion said with an overabundance of relief. Truth be told, he was grateful to have been spared the embarrassment of having to present the day before at Hazon Labs' weekly show-and-tell Thursdays. By his reckoning, he needed twelve to fifteen hours to clean up all the modules. He'd come into work on a Friday, typically an off day at Hazon Labs and throughout Israel, to work without the constant hum of interruptions. So much for that plan…

"Our 'fans' are out in full force today," Joshua said, referring to the parking lot protesters who gathered for morning coffee in Hazon Labs' back parking lot. The group was mostly a nuisance, calling Hazon employees heretics, one of the nicer epithets, as part of their morning routine. With the first anniversary of October 7 approaching, there was a perceptible rise in the number of HaMikdash3.0 detractors, plying their anti-Semitic world domination conspiracies to the masses across social media. Of greater concern were the technically proficient among their "fanbase" — the digitally savvy, anti-Semites who might target HaMikdash3.0 and its members.

"Tricky business, dodging them on my bike," Joshua joked.

"At least, they haven't resorted to throwing eggs at any of us."

"Yet," Joshua said with a generous smile. "I can think of better ways to spend my Fridays."

"Me too," Tzion thought, then realized his remark might be misconstrued. He believed in the project and wanted Joshua to know giving up a Friday was a small price to pay. "HaMikdash is too important to let the shits win," Tzion said, affirming his thoughts.

"Hopefully, the Big Guy upstairs appreciates your sentiment and the overtime," said Joshua doffing an imaginary hat and casting of his eyes upward.

Tzion knew the casual conversation would soon turn serious. No doubt his boss wanted to look at what he *was* supposed to present the day before. Joshua was always fair, but demanding, especially with the HaMikdash3.0 launch just around the High Holidays' corner. He was supposed to have been ready yesterday and excuses definitely wouldn't fly. As the company's lead developer, Tzion knew Joshua trusted him to bring the HaMikdash3.0 project home — on time and, ideally, on budget. Tzion liked Joshua, admired him, loved working for Hazon Labs, agreed with the company's mission, and didn't want to disappoint the team or himself, despite the project's many challenges.

A first-generation Israeli, Tzion was the first in his family, the eldest, to be born in Israel following the 1991 airlift of 14,325 Ethiopians during Operation Solomon. Like others in their Ethiopian community, his grandparents walked hundreds of miles from Gondar to Addis Ababa to finally come home to Zion. His parents, Yafa and Asef met in a temporary refugee camp housing the new arrivals. Only teenagers at the time, once found, they'd never parted from one another. Tzion was the first in his family to attend university; though for a time there was a question whether he might also be the first in the family to be sent to prison.

During his early teen years, Tzion rebelled, shunning his family's "old country" ways and alienating them, much like the alien he felt himself to be. He identified with other non-conforming rejectionists, a multicultural blend of street punks who spoke Hebrew in half a dozen different accents. By his twelfth birthday, Tzion could swear in as many languages. He sought out "others" like himself, hanging out in the parks. Their collective mantra was to do as little as possible, except when it came to causing trouble. Petty crimes mostly, but criminal, nonetheless. Tzion's saving grace was that he was smart and naturally excelled in school without much effort. He took only 5-point-level subjects — the highest academic achievement level in the *Bagrut*, Israel's high school matriculation exams. With a high profile, he placed well in the IDF, served even better, and finally grew into taking himself and his responsibilities seriously. After completing his thirty-two months of mandatory service, he declined offers to pursue an Officer's training course as recommended by his Commander.

Instead, he attended Ben Gurion University of the Negev, graduating with top honors with two first degrees, one in psychology and the other in computer graphics. Hazon Labs was his first career move, and hopefully his last. The dual degree combined with an artistic eye, a trait he owed to his photographer father, helped him generate HaMikdash3.0's sophisticated User Experiences (UX) and User Interface (UI). Working at Hazon Labs also allowed him to open the books on his own *Torah* learning; an opportunity he'd missed in his youth but which he now accepted and appreciated as an adult. Tzion knew this fresh perspective helped him craft engaging and meaningful HaMikdash3.0 storylines. His grandfather, Mekonen Beru, a *Kessin*, would have been proud to see his prodigal grandson finally find his way home. He hoped that somehow his grandfather knew he'd not only rejoined the ranks of the Jewish people but that through his work on

HaMikdash3.0, he honored *Beta Yisroel*'s historical and religious link to the Israelite tribe of *Dan*. Tzion's grandfather served as the priest/Rabbi for the immigrant Ethiopian community in *Beit Shemesh* until his passing in 2013… four years before Tzion finally found purpose in life. He credited an outdoor adventure group that took him, and other misfits, hiking, biking, and exploring the Judean Hills surrounding *Beit Shemesh*. Connecting to the land changed him, giving him a sense of belonging. He also discovered a passion for photography — an activity he and his father could share. Ironically, or by that confluence of events often consigned to chance, the ancient city of *Beit Shemesh* and the surrounding Judean Hills bordered the region historically linked to the tribe of *Dan*.

Tzion stopped believing in chance and knew that events "conspired" under what was known collectively as *Hashgacha*. Divine Providence operated on an individual level under the label, *Hashgacha Pratis*, and worked together with Divine Providence at the community or general level, *Hashgacha Klali*, governing all things, both great and small. The trick was in recognizing providence at work — an awesome wow experience, yielding insights if one knew how to look. Tzion knew the governing hand of Providence guided him in his work on the HaMikdash3.0 project. He'd only been on the job as project manager for a day, when, without consulting anyone, he named the HaMikdash3.0 product demo avatar, *Ari of Judah*.

He derived the name from the term, "Lion of Judah," which was co-opted by Ethiopia's rulers through the ages who'd laid claim to Queen Batsheba's liaison with King David as a status symbol. Tzion substituted the Hebrew word *Ari* for lion, a subtle change but an ongoing homage to Tzion's heritage and personal journey. With a confidence born in truth, he named the company's signature avatar, *Ari of Judah* — a most excellent name choice. He recalled standing nervously in front of the Hazon Labs' team in a long-ago Thursday show-and-tell session. With the benefit of 20/20 hindsight, he realized that he probably should have asked for input on *the* avatar's name as it would become HaMikdash3.0's digital ambassador. But all his worries vanished when he unveiled "Ari of Judah" for the first time. The big reveal was met with rousing applause, and a polysyllabic enunciation of *mi-tzu-yan*, meaning excellent with an exclamation point, from Joshua.

His grandfather would have appreciated the nuanced references to Ethiopia and a reminder of *Beta Yisroel*'s true tribal claims to the Lion of

Judah title. Tzion missed his grandfather and remembered the old man's heartache in having to fight for Ethiopian religious traditions and rights, challenging Israel's predominant Ashkenazic and Sephardic religious authorities. Most contentious was the Chief Rabbinate's challenge to the *Beta Yisroel's* authenticity as "real Jews" demanding that the early immigrants undergo a symbolic conversion to Judaism. Not surprisingly, the embers of resentment lingered for years. Thankfully, calmer heads finally prevailed and time-honored Ethiopian traditions — practices that had ensured the survival of their isolated Diaspora community across the millennia — were gradually accepted and respected. Nonetheless, the Ethiopian community faced additional challenges, not the least of which was learning how to adapt to the realities of modern Israeli life and the religious fluency of contemporary Judaism.

Fortunately, Tzion's younger siblings, nephews, and nieces were no longer viewed as outsiders among their non-Ethiopian peers, and guests at a *Bar/Bat Mitzvah* celebration or wedding were color-blind to any differences. The country and the people had made great strides in embracing the diversity reflected in the Jewish Diaspora — a mosaic of rich cultural textures, woven into an enriched tapestry that continues to evolve… a dynamic work in progress.

"I should warn you… the modules are still a little rough," Tzion said, rubbing his forehead and flicking away a small bead of sweat that threatened to drop onto his keyboard.

Rough was most definitely NOT what Joshua wanted to hear. He tried to contain his disappointment, steeling himself against whatever "rough" might mean. With the official launch set for Sunday, October 29, the time on the countdown clock was fast running out. Unfortunately, with the upcoming Jewish holidays the work-weeks would be shortened, leaving Hazon Labs with only half that number of official workdays. No, "rough" definitely wouldn't cut it, Joshua thought. He slipped on the prototype wrap-around VR/AR glasses and then turned his attention to the 48" ultra-wide, curved monitor perched ergonomically on Tzion's desk.

"How 'bout we just run it," Joshua said, softening his tone, but bracing himself against what "rough" might mean. Sensitivities notwithstanding, he needed to review the storyboard and planned to watch the module from dual perspectives: as the company's CEO and as a first-time customer.

Tzion took a deep breath and engaged the opening video sequence to the HaMikdash3.0 demo.

Onscreen, the hands of a clock spin rapidly backward in Time while a companion solid horizontal green timeline bar recedes from right to left. Scripted in bold block letters and measured in centuries, the numbers zoom in and out of a colorful montage of blurred but discernible bits of History, effected using microsecond pauses on the still images.

In the background, mournful music plays softly, an evocative tune. The date, 587 BCE/BC appears, then zooming out a small part of an image comes into sharp focus. The image zooms out further to reveal a painting titled, "The Flight of the Prisoners" by French artist James Tissot. The image is of the Babylonian exile of the Jews in muted pastels; a line of weary travelers fills the screen as a mournful clarinet solo of Al Naharot Bavel, "By the Waters of Babylon" plays softly in the background. The painted scene comes alive, transformed with vivid colors, terracotta, pinks, purples, and blues. The long procession of the weary — mothers, fathers, and children, the old and the young — drag themselves away from Jerusalem to face the Exile. In the background, smoke rises to the heavens as the walls of Jerusalem are breached and the city burns.

The animation pans into the city, a scene of devastation throughout Jerusalem's ravaged streets, following a path to the ruined Temple. As if delivering a live report from Jerusalem, the Narrator's resonant baritone somberly describes the devastation. "Solomon's Temple is destroyed; Jerusalem is in flames." Overcome, the Narrator inhales sharply as a giant stone block crashes to the ground, words engraved in square-lettered Hebrew script can be seen in the rock face, לבית התקיעה *(le'Beit HaTekiah); the English translation "To the trumpeting place" emerges from the Hebrew text. The stone settles among the dozens of large blocks of hewn limestone at the base of the Temple Mount's west-facing retaining wall.*

The Narrator sighs, a slight quiver constricting his already strained voice, "And so it came to pass that King Zedekiah, the last of the Kings of Judah, saw Jerusalem, the City of Gold, consumed in flames. Her orchards and groves burned, her walls breached, the people driven into exile... the Temple destroyed.

"Zedekiah gambled and lost when he shifted his loyalties from the Babylonians, who had installed him as King and instead sided with the Egyptians. Whether his decision was borne of ego or naivete, in revenge the Babylonian ruler Nebuchadnezzar delivered a death blow to the Holy City, wrenching her children from under her sheltering protection, and exiling them to Babylon."

The figure of a man, hiding in the shadows, suddenly appears in the scene. Frightened, he enters a darkened cave; in his outstretched arm, a flaming torch lights the way. He races through a maze of branching tunnels, turning this way and that, pausing, breathless, listening... his pursuers are closing in on him. In the distance, giant shadows skitter across the limestone walls. The frightened figure hears the echoes of soldiers running through the cave. Frantically, his head turns to the left and right trying to discern their direction. They're close... too close. An army of shadow soldiers march steadily across the cave's walls.

"Zedekiah flees the city, hoping to evade his Babylonian pursuers. He escapes through the warren of interconnected caves and tunnels stretching from Jerusalem's double-walled gate in the south out to the plains of Jericho in the northeast. The year is 587 BCE/BC. The Temple is no more, its treasures lost. The people, and G-d's spirit, the Shechina, exiled."

In a sweeping shot, only the flames remain, raging in vibrant oranges, yellows, and reds set against the stillness of a black sky. The image fades to a painting by artist Romain Cazes, "Captivity of the Jews in Babylon" showing a small group of people gathered near the water's edge, sitting beneath the branches of the willow trees. The painting comes to life at first with only the slow sweep of the willow branches, then with the people, weeping, swaying in tandem with the branches' movements.

In a mournful voice, the Narrator speaks the words of Psalms 137, spoken first in English, then sung in Hebrew. The music heard earlier plays softly in the background, now with lyrics in Hebrew and a voiceover in English.

"By the rivers of Babylon, we sat and wept when we remembered Zion. In the willows, we hung up our harps. There, our captors tormented us, mocked us, demanding we offer up a song, 'Sing to us the song of Zion. But lo? How can we sing the song of G-d in this foreign land?'"

After a pause, the Narrator continues, "Written by the prophet Jeremiah, the words of Psalm 137 foretold of the destruction, but his warning went unheeded. Today, these same words are sung before reciting the Grace after Meals blessings, the Birchat HaMazon — a testimony to the ongoing exile, a forever reminder of what has been lost…"

The scene spins into a whirling blur of rapidly changing images as Time rushes forward. The scene shifts to modern-day Jerusalem — a jarring two-millennia time jump in the blink of an eye. The narration resumes. "The Time has come to rebuild the Temple, the third Holy Temple, the Beit HaMikdash version 3.0. The time is now to recover the lost artifacts, repair a broken world, and bring peace to all Mankind."

    Joshua furrows his brow, wondering what Tzion was worried about. He could find nothing "rough" about any part of the introductory scenes. As far as he was concerned, the sequence was magnificent. The scene was set, captioned text scrolling, images rendered, and the motion capture and audio in sync: check, check, and double-check. All appeared to be a go for the opening gambit, introducing player-members to HaMikdash3.0. He patted Tzion's shoulder in recognition of a job well done for delivering a technically elegant and emotionally charged experience. The high-praise word, "nice" had just formed on his lips, when the storyline's narrator said: "Will you accept the cha-cha-cha-challenge?"

    The word "nice" was instantly appended with a long snort, a groaned aye-yai-yai-yai, and a silent expletive. Joshua inhaled deeply hoping to contain his infamously short fuse, a noted character trait encoded in his *Kohanic* genes. He looped his finger on the bridge of the prototype wrap-around VR/AR glasses and slowly pulled them down to the tip of his nose. His seafoam-colored green eyes were set in an open stare, wide in disbelief. He stared at Tzion, who, in addition to managing the HaMikdash3.0 project, was also the lead developer on the *Zedekiah's Cave* (ZC) storyline and game module.

Tzion blanched a shade lighter than his smooth, mocha-colored skin and felt a warm flush fill his cheeks. He grimaced, acknowledging the audio bug. "I know," he said, desperately wanting to stop the demo run, knowing there were more unpleasantries yet ahead in the not-quite-finished ZC sequence.

While taller than most Ethiopians, Tzion felt himself grow smaller as Joshua — a beefy six-foot-tall, ginger-haired computer whiz with black belts in multiple martial arts disciplines, including *Krav Maga* — took a step closer, arms folded across his broad chest. The large editing and screening suite should have afforded Tzion some breathing room, but didn't as Joshua took another two steps forward to stand to his immediate right.

Joshua braced himself again for the continuation of whatever "rough" might also mean for the ZC module. "And Zedekiah's Cave module?" Joshua asked, almost too afraid to hear the answer.

"Well..." Tzion started to say but was preempted by Joshua, who softened his tone, realizing that sending his blood pressure into the stratosphere wouldn't serve him or Tzion.

"Let's just run it, okay," Joshua said, hoping to put his best programmer at ease. He felt for Tzion, realizing his project manager had come in on Friday — the country's official day off — to clean up the demo without the usual Hazon Labs' frenetic distractions. His included. Joshua had interrupted Tzion's fixing of the "roughs" that needed his attention. He also recalled that this *Shabbat* Tzion's youngest brother Zev was celebrating his *Bar Mitzvah* — Judaism's coming-of-age ceremony for boys at age 13 — which made his presence in the office all the more impressive but also worrisome. No matter how painful the next few minutes would be for him, or Tzion, Joshua needed to see more of HaMikdash3.0.

Everyone was running on empty, himself included. He'd barely slept, having made it home to his apartment in Jerusalem's *Baka* neighborhood at 3:30 that morning. Only to rush back to the office a few hours later to pick up the forgotten presentation he'd worked on for most of the night and well into the morning, all for a speaking engagement he could have well done without. For him, every day was a workday; Fridays were no exception, and with the launch date looming large, chasing out to Reichman University was an unwelcome disruption. But there was no way Joshua could refuse. Reichman's end-of-the-summer term seminar was billed as a Memorial lecture in honor of his grandfather, Jacob Katzenstein who'd endowed a chair in the University's School of Sustainability — a fact the University's Chancellor shamelessly leveraged. Even so, part of him wanted to cancel the lecture, feigning some mysterious illness to get out of one hour plus travel time from Jerusalem to Herzliya, not including the lecture itself.

The official Hazon Labs intranet calendar displayed a T minus 34 days countdown, replete with hours and seconds; a weighty reminder that conveyed a proper sense of urgency to the tasks at hand. They did not have a go/no-go option… only a go option. Joshua had steadfastly refused to budge on a post-*Sukkot* holiday/post-Oct7 release date. They'd already "blown" the unabashedly opportunistic launch date of *Tisha b'Av* (9th day of the Hebrew month *Av*), a day marked by numerous national tragedies for the Jewish people, including the destruction of both the First and Second Temples in 586 BCE and 70 CE, respectively. Oct7 joined the ranks of national tragedies to be commemorated, and to be forever immortalized with newly scripted *kinot*, soulful elegies, which would be included in recitations on *Tisha b'Av*, a day of mourning, fasting, and reflection.

Tisha b'Av would have been the perfect launch date for HaMikdash3.0, but also the worst. While 3.0 was primed for release for what Joshua called, "a perfect, contextually congruent marketing opportunity" at the last minute, he nixed the launch. Joshua was willing to be irreverent, even bearing the contempt of his critics, but HaMikdash3.0's announced "Tish" launch was met with vehement criticism, leveled at the company and at him personally. Heeding the advice of his team, Joshua decided the golden opportunity was a shade too insensitive, even for him. Besides, he would have risked alienating HaMikdash3.0's flock of religious supporters who might wither under peer pressure to "abandon their fool's errand," or be threatened with the almighty *Wrath of G-d*. He'd won over many of his adherents by positioning HaMikdash3.0 as the solution rather than the problem. While motivations and definitions of a Higher Power might differ, the so-called "dawning of the age of Aquarius" — which promises a quieter, simpler time of love and the end to wars — was an attractive concept, even to those in the atheist and agnostic communities. If 3.0 could usher in the new era, then so be it. Though some, no doubt, probably hoped the whole thing would implode on itself, and finally rid the world of all those pesky religious nuts. Thankfully, the Satanists hadn't given HaMikdash3.0 their official endorsement, or invited him to join their ranks, even though his most ardent detractors did label him the Devil, anti-Christ, and a few other choice epithets and anti-Semitic tropes.

The delayed launch was met with both disappointment and relief; the accountants and Board in the former group, and the Hazon Labs team in the latter. As it turned out, the delayed launch was a true godsend. Or maybe it was his *Opa* whispering in his ear, "Try not to piss off too many people, Joshie… at least not all of them at the same time." Joshua was glad he'd heeded the inner voice, whatever or whoever the source. Hazon Labs' teams used the extra time to add a new storyline module about the 1492 expulsion of the Jews of Spain with the Alhambra Decree. The 1,500-year-old Jewish community was given a choice, convert to Christianity or be expelled with the deadline on the 9th of *Av*. Death sentences were reserved for those who either refused to leave and/or publicly denounced the decree refusing to convert, and by default encouraging others to resist.

To celebrate the new launch date, the team gathered for a Hazon Labs family-style dinner, replete with Ladino music strumming in the background and Spanish-themed foods, catered by best-selling cookbook author and chef, Jamie Geller, all of which set the stage for a pivotal "aha" moment. A critical rectification of a massive *faux pas* that would have left HaMikdash3.0, and the company, open to justified cries of racism and Ashkenazi elitism. While the Hazon writing teams had done a stellar job integrating pan-religious perspectives into the various storylines, they'd nonetheless taken an almost exclusively Ashkenazi perspective, a default Eastern European point-of-view, and an unacceptable error. As the group chowed down, Tzion casually compared Chef Geller's non-seafood chicken and sausage paella with *Doro Wat*, a slow-cooked Ethiopian stew made with chicken, onions, garlic, ginger, and a spice blend. The comparison kicked off an offering by the group of other family feasts and food traditions, and a one-pot, slow simmer, cook-off challenge was set for the following week. Tzion put up his mom's *Doro Wat* up against graphics specialist Orah

Sharabi *Mandi* — a traditional Yemenite dish made with chicken or lamb, and rice cooked with a spice blend of cumin, cardamom, and cinnamon.

With a full stomach, and a licensing deal struck with Jamie Geller to be HaMikdash3.0's culinary guide, Joshua's high-octane creativity took off, eager to remedy the significant diversity and inclusion oversight. At the following Thursday show-n-tell session, Joshua presented the elaborated storylines, infusing them with a deliberate, rich multicultural texture and *ta'am* (flavor). The entire Hazon Labs team — all twenty-five employees, a mini-United Nations, albeit made of friendlies — elaborated the constructs further, sharing family recipes, traditions, and *niggunim* (song tunes) that reflected the diversity of modern Israeli society, Muslim, Christian, and Jewish, bringing the cultural richness from Arab, Druze, Mizrachi, Sephardi, and Ashkenazi peoples with the ingathering of Jews and ethnic minorities from around the world.

The new storylines not only reflected the modern-day miracle and prophetic sign of the ingathering of the Jewish people to the land of Israel but of uniting people under a "One G-d" principle. From the far corners of the Andes and mountaintops of Tibet to the tropical islands of the Caribbean and Hawaii and across the dispersed First Nations of North America, the hidden connections to Judaism had brought the forgotten and the lost home. Judaism found new adherents, converts from across the globe whose souls could not deny their connection to the Jewish people despite raging anti-Semitism — a word that neatly summed up Jew-hatred, but which inadvertently sanitized and compartmentalized an insidious evil spawned in the depths of hell that defied logic or reason.

Joshua translated his newfound awareness and respect by personally scripting two co-related storylines. "Lost and Found in *Silwan*," a geolocation challenge where players followed clues to identify the modern-day location of the Yemenite village established in the late 1800s on the barren hilltop adjacent to the Mount of Olives cemetery. He linked "Lost and Found in Silwan" to *Al Kanfei Nesharim* (On Wings of Eagles). The magnificent storyline to the airlift of an estimated 49,000 Yemenite Jews, more popularly known as "Operation Magic Carpet," that took place between June 1949 and September 1950.

The "Wings" storyline began with the "Song of the Wind" taken from the esoteric text known as *Perek Shira*, meaning Chapter Song. *Perek Shira* links G-d's creations with a specific verse or part of a verse from the entirety of the *Tanakh* — the *Torah*, Prophets (*Nevi'im*), and the Writings (*Ketuvim*). While the authorship and date of origin of *Perek Shira* are unknown, the text offers insights into Creation and lessons that each can impart. Conspicuously absent from the song is Man who is charged with learning *from* the song.

The opening sequence of the storyline was pure Joshua, transitioning real-world footage of an eagle in flight to an animated eagle, circling over the city of Jerusalem. The eagle was then transformed into an airplane with a quote from *Isaiah 43:6* appearing onscreen. Joshua chose to do the voiceover narration himself.

"The Wind is saying, 'I will say to the north, Give up; and to the south, Do not withhold. Bring My sons from far, and My daughters from the ends of the earth."

HaMikdash3.0's multicultural outreach found champions from across the globe. *Bashir Aboud* reached out to his father's family in Lebanon, Christian Arabs, and keepers of their family's full history of travels across the deserts of the Middle East for an upcoming storyline on the Sheiks of Arabia. HaMikdash3.0 captured the attention of diverse peoples, including First Nations Chief Joseph RiverWind of the Arawak Taino Nation of South America and the Caribbean. RiverWind. The Chief, a champion of indigenous people, took the public stance, not only noting the significant parallels between Indian tribal traditions and Jewish customs from taking an ark into battle to establishing land-based tribal affiliations, but also appreciating the inspiration his people could draw from the Jewish people's resilience and return to their indigenous homeland after a 2,000-year exile.

In 2021, curious connections between First Nations and Israel, led Geneticist Donald Yates, himself a descendant of the Cherokee tribe, to analyze the DNA of sixty-seven members of his tribe. The surprising data showed that of those tested, approximately one-third of their genes were more similar to people originating in the Middle East and Europe, rather than East Asia as had been previously thought. With Chief RiverWind's permission, the development team included a Native American-themed vision quest in HaMikdash3.0 with a cameo appearance of the Chief's avatar. The fact that Hazon Labs' name translated to Vision Labs in English was not lost on either Joshua or Chief RiverWind. Joshua asked Eric "Arik" Anders, the company's Chief Marketing Officer, if he had anything special he wanted to contribute. Arik appreciated the gesture, but reminded his boss he was in the process of converting to Judaism, and liked to keep his former life separate from his current.

The newly expanded content included educationally driven material, religious and regional rituals and practices, language study, art, shops, and foods to showcase the company's newfound diversity agenda. Joshua offered a *mea culpa* for not catching the ethnocentric oversight sooner, and for not reflecting an all-embracing pluralism and inclusivity across the Abrahamic religions and other belief systems. As CEO of Hazon Labs, Joshua wondered how he had forgotten the HaMikdash *vision*, a utopian wish reflected in *Isaiah 2:2-4.*

> *And it shall come to pass in the end of days, that the mountain of the LORD'S house shall be established as the top of the mountains, and shall be exalted above the hills; and all nations shall flow unto it. And many peoples shall go and say: 'Come ye, and let us go up to the mountain of the LORD, to the house of the God of Jacob; and He will teach us of His ways, and we will walk in His paths.' For out of Zion shall go forth the law, and the word of the LORD from Jerusalem. And He shall judge between the nations, and shall decide for many peoples; and they shall beat their swords into plowshares, and their spears into pruning hooks; nation shall not lift up sword against nation, neither shall they learn war any more.*

In retrospect, the glaring oversight was obvious, but not the question of why no one else on the team had spoken up. The war had messed up people's thinking in ways they weren't even aware of or had yet to appreciate. Joshua hoped the new focus would provide the Hazon Labs team with a desperately needed *chizuk*… one that would help carry them through the first anniversary of the October 7 massacre. As a company, Hazon Labs had juggled the demands of "Operation Iron Sword" as employees were called up for reserve duty; and the ongoing guilt of continuing on with "business as usual" safely ensconced in their Jerusalem offices. While the war with Hamas raged on and the losses among family and friends mounted, Hazon Labs' employees volunteered by picking and packing fruit and vegetables on farms whose workers had gone to war or returned to their home countries. They also donated clothing and toys to displaced families living out of suitcases in hotels scattered throughout the safer parts of Israel.

They also built and launched several Apps to assist pro-Israel activists in countering the blood libels and mis-/disinformation about genocide and ethnic cleansing which didn't hold true before October 7th and certainly not after. They advocated on behalf of the men and women who'd been subjected to rape and other gender-based violence; and, challenged those who denied Israel's right to defend itself and its efforts to bring home the hostages. Unfathomably, the haters managed to even take issue and somehow justify the kidnapping of children; two of which were still being held by Hamas and their ilk. The red-haired siblings, four-year-old Ariel and Kfir, his nine-month-old brother, along with their parents Shiri and Yarden had been kidnapped into Gaza on October 7th from Kibbutz Nir Oz. Rumors swirled that they had been killed or sold. Whatever the truth, almost a year after October 7, they were still in Gaza. The Hazon Labs' team did what they could, but it was never enough…

The emotional trauma of Oct7 was compounded by questions about the political, military, and intelligence failures and mismanagement in response to the attack, but also the failures that lead to Oct7. How could Hamas have built 500 kilometers of tunnels under the noses of the Southern Command, surveiled Israel's defenses at the fence, and openly trained on gliders for the operation called *al-Aqsa Flood* with impunity? Questions, but where no answers would ever be good enough no matter how many official inquiries were held. One could only hope that the lessons had been learned and that "Never Again" truly meant never again.

While much of the political and ideological sparring between the left and the right, secular and religious, was set aside amid mobilizations and calls-to-arms in both military and civilian arenas, there was little time or space to mourn the heroes and angels, or grieve for lives left unfulfilled, or attend to the country's collective struggle with PTSD. The impact of Oct7 was still raw and would be for years to come. In some ways, Israel became united as never before but was also broken as never before. No one was left unscarred. Joshua's decision to forge ahead with the launch continued to be controversial. He silenced most of the critics, pointing out that no time would ever be a good time to launch HaMikdash3.0 as the country was still at war and, barring a miracle, would be at least for the foreseeable future.

The intended *chizuk* worked as the Hazon Labs team poured themselves into the increased workload. No one at Hazon Labs could argue with the significant improvements in diversity, and multiple voices and languages now given their due expression. "Live Authentically" became one of the company's slogans and was prominently placed on the company's merch. They took full advantage of the release date's delay, making additional UI/UX upgrades to both the User Interface (UI) and User Experience (UX), expanding HaMikdash3.0's avatar generator, Virtuoso, which now carried a full range of body types, skin colors, and authentically accented AI-generated speech and language options.

The value-added changes meant the HaMikdash3.0 community could grow organically, offering player-members an endless array of interactivities beyond any previously stated user-engagement goals. The Authenticity module was expanded to allow members to contribute content, including storefronts, gift shops, restaurants, and study groups to enrich and elevate the community space. Joshua E. Katz's vision was embedded in the company's name, *Hazon*, but his personal perspective stopped short of openly stating or believing that HaMikdash3.0 was part of any prophetic vision. He did, however, hope HaMikdash3.0 would accelerate the long-ago prophesied coming of the *Moshiach*/Messiah, albeit for selfish reasons.

The clock was ticking for all of them. According to Jewish tradition, the Hebrew calendar would run out at the year 6,000 mark, setting a countdown clock for the *Moshiach's* arrival as relatively imminent with the upcoming start of the year, 5785. While precise calculations or predictions are strictly *verboten*, it didn't take a rocket scientist to figure out there were "only" 216 years to go. The more hopeful believed "Time" would be credited for the 210 years spent enslaved in Egypt, meaning the world was at T minus 6 years and counting. If so, the Time remaining before the Messiah's appointed arrival could be counted on two hands, and soon only on one with the start of the Jewish New Year 5785 in six days.

Joshua believed HaMikdash3.0 would help speed that timeline along. The Faithful had always believed in the coming of the Anointed One, singing with a longing heart: "I believe with perfect faith in the coming of the *Moshiach*, and even though he may tarry, I will wait for him, every day, every day." Since Oct7, people who'd never believed in the *Moshiach* looked to the Heavens and prayed for an end to baseless hatred and most importantly for the return of their loved ones in the *Techiyat HaMei'tim* — the Resurrection of the Dead. Joshua believed and welcomed the day.

But what Joshua didn't know, or could have known, was that Time was also running out for him — a plan formulated long ago by Heaven for the role that Joshua E. Katz would play in the days to come… in these the End of Days.

The Archangel Uri'el heard a distinctive, "Ahem" but dared not look at which of the other Archangels, *Seraphs*, or G-d forbid one of the *Chayot HaKodesh* might be looking over his shoulder. Placing a wingtip on the virtual keyboard, he kept it on the backspace button and erased the cryptic, pseudo-warning regarding Joshua E. Katz. Team Katz had recently received a new mandate which placed additional restrictions on what could, and could not, be entered into the Angelic Record. Freewill notwithstanding, concern centered around any undue influence, or interference, with the course of Human events. No hints or saves would be allowed.

Uri'el's lion's face purred softly like a kitten, glad to have dodged a formal reprimand from the often-mercurial *Kochot*, the Powers That Be, with their sharpened claws and justice-wielding quills. Checking to make sure the Others had left, Uri'el turned his attention back to the Angelic record. He'd barely turned the page for the new entry when suddenly his feathers stood on end — statically charged because of the "who," or more accurately the "what" was behind the incoming call to Joshua E. Katz's cellphone.

Chapter 2

For as long as Joshua could remember he could sense incoming calls before his phone rang or vibrated in his pocket. Having served in Israel's 8200 signal intelligence unit, he attributed his ability to detect subtle frequency shifts, a kind of "Spidey sense" that earned him the reputation as a Super-Detector. The "SD" acronym, however, bothered him as did the "SS" Super-Sensor acronym, both labels for elite Nazi units, and a designation he could well do without. His friends called it uncanny, weird, spooky, and a voodoo-hooey-type sixth sense. While he could never explain it, Joshua suspected there were others like himself, but who kept their unique sensitivities, a.k.a. abilities, to themselves.

On cue, with barely a two-second delay, Joshua's phone vibrated alerting him to an incoming call. Annoyed, he furrowed his brow at the interruption and sneered as the caller ID showed it to be a blocked number. Unfortunately, his abilities didn't extend to mind reading. The blocked caller ID was troubling since very few people had his cellphone number. In general, Joshua preferred Face-to-Face conversations or email communications with an economy of words. He'd left clear instructions with his admin, Tamar, that under no circumstances was she ever to give out his cellphone number or disturb him with a transferred call unless it happened to be the Nobel Prize committee phoning to let him know he'd finally been nominated for a Peace Prize. A running joke in the company; Joshua, however, was dead serious.

Tzion heard Joshua's phone's humming vibration and offered a quick prayer of thanks for the interruption. Hopefully, his boss would take the call and go away, sparing him from further embarrassment. The Zedekiah Cave (ZC) module wasn't all that bad. The problem was he'd discovered an inexcusable graphics glitch long after the video had been shot, but not before he started editing and rendering the footage for the animation sequences. Supervising and coordinating the graphics, motion capture, and game development teams had been so overwhelming that he'd only just been able to address the problem with the ZC storyline. He thumbed the image game blocks on his wrist — Hazon Labs version of worry beads with *some* stress-relieving benefits. He'd created an image set with pictures of his family's Ethiopian village interspersed with the rolling Judean hills near *Beit Shemesh*. Everyone at Hazon Labs had their own set of customized image blocks, a minimally disruptive way to decompress and reset attention using a personalized figure-ground visual illusion. Each set also included a retractable USB thumb drive with fingerprint identification for login and continuous user verification, and a few other handy gadgets.

Joshua declined the call with a dismissive glance at the cellphone's display. Tzion's last hope was if his boss chose to review one of HaMikdash3.0's other twelve scenarios. "Please, please, please," he whispered in silent prayer, "just not Zedekiah's Tears." Unfortunately, neither luck, hope, nor prayers were on his side, and the tears were about to be his own.

With a twirl of his index finger, Joshua signaled they should continue with the sandboxed simulation, indicating that Tzion should proceed to the next sequence. The prompt was sufficient for him to respond to the stuttered call to accept the cha-cha-cha-challenge.

Speaking softly into his headset, he said, "Yes." The command triggered a vertical window-blind animation, revealing an expansive view of Jerusalem's Old City that filled the screen as the background image. The interface displayed HaMikdash3.0's thirteen (13) core storyline options; eight were set into each of the Old City's official gates including the sealed Hulda/Triple Gates at the base of the Temple Mount's southern exposure. For the 3.0 version, none of the storylines involved the famous/infamous *Sha'ar HaRachamim* — the sealed gate through which the *Moshiach* would enter the Temple Mount. Joshua had a different scenario already worked out for that gate in a later version of HaMikdash and smiled at the thought.

The onscreen background image was expansive, panning out of the Old City south to *Ir David* (the City of David) to the Pool of Siloam then to the *Givati* Parking Lot excavations and the closed-to-the-public Pilgrimage Road. To the east of the Old City, glowing activity icons highlighted the *Har HaZei'tim*/Mount of Olives cemetery and the nearby "Lost and Found in *Silwan*" storyline. In the north, users could visit the "Temple Mount Sifting Project" near Hebrew University's Mount Scopus campus. Each scenario blended animations of real-world locations with gamified interactivities and knowledge quests. The dozen "Under Construction" signs scattered throughout the image map held the promise of additional interactives currently under development.

The company's twenty-five employees and consultants were all part of THE greater development team. The eclectic and talented group of illustrators, historians, writers, and a core group of software and hardware engineers brought diverse and mostly complementary views to the project, with the usual friction expected in working with creatives, introverts, and mega-egos. While building the team was easy; keeping the company and the team running smoothly in the company's day-to-day operations proved more challenging for Joshua. With the war, attention was easily diverted to the latest news reports, hostage releases and rescues, body recoveries, and funerals to be attended.

The first hostage releases in November 2023 were cause for celebration, though mixed with healthy concern at the release of hundreds of convicted terrorists from Israeli jails in a 1:3 ratio. The concern was justified. Hamas leader Sinwar, mastermind of the October 7 slaughter, had been released in 2011, together with 1,024 other prisoners from Israeli jails, to secure the freedom of IDF soldier Gilad Shalit who'd been held by Hamas for over five years. By November 30, 2023, one-hundred-five civilian hostages had been released, 81 people from Israel, 23 Thais, and one Filipino. The brief moment of hope for the remaining hostages ended when Hamas broke the cease-fire agreement. Joshua scrambled in late December 2023 to arrange a team-building exercise at the Temple Mount Sifting Project (TMSP). The competitive treasure-finding tasks, water fights, and actual mudslinging offered the team a much-needed and well-deserved decompression. The sifting project became the newest 3.0 module, providing the team with an object lesson on how to optimize HaMikdash3.0 storylines and enhance user engagement. The Temple Mount Sifting Project storyline leveraged real-world Online to Offline (O+O) crossover activities with opportunities to promote Israeli tourism and the economy, an agreement inked with Israel's Ministry of Tourism. To further the collaboration, "Helper" avatars, identified by baseball caps bearing the official Ministry of Tourism logo, were strategically placed across the HaMikdash3.0 landscape to assist users. In HaMikdash3.0, the real-world, hands-on, crowd-sourced TMSP project was mirrored in the online experience as users were challenged to recover fragments of stone, glass, wood, bone, and pottery shards from buckets filled with mud and rubble.

The digital version of the "thousand-ton" rubble pile held many treasures and found objects. In the real world, the rubble had been illegally excavated from the Temple Mount in 1999 and unceremoniously dumped in the *Kidron Valley*. While the recovered objects had lost their *in situ* archeological and historical value, each find was nonetheless priceless. With HaMikdash3.0, they could digitally represent how the objects, the parts, had once belonged to the whole… the Temple.

The TMSP development team collaborated with Biblical archeologists from the Israel Antiquities Authority, Hebrew University and *Ir David*, selecting real-world found objects for the interactivities. By launch time, they would deliver a dozen puzzle-styled reconstruction scenarios with the missing pieces to be recovered from the sifting interactive. Users could adjust the skill level, varying the size and minimum number of "finds" a.k.a. puzzle pieces with matched points earned and progressions. While not everyone liked puzzles, real or digital, the 3D-like puzzle pieces added a new dimension to the interactivity. Users were required to download a 3D viewer and apply their visual-spatial skills to manipulate the puzzle pieces, rotating, flipping, and turning the found objects across the X, Y, and Z axes. The depth feature allowed Time, typically the fourth dimension, to provide Historical context within the three-dimensional virtual space.

After the launch crunch, the team could focus on developing twenty-four additional story-game scenarios, half in Jerusalem, and the other twelve set outside of Jerusalem, including in Hevron/Hebron at the *Ma'arat HaMachpelah/Ibrahimi Mosque* (Tomb of the Patriarchs and Matriarchs); at the Sea of Galilee as a fisherman (Fishers of Men) quizzed participants on the Bible; in *Qumran* with the discovery of the Treasures of Copper Scroll; and, at Rachel's Tomb as well as in Bethlehem proper for a special Christmas storyline heralding Jesus' birth.

The possible scenarios and storylines that could be developed were limited only by their imaginations. Thankfully, HaMikdash3.0's thirteen scenarios were robust enough to give them a head start before needing to deliver a 3.1 upgrade. Part of HaMikdash3.0's user engagement and promotional strategies was to allow the virtual world to develop based on user-defined activities, contributed content, and other participatory opportunities including storefront shops and businesses opened by 3.0 members. To further promote user engagement, members would be encouraged to propose location-based, game scenarios in open competitions that would be reviewed, ranked, and voted on by other HaMikdash3.0 members and complemented by a group of experts to ensure historical, religious, and cultural accuracy. They decided to link one user-supplied scenario competition to early registration, a bonus for pre-registered users.

Choosing the initial thirteen storylines for 3.0 had been challenging, forcing the team to adopt a "less is more" approach. The enthusiastic brainstorming sessions generated dozens of intersecting storyline ideas that filled three whiteboards and Dry Erase flip chart pages plastered on every bit of wall space in the conference center. Joshua eventually had to rein them in, focusing only on the first thirteen. He reminded them there would always be more storylines — some more compelling than others; and one, like the *Har HaZei'tim* storyline, which hit a little too close to home for Joshua.

If home is where your family is, then *Har HaZei'tim* was home for Joshua — his parents and grandparents were buried in the mountaintop cemetery, among the graves that could be traced back to the First Temple period. Joshua attempted to build the *Har HaZei'tim* storyline himself, but in a miserable crash and burn spent most of the time crying over his keyboard... literally. After several failed attempts, he smartly turned over primary production responsibilities for the *Har HaZei'tim* storyline to Tzion. He was already overseeing the whole of HaMikdash3.0 and building the Zedekiah Cave storyline, so what was one more in the grand scheme of things? Lucky number 13. While Tzion was honored by the task, he cried a little too.

In the end, Joshua knew he'd made the right decision. Tzion had done a stellar job, providing HaMikdash3.0 members with opportunities to earn participatory points in the virtual cemetery by performing various tasks. In addition to repairing destroyed headstones, collecting name rubbings, placing a remembrance stone on a grave, lighting a memorial candle, and picking up trash that littered the *Kidron Valley*, members could earn bonus points for recovering the names of the dead. The challenging task required online genealogical research to recover the names from the thousands of shattered headstones, some degraded by time, and thousands more deliberately destroyed during the Jordanian occupation of the Old City and East Jerusalem between 1948 and 1967.

Hopefully, Tzion had executed Zedekiah's Cave with the same attention to detail. Joshua nervously fiddled with his own set of image blocks.

The plain white blocks lacked any visible images; his could only be seen under UV light.

"Let's run Zedekiah's Cave. I want to see how the transition to the Temple Mount works," he said, then watched his lead developer physically squirm in his chair.

Tzion blew out a frustrated breath, knowing he'd better own the major league snafu sooner rather than later. "Upfront, my apologies, Joshua. No excuses. It's just that I've been spending most of my time supervising everyone else and well, ZC sucks. Actually, it's not all that bad, but there's an issue."

Joshua raised his eyebrows at Tzion's admission.

"But the other scenarios are perfect!" Joshua looked at him askance. "No, really, *b'emet!*" Tzion said, invoking the Hebrew word for "in truth."

Joshua smiled. He trusted Tzion to get it right, just hopefully within the constraints of their very tight timeline. "Let's just get through it, okay?" he said, wondering how bad their version of cave spelunking could be.

"Okay, this is the male avatar sequence," Tzion said, adjusting the specially designed glove that controlled character movements, and reengaged the demo.

Onscreen, the company's signature avatar steps into the frame and looks over his shoulder, half-turning his body... an invitation. The avatar then turns to face the user. On the front of his T-shirt is an illustration of Avera Mengistu, Tzion's cousin, and Hisham al-Sayed.

The two young men, both with mental health issues, had wandered into Gaza in 2014 and 2015, respectively, and had been held hostage by Hamas ever since. The terrorists not only refused to free them or for the International Red Cross to visit them, but also rejected calls to release the bodies of two IDF soldiers, Lieutenant Hadar Goldin, and Staff Sergeant Oron Shaul, killed during Operation Protective Edge/*Tzuk Eitan* in 2014. The parents of the four waged a tireless battle for their release, holding concerts and weekly rallies to help raise awareness and staging protests outside the *Knesset* and meeting with committee after committee. While met with sympathetic ears, their decade-long battles didn't change their reality as Hamas steadfastly refused to release either the dead or the living. Despite their efforts, they became part of the background noise, failing to gain sufficient momentum to raise the ire or urgency needed for *Pidyon Shevuim*, the Redeeming of Hostages. The religious obligation ranks among the greatest of *Mitzvot* (Commandments) that can be performed.

Before Oct7, the families of Goldin, Shaul, Mengistu, and al-Sayed suffered terribly with no word of their loved ones except for the doctored photos and videos released by their Hamas captors, which only deepened their families' psychological torture. The International Red Cross and Human Rights organizations stood silent; a collective failure that didn't even meet the bare minimum mandates of their mission statements or presumed Humanity. The world failed them, but Israel also failed to bring them home. In an all-too-prescient glimpse into the future, after Oct7 Israel was confronted with "redeeming" 251 hostages, the living and the dead, kidnapped by Hamas, along with the heads of those decapitated in the rampage. Horrific trophies taken as souvenirs or to be sold in Gaza… the going price: $10,000. To date, only the severed head of 19-year-old Sergeant Adir Tahar had been recovered. It had been kept in a freezer for two and a half months. These too needed to be redeemed in a macabre horror show without end.

In the wake of Oct7, an overdue reality emerged among Israelis who questioned why they had ever tolerated genocidal maniacs on their doorstep? Was it a perpetual underlying sense of victimhood that stood at odds with a tolerance born of arrogance, or deep-seated guilt over some nebulous offense? After Oct7, the families of the four 2014/2015 hostages joined the hundreds of families, and a nation, praying, hoping, and demanding that *all* of the hostages held by Hamas, those still alive and the dead, would be released, brought home. But the days and months marched on.

Tzion honored his cousin Avera by placing a picture of him, ten years out-of-date, on the avatar's T-shirt. Above it, was a yellow ribbon in honor of all the hostages still held by Hamas — a poignant symbol that became synonymous with the slogan, *Bring Them Home.*

Joshua gently squeezed Tzion's shoulder and swallowed hard, biting back the tears that lived just below the surface — an ongoing nationwide PTSD metered across the diversity of Oct7 experiences and the war that followed. The brave but senseless deaths of hundreds of IDF soldiers and reservists killed in action; news of confirmed hostage deaths from October 7th or those killed during their captivity; or, the deaths of three hostages mistakenly killed by the IDF; the bodies of dead hostages recovered in groups behind tunnel walls — all were parsed in news feeds, the details punctuated by a temporal crevasse that reopened wounds just as a scab had begun to form. All the while rockets and drones filled the skies, launched from the Houthis in the south, Hezbollah in the north, and Gaza in the east, sending people racing into bomb shelters where available and if time allowed. Twelve Druze children in the Golan town of *Majdal Shams* were murdered by a Hezbollah rocket that landed in the middle of a soccer game in July 2024. The Iranian barrage of 300 drones, rockets, and ballistic missiles launched at Israel's population centers in April 2024, but which were intercepted with 99% accuracy, exceeding the system's specifications. Truly miraculous, but which meant little to the bereaved Bedouin family mourning the death of their precious seven-year-old daughter, *Amina al-Hasoni,* who was killed in Iron Dome's 1% defensive failure. The immediate calls for restraint following the deadly assault… deadly for its intended outcome as an enfeebled U.S. government tried to contain Israel's response. Calls to "Take the win" amounted to a hollow victory, ignoring the intent of what might have been, and which was certainly the intended outcome by launching rockets at Israel's civilian population. "Take the win" for what? Surviving the genocidal intentions of Israel's enemies, whose so-called leaders hid in underground tunnels or lived in the lap of luxury in 5-star hotels in Doha. Leaders who continued to pad their billion-dollar bank accounts while trumpeting the miserable state of the Gazan population across the digital airwaves.

In Israel, defiant anger combined with profound sadness left no space for even a single breath in between. Life became an emotional rollercoaster where tears or rage could emerge without warning, prompted by simple truths, a song, a kind gesture, or even a smile. Oct7 could never be forgotten, because "never again" had happened right under the watchful eyes of the Field Observers, *tatzpitaniyot,* whose repeated warnings were largely ignored. Some suggested the warnings, though deemed credible, were callously used as a political timebomb gone awry — one that left 1,200 dead, 251 kidnapped by Hamas, and nearly 100,000 residents of Northern and Southern communities internally displaced as rockets, ballistic missiles, and suicide drones continue to rain down across Israel.

But perhaps one of the hardest to reconcile was how easily the world dismissed the horrific crimes perpetrated by Hamas. The monsters of October

7 didn't just kill people, shooting them down like dogs, but burned people alive; beheaded adults and babies; and mutilated and desecrated bodies gleefully, even playing with chopped-off body parts. As Tzion thought of that day, which he did often, he couldn't help but wonder how his cousin, Avera, had endured ten years in captivity with these cruel animals. Tzion also knew the true horrors of the day had not yet emerged as the survivors had only recently begun speaking of the horrors they witnessed, the rapes of both men and women, and the brutality of the assaults. He couldn't understand the silence, especially from the women's groups dedicated to fighting against sexual violence.

Was their hatred of Jews so absolute that they couldn't even muster an ounce of empathy or find their own integrity? Their collective silence conveyed either tacit approval or denial of the truth... both equally despicable. Forty-seven minutes of video footage from Oct7 didn't spur their conscience, nor did the 60-minute documentary, "Screams before Silence" produced by Sheryl Samberg, former CEO of Facebook. The documentary provided never-before-heard eyewitness accounts of the atrocities from victims and survivors of the Nova Music Festival who had watched helplessly as their friends were brutalized. Tzion didn't have to imagine what the hostages endured at the hands of their captors... some images stayed with you; emblematic of the horror. Naama Levy, a 19-year-old *tatzpitanit* being dragged from the back of a Jeep, the tendon of her Achilles' heel cut to prevent her from running away, and the seat of her sweatpants covered in blood. She'd been taken from the Nahal Oz Army base together with Agam Berger (19), Liri Albag (18), Karina Ariev (19), and Daniella Gilboa (19), all still in their pajamas, as the video of their abduction surfaced. As the Jewish New Year 5785/2024 approached, the country held its collective breath hoping the female soldiers along with Romi Gonen (23), Emily Damari (28), Arbel Yehoud (29), Doron Steinbrecher (30), and Shiri Bibas (32) and her children, four-year-old Ariel and nine-month-old Kfir, would all be returned alive.

Tzion touched the Hostage and Missing Families Forum solidarity dog tag with the Hebrew inscription, "הלב שלנו שבוי בעזה" (My heart is held captive in Gaza) that he, and much of the country, wore. He cleared his throat, then clicked on the *Ari of Judah* avatar. The point of view shifted, assuming an over-the-shoulder look. The back of the avatar's T-shirt revealed a swatch of aquamarine blue and purple colors, the color of *tekhelet* — the Biblical blue-purple colored dye extracted from a marine snail.

Using his gloved hand, Tzion hovered over the avatar's T-shirt. A small question mark icon pop-up appeared on the screen, alerting the user to an Information Cube (I-Cube). Like the Ministry of Tourism guides, the I-Cubes offered player-members relevant information and historical context to enhance their HaMikdash3.0 experience. The difference was that I-Cubes could be stored in a player-member's dashboard.

Tzion clicked on the sapphire-colored cube, which covered the history of *tekhelet*, its purpose, and the connection to the Ten Commandments that were "written" on sapphire stone tablets.

"I like your color choice," Joshua said admiringly.

"I've been refining the *tekhelet* RGB," Tzion said, referring to the mix of Red-Green-Blue pixel percentages from a 16-million color box of digital crayons. "The *Tekhelet Factory* folks say it's spot-on to the dye color they use for *tzitzit* strings," he said. When Tzion visited the *Tekhelet Factory*, he picked up a package of strings; a gift for his brother Zev's *Bar Mitzvah*. Looking at the package on his desk, he chided himself for not giving his brother the present sooner.

With Zev's *Bar Mitzvah* tomorrow, there wouldn't be enough time to replace the white strings on the four-cornered *tallit* and knot them with the new *tekhelet* ones. He'd been too busy to think ahead and would have to think of some way to make it up to his brother. Tzion was looking forward to the celebration; it had been a long while since he'd been inside the *HaNarkis* neighborhood *Beit Knesset* where his *Bar Mitzvah* had been held.

"Strange how *tekhelet* comes from shellfish," Joshua said, then added, "it being not very kosher and all," punctuating the comment with a confused frown on the unholy to holy transformation.

"Above my pay grade," Tzion smiled.

"And mine," noted Joshua. "I know I've told you this before, but the Ari avatar is brilliant, by the way," referring to the name, "*Ari of Judah*" written in bold block letters across the T-shirt's shoulders, like a football jersey.

HaMikdash3.0 allowed avatar names to be displayed in multiple ways, including with a simple, floating balloon above an avatar's head, embedded in an article of clothing, or placed on a shoulder badge, tattoo, or jewelry. The system was designed so that users could apply any "skin" to a selection of base avatars with different epidermal tones and add other character attributes and personalization features, including promoting causes on clothing; each feature was designed to add richness and depth to a user's online persona. HaMikdash3.0 members could even upload personalized graphics and face images into Hazon Labs' caricature generator to customize their avatars in Virtuoso, HaMikdash3.0's user-profile builder and avatar creator.

Many of HaMikdash3.0's advanced features were free; a subset, however, were only accessible through in-app purchases using *ShekCoins*, (*Shekel Bitcoins*), the site's issued bitcoin currency. *ShekCoins* could be earned through gameplay, banked directly, or allocated to real-world charities and other non-profit projects. Joshua discouraged long-term banking of *ShekCoins*, i.e. hoarding, by placing a time limit on how long *ShekCoins* could be kept in a member's online wallet; and, awarding points and rewards to members for giving *tzedakah* (charity). Each member was given a starting bank of *ShekCoins* with monies allocated from their subscription fees. *ShekCoins* were also given to those whose subscription fees had been waived. Joshua's goal was to keep HaMikdash3.0 accessible to all, regardless of income, while promoting the concept of *Tzedakah* and suitably rewarding members for their generosity, charity, and acts of kindness. Not surprising, the algorithm dinged misers and hoarders with a gentle warning.

Joshua's phone vibrated again. Another blocked number, the same or maybe different. Again, he didn't answer it and turned his attention back to Tzion. "*Slicha, ani eetcha*," meaning "Apologies, I'm with you." A truthful acknowledgement of the distraction in an ever-demanding, short-attention-span world filled with endless interruptions, and confirming to the recipient that they *now* had the speaker's undivided attention. Or, at least until the next priority distraction took its place.

Tzion re-initiated the onscreen sequence.

> *The Ari of Judah avatar stands before a black screen. A faint, single point of pulsating light is seen in the distance. Tzion had engineered a partial pause that allowed a subset of features to remain active... a prompt to facilitate user re-engagement.*

> *With a single click of the mouse, Ari of Judah takes a single step forward then promptly tumbles down an unseen flight of rock-hewn limestone stairs, and into a dark cave. Onscreen, a retake prompt with both text and audio is presented. "Care to try that again?"*

Ari of Judah virtually brushes himself off. He throws a disgusted, dagger-filled glance over his shoulder before running his hand through his short-cropped hair; an action modeled on one of Joshua's signature mannerisms.

Tzion heard Joshua chuckle, then tapped the "Yes" option. Building-in humor, easy wins, and second chance re-takes into gameplay were critical to HaMikdash3.0's design, as were the near-endless challenges that would ideally keep members engaged.

To incentivize pre-launch registrations, Hazon Labs offered a $250,000 grand prize to one lucky registered user. The first early enrollment drive was linked to the *Sefirat HaOmer*, the 49-day counting period between *Pesach*/Passover and *Shavuot*/Pentecost holidays. The pre-launch enrollment promotion was designed to boost the company's early revenues — a move that kept the accountants and investors happy, and off Joshua's back. The $250,000 inducement fell short of a *quid pro quo* lottery requiring users to pre-register/enroll/buy a subscription to qualify, which would have had HaMikdash3.0 run afoul of legal. But since HaMikdash3.0 also offered a fee waiver to anyone requesting one, the lawyers insisted they couldn't be accused of running a lottery scheme. The $250,000 prize monies were placed in a trust account, the day before any subscription fees were collected.

If their legal arguments were challenged, Joshua would reveal the truth behind Hazon Labs' pre-launch registration efforts, though he'd leave out the more desperate parts of the story… His story. The actual reason had little to do with the company's balance sheet or delivering a healthy ROI to Hazon Labs investors, though they would all benefit by default by a successful drive. The truth behind the enrollment drive was hidden in plain sight along with the rest of the company's proprietary information and guarded by a mandatory, iron-clad non-disclosure clause signed by its employees and consultants. Joshua's *truth* operated under the guise of a clever marketing ploy, stamped "top secret" and put into the vault, along with the quarter-million cash prize.

The "top secret" goal was to identify and "anoint" a player-member as HaMikdash3.0's *Kohen Gadol* (High Priest); a position first held by Aaron, Moshe's brother, in the 14th century BCE/BC. The "how" to the goal was a stealth program installed in a far-back corner of HaMikdash3.0, which scoured user-profiles and mined publicly sourced data about each

HaMikdash3.0 member. The collected and extracted data was then automatically fed into Joshua's Dimensional Torah Codes program (DTC) which would search the entire text of the *Torah*, mapping encoded words associated with each player-member.

Like other *Bible Codes* analyses programs, the search was linear, searching for non-contiguous letter strings that revealed hidden words and ideas in the gaped information. But Joshua's DTC added two features. The first viewed the *Torah* text as a continuum, connecting the last letter of the last word of Deuteronomy, a *lamed* (ל) in the word, *Yisroel* (ישראל) to the first letter of the word in Genesis, a *beit* (ב) in the word, *Bereshit* (בראשית). The second feature relied on a dimensional continuum of how the letters of the *Torah* aligned themselves vertically and horizontally in a wrapped Torah scroll configuration — the same configuration of how it was rolled and unrolled each *Shabbat* and on Holidays throughout the year. The dimensional program virtually rolled and unrolled a scroll, taking slices through the text and building a dynamic analysis across X, Y, and Z-axes. Joshua viewed the dimensional analysis as a kind of virtual CT, extracting data from the slices and then reconstructing these *in situ* for visualization.

The combined linear and dimensional analyses could be compared for any individual, yielding new and different insights, and hopefully bringing Joshua closer to finding the *Ones*… the *Kohen Gadol* and the other One. Given enough time and users, Joshua knew the DTC program would be able to identify the *first One*. A part of him hoped the appointment of a *Kohen Gadol*, even a virtual one, would be sufficient to shake the Heavens and move mountains. Literally. No doubt Jérémie "Jay" Sofer, his best friend and *sgan*/second-in-command, knew HaMikdash3.0's true mission, an absolute ground truth from which Joshua had never wavered. He understood the risks to his *Nefesh*, mortal soul, and its four Celestial counterparts, levels of soul consciousness: *Ruach*, *Neshama*, *Chaya*, and *Yechida*. His search for either of the chosen "Ones" would likely merit him a lengthy stay in *Gehinnom* to exact, in full measure, his soul's rectification. On Earth, it might just get him drawn and quartered. But if all went according to plan, he'd force G-d's hand to bring on the actual Messiah and resurrect the dead. His dead.

Timing notwithstanding, a chill ran down Joshua's spine as once again his phone buzzed, prompting Tzion to pause the scene. Joshua barely glanced at the screen to see "no name" pop into view and promptly dropped the phone into his back pocket.

"Sorry about the constant buzzards, Tzion." Unfortunately, turning off his phone wasn't an option. In general, he needed to be available 24/7, plus he was waiting for Jay to drop off the car for his run out to Reichman University. "Tzion, honestly, I'm not sure what you're so worried about. I like what I'm seeing so far. Really."

"Thanks, boss. But you may want to hold off on my bonus," he said, offering a lopsided grin topped by a furrowed brow.

"*Yalla*," Joshua said, adding "But maybe speed it up."

Tzion engaged the sequence, running it at 1.25X speed which had little perceptible effect on the audio or visuals.

> *Onscreen, Ari of Judah turns his head, looking to the left, then the right, and spies a torch affixed to the cave's rough limestone walls. He tries to remove the torch, but it doesn't budge. Thoughtfully, he leans in and grazes his hand over a simple letter-number-symbol substitution code etched into the limestone walls. He examines the torch's metal base which has a series of six rings stamped with the 22 letters of the Hebrew alphabet plus the five (5) sofit/ending letters of kaf, mem, nun, pe, and tzadik (ץ,ף,ן,ם,ך respectively)*

> *Using the specially fitted glove, Tzion virtually works the scytale-like cipher device, rotating the rings to spell out the name, Zedekiah in Hebrew, צדקיהו. He'd deliberately made the solution an easy-to-crack code, and an easy-to-guess password even without a cipher, foreshadowing more interesting letter-number-symbol challenges to follow.*

> *With the torch's scytale base encoded, a plus sign followed by a set of points, +50, +275, and a Time bonus +500 scrolls upwards, followed by an audible click as the torch is released from the magnetic mount. Ari of Judah nods, but the torch doesn't light. The avatar shakes it a few times as if it's a Faraday-type flashlight, but to no avail. Ari of Judah carefully looks down into the torch's cone then takes a closer look at its base and notices a keypad. Once again referring to the letter-number-symbol substitution code, Ari of Judah*

"air writes" the summed numerical value of 215 for the Hebrew letters in the name צדקיהו *and punches in the number sequence, 2-1-5. The torch lights. Its flame casts just enough light for Ari of Judah to see within his immediate personal space of approximately six feet, dalet amots.*

"The intensity of the flashlight changes based on speed, accuracy, and tasks completed," notes Tzion.

"Nice. Very nice."

With the torch lighting his way, Ari of Judah safely descends the steps into the darkness below. A baritone voice, which sounds like a cross between Arnold Schwarzenegger and Count Dracula, speaks. "You are entering Zedekiah's Cave. Here, King Solomon's Master Masons quarried the special Meleke limestone used to build the First Temple. You, Ari of Judah, have been chosen to help build the 3rd Temple… HaMikdash3.0."

Joshua chuckled ever so lightly, truly pleased. Tzion glanced up in time to see Joshua's smile.

Onscreen Ari of Judah raises the torch and looks at the cave's ceiling. The cartoon-styled image of the actual cave reveals a mix of graffiti, tool marks, and the sharp, ninety-degree edges of previously quarried limestone.

"Zedekiah's Cave holds many secrets, cryptic codes, and clues carved into walls to guide you through secret passages up to the Temple Mount or through other paths stretching out to the northeast to the plains of Jericho, a distance of 27.3588 kilometers. What awaits you is a great treasure, but your first task begins by finding your way to a pool of water, fed by an unknown water source, located deep in the bowels of the cave."

A still shot of a raised platform brimming with water appears on screen. "These are the 'Tears of Zedekiah' the tears shed by Zedekiah for his murdered sons, killed by Nebuchadnezzar.

"Your task is to fill the limestone cup with Zedekiah's Tears. But how? You will have to work for your reward. You must master

the secret of the shamir, mining the quarry, producing a building block worthy of the Temple, and deciphering the code to learn the Freemasons' secrets for raising a five-ton stone block to its place on the Temple Mount. Then, and only then, will 'thy cup runneth over'."

"I took some literary liberty with the translation," Tzion said, with an innocent shrug

"For a good cause," Joshua said, adding a wink. During their bantering, Joshua caught a glimpse of a fleeting shadow crossing *Ari of Judah's* path, a mere two-tenths of a second, the length of an average blink. "Very nice. Subtle," Joshua remarked, punctuating the comment with a chuckle.

"I've designed a variety of *sheidim*," Tzion said, referring to the dark creatures rife in HaMikdash3.0's scenarios; each kind is designed to foil or foul the user's actions. "I created an image mask so we can drop them in or take them out of any scenario."

"Can't escape them. They are everywhere, after all," Joshua said, casting his eyes all around him at the unseen beings occupying the multi-dimensional spaces extant with their own "relative" reality.

"I've put a limit on the number of *sheidim* masks per scenario, and on any user avatars with similar nefarious attributes as well."

"Good. I don't want us creating a Hell space filled with demons," Joshua said. The topic had come up at one of their team meetings early on as they worked out HaMikdash3.0's no-go scenarios. Joshua knew of demons and had more than a few of his own, but he had no desire to turn HaMikdash into a Middle Earth version of *Gehinnom*, a.k.a. Hell.

"*Yalla*," he said, indicating that Tzion should *hemshech*/continue with the rest of the scene.

The shadow's brief onscreen appearance prompts an AI-driven fear response. a dizzying flip of Ari of Judah's head from side to side, as he tries to track the elusive shadow figure. The figure is creepily glimpsed standing right behind Ari of Judah.

"Ari of Judah, beware. Be AWARE. Dangers and hazards surround you. Dark forces will block your path and try to lead you astray, to keep you from completing your tasks and reaching your goal.

Beware of the shadows. Beware of the whispering stones. Beware of the creeping creatures that live in the tombs below.

"Leave now or continue your quest? Choose wisely…" Without hesitating, Tzion clicked the "yes" button, then using the interactivity glove walked Ari of Judah forward, following the steps slowly down, deeper into the cave. A vigilant Ari of Judah is acutely attuned to his surroundings. He enters a large, high-ceilinged cavern, extending the torch into the space in front of him. The cavern visibly brightens.

"You have entered the Meeting Place, the Hall of the Freemasons. Here in King Solomon's quarries, the Freemasons meet each year. Here, they honor King Solomon, their first Grand Master. Here, you will quarry limestone and discover the key hidden in the Masonic symbols.

"Look, and you will see. Listen, and you will hear in this place of sound and music… a meeting place for song and service."

A cartoonified image of the popular Jewish reggae rapper, Matisyahu, is projected onto a cavern wall, along with a crowd of cheering avatar fans as the Matisyahu avatar sings his hit song One Day.

The concert projection fades. Ari of Judah looks to the cavern's floor where a colorful poster promoting a Matisyahu concert lies at his feet. A thin trickle of water flows over the page, smudging the print on the poster dated April 3, 2024. The water continues to wash away the text, revealing a map drawing of the cave and a hidden cavern below. As Ari of Judah bends to pick up the map, a gust of wind blows through the cave lifting the map into the air, out of reach.

The scene zooms out. Ari of Judah chases after the paper racing through the cave, slipping and sliding on the slick limestone. "He" barrels forward to a rock-hewn crevice and skids to a stop before a chest-high ledge brimming with water flowing over the top.

The narrator speaks. "These are Zedekiah's Tears. You have arrived."

Ari of Judah reaches his hand out to touch the continuous trickle of water, dripping into the pool of water from an opening in the rocks above. In the center of the ledge is a cup fashioned out of limestone.

The scene is perfect, except for one minor detail; the cup is upside down and rather than the water filling the cup, it bounces off the upturned cup, spraying droplets off to the sides.

Joshua was momentarily speechless, but if actions could speak louder than words and fury is measured by silence, then his punching the wall spoke volumes.

"Oh, come on, Tzion. This is the rendered footage. You guys shot this stuff months ago! Didn't anyone notice the damn cup was upside down?"

Tzion spun around in his chair to face his boss. "Honestly no, not until I started editing."

"Un-be-lie-va-ble," Joshua said, hyphenating each syllable. He ran his left hand through his short-cropped reddish blonde hair wishing he had more to pull on.

"I know it looks bad, but I think I came up with a way to save it as is…"

"Do I *really* want to know?"

"Honestly, I think it might be even better than the original gameplay scenario."

"Gimme," Joshua said with a heavy sigh.

"Okay. As play progresses, the center of the cup gets progressively worn down as players earn points with each ZC task performed. We can adjust the erosion rate and when they hit a pre-set threshold, the cup forms a kind of thick, hollowed-out ring. And…"

Joshua cleared his throat, cutting Tzion off. "Ugh, Lord of the Rings dinging any bells?"

"No, no, no, not like that. The water wears down the cup, hollowing it out, and only then can the water start to fill the shelled-out cup up to a pre-set meniscus. It extends gameplay but doesn't change the fundamental storyline since we can still use the weight of the water to trip the lever." Tzion hadn't taken a single breath during his scrambled-eggs presentation. Finally pausing, he inhaled sharply and waited expectantly for Joshua's reaction.

"Hmmm, interesting… so a cup in formation, not a ring, that still gets filled."

"Yep. We can even elaborate gameplay by adding an acid-base chemical reaction challenge as a bonus since the cup is made of limestone, and even linking it to a possible explanation for the *shamir's* mode of action. Anyway, successful task completion speeds up the rate of erosion. We could even have symbols appear on the side of the cup which can be integrated with another storyline."

"The Copper Scroll," they said in perfect unison, smiling.

Joshua held up his hands, a clear "enough, stop" signal, then drew a finger across his lips thinking. A single thoughtful, harumph escapes.

"So, what'd ya think?"

"It's still a little lemon-lemonade-like, but then I kind of like lemonade," Joshua said. Then, dropping his voice a couple of octaves, adding, "kind of." He gave Tzion a thumbs-up sign, then made a beeline for the door.

"I might have to reshoot some MoCap footage," Tzion shouts after him.

"Permission granted, not that you need it. Now get out of here. *Shabbat Shalom* and *Mazal Tov* on your brother's *Bar Mitzvah*," Joshua said as the door to the screening room eased closed with a slow pneumatic hiss and the unmistakable sound of Joshua's phone buzz-humming again.

Only this time, the vibration was heralded by a welcomed ringtone — a *Tekiah Gedolah shofar* blast lasting for 14.9 seconds, followed by a series of *shofar* sounds — followed by three punctuated *shevarim* wails, and the *teruah's* rapid nine tutting sounds, blasting out the news: HaMikdash3.0 had hit its next pre-launch registration milestone — 1.5 million member-players.

Hazon Labs' security cameras captured Joshua's smile and the incomplete thought as he stepped outside into the mid-morning sun, "Jimi…"

Chapter 3

"Jiminy Cri-. Crickey!" Archangel Uri'el (אוריאל) thundered. How in the h-e-double toothpicks am I supposed to get any work done around here!" he grumbled under his breath, releasing a growl from his lion's face that inadvertently triggered a small underwater earthquake centered fifteen miles off the coast of Manaus.

"One hundred thousand screaming Guardian Angels in the last half hour alone, and all singing out of tune." He lifted his eyes to one of the Heavenly Realms above his own. "Where are the Levites' melodious songs when you need them?" He sneered at the cacophony's source... 1.5 million Guardian Angels. "Really?"

He considered his next action for only a moment as the strident noise levels rose to a crescendo that might easily trigger an avalanche if there were snow or mountains in the Heaven of Heavens. Uri'el's genius flesh-and-blood charge had programmed *his* alerts to sound a *shofar* blast whenever HaMikdash3.0 enrolled a new member, including a 5X multiplier when they reached an enrollment milestone. Unfortunately for Uri'el, he/she/it was forced to listen to every 2.99-second-long digital *Tekiah shofar* blast with EVERY new member that HaMikdash3.0 signed on, and which had the "bonus" side effect of creating a new Guardian Angel (GA) in Heaven *every* bloody time. That wasn't exactly true. Joshua's 2.99 seconds-long *tekiah*, fell just shy of the required angel-making 3.0 seconds. THE Supreme Celestial Council decided not to penalize Joshua or HaMikdash3.0 for the slightly shorter-than-required *shofar* blasts. Instead, they applied a summative formula that allowed individual *tekiah* blasts to be combined to reach the minimum time length for properly generating a Guardian Angel. Some rules could be adapted with end-around fixes; others were top-down commandments from Above and could not be amended. Any GAs-in-development were held in reserve and carried over to the next *shofar* blast to complete the GA-generating process. It seemed like an equitable solution.

Uri'el couldn't be sure, but he suspected that Joshua Katz knew exactly what he was doing by creating an army of Guardian Angels (GAs). As much as he hated to admit it, they would need all the help they could get in the coming battle... but that discussion was best left to another day.

"Talk about protection," he said, scratching his head with the tip of his wing. For now, the newbie GAs needed to be corralled into service, and it fell to Uri'el to gather the proverbial troops. He had no choice in the matter. Each of HaMikdash3.0's Guardian Angels was linked to *his* chimerically shifted Archangel/Cherub frequencies, vibrating between 690-790 Terahertz (THz) in the purple-violet (*argamon*) portion of the visible light spectrum. His frequency shone forth even though he was providing a temporary home for one of the Ark of Covenant's *Cherubim*, but more on his centuries-long chimeric dilemma later. For now, the noise level was enough to wake the proverbial dead, though technically there weren't any dead in Heaven. Rather, freed from the shackles of their human form, souls continued to evolve.

When Uri'el could stand the noise no longer, he flicked his winged wrist and silenced all the GAs around him. The newbie angels continued their chatter and chanting only in a narrow FM radio band, offering Uri'el a welcomed respite.

"Ahhh, much better! Now where was I? Ah yes, but first…" With a Cheshire cat grin, which admittedly looked ridiculous on his lion face, he decided a little payback was in order. He primed a series of *machlokot* — disputes — which would invariably lead to hours of endless debates in the hallowed Earthly *midrashot*, centers of learning.

The first question was an obvious one. Uri'el placed it into the open mind of a Gen-Zer who'd been weaned on an unhealthy diet of digital milk — no judgment intended. He quickly gave the Big Guy a thumbs up making sure the *Kochot*, a.k.a. The Powers that Be, knew that he knew his place. And so, he began the entry…

> *"Did sounding a digital shofar with the click of a mouse count towards fulfilling the mitzvah, the commandment? Did sounding the shofar off-season count as a sin rather than a blessing? And if the tekiah blast came just short of the required three seconds as with the HaMikdash3.0 sounds, was one obligated to say the bracha, the blessing?"*

The questions were theoretical on Earth, suitable fodder for endless study hall discussions; in Heaven, however, the population explosion of HaMikdash3.0-generated Guardian Angels was already a vexing, overcrowding problem with no relief in sight. Relatively speaking. Yes, angels take up space, albeit in ten dimensions across the seven Heavens.

Pleased, Uri'el returned to his official record of angelic reflections and considered how best to craft the next part of his entry. The key to his treatise would be the sixth letter in the Hebrew alphabet, *vav*. He dipped his feather quill into the ink well to continue his entry. Other Heavenly Creatures preferred to instantly transfer their thoughts onto parchment, a bit of hocus-pocus osmosis where thought energy flowed, transmuted from one form into another. Uri'el was old school, preferring a more traditional approach for his contributions to the Angelic record. According to the Rules, each Archangel was given charge over a portion of the 600,000 soul groups, the root souls, and was responsible for recording the salient details in the official Chronicle of past, present, and future events in a simultaneous confluence of Space-Time.

While *Matat* — the safest way to refer to the Archangel *Metatron* — was Heaven's official scribe, each of the Archangels was also required to submit a personal chronicle, a diary. Uri'el, an Archangel by design, already held a highly respected position in the hierarchy of Celestial Beings but had been "temporarily" raised to a *quasi-Cherub* status attendant with the responsibilities and facial features. Overbooked, overworked, and overscheduled, didn't begin to cover his new responsibilities leaving him with little more than a femtosecond of extra time on his proverbial hands, or wings as the case may be. His status quo *status* would hold until the Holy Ark of the Covenant was safely restored to the *Kodosh HaKodashim* — the Holy of Holies — and his resident *Cherub* could be returned to its place of honor. Rumor had it that the other *Cherub* was missing in action. Uri'el wasn't so sure. He suspected at least one of the *Cherubs* was commanded to stay with Ark at all times. He got "stuck" with the other one, but hopefully not for too much longer. In the grand earthly scheme of things, a 6,000-year cycle, things would move along quickly. Especially now.

"Now where was I? Ah yes."

Like my kind, I am generally tasked with only one job/task/mission at a time. The approach focuses absolute attention on whatever needs doing, watching, helping, or protecting, and to effect the confluence of past, present, and future events to a given end (though none would dare call it interference). Our intention might be on an individual, but more often it is on a soul group or a soul root if, Heaven forbid, its progression begins to regress. It was rare to see the complete restoration of a soul group or the gathering of sparks in a single individual. Such transmigrations, however, can become more common, especially in times of change when it is necessary to effect a shift in the course of Human events. That is the situation today, and as it will be, in the coming days for my ascendant charge, Joshua E. Katz, born of a Priestly family in the Great Assembly of Kohanim.

Sometimes, when it is a critically important task, such as when the fate of Mankind hangs in the balance, as when evil — true evil — threatens the continued existence of Man, an Archangel will often work with a host of Guardian Angels (GAs)…

Looking out of the corners of his eyes, Uri'el cast a dismissive glance, sneering in the general direction of the newbie GAs. "G-d help me," he whispered. He shook one head after the other as he caught a glimpse of a trail of GAs climbing the proverbial walls, hopping and loping about in Parkour heaven. Impressed with their athletic abilities, he identified the five most talented of the bunch, recording their identity numbers for future, high-altitude missions.

For the moment, he closed the page on Joshua E. Katz and picked continued with the general Angelic record, his personal musings.

Uri'el and Ari'el — the story of the light and the lion. He paused, thinking it would make a decent title for a book or movie in the same vein as C.S. Lewis's novel, "The Chronicles of Narnia: The Lion, The Witch, and the Wardrobe."

Our names differ by a single letter in the Hebrew alphabet: a vav (ו); its corresponding numerical value is 6. The number 6 is widely accepted as symbolic of the six days of Creation. The Hebrew word, בראשית, Bereshit, which translates to "In the beginning," also has six letters. Coincidence? I think not.

The vav holds a special place in the first sentence of the Bible, connecting Heaven and Earth. In Genesis 1:1, the sentence: 'Bereshit bara Elo-kim et ha'Shamayim <u>v</u>'et ha'Aretz' translates to 'In the beginning, G-d created the Heavens <u>and</u> the Earth.' The vav is not *a mere Boolean operator; rather, it signifies the mirroring of activities between the two realms, between Heaven and Earth, forming an intimate connection. My fellow Celestials and I have been since the beginning of Man's time (and before), so it is fitting that it should fall to us to help mediate this challenging time in Human history. Still…*

Uri'el covered his four faces with his wings, shielding his eyes and thought-transferred the rest.

Ironically, centuries before the advent of computers, the revelation of the hidden had already begun. Mankind was more perceptive than we Celestials generally gave them credit for…"

"Strike that," Uri'el said not wishing to incur the wrath of the female contingent, then continued with the thought transfer.

Man/Woman was smarter than we Celestials gave him/her credit for being, though Heaven forbid should any Angel, Archangel, or other Higher Being ever admit to the unspoken sibling rivalry, the competition between our kinds. It didn't take long for them to gain insights into the power inherent in the Hebrew letters. However, it took time before the Earth dwellers (gender-neutral pronoun, deemed acceptable) applied their knowledge to the Word of G-d and began unraveling the Word's esoteric layers, decoding the hidden meanings embedded in the text of the Torah.

Uri'el's faces all smiled at once as he cleverly negotiated the gender trap.

By the time most Earth children reach the age of three, they've learned their ABCs; some even know it to the end of the alphabet. By age 4 or 5, many can recognize the letters as distinct and not merely relegated to their role in a sing-song melody. Unlike the alphabet, cardinal numbers, ordinals, in particular, can be challenging at any age as many mathematical concepts can be abstract. Does 1+1 equal 2 or is there a Gestalt, where the whole is something other than, more than, the mere sum of its parts?" But I digress.

Children growing up in bi-/multilingual families confront additional challenges, or benefits as some suggest, tackling number and letter songs and rhymes in multiple languages which can facilitate learning, maximizing lateral thinking and neuroplasticity. Children, attending a religious or synagogue-based preschool, are simultaneously taught the Alphabet alongside the Aleph-Beis: the 22 letters of the Hebrew alphabet (27 if you count the ending sofit letters, typically found only at the end of a word, save for a few exceptions). Note also the linguistic crossover between the words: alphabet, alpha-beta, and aleph beis are apparent. Note, the difference between "beis" and "beit" reflects pronunciation differences between Ashkenazi and Sephardi Jews, or between Israelis and others.

As I was thinking, the tunes for the ABCs and Aleph-Beis are decidedly different. The direction in which the letters are written is opposite, and the letter shapes are distinctly dissimilar. While the first two letters, A-Aleph and B-Beit, are phonetically aligned, the similarity ends at the third letter C-Gimel, but picks up again with D-Dalet, only to diverge again. While certainly confusing for young children, dual language instruction paves the way to understanding the language of the Bible, the Torah.

The letter, Aleph, is one of several letters used to symbolize the unity of G-d... the G-d of all Creation. This unity is exemplified in the Shema prayer, the declaration of faith and belief: 'Hear, O' Israel, G-d is our L-rd, G-d is One' — recited in the morning and evening prayers, respectively, and then a version of which is said before retiring to bed. The Shema is a prayer of sanctification and often used as a symbol of resistance, urgently recited throughout the ages when the embers of hate sent Jews into the next world... the last utterances of the persecuted whispered or shouted Al Kiddush Ha-Shem, Sanctifying G-d's Name.

Uri'el paused respectfully to honor the memory of the innocents brutally killed by Hamas at the Nova Music Festival and in the surrounding Kibbutzim on October 7th. He held the moment for the heroes killed and injured defending the south from the Gazan invaders.

Until Oct7, it had been some time since Heaven had heard the volume of strangled and terrified cries of the Shema prayer. The

Holocaust years were filled with such prayers spoken with dying breaths, but Oct7 stood out as a singular event in contemporary Jewish history. The cries of the innocent shook all seven Heavens from the highest point to its very foundations, and in the months that followed, the anguished tears of loss continued to flood the Heavens.

While Islam's 'martyrs' commit heinous crimes and seek death in the name of All-ah, claiming to glorify All-ah by their evil, Judaism celebrates the sanctity of life and it is only when a Jew is murdered because of their faith or Jewish identity that it is said that they have died as true Holy martyrs sanctifying G-d's name. On October 7th, that distinction was never more clearly evident as the words of the Shema prayer passed the lips of hundreds of terrified young people at the Nova Music Festival, crying out with their last breath. On Oct7 as the forces of evil defiled All-ah's name, G-d's name, with every life they took, with every world they destroyed, the souls of those who they murdered were lifted to the Heavens to stand at the right hand of G-d beside the Kiseh HaKavod — the Throne of Honor, the Glory Seat. Martyred in life for the sanctification of G-d's Name, Al Kiddush Ha-Shem, these Holy Ones were already consecrated. For those murdered Al Kiddush Ha-Shem, the Jewish ritual of taharah, preparing and purifying the dead for burial, is not necessary as they are considered to be already pure, purified in their sacrifice and effecting a rectification of their souls.

Uri'el paused his thoughts again, allowing the sweet sounds of the song, *Elokai Neshama*, to fill the space around him.

Elokai Neshama shehnatata be tehora he, Kol Z'man she'haneshama bekirbee modeh ani l'fanecha... My God, the soul You put in me is pure. As long as the soul is in me, I thank You..."

The pure soul of Yehuda Bacher, a pure light, joyously sang the words while driving in his car in the days before he was murdered on Oct7. Some saw the looming shadow of the *Malach HaMavet*, the Angel of Death pass over Yehuda's face as he sang about the *neshama* — the heavenly soul, the counterpart to the earthly *nefesh*: "You created it, you designed it, you breathed it into me, you guard it within me, And you will take it from me, but will return it to me in the future, eternally." No more prescient words were ever spoken. His tragic murder on Oct7 brought these simple words to a world in need of soul-full comfort. Uri'el allowed himself another moment in Yehuda's Light, then returned to the Celestial record. It wouldn't do for the GAs, or worse his fellow Angelics, to find him crying like a baby. Unfortunately, he was a little late reining in the tear rolling down his cheek as one of the GAs waved a cloud box of Kleenex® for him to use.

He accepted the kindness with a grateful nod of all of his heads. Guardian Angel number: 730.71 (GA-730.71), however, mistakenly took the gesture as an invitation. The little guy promptly hopped on Uri'el's winged shoulder, sporting a silly grin, pleased as a peach with his newfound perch. Uri'el was about to flick him off when he heard his mind's ear, say, "The World stands on three things, *Torah, Avodah, Ve'Gemilut Chasadim* (Torah, Service of G-d, and Acts of loving-kindness)." All true, but which did not apply to Celestials, except GA-730.71 was familiar with *Proverbs 1:2*, and stood just a little taller, all 2.5" of him.

Ostensibly, Uri'el was in charge of training the GAs and recognized the good lesson he could impart to them before they'd officially be called up to the front lines. He turned his Human face to GA-730.71 and thought-transferred a simple "thank you." Overwhelmed, the little guy demurely lowered his head and turned a spectrum of colors from lavender to indigo.

Now where was I, Uri'el wondered.

Ah yes… the Hebrew letters and their hidden meaning; the perfect segue back to the story of technology whiz-kid Joshua E. Katz. Uri'el smiled at the letter "E" in Joshua's name, nodding deferentially to its Hebrew source; though it was not the letter, Ayin (ע) but the letter, Aleph (א).

Continuing. With the aid of computers, one can search for interesting relationships, applying word-letter-number combinatorics. These number manipulations are part of the mystical nature of the Hebrew letters, the words they form, and what may be formed, called into being, from them. Such is the power of these otiot which G-d combined to create the world. For seekers, the esoteric mysteries embedded in the text of the Torah are conveyed in the absolute prohibition to neither add nor subtract; or, to change even a single letter of the text.

Should a hand-written Torah scroll have any such defects it is rendered *pasul*, unusable for ritual purposes, despite the laborious effort and cost of handwriting a Torah scroll. The prohibition against modifying the text also applies to a subset of unusual letters found in the Torah, which by design, can appear inverted, broken, or written larger or smaller than the other letters.

Owing to the vagaries of language and the scattering of the Jewish people to the four corners of the world over the millennia one would expect to see errors in translation or transmission to occur in a hand-copied document be it from spontaneous mutations or simple transcription and/or translation errors. Yet today's texts match with near-perfect identity to thousand-year-old scroll fragments found in ancient libraries around the world and those recovered in the caves of Qumran along the shores of the Dead Sea. The question, of course, is why? Granted, it is the word of G-d, but why should such a rigid preservation process be applied to the Torah's text? Why? Why is each letter (and letter part) of the Torah given preeminence, none above another, all deemed essential?

As the authoritative words of G-d delivered to Moses on Mount Sinai, all 304,805 letters comprising 79,976 words carry inherent holiness and, by default, intrinsic value of immeasurable nature. But while the absolute fidelity of the letter sequence has been carefully guarded, the letters and words have nonetheless been subjected to a wide range of mathematical, thematic, and linguistic machinations through the practice of Gematria.

A simple/not-so-simple explanation of Gematria is included here for reference. In numerical terms, each Hebrew letter corresponds to a number. The letter aleph (א) equals 1, beit (ב) equals 2, and so on through the letters of the Aleph Beit (alphabet) through to and including the letter yud which equals 10. But then, the numbering logic changes using increments of 10. The kaf (כ) equals 20; lamed (ל) equals 30 until the letter kuf (ק) which equals 100. From there, *the letter values are in increments of 100 from the resh (ר) which equals 200, then shin (ש) equaling 300 to the last letter of the Aleph Beit, the taf (ת) with a value of 400. Another exception is the letter aleph, which can also be assigned the numerical value of 1,000.*

Uri'el paused long enough to see the GAs lined up in neat pyramid stacks of five hundred each, trying to follow his treatise on *Gematria*, feverishly scribbling and comparing notes. The confusion on their faces was matched by a strong wind created by their raised, waving wings, giving him pause. Even GA-730.71 apologetically hunched up his winged shoulders as lost as the others.

Perhaps, an example, he announced, earning him a chorus of inaudible sighs and wing claps. The word for water is mayim (mem-yud-final mem) מים *which has a numerical value of 40 + 10 + 40 = 90. Numerically then the word mayim can be related to other words or phrases with the same numerical value, such as the Hebrew word for king, melech (*מלך*) whose letter combination also has a numerical value equal to ninety (40 + 30 + 20 = 90).*

The mathematically adept among the GAs worked out the calculations themselves and gave him a thumbs/wingtip-up sign.

Words can have an alternative, simple numerical value if they contain any of the sofit letters of chahf (ך), mem (ן), nun (ן), and pe (ף). As such water has an alternative value of 650 (40 + 10 + 600) where the mem sofit (ם) has a value of 600, but that is a discussion for another time.

There are other types of Gematria calculations beyond simple sums, including differences, first and/or last letter reconstructions, and word root comparisons designed to elucidate relationships between words and spaces which share the same numerical value or conceptual in a fascinating exploration into the many layers of the Torah. This literal, one-dimensional perspective, can connect the seemingly unconnected through numbering parallels and letter-number manipulations with simple letter rearrangement, addition, and/or subtraction algorithms applied to the primary text.

He glanced at the GAs to make sure they were following his dissertation and was pleased to see a majority of the GAs giving him a solid two-thumbs/wings-up sign.

> *The use of computers allows for an elaborated probing of the Torah's hidden layers, applying advanced algorithmic models and supercomputing Artificial Intelligence tools to uncover the hidden. But long before the advent of computers, the erudites were granted insight into this hidden Torah world. Rabbi Bachya ben Asher, a 13th-century Spanish mystic, explored the Torah's very first sentence to find its hidden meaning. He looked to identify discernible patterns between the letters based on an equidistant spacing, a skip distance between the letters, and from those letters to construct words or concepts that ignored the spacing gaps to form new words (and worlds).*

Uri'el looked again at the GAs and was relieved that many had fallen asleep; relieved, since he didn't feel like explaining the nuances of the encoded secrets in the *Torah*. Even GA-730.71 had tucked himself into a feathery bed.

> *Without the benefit of a supercomputer, Rabbi ben Asher calculated the length of the lunar cycle based on the day and time of the moon's birth at Creation by regrouping a subset of the letters. Using a letter-number calculation, he obtained a value for the length of the lunar cycle equal to 29.530594; a value which astoundingly differs by only 0.000006 when compared to NASA's own 2007 satellite-based observations of 29.530588 ... a surprise to some, but not everyone.*

> *These kinds of explorations and discoveries continued through time. In the 16th century, Rabbi Moshe Cordovero, a revered scholar and mystic from Safed, a city in Israel's north, wrote about the 50 Gates of Understanding — 50 ways to understand the Torah...*

On cue, the HaMikdash3.0 Guardian Angel Acapella group began humming the tune of Paul Simon's 1975 hit song, "50 Ways to Leave Your Lover" to which Uri'el promptly plugged *all* his ears. To convey his displeasure, he turned his lion face to them. Like naughty little children, they started giggling in the corner. His human face glared at the mischievous group, which he followed quickly with an angry roar from his lion. Not to be outdone, his eagle offered up a high-pitched, ear-splitting squawk and, lastly, a threatening guttural bray from his ox face. For once, he was happy to put his *Cherub* features to good use.

"Not another sound," he cautioned them, splaying open his wings. GA-730.71 woke up long enough to join the rebuke, scowling and pointing a rigid wing finger at his fellow GAs. The group retreated into a tight huddle, or as much of a tight huddle as a 1.5 million-strong army of Guardian Angels could muster.

Settling back into a meditative state, Uri'el continued his entry.

In Rabbi Cordevero's description of the 30th Gate of Understanding, he wrote the following: 'The secrets of our holy Torah are revealed through knowledge of combinations, numerology (gematria), switching letters, first-and-last letters, shapes of letters, first– and last– verses, skipping of letters, and letter combinations. These matters are powerful, hidden, and enormous secrets. Because of their great hiddenness, we cannot fully comprehend them. Further, to see different angles through these methods is infinite and without limit. On this, the Torah says, 'its measure is longer than the world.'

Over the centuries, Rabbi Cordevero's curious words challenged many to knock on the Torah's secret gates. Notable among them was Rabbi Chaim Michal Dov Weissmandl, a Slovakian scholar who lived during the tumultuous times of both World War I and II. Weissmandl developed an ingenious method to help him decode the mysteries of the Torah. Painstakingly, he arranged all 304,805 letters into 10x10 arrays and printed them on white index cards to help him better visualize cryptic patterns and illuminate additional equidistant letter skip patterns. He scanned for emergent patterns that generated words, concepts, names, and historical events and transformed the lines of text into coherent, non-random patterns, despite the spatial separation of the component letters. Following his death in 1957, Rabbi Weissmandl's students published a book with his discovered Torah codes. The book, titled Toras Chemed

(תורת חמד) combined the roshei tevot, the first letters of Rabbi Weissmandl's name to form the word, חמד: Chaim (ח) Michal (מ) Dov (ד) — a fitting homage to the man and the mathematics of Gematria which enriched his, and their, study of the Torah.

Rabbi Weissmandl is credited as the modern torchbearer, the forerunner to contemporary scholarship into the hidden Torah codes. These studies have engaged students, scholars, researchers, statisticians, mathematicians, and computer experts, including Joshua E. Katz — Yehoshua Eli…

Uri'el caught himself before putting too much into the record. Eventually yes, but not at this particular point in Time. Any misstep could inadvertently affect the outcomes of events and not necessarily in a good way. In the next instant, Uri'el deleted Joshua's Hebrew name and inserted his English name, punctuating it properly with a period.

"That was close," he said, then continued the thought writing.

The rapid evolution of computing capabilities in the late-20th century combined with advances in image processing made the study of the 'infinite' that Rabbi Cordovero described in the 16th century possible. With computers, the textual and textured nuances of the 30th Gate of Understanding could finally be released from its previous password-protected, encrypted status.

Voodoo notwithstanding, cutting-edge AI-driven, Deep Learning algorithms are a dark mystery, veiled behind a cloak of unrestrained checkpoints and endpoints, and relational permutations with emergent learning capacities. Deep Learning presents ITself alternatively functioning as a fully differentiated, autonomous semi-sentient entity or a de-differentiated cancer lacking internal regulatory controls — a scary binary beast. In either case, AI is perfectly suited to building esoteric-squared connections that might finally unlock ALL of the levels at the 30th Gate of Understanding, and perhaps even beyond. For over forty years, a dedicated group of researchers have pursued scholarly research into the mathematical and statistical validity and uniqueness of Torah Codes. Known as the Gates Working Group, their name is not an ode to the founder of Microsoft, but rather a reference to the Sha'arei HaBina, the Gates of Understanding.

For other people, the Torah Codes represent an interesting intellectual digression; for others, useful tools for engaging seekers and searchers, or the spiritually wayward to look upward and inward. But perhaps the most challenging task for the Codes is to draw in the skeptical, disenfranchised, and hyper-rational Modern Man or Woman to discover a deeper meaning in Torah study, to peel back its many layers and open its gates of understanding beyond a simple reading of the narrative. For others, the embedded codes merely confirm an already accepted truth salted with a renewed appreciation for the omnipotent writer of the Torah, a.k.a. G-d.

General knowledge of the Torah Codes has been spread through Aish HaTorah's Discovery Seminar. The outreach program is designed to help engage people of all ages in Judaism and Torah learning. For reference purposes only, for just under $50 (USD), you, too, can be a 'master' of the codes, at www.biblecodes.com; inquire about free shipping. It should be noted, however, that the program carries an unambiguous legal disclaimer along with a stern warning: the product is intended for educational and/or entertainment purposes. The disclaimer can also be generally applied to any study of Torah Codes, reflecting only what is known of past and present events, and which cannot and should not, under any circumstances, be used as a prediction tool or a modern-day divining rod. The study of Torah is for Torah's sake, and such knowledge should not be used to try to derive or predict the future, or Heaven forbid, to attempt to influence future events.

Whether one holds to thirty, fifty or thousands of Gates of Understanding to the Torah through which to apply a literary, historical, anthropological, or theological lens, the words of Rabbi Yochanan Bag-Bag can be applied, 'Turn it and turn it, for everything is found within it.' These cryptic words found near-perfect resonance with Joshua E. Katz in the 'Dimensional Torah Codes' (DTC) search algorithm he developed. With a single tap on a keyboard shortcut, the linear reading of the Torah was elegantly transformed into a dynamic three-dimensional tapestry, a colorful weave of interconnected threads conveying dates, names, and places — the contextually bound history of Mankind.

With Joshua's program, the Z-axis became a dynamic force, bringing different letters and word groups into proximity in a non-linear type of skip distance analysis. The program illuminates the spatial characteristics of the Torah and its codes in their natural configuration, i.e. as a rolled scroll. The programming requires this virtual scroll to be rolled and unrolled as it would naturally be done for the weekly Torah reading. The approach brings letter combinations into new dimensional configurations, transforming the finite into the infinite to encompass the nearly 6,000 years of this World's history. The key was to let deep learning do a deep dive into the text, generating elegant spatial transformations and compelling visuals. Joshua's work adds a rich, new layer to Torah scholarship, a gate of understanding approaching the 'infinite' alluded to by Rabbi Cordovero in the 16th century...

"Oh, for the love of G-d, not again!" Uri'el shouted, ready to tear off his wings if he heard one more tinnitus-ringing digital *shofar* vibration. "Enough already," he shouted. It wasn't even the High Holidays when hundreds more legitimate *shofar* blasts would be sounded, generating another legion of Guardian Angels. Uri'el suspected Joshua E. Katz had cooked up something special to celebrate the Jewish New Year for all 1.5 million plus newly inducted netizens of HaMikdash3.0 with a unique *shofar* twist. Strange, he thought, why wasn't he privy to those particular details in Joshua's mind?

Distracted, Uri'el noticed one of the newbie guardian angels, number 755.23, tugging on the hem of his "pants" if he was wearing any. Having gotten Uri'el's attention, the little guy animatedly started speaking. But having been silenced earlier, he was hard to understand without a voice. He finished saying whatever was on his mind and impatiently crossed his little angel wing arms in front of him as if waiting for an answer.

"Mind repeating that? I seemed to have missed that in the first go-round," Uri'el said, snapping his fingers.

With a nails-on-chalkboard whine, GA-755.23 said, "I asked, what are you doing, and well… I wanted to know if you needed any help?" The dopey, but sweet, Guardian Angel said, adding a silly grin to his question/offer to help.

Uri'el had been prepared to send the annoying little angel away without a second thought. The little twirp had no idea he was addressing an Archangel with mondo *Cherubic* elements. Considering their size difference, Uri'el thought it was kind of ballsy of the munchkin to even ask. He glanced over to GA-730.71, tucked in for the day/night on his left shoulder, whistling out a snore. With each exhale, he sent a winged feather fluttering like the character Sleepy in the Walt Disney animation of "Snow White and the Seven Dwarfs." The original and not the ridiculous live-action re-make that took political correctness into the realm of the absurd, and further discriminated against dwarfs, Little People, or whatever the politically correct term was these days.

He did have other shoulders to offer GA-755.23, and recalling the kindness proverb adopted a more generous visage, "I appreciate the offer, but no thank you. And to answer your question, when we, my fellow Archangels and I…"

"Whoa, are you telling me that you're like a real Archangel?" GA-755.23's eyes bugged wide open, ready to pop out of his head and would have had they been spring-loaded. "OMG, I can't believe it. And here I thought you were just like us, only bigger. Lots bigger!" The enthusiastic rambling quickly drew the attention of the other GAs. To distinguish himself from the pack, GA-755.23, promptly leaned in as if taking a selfie with Uri'el, pointed and mouthed the word, "Archangel" with two big thumbs up.

After giving GA-755.23 his autograph, Uri'el said, "Now, if you don't mind."

"Hey, consider me gone," GA-755.23 said, delivering a crisp salute with his little right angel wing, but which nearly took out his eye.

To continue. The records kept above can filter down to Mankind/Womankind, a kind of stream of consciousness, the flow that the adepts, creatives, and other folks can tap into. We Celestials are the creative engine that keeps on giving.

"Hmmm, interesting," GA-755.23 said, trying to free himself from the tangles of Uri'el's lion's head mane.

"I thought you'd gone," Uri'el said, sinisterly dipping all of his heads.

"Got a little hung up here," he said, finally freeing himself. "I'm outta here bossman, angel man, archangel man!" GA-755.23 said, then flew off like a drunken lightning bug to join the other Guardian Angels, then zipped back. "And not to worry, I'll keep the riff-raff out of your hair, I mean fur, I mean feathers. You know what I mean. Later dude."

The other Archangels couldn't help but laugh. Guardian Angels were helpful on Earth but were pre-programmed to annoy other Celestials — an inverse relationship between annoyance in Heaven and helpfulness on Earth, making this particular group of Guardian Angels a powerful force once they hit the road below. With a sudden awareness of the solemnity of the tasks ahead, Uri'el looked at the growing army of Guardian Angels with a new appreciation. These were true Guardians. Each had been called forth because of their interaction with someone in the Katzenstein/Katz soul root — a relationship spanning the generations of Man/Woman throughout the millennia. They were called into service to ensure that this generation's scion would complete his tasks… his soul's mission in a final rectification.

If all went according to plan, which it would have to in the end, Uri'el and the other Archangels would likely need the help of all the generated Guardian Angels to effect the end they all hoped for, which even THEY longed for since the dawn of Man's Time… a rectification to be reached in the End of Days — *b'Kaitz HaYamim.*

Chapter 4

The *shofar* sounds blasting from his cellphone heralded HaMikdash3.0's latest enrollment milestone. The long *tekiah* lasted only fifteen seconds, but long enough to trigger an ocular migraine in Joshua E. Katz's brain. To be more precise, his right eye, filling his field of vision with a scintillating scotoma. The word scintillating failed to adequately describe the shimmering zig-zag disruptions that could send Joshua into quiet mode, an enforced time-off away from the computer screen's glare and low-frequency strobe effects.

After leaving Tzion's office, he automatically pushed the dual-purpose VR/AR glasses he'd been wearing up on his forehead. He took two steps into the parking lot, squinting against the late morning autumn sun, and drew the dual-purpose glasses back down to the bridge of his nose to shield his eyes. He waved to Jay/Jérémie, who was waiting more or less patiently by a black Range Rover emblazoned with Hazon Labs' logo on the spare wheel cover and passenger side door panel. Joshua swept his hand across the name, acknowledging his good fortune, and braced himself against the distortions to his depth perception the migraine caused. Compared to other types of migraines, the ocular type was relatively rare and thankfully not always accompanied by brain-exploding pain; not always, but frequently enough in Joshua's case.

"Mazal Tov, you did it! 1.5 mill," Jay exclaimed as Joshua circled to the driver's side, though Jay didn't move out from the open door.

"A 'we' function, Jay. I… we couldn't have done it without you," Joshua said, offering the barest of mirth-filled smiles which faded in the next moment.

"You look like death warmed over," Jay said, already having decided to do the driving, both ways, rather than risk life and limb by allowing Joshua to get behind the wheel.

"Me thinks, this burning the candle at both ends has finally reached the end of its wick," Joshua said, managing another feeble smile.

"Seriously, are you okay?" Jay asked, already knowing what part of the problem was… Tzion's Zedekiah's Cave (ZC) presentation didn't go exactly as planned.

"You probably already know the ZC demo has issues."

"I'm sure Tzion will get it done."

"I know. But I'm also having one of those lovely headaches again," Joshua said, massaging the concrete knot at the back of his neck.

"Did you take something?"

"I think staying conscious during my talk takes priority over any pain relief. Though, I plan on being comatose afterward."

"I'll drive," Jay said, nodding to the passenger seat. "Try to catch a few z's until we get there."

"Like you don't have better things to do."

"Not so much today. Some last-minute shopping for *Shabbat* is all." Jay said, knowing that no matter what time he got back to Herzliya, the neighborhood *makolet*, convenience store, would be open until minutes before candle lighting.

"You sure?" Joshua said, knowing Jay took his *Shabbat* preparations seriously. They both "blamed" HaMikdash3.0 for Jay's religious conversion from a decidedly secular status with an Eastern-influenced spiritual/cultural interest in Judaism to a "getting there" status from an observance perspective. The same bug seemed to have affected many of Hazon Labs' employees which Joshua encouraged, though he was careful to not get infected himself.

"Positive," Jay insisted. "There are enough distracted Israeli drivers behind the wheel as it is. Wouldn't want to lose you at this point... at any point for that matter."

"Not to worry, even *if*, I've got a good *sgan*," Joshua said with a wink and slapped his second-in-command, on the back before crossing back over to the passenger side.

Standing across the roof from another, Jay said, "That you do, *achi*."

"I'll owe you one," Joshua said with a slight shrug.

"Be careful, I might just try to collect on those 'ones' one day, in equity," Jay said, with a wide grin and a wink, though he was already a 49% partner in Hazon Labs; the differential acknowledging HaMikdash3.0's original idea source and patents. He rapped on the Rover's roof, then climbed behind the wheel. He keyed, "Reich–" which was sufficient input for *Waze* to offer a Reichman University option and to build a real-time map of their best/fastest route to the Herzliya campus. He was rewarded with a "Cheerio, let's go," delivered with an upper-crust British accent.

"I'll kill myself if I have to listen to Monty Python the whole ride," Joshua groaned.

Jay promptly lowered the voice direction's volume.

"You're not even British, man!"

"Quite true," Jay said, affecting a pish-posh accent that couldn't be attributed to any particular country, adding, "it reminds me of my fine European heritage."

"In which lifetime? You're more Israeli than I am," Joshua said, flicking his index finger under the tip of his nose in Jay's direction. "Thanks for driving."

"Sababa," Jay said, using the familiar Israeli expression which alternatively meant cool, great, or no problem, depending on the context.

"Ready to run the gauntlet?" Joshua asked, referring to the regular Friday protestors, encamped across the First Station parking lot. Having been granted a reprieve from driving, Joshua just wanted to close his eyes. Unfortunately, that would more than likely prompt a social media firestorm, complete with snaps of him sleeping on the job and not exactly the message he wanted to send in their final push to the HaMikdash3.0 release. As Jay pulled across the lot, Joshua gave the crowd a slight Queen of England wave, followed by a "thumbs up" sign. The protestors answered by re-doubling their chants and sign-waving for his benefit, and likely their own, before going back to their coffee klatches.

Fortunately, these guys had no qualms about showing their faces, which the parking lot security cameras captured and reviewed each Friday. The feed was automatically sent through a facial recognition program, looking for any new faces. These were promptly vetted through open-source resources looking for real troublemakers, vandals, and criminals. They were mostly harmless.

Of greater concern to Hazon Labs were the faceless hacker elites, collectively known as Anonymous. For whatever reason, which still defied explanation except maybe for the attendant publicity, they had joined the Boycott, Divestment, Sanction (BDS) cult pursuing anything and everything with an Israel connection. Their *raison d'être* put Hazon Labs and HaMikdash3.0 squarely in their crosshairs.

"By the way, how are your kiosks doing?"

"My kiosks?" Jay asked, eyes wide. He didn't mind taking ownership of the kiosks, but it would be good to spread the blame around if necessary for failing to deliver, just in case.

"You know what I mean."

"I bring ye' tidings of comfort and joy."

"Jay man, my brain hurts, please don't start singing," Joshua groaned as he brought both palms to his face in what resembled Edvard Munch's iconic "The Scream" painting. Jay's singing voice could set dogs howling and cats screeching.

"We're great on that front. Security cams are running, and we've strategically distributed a dozen virtual reality T-osks throughout the city."

"T-osks? Can't we call them something else, anything else? Sounds like we're brewing tea or building a mosque," Joshua grimaced.

"It stands for Temple Kiosk, pretty clear to most folks. They are *my* kiosks after all."

Joshua rolled his eyes and let out a short snort. "Why not V-osk for Virtual Kiosk?"

"Too vanilla. But if you insist, I'll run it past legal to see who else is using it. I'm guessing we'll probably run into a trademark issue."

"You said twelve -osks, what happened to *our* lucky number 13?"

"Keeping that one close to home, on the *mesila*," Jay said, referring to the popular walking, running, and biking path around the corner from Hazon Labs' offices at the JVP Media Quarter. The *mesila* started on the north at First Station, Jerusalem's original train station that once served as the main railway, connecting Jerusalem and Jaffa.

The rehabilitated *mesila* followed the original train route through the *Emek Refa'im* neighborhood into *Mekor Haim*, *Talpiot*, and *Beit Safafa*, ending near Teddy Kollek Stadium in the *Malha* neighborhood. The route included original rail ties, fasteners, go/no-go signal boxes, and historical information in Hebrew, Arabic, and English. Built during the Ottoman Era in 1892, the First Station building retained much of its original charm with exposed tracks, original fixtures, and weathered wood painted in Jerusalem blue, a mix between pale light blue and turquoise. As a venue, First Station boasted restaurants, shops, an events stage, and a Thursday-Friday kiosk-styled vendor market.

"The diverse mix of walkers, local and otherwise, who use the *mesila* should give us additional market data inputs," Jay remarked about First Station's popularity with neighborhood folks and tourists who could rent bicycles and other foot-powered movers. "Come Sunday, I'll run diagnostics on each of the units. Make sure we haven't shaken anything loose during transport."

"I'd hate for any -osks to go on the fritz, or worse electrocute someone," Joshua said, with a snorting chuckle.

"Not a great way to start off!" Jay said, glancing over to Joshua who'd bunched up his sweatshirt as a pillow and was resting his head against the window.

"Death by Kiosk" wasn't likely; though they both knew the bigger problem with the V/T-kiosks would be from vandals armed with spray paint, baseball bats, and other weapons of choice. While each unit had a built-in, forward-facing camera for capturing vandals, Jay strategically positioned each unit near a city security camera to record a wider field, i.e. vandals-on-approach. He wasn't being paranoid, just realistic.

"Worst case, we can use the publicity to put HaMikdash3.0 on the infamy track," Jay said with a smile.

"I prefer fame, at least for now," Joshua said, adding a smile and contemplative wide-eyed, eyebrow-lifting smirk of his own. He tapped the thumb drive in his pants pocket, the visuals for his presentation, then closed his eyes intent on eliminating the competing visual strain on his brain.

Sleep never came easy to him. His mind was always racing, now more so than usual. He was juggling a thousand and one moving parts before HaMikdash3.0's late October release. While trusting others didn't come naturally to him, he was smart enough to know he couldn't do it all. He needed to be able to count on his people and not worry about them doing their parts in a HaMikdash3.0 Gestalt where the amazing whole they were building would soon be something other than — indeed greater than — the sum of its parts.

The adage, "You don't get a second chance to make a first impression," didn't only apply to meeting new people, but also to product launches, and his Reichman University talk was part of that all-important howdy-do gathering for capturing more eyeballs. He reviewed his remarks in his head, especially the high points he prepared with the attendant PowerPoint® visuals.

HaMikdash3.0 was more just than a gamers' paradise or a mecca for social voyeurs — the casual gamers and social butterflies who could appreciate a bit of dissociative role-playing. These were among the early adopters, eager to be first in line for the latest (and greatest) "it" thing. But Joshua's primary target audience was the spiritual thinkers and seekers, people of all faiths and beliefs, looking for a meaningful forum with other like-minded souls. The spiritual aspects of HaMikdash3.0 were embedded in the experience and would organically evolve, raising HaMikdash consciousness in a long-overdue awakening. Admittedly, sometimes the lines blurred between HaMikdash's soul work and its gaming personae. With the latest milestone over 1.5 million people were already part of the HaMikdash3.0 family. Membership numbers had already grown beyond their modest quarterly projections, but not beyond Joshua's vision for HaMikdash3.0 in the real world. The site was already garnering favorable reviews, even though users could only access a limited number of its features. Page rankings showed that the Bible reference pages had the second-highest hit rate and among the longest page views as members built up their Scenario Knowledge Packs, meaning that even now, HaMikdash3.0 was capturing users from its primary target market with crossovers to its secondary market objectives. Notably, the longest page views, measured in hours not minutes, was with the Virtuoso Avatar Design Sequencer (VADS) and Authenticity program used by every new member for creating their avatar and online personae.

The advanced AI-based character generator leveraged a reference library of facial attributes to generate nuanced character faces and features for personalizing reactions and attitudes to create a more dynamic and authentic user experience. It was a hot, go-to repeat area with users updating their characteristics, at least according to usage stats. For those members who elected to forego the safety of online anonymity, VADS also allowed users to upload personal images that were then *cartoonified*, transforming the user into responsive "living, breathing" animated avatar twin. Joshua figured that people who still hadn't checked out HaMikdash3.0 would likely do so for a first look at the image and AI-based technology innovations.

Hazon Labs also used an advanced image-based system for user authentication and verification. While the threats from malicious human black-hat attacks continued to give them the usual 24/7 headaches, they were able to keep the non-human bad actors at bey. To test the system, Jay enlisted the services of a group of recent 8200 graduates to try and hack the system — *try* being the operative word. They failed gloriously and two were brought on board as part of the company's red-alert, White-Hat team. Secure user transactions and interactions were essential for any application. For HaMikdash3.0, protecting subscriber data came with unique challenges. Threats ranged from real-life stalkers, like Anonymous, to *Jihadi* lunatics, the *Jihadnikim*, who viewed HaMikdash3.0 as an assault on *al-Aqsa* and the Dome of the Rock and which lumped its subscribers into the "valid targets" category.

Considered naive by many, even his supporters, Joshua honestly believed that a virtual Temple service might be THE non-violent solution to the Temple Mount situation since his approach did not infringe on the actual physical space. Only, he couldn't have been more wrong. Save for HaMikdash3.0 supporters and Hallelujah believers, HaMikdash3.0 "enjoyed" critics from across the religious and political spectrum, plus a handful of anarchists. Joshua planned to include brief remarks in his Reichman talk about that particular aspect of the Hazon Labs' journey. He also planned on introducing Jay, who enjoyed the limelight far more than he did but was rarely asked to speak.

They were quite the pair, though once a trio…

Where Joshua was tall and muscled, Jay was tall and lean standing at 1.98 meters. Belgian by birth, and Israeli from the age of nine when his family made *Aliyah*, Jay was promptly recruited to the *Neurim* program for gifted athletes. He had a natural swimmer's physique, longer in the body than his legs and tapering to a narrow waist, and a wingspan that rivaled U.S. Olympian great Michael Phelps. Jay swam for Israel's National team but failed to qualify for the Olympics thanks to a blown eardrum in a scuba diving mishap in *Eilat*. The resulting bouts of vertigo also kept him from qualifying for *Shayetet 13* — Israel's special forces unit, a powerhouse cross between the US Navy Seals and the UK's Special Boat Service.

Fortuitously, he landed in the IDF's elite signal intelligence technology unit 8200, *Shemona Matayim* — a good third-choice IDF placement. His second choice/placement had been the Air Force. Vertigo notwithstanding, Jay was at the upper-height limit for fitting comfortably in an F-35 cockpit without a helmet, and flying helicopters, while cool, wasn't his style. Cockpits weren't designed with adjustable seats or for people who shopped at the not-so-local "Big and Tall" stores. Nonetheless, he and Joshua earned their private pilot's licenses and went in together on a time-share lease on a Cessna Citation X jet. During their service, Julia Morgenthau became their third "J" partner in crime, J3 — the third musketeer in their 8200-alumni technology triumvirate. They smashed through their military service with plans for co-founding a startup after university. They agreed to limit their academic pursuits to first degrees, BA/BS, or accelerated programs that combined first and second degrees to get them on the startup track without too long of a delay.

For a technology entrepreneur, "graduating" from the 8200 unit was often a golden ticket to success, that, and Air Force service — a different kind of elitism. After their tenure with 8200 ended, Joshua started dating Julia, a 1.75m tall auburn-haired beauty. She was headed to Ben Gurion University's aerospace sciences while Joshua was accepted to the Technion's advanced computer vision program. Their busy school schedules combined with a 121-mile commute each way, which wasn't much in the grand scheme of things unless you accounted for Israeli traffic and a disturbing offensive driving mentality, proved to be their undoing. Whatever awkwardness there might have been between Julia and Joshua after breaking up would have quickly been set aside for the sake of HaMikdash3.0. Without reserve, Julia would have loved every minute of Hazon Labs' meteoric rise, not to mention their workload would have easily been cut in half with her on the team.

Historically, Joshua + Julia + Jay was always greater than the sum of their work effort. Her mind had once worked like a supercomputer; her multi-colored polished nails flying across a keyboard to the beat of a hummingbird's wings, pouring out elegant code to a rhythm only she could sense. Admittedly, Jay was probably a little in love with Julia too — not that it mattered anymore. A scuba diving accident off the coast of Crete left Julia not only a quadriplegic but her once brilliant mind had been starved of oxygen for too long, leaving her unable to communicate even a single thought. Persistent vegetative states had that effect.

Jay always kept Julia in mind whenever he said the *Asher Yatzer* blessing. The profound prayer is recited after leaving the bathroom and praises G-d for the human body's intricate inner workings and miracles of its interconnected processes. Jay held no delusions or illusions about the prayer affecting Julia's current state; any meaningful recovery required intervention from Above, which for whatever reason, was withheld all too often from those who needed it most.

He glanced over at his friend with an uncanny Spidey sense.

"May I help you," Joshua said, without opening his eyes or moving a muscle.

"Just thinking about Julia, I was on autopilot."

"I thought we were trying to avoid an accident by you taking the wheel?"

"Noted," Jay said, glancing at the Waze navigation screen.

"I miss her too. You're still visiting her, you know… there?"

"Yeah." *There* was a long-term nursing care facility for people, many under the age of forty, with traumatic brain injuries. Per capita, Israel had more than its share of TBIs. Joshua had seen the inside of enough facilities when his *Savta* Rachel died after a long battle with breast cancer in Sheba Medical Center's hospice care. No matter how cheerful, kind, or sensitive the staff, or how much green landscaping and trickling water gardens there were for a temporary break from reality, the outcome was invariably the same. The variation on the theme was repeated with Joshua's grandfather Jacob, though the time between his being diagnosed with prostate cancer and his death was *only* eighteen months. The outcome was the same in either case… gone.

Jay was grateful his parents were still alive and relatively young, which offered no guarantees except maybe on actuarial tables for a long life. *Baruch Ha-Shem* (Bless G-d). He'd been fortunate. Joshua, not so much. Jay probably knew more about Joshua's past than anyone, including how his parents had died a couple of weeks before his *Bar Mitzvah*, and which was how he'd come to live with his Holocaust survivor grandfather Jacob Katzenstein — his *Opa*, his Mentor, and Champion. Jay knew it was especially bittersweet that Jacob hadn't lived to see what Joshua had built in HaMikdash3.0.

Joshua was two years into an accelerated program at Technion when Jacob was diagnosed with prostate cancer. By then, Jacob was Joshua's only family, and which relegated school and his thesis research project to a status somewhere below an afterthought. Joshua's thesis advisor, however, thought otherwise and was eager to see Joshua's multi-dimensional visualization project realized. After emphatically saying, "NO" to continuing his studies, Joshua's former thesis advisor, Ezra Noiman, a.k.a. he who shall not be named, attempted to *acquire* the project for himself, claiming the authority of the University and as Joshua's advisor/mentor. All technically true.

The ensuing intellectual property battle between Joshua E. Katz, plaintiff, and the Technion -Israel Institute of Technology, represented by the IP heavyweight law firm headed by Stanton Golby, began in earnest. The University smartly dropped the counterclaim while Joshua's former thesis advisor foolishly pursued the matter. Joshua never wavered in his claim thanks, in no small part, to Jacob — the inventor of record on fifteen separate materials science patents. Championing his grandson, Issac's two favorite cheers were, "Beat the bastard!" and "Give 'em hell, Joshie," co-opting the "Give 'em hell, Harry" phrase which on some level likely gave Jacob the will to live as long as he did.

As Joshua sat vigil by his grandfather's bedside in the hospital, at home, and finally at the Chaim Sheba Medical Center's Cancer Hospice, he left the legal wranglings to the attorneys while independently continuing the research project that improved visualization capabilities for identifying contextual connections between spatially separated words. The Large Language Model (LLM) model he developed had general applications for advancing word searches, text analysis, and image captioning capabilities. The idea was borne from Jacob's interests in *Aish HaTorah's* Discovery program — an educationally-driven outreach/*kiruv* program that used some of the *Torah's* hidden mysteries to spark an interest in the less-inclined in Judaism. In the last years of his life, Jacob credited the Discovery program for helping him reconnect him with Judaism.

Jacob had grown up in the town of Saabrücken in southern Germany, steeped in Jewish practices. But even as a young boy he found his teachers often ignored the nuanced aspects of *Torah* study or to include the spiritual richness of the *Kabbalah*. Hidden from the masses for centuries, the eventual translation of the original texts of the *Zohar* (Book of Splendor) and *Sefer Yetzirah* (Book of Creation) and the commentaries to multiple languages, and later with the advent of the internet, knowledge of the esoteric became accessible to all. Ironically, or perhaps not all that surprisingly, much of the hidden wisdom was intimately linked to mindful practices and meditation in an East meets West unification. After the Holocaust, Jacob lost whatever remained of his faith only to re-discover it at the end of his life. He wished there had been more time in *this* life to dedicate to learning. As it turned out, the afterlife gave him all the time he needed in the *next* world to pursue his studies of all of the *Torah's* Gates of Understanding.

Jacob supported both *Aish HaTorah* and *Kabbalah*-oriented programs, believing that opening the spiritual floodgates could help empower young people's Jewish identities in the face of rising anti-Israel and anti-Semitism on college campuses. The disturbing state of affairs existed long before Oct7, but which was transformed into very public and aggressive displays thereafter. Jacob had emerged from the hell fires of the Holocaust, the sole survivor of his family at the age of twelve, and recognized the all-too-familiar warning signs… the academic boycotts as conference abstracts were rejected, and lectures stormed by hecklers or canceled; musicians pressured to cancel concerts in Israel; venues breaking contracts citing security concerns; and, authors unable to find representation or dropped by their longtime management companies. Jacob shared his concerns with Joshua, though his intention was not to frighten his grandson. Rather, he sought to empower Joshua in his Jewish identity, and complemented that pride with advanced martial arts training that he insisted his grandson also pursue. The existential threat for Israel was ever present, though Jacob hoped that the blind hatred from many of Israel's neighbors wouldn't extend beyond her borders to encompass the world. Unfortunately, he'd been wrong.

After Oct7, the simmering cauldron of anti-Israel and anti-Semitic hatred exploded. Joshua wished his grandfather had lived to see him apply the multi-dimensional visualization tool to the *in-situ* analysis of the *Torah* codes. But at the same time, he was grateful his grandfather hadn't lived to see the rampant Jew-hatred and blood libels masquerading as pro-Palestinian activism, and which now permeated every corner of the globe. Joshua needn't have worried either way. He'd given Jacob years of joy, especially in the last year of life. Beaming with grandfatherly pride, albeit from his hospital bed, Jacob listened as Joshua shared the daily progress reports on the development of the multidimensional visualization technology.

The looming prospects of his death didn't dampen Jacob's spirits on Earth… or in Heaven. For a time, Jacob's *neshama*, his higher soul, took up near-permanent residence at Uri'el's side to help prevent G-d's divine anger from being co-opted by evil forces during the *regah*, the 1/58,888 parts of an hour, 0.061 seconds of every day, which put Joshua at high-risk. The *regah* changed from day to day and generally could not be predicted, except by a few chosen prophets. Ironically, *Balaam*, the non-Jewish prophet, could see these "moments" and sought to exploit one, or two, to curse the wandering Jews in the desert. As the *Torah* tells it, *Baalam* tried twice, but failed both times, bestowing a blessing on the Jewish people instead of a curse. Smartly, Jacob's *neshama* also took out a Celestial insurance policy, protecting Joshua and HaMikdash3.0 from liability and any resulting retribution should the thin line between the sacred and the sacrilegious be crossed, or should his chip-off-the-old-block grandson push the bounds of irreverence a byte too far.

By early September 2021, Uri'el knew Jacob's earthbound *nefesh* didn't have many more days with his grandson. Jacob also sensed the end was near and as the appointed time neared, his *neshama* prepared for the arrival of his *nefesh*, his earthly soul, which would then join with his other soul parts waiting in the wings. Uri'el respectfully bid Jacob's *neshama* goodbye and safe travels as it continued on to its next journey with a respectful nod from his human face and a half-salute with his wing.

And it shall come to pass in that day, That a great horn shall be blown; And they shall come that were lost in the land of Assyria, And they that were dispersed in the land of Egypt; And they shall worship the Lord in the holy mountain at Jerusalem.

— Isaiah 27:13

CHAPTER 5

"You're humming," Joshua said, his voice heavy from sleep.

"Sorry, I didn't mean to wake you," Jay said. Unconsciously, he'd been humming the tune to *Ve'Haviotim*, thinking that Joshua would likely be going up to the Temple Mount on *Yom Kippur* to honor Jacob by walking in the footsteps of his *Kohanic* ancestors.

"No worries, I was somewhere between sleep and dreamland," Joshua said, offering his best friend a thin, closed-lip smile.

"I've been meaning to ask, I was planning on going up to the Temple Mount on *Yom Kippur*, did you want to coordinate going together?"

"Thanks, but I'm still undecided."

"Really?" Jay said, surprised by the ambiguous response.

"Can't you just see the headlines now, 'HaMikdash3.0 CEO storms *al-Aqsa*' or 'Temple Mount under siege by digital wannabees,'" Joshua quipped.

"I see you've given this some thought."

"Anders actually brought up the ramifications of my going up. I can't disagree with his assessment, but…"

"But is right! Our brilliant Marketing Guru might be technically right, but it's Jacob's *azakara*," he said, referring to the anniversary of a person's death. "You are human after all, much as you try to downplay it."

"If I decide to go, I'd definitely appreciate the company."

"Deal," Jay said, then with a quick glance at Joshua added, "you might as well close your eyes again. Waze® says we've still got another twenty-five minutes to go."

"Better yet, maybe you can just wake me up when September ends," quoting the title song by Green Day.

Ironically, the lyrics to *Ve'Haviotim* were already on Joshua's mind when Jay started humming. He'd been thinking about Jacob and his last wish… to bless Joshua with the Priestly Blessing on the Temple Mount, *Har HaBayit*. When his grandfather was diagnosed with prostate cancer, Joshua prayed as never before that G-d would grant his Opa a *Refuah Shlema*, a complete healing. In a way, his prayers were answered. Jacob's suffering ended… a different kind of *refuah*. G-d was funny like that. Joshua closed his eyes, remembering the *Har HaBayit* memory with Jacob.

* * *

Yom Kippur, 2021 (5782)

A private ambulance transported eighty-eight-year-old Jacob from Ramat Gan's Chaim Sheba Medical Center Cancer Hospice to Jerusalem. Not surprisingly, traffic going into the city was horrendous. On most days, life in Jerusalem could be described as frantic, frenetic, and frenzied; in advance of *Yom Kippur*, it was a *farkakte* nightmare. At sundown, however, an austere silence would veil the city, and much of the country, as the traffic snarls would grind to a halt and streets would be closed to everything but the non-motorized and foot traffic. On the *Ayalon*, Tel Aviv's main highway, families with bicycles, tricycles, and strollers zoomed about well below the posted speed limit of ninety kilometers per hour. The 25-hour-long *Yom Kippur* observance is typically filled with prayer and fasting, a time when people are likened to angels and wear white as their sins are laid bare before the Almighty in a last-ditch pitch for forgiveness.

Joshua traveled in the ambulance with his grandfather, while Jay took point in Jerusalem. He handled logistics and arranged their stay at the *Aish HaTorah* guest house, which gave them easy wheelchair access to the *Kotel* Plaza and the Temple Mount. At 9 o'clock on *Yom Kippur* morning, they joined a group of thirty-six men, women, and families with children, ascending the Temple Mount. Jacob sat regally in his wheelchair, resplendent in a white and gold *tallit* and matching *kittel* — a mid-thigh length overcoat made of linen traditionally only worn on *Yom Kippur*. He had purchased the *kittel*, especially for the occasion. Joshua donned a white T-shirt and tan pants, the closest he could come to the white and gold-colored clothing typically worn on *Yom Kippur* by *Kohanim*. Jay had foregone the white clothing tradition and was smartly dressed in black slacks and a light blue shirt. He intended to give Joshua and Jacob time alone and tried to beg off going up to Temple Mount with them. But Joshua insisted.

Assisted by Jay, Joshua pushed his grandfather's wheelchair across the *Kotel Plaza's* stones and up the *Mughrabi* ramp to the *Hallel Gate* — the only entrance to the Temple Mount open to non-Muslims. As the *Yom Kippur* 5782 prayers continued among the penitent petitioners at the Western Wall below, the ascending group sang the passage from *Isaiah* 56:7, a rallying cry for unity of belief in only one G-d and peace on Earth. The words to *Ve'Haviotim* caught in Joshua's throat and tears welled in his eyes as he kissed Jacob's cheek. He pushed the wheelchair up the wooden ramp in silent reverence as his grandfather "shuckled" back and forth, tears flowing freely down the old man's face.

With a sense of knowing what the next few hours would bring, Joshua tightened his grip on the wheelchair as if doing so could keep his grandfather with him. Joshua pushed on, willing his feet forward to the *Hallel Gate*. Formally known as the *Mughrabi Gate*, it was unofficially renamed to honor the memory of thirteen-year-old, *Hallel Yaffa Ariel* (HY"D), killed on June 30, 2016, when a Palestinian terrorist broke into her home in *Kiryat Arba* and killed her while she slept. Each month, her mother Rina leads an ascent to *Har HaBayit*. The timing is centered around *Rosh Chodesh*, which marks the start of each new month on the Hebrew calendar, when songs of praise and thanksgiving are recited in the traditional *Hallel* prayer. In the hearts of those who ascend the Temple Mount, the entry to *Har HaBayit* could have no better name than *Sha'ar Hallel* which translates to "Gate of Praise" to honor the memory of this young girl whose life was cut short by evil, but whose legacy of praise lives on.

Just outside the gate, Joshua watched as several men dropped to the ground, prostrating themselves before crossing over the threshold onto the Temple Mount. Surrounded by the Border Police, the group moved *en masse* toward the designated prayer area along the Temple Mount's far Eastern wall. The well-worn paving stones passing beneath the wheelchair's grinding wheels bore the indented mark of *mezuzot*. Many had once been doorposts and lintels in the Jewish Quarter which was destroyed during the Jordanian occupation between 1948 and 1967. By some convoluted notion of Grace, these stones "merited" a place on *Har HaBayit*, albeit underfoot.

Joshua wanted his grandfather to have a meaningful experience on *Har HaBayit*, though how much praying would be possible was out of his hands. Generally, any obvious open Jewish prayer was strictly forbidden…

a swaying movement, or a 180-degree pivot that carried *tzitzit* fringes flying with each side-to-side turn, or the silent movement of parched lips in prayer, let alone prostrating oneself in a deep *Aleinu* bow of submission — none were permitted, though who was watching at the time dictated to what degree these Jewish prayer practices were allowed.

Their group followed the prescribed route along the southern portion of the Temple Mount, skirting past the *al-Aqsa Mosque* and then continued along the easternmost path. The routing ensured they would avoid any potential approach to the presumed spot of the Holy of Holies, an area demarcated by the Foundation Stone, the *Even HaShesiah*, inside the Dome of the Rock. The long-way-around route took into account that the Foundation Stone was believed to extend well beyond the confines of the Dome of the Rock where only a part of its surface was visible.

The *Wakf*, the *Islamic Authority* overseeing the Temple Mount, prohibited Jews from stepping onto the elevated plaza surrounding the Dome of the Rock. The Border Police escort, which accompanied all Jewish groups, enforced the prohibition but which apparently didn't apply to kids playing soccer in the open space. The Dome of the Rock itself was strictly off-limits to everyone except Muslims and the few dedicated archaeologists who ventured inside with coveted special permissions. Other exceptions fell under the security banner when riots broke out on the Temple Mount or when Muslims barricaded themselves inside *al-Aqsa* or the Dome of the Rock and attacked the police.

The walls inside of the ornate Dome of the Rock structure are covered with *Quranic* verses written with calligraphic flair, and at its center stands the Foundation Stone. Photographs of the Foundation Stone show a worn indentation, which according to some is believed to be where the Ark of the Covenant had once rested on the stone's surface within the Holy of Holies of the Jewish Temple. The current location of the Ark of the Covenant is the subject of intense speculation and far-flung possibilities, including being hidden in the Vatican's secret archives along with other Jewish treasures. That possibility is further fueled by a relief sculpture on the Arch of Titus that famously depicts the seven-branched golden *Menorah*, though nothing resembling an Ark is evident. The possibility that the Ark, which disappeared in 586 BCE, had been miraculously found and subsequently taken as a prize during the conquest of Jerusalem in 70 CE/AD was not outside the realm of possibilities. The time gap, however, was difficult to reconcile and its unknown whereabouts in the interim required a major logic leap. But if not in Rome, then where?

Other historians and religious pundits believe that the Ark of the Covenant was given to Queen Bathsheva, mother of the future King Solomon, for safekeeping when she returned to Ethiopia, and it has remained there ever since. Today, the High Priest of Aksum still stands guard at the Church of St. Mary of Zion as the Ark's Protector and is the only person allowed to enter a sacred chamber. The most intriguing idea is that the Holy Ark never left Jerusalem. Excavations under and near the Temple Mount had previously uncovered an array of dead-ending caves and caverns where the Ark might have been hidden for safekeeping. Fueling the possibility, researchers found a mysterious "plastered" wall in a water cistern that previously held water for the Temple Service but have not searched beyond it.

Some ground truths remain elusive; no one, save for the Almighty, and maybe a couple of *Cherubim*, knows with certainty what became of the Ark of the Covenant. In Jewish circles, the Ark of the Covenant disappeared in 586 BCE during the Babylonian destruction of Jerusalem. Its whereabouts remain unknown… hidden until the final Temple, the third *Beit HaMikdash* would be rebuilt. Joshua's favorite idea about the Ark's location came to him one night in a dream; an idea planted in his mind by a helpful Archangel named Uri'el. He couldn't recall how the dream started and only remembered standing in the Holy of Holies watching the *Cherubs* swooping around the chamber. Normally, their wings were extended over the *kaporet*, the golden lid of the Mercy Seat where the *Shechina*, the Glory of G-d, rested. In the dream, though, after the acrobatic display, their wings stretched out in front of them and began moving in a wavelike motion that buoyed the Holy Ark, the *Aron HaKodesh*, into the air and up to the Heavens. Joshua continued watching until the Ark and the *Cherubs* disappeared from view in a brilliant, blue-colored starburst that lit up the dreamscape's night sky. Wherever the Ark of the Covenant might be today, its mystical powers still captivated the faithful, and Joshua wasn't about to let a good dream go to waste. HaMikdash3.0 planned to include a scenario that challenged players to discover the hidden location of the Ark and harness its power, albeit, of the virtual kind.

As their group continued their walkabout on the Temple Mount, they arrived at the far Eastern walking path, accessible by a short flight of six stairs. Easy enough for the group, but an impossible obstacle for someone in a wheelchair.

"Jay, can you wait here with Opa," Joshua asked but didn't wait for an answer. He caught up with the lead Border Policeman, one of five escorting their group. The entire group paused while Joshua made a special and necessary request.

"You go there," the Border Policeman suggested, referring to the immediately adjacent unpaved path strewn with boulders of varying sizes, overgrown with weeds, and some unknown kind of buzzing insect.

"I don't think so," Joshua said, skeptically looking at the officer.

The semi-private conversation drew everyone's attention, from English, French, and Hebrew speakers alike. In Israel, your business is everyone's business. The other Border Police soon found themselves being questioned about the problem, while others complained about the delay and the heat, and just wanted to move ahead.

"My grandfather is sick. Would you push your grandfather over that? It's too much."

"Carry him, bring the chair after. You push."

From Joshua's perspective, the officer was being unreasonable. In the Guard's defense, this was probably group #20 for the day already, and he may, or may not, have been favorably disposed to have to carry on with the task for the rest of the morning.

"I don't think you understand." Joshua immediately recognized his mistake but didn't have time to soothe the Guard's bruised ego or the challenge he'd made to his authority.

"You go back. Now!" The Border Guard announced; it was not a suggestion, but an order.

Joshua counted to ten, then started eating a mega-slice of humble pie.

"Look, I apologize. I'm not trying to cause any problems. Couldn't we follow that other path," referring to a mostly paved, parallel walkway. "We'll join up with the group by the *Ezrat HaNashim*," referring to the area where groups stopped to pray, known as the Courtyard of the Women.

Joshua figured he could wheel Jacob onto the perpendicular paved walkway, pray, and then return to the other parallel path until again joining the group by the *Sha'ar HaRachamim*, the Mercy Gate.

"Please."

The Border Guard officer sneered at Joshua, then relented. "Aach, go," adding a dismissive wave. "You too," the Guard added, pointing to Jay, "help him."

As they approached the alternative path, Jacob reached his hand up to Joshua. In a trembling voice, barely speaking above a whisper, "I'm sorry for being such a bother, Joshie."

Joshua leaned in, "Opa, it was me. I didn't handle it, him, very well," nodding toward the Border Guard who dogged their every step since having an escort was still required. What did he think, they'd try and storm the *al-Aqsa Mosque*? If the thought had ever crossed Joshua's mind, they'd make a break for the Dome of the Rock. Joshua thought, smiling to himself.

"Thank you, Joshie. You too," Jacob said, looking over to Jay. "I needed to come here, today," then after a brief pause, added, "especially today."

Nothing more needed to be said until they arrived at the *Ezrat Nashim*, the Women's Courtyard. Here, Jacob Katzenstein, barely able to breathe, lifted his *tallit* over his head and rose upright out of his wheelchair. He pulled Jay in for the blessing, placing his hands in the traditional Priestly configuration, a double-handed, "live long and prosper" split finger popularized by Star Trek's Leonard Nimoy. Each of his hand formed the Hebrew letter, *Shin* — an emblematic symbol for G-d's name, *Shad-dai*. And there, Jacob blessed his grandson for the last time.

"[May] G-d bless you, and guard you; [May] G-d make His face shine unto you and be gracious to you; [May] G-d lift up His face unto you and give you peace."

As Jay and Joshua eased Jacob back into the wheelchair, Joshua intoned a silent prayer, again wishing for Jacob to have a *Refuah Shlema*. Then in the last hour before the pearly gates of Heaven closed during *Neilah*, the concluding prayer service on *Yom Kippur*, G-d answered Joshua's prayer and ended Jacob Katzenstein's suffering.

Dying on *Yom Kippur* is auspicious, with but one exception. When the Temple stood, the *Kohen Gadol*, the High Priest, would enter the Holy of Holies to petition on behalf of the people, asking that G-d should forgive the people's sins and stay Satan's (שטן) hand. The High Priest's *Avodah* (Service) included bringing a sin-offering sacrifice of an unblemished bullock and was offered with a confession of his sins and those of the people. Entering the Holy of Holies on this day was not for the faint-hearted and the death of the *Kohen Gadol* on *Yom Kippur* was viewed an ominous sign for the Jewish people. In other words, "You (and/or the people) have been found wanting" and the sentence carried out swiftly. Since the Holy of Holies could not be entered by anyone other than the *Kohen Gadol*, tradition held that a rope was tied around his ankle such that if he died while making his petition on behalf of the people he could be pulled out. Whether there was any symbolism attached to Jacob, a *Kohen*, dying on *Yom Kippur* only Heaven knew, along with anyone else with an appointment with the *Malach HaMavet*, the Angel of Death, on that day.

The words *Baruch Dayan HaEmet* (Blessed be the True Judge) are usually said upon hearing of a person's death. But G-d sometimes asks a lot from people… too much from Joshua who consciously refused to speak the words. He couldn't bring himself to proclaim the righteousness of the pain he felt at his Opa's death, or in the decade and a half before then when he buried his parents. For Joshua, *Yom Kippur* was a day of mourning, of memory, and which wasn't relieved at the end of the fast with the sounding of the *shofar*. While Jews around the world heaved a collective sigh of relief, grateful for surviving the day and with any luck to have their sins forgiven, Joshua could find no such comfort.

Later that night, Jacob's body was lovingly wrapped in his new gold and white kittel which became his burial shroud. He was buried in the family plot on *Har HaZei'tim* near Joshua's parents David and Shoshana Katz, who had preceded Jacob in death by fifteen years. Jacob was laid to rest in the plot next to Oma Rachel, his wife of thirty-five years, to his right. To his left stood the memorial stone bearing the names of his loved ones murdered in the *Shoah*, the Holocaust. The names of Jacob's parents, Esther Malka and David Katzenstein, and his five siblings, Channa age 12, fraternal twins Yehoshua and Mushka, age 10, Pinchas, age 5, and Nechama, just 18 months old. Beneath their names, were the Hebrew words, *Ha-Shem Yikom Damam*, which translates to, "May G-d avenge their blood." Joshua wished there was an intermediate term between BDE and HY"D since he couldn't praise G-d for taking away his grandfather or claim murder.

With the exception of close familial relationships, Jewish tradition does not allow *Kohanim* to come in contact with a dead body, and all the more so to enter a cemetery where contact with *tumah* (impurity) was unavoidable.

The exceptions, however, did not extend to grandparents even though after Joshua's parents were killed Opa Jacob became his legal guardian. In truth, from the age of thirteen and for the following twelve years, Jacob was Joshua's father. Still, Joshua stood on the walkway just outside the cemetery, an area marked as the *Derech HaKohanim*, the Path of the Priests. Jay stood just inside the cemetery, listening to the eulogy (*hesped*) which was given by the former Ashkenazi Chief Rabbi Meir Israel Lau, a child Holocaust survivor himself and Jacob's close friend. Joshua declined to speak, begging off when Rabbi Lau turned in his direction. What more was there to say…

Jay took up the first shovelful of dirt, shaking it gently onto Jacob Katzenstein's shrouded body wrapped in a *kittel* and overlaid with his new white and gold *tallit*. He looked over to his best friend, the sole surviving member of the Katz/Katzenstein family, and with a nod gathered up another shovelful of dirt on Joshua's behalf. When he looked up again, Joshua was gone.

* * *

A YEAR LATER… RAMAT ILAN APARTMENTS, GIV'AT SHMUEL. OCTOBER 23, 2022

After Jacob's funeral, Joshua and Jay did not speak or see one another during the following year. Jay was busy working on a start-up idea, a solution for tracking fraudulent credit card transactions. After finally going to bed at two in the morning, less than an hour later he heard a loud banging on his apartment door that promptly woke every dog in the 19-story high-rise building. He picked up a cricket bat and adopted a defensive stance, ready to swing at the intruder. He flung open the door, rattling a framed poster off the wall, and managed to stop mid-swing before clobbering Joshua. He was greeted by a familiar two-fingered cross — an "I surrender" sign from his former *Krav Maga* sparring partner.

In a torrent of manic excitement and all the fanfare it deserved, Joshua explained HaMikdash3.0 — his big idea. J2 signed on as J1's Executive Vice President and second-in-command, working full-time and a half to build the virtual space. Together, they ran code, storyboarded scenarios, recruited staff, found offices, and were off and running in record startup time. The company benefited from initial pre-seed monies from patent royalties from Jacob's estate, then went directly for Series A funding one year later. They raised a modest $18 million before the start of the High Holiday season in September 2023, setting their sights on a mid-summer 2024 launch. Then October 7th happened on a festive *Shabbat* morning as Israelis celebrated the combined holidays of *Shemini Atzeret*, the last day of *Sukkot*, together with the *Simchat Torah* holiday. The holiday, marking the end of the one-year cycle of reading the entire *Torah*, and the start of the next cycle, is repeated year after year and reflects the continuity and centrality of the *Torah* to Jewish life. But *Simchat Torah 5784*, October 7, 2023, the 22nd day of the Hebrew month of *Tishrei* changed Israel forever.

Sirens sounded in the early morning hours throughout the country as a barrage of Hamas rockets from Gaza targeted major population centers in the South, along the Coast, and even reaching Jerusalem. People scrambled to their bomb shelters, reaching out to family and friends; reservists rushed to help, and IDF soldiers on leave were called in. The Oct7 horror show began at 6:29 that morning as a rampaging horde of terrorists breached the security fence separating Gaza from Israeli communities in the South. Chaos reigned that day with too many unknowns as the flow of information out of the South was conveyed in desperate text messages. Little by little the horrors inflicted on the people living in communities and towns in the Gaza Envelope and the thousands of partygoers attending the Nova Music Festival emerged. With sickening irony, the Nova Music Festival was billed as one for "friends, love, and infinite freedom" … a far cry from the horrors inflicted on 370 partygoers and the hundreds of survivors, physically and emotionally scarred who lived to speak for those who could not.

Throughout the day, details about the horrific nature of the massacre emerged, defying the rational mind's ability to believe. As each hour passed, the number of dead rose steadily from fifty to a couple of hundred, to over a thousand murdered with a genocidal brutality that was then, and still remains, difficult to comprehend. The final count of the dead would take weeks as bodies were extracted from incinerated cars and burned-out homes, contractures grotesquely freeze-framing their last moments of agony. Body bags filled with only parts, bones, and ashes; bullets obliterating faces and private parts; bodies tied together by razor wire where only an X-ray could delineate where one body started, and another ended. Bodies piled together in a heap and set on fire, delaying the identification of the dead from the remaining charred bits of flesh and bone. Homes were ripped apart and incinerated by RPGs, anti-tank missiles, and chemical weapons that melted both metal and concrete, leaving behind only charred shells.

Gaping holes punctured the veneer of peace promulgated by members of the southern *Kibbutzim*. They had been betrayed by those they'd helped; by those they'd shuttled to hospital appointments; and, by those they'd broken bread with over the years as detailed maps of *Kibbutzim* replete with names and addresses of the residents were found on the captured and dead terrorists. Captured on Go-Pro cameras and cellphones, the live-streamed brutality was posted with gleeful pride on Telegram and other social media platforms giving the world front-row seats to the horrors of Oct7. By the end of the day, and into the night, many were still waiting to be rescued from communities throughout *Otef Aza*. By the end of the day, stories of heroism emerged, witnessed by the survivors and the rescuers, and the vaunted Israeli resilience became a *tour de force* as citizens mobilized to support the IDF and reservists who'd run to fight, to save, to help even before officially being called to duty.

Over twelve hundred men, women, and children, old and young were brutalized — a count that took weeks to complete as bodies were still being recovered days, weeks, and months later. On August 6, 2024, nine months after Oct7, the last missing person, *Bilha Inon*, age 75 from the community of *Netiv HaAsara* was finally identified. After further forensic analysis of the evidence found near the burned-out house she shared with her husband, also killed on October 7, she was officially declared dead. Notwithstanding the upcoming anniversary of Oct7, over 1,200 *Yahrzeits* would be marked on *Simchat Torah* 2024 by families across Israel as the national trauma continued.

Oct7 didn't end for the 251 men, women, and children, soldiers and civilians, young and old, citizens of a dozen different countries, among them Jews, Christians, Muslims, Druzim, Buddhists, Bahá'í and Hindus, the living and the dead, who'd been taken as hostages into Gaza. Oct7 didn't end for their families who desperately sought their release, or a visit from the Red Cross, or proof of life… all of which had been denied them. For weeks, they received no word about their loved ones.

The closer Hazon Labs came to HaMikdash3.0's post-*Sukkot* launch date a year later, the more subdued Joshua became. His brooding bordered on a depression that went far beyond a startup's roller-coaster ups and downs. Jay suspected that Joshua's moodiness had less to do with the HaMikdash launch and more to do with the season, the upcoming High Holidays, specifically *Yom Kippur* — the holiest day of the year on the Jewish calendar; the Day of Atonement, *At-One-Ment* — and the second anniversary of his Opa Jacob's *yahrzeit*. So much had happened during the three years since Jacob's passing. Jay expected that with the HaMikdash3.0 launch looming large, *Yom Kippur* this year would be even more difficult for Joshua — a confluence of the past, present, and future — memories, hopes, and dreams, and the memory of the last journey Joshua and his grandfather had taken together. Jay felt privileged to be part of that last journey and to be able to help Joshua as best he could then, and now.

※ ※ ※

"Gotta hurry. Be Quick, Jackie. No worries. Jackie be nimble, Jackie be quick," she said. Talking to herself was normal, relatively speaking. But then her point of view was the only one that mattered.

"A job done well is a job well done because doing a job well is how it gets done." The word salad sounded like one of the viral parody videos of the U.S. Vice President rounding the net. Maybe she should become the Veep's speechwriter? She chuckled softly, then allowed it to blossom into a full-blown cackle.

Hmmm… maybe she needed a signature laugh too. Something sinister, evil, but not ghoulish. "Practice makes perfect because perfection takes practice." This was too good… she was definitely on a roll. With a simple click of the touchpad, silent as it was, she opened the laptop's video camera to record her latest witticism, almost forgetting she needed to be offline for at least the next two hours. "Stupid, stupid, stupid how can you be so stupid?" It was a rhetorical question. She wasn't stupid by any metric, not with a genius IQ hovering in the low 160s. But she did forget shit sometimes.

She glanced at the time on the taskbar, then closed the file pleased with her handiwork. The timer would auto-load the cyberattack sequence, all she had to do was make sure she was nowhere near any device that could link her to the assault on Eazon Labs' main servers.

"Done, done, and done," she announced, following it up with a little jig around her computer chair. She shut down the desktop computer and then disconnected it from the apartment Wi-Fi, then grabbed her company laptop from the side table. Disgusted, she brushed away the rolling papers, stray pot seeds, and bits of ash. Ez was a pig, leaving his shit all over the place. "Asshole," she said loud enough for him to hear, if he wasn't still asleep. Still, in "happy dance" mode, she checked for a stray roach, but without any luck. "Asshole," she repeated, thinking he probably chewed it down. Anyway, it was probably better for her to keep a clear head.

Jackie Allon zippered her laptop into her backpack and headed for the door. It would take her less than twenty minutes to get to Hazon Labs on her electric bike. She planned to time her arrival well after the fireworks started. "Damn," she said and did an about-face at the door.

What was she thinking? She dropped her bag by the door and pulled the T-shirt over her head. She tugged on her wetsuit shorts, but the restrictive neoprene, designed to fit snugly, didn't budge. Ez could deal with the roadblock himself as she jumped back into bed. She'd nearly blown her cover story. "Jackie's got her list but didn't check it twice!" she grumbled to herself.

She jumped onto the bed, nudging the Professor with each bounce up and down. Finally, his light snoring stopped. She dropped down to the bed and pulled away, as each exhale sent the stale stink from his breath her way.

"Wake up, I've got to kill some time," she announced, nudging him again more forcefully, rocking his hips back and forth. "Come on, today's the big day."

"Already?"

"Friday. Just like we planned."

"Then why are you still here?"

"Because I wuv you," she said, nearly choking on the words. Ezra Noiman, the Technion's former superstar professor, had been useful to a point, a sounding board when he wasn't stoned or drunk, or both. She'd found him wallowing in a bar, ranting against the same bastard she hated, and took pity on him. He'd spiraled after losing the lawsuit against Katz. The University was none too pleased with him either, grant monies dried up while he pickled his liver, earning him an extended stay in rehab. His fall from Grace was all in the public record. Ez could be summed up as a self-destructive, narcissist which dovetailed nicely with her borderline personality disorder. Borderline, my ass. She was a full-blown sociopath, with the smarts to know how to hide it most of the time. The rages, though, left her mostly unemployable. The Professor had provided her with the one kernel of information she needed to beat the bastard. She'd do it for herself and for him.

"How much time we got?" he asked, scratching at his two-day-old stubble.

"Long enough," she said, stroking him then giggled. "Well, not yet."

He took the challenge, slowly becoming aroused, less by her than by the thought of finally taking down Joshua E. Katz. "I'd love to see the little shit's face."

"Speaking of shit-faced, you might want to go easy on the booze. Maybe keep a clearer head for the next few, I might need you." Unlikely as that might be.

"I've never been clearer," he said, flipping her roughly onto her stomach. "You?"

"In perfect sync," she said, lifting her ass in the air. She'd have gladly set about destroying Joshua even without any prodding from the loser Professor. She never called him that to his face. He could be useful when he wasn't too drunk to perform. Noiman was best when he had his shirt off. Still, hot with the cut abs and the sexy curve below his waist that defied all logic since the man didn't work out unless lifting a liter bottle of booze every day counted as exercise. Sex was a bonus when he could perform. He'd gone at Joshua Katz using a frontal assault and failed. Backdoors were always better. Always.

"Ready when you are," she said, glancing over her shoulder.

"How much time have we got?"

"Roughly two hours," she said, placing a heavy emphasis on the word, roughly.

"Perfect," he grunted then easily pulled down her wetsuit pants and forcefully entered her backdoor.

Chapter 6

Human thoughts create infinitesimally small vibrational disturbances, frequency shifts that can be detected even in their fractional parts. This "Open-Source Intelligence" (OSINT) is an invaluable source of information. Parsing the information, however, can be challenging since the data stream seems to lack a shut-off valve or flowmeter. As such, no conversation can ever be considered truly private under "Open Source" rules. Ripples from Earthbound conversations often hit Heaven's home, disrupting worldwide operations. Uri'el had been unsuccessful in closing off the flood of TMEI — Too Much Emotional Information — pouring in and was deeply impacted by Joshua's last thoughts about Jacob Katzenstein's death. He'd also heard "her" plotting the cyberattack targeting HaMikdash3.0 and Joshua.

Humans… he often wondered why G-d even bothered?

Uri'el shook off the distraction and, with great effort, focused on his current task, completing the Angelic record on the Hebrew letter, *Aleph*. One would think enough had been written about the letter, but the gates of understanding extended well beyond the official 50 Gates of Understanding. With Earth's Time acceleration, currently running at 1.25X speed, Uri'el took advantage of the moments when he could prioritize his angelic duties.

> *The Aleph (א) can be viewed as a combination of other letters, namely the 6th letter Vav (ו) rotated to approximately -315°, a 45° counterclockwise drop, and framed by two oppositely placed Yuds, one set above the vav on the downslope, and one below towards the head of the vav. The word vav translates to hook, a connector, a connecting hook used in constructing the Mishkan, G-d's dwelling place on Earth before the Temple was built. The configuration of the Aleph also embeds meaning in its conformation, establishing a connection between Heaven and Earth — a separation between the waters above from the waters below, a completion guided by the Hand of G-d, the Yad of G-d's work (yud).*
>
> *The letter Aleph has a simple numerical value equal to 1 or sometimes 1,000 depending on the context. The Aleph also has a second*

value derived from the combination of the letters used in its construction: Vav + Yud + Yud (6 +10 + 10) which equals 26. As noted previously, Gematria rules allow us to identify other words with a similar numerical value. The number 26 is also the sum of the letters of the Tetragrammaton the ineffable Name of G-d given as Yud + Hei + Vav + Hei, or 10 + 5 + 6 + 5. Again, twenty-six.

In Gematria, one can also consider the role of the letter Aleph in different words. For example, the word for blood is dahm (דם), and the addition of a single letter Aleph transforms the word into ah-dam (אדם) which means man. We can continue the exercise by adding the letter hey (ה) at the end of the word for man to generate the word, ah-damah (אדמה), meaning "of the earth" which elegantly describes Man's origins from the dust of the Earth.

Another example relevant to the story of Joshua E. Katz is the word (אמת) emeth, meaning truth, which has a numerical value of 441. Emeth is the word said to have been written on the forehead of a Golem to animate it (the appropriate use of an "it" pronoun) from an empty shell formed of mud and clay, to a kind of alive state, sans a soul. But when the letter א is removed from the word אמת it becomes מת, meaning death; it is said that the Golem would then return to its original form, a pile of clay or mud.

Oh, what a difference a single letter can make, especially when it is an א! I offer now wisdom and insight on the word, אדם. What is Man? He is not Adam Kadmon, the primordial man 'borne' of the primordial light, so Adam Kadmon is not a man by any stretch of the definition, but a unique creation. Adam Kadmon is transcendent, confluent with the Sefirot, the Emanations of G-d, undifferentiated within the divine blueprint for all creation, but extant before creation. But what of Man, the Earthly being? Adam HaRishon, the First Man, he too was an empty vessel 'borne' of the dust of the Earth until G-d's breath transformed him, animating him from a Golem-type being with the Ruach HaKodesh, a holy breath breathed into him. Adam HaRishon was a unique vessel infused with the Light of all the souls that would ever be, a reflection of the Divine Light. But like many of the stories of Man (no *judgment intended here), sin reared its proverbial ugly head, and the vessel shattered. The differentiated Light yielded 600,000 root souls from which millions and millions of sparks became part of Creation, but where each spark continued, and continues, to hold a fractional part of the Primordial Light. This microcosmic splintering mirrors the cosmic Shattering of the Vessels, the Shevirat HaKelim. Such is how it is, above as below; same yet different like the two Yuds one placed above and the other below, separated by the angled Vav. Ah, the beauty of the letter Aleph.*

These are the times of Rectification, a tikkun to refine the sparks and restore them to their source… a time to bring together what is above and what is below in this particular present — a confluence of past, present, and the future as this Time approaches its End.

I digress from the Aleph to describe the exquisite beauty of the Hebrew letters and their nuanced relationships as told by the words for water and heaven — מים *and* שמים, *respectively, an honor to the letter Shin. On the second "day" He (capital H, the Big Guy) placed the rakiah — a dome-like structure to separate the waters above from the waters below to create what people call Heaven and Earth. This is the lowest rakiah. Of note, while G-d is everywhere, Heaven is the space-place typically associated with G-d whose other name is Shad-dai — one of seventy-two Divine names. The name is symbolically represented by the letter Shin,* ש. *When found in the Torah, the letter Shin is given special prominence, written with three crowns known as tagin. The Shin is one of only seven letters in the Hebrew alphabet to merit the crowns. The letter resembles flames, as the word for flame is Aish,* אש. *The letter Shin is constructed from a combination of Vavs and Yuds; the flames are formed with the letter Vav, and at the top of the three Vavs are Yuds, whereas at the bottom, the Vav joins the three flames. The tagin crowns top the farthest left Yud. The letter Shin has a numerical value of 300, which can be viewed as three times one hundred, a threefold state of perfection that man/woman can obtain in thought, speech, and action. The Shin is the root of the word, shuva, meaning return or repentance, and where* the word, kapper, to atone, also has a numerical value of 300. By extension, Yom Kippur can be seen as the impetus, the driver, to effect perfection throughout the year.

An important note. The Heaven referred to previously should not be confused with the Heaven of Heavens or any of the higher Heavens and the realm of me and my kind, and which is indicated by the use of the letter, Hey — which precedes the word שמים as in הַשמים i.e., The Heavens... which can be read as the uppermost of the Heavens or to include all of the Heavens.

Continuing. The doorposts of Jewish homes are generally adorned with a mezuzah, placed on the right, front-facing door jamb at a minimum at the entrance, with additional "semi-optional" placements on interior walls for an elaboration on the core mitzvah. The mezuzah is the housing, the covering which encloses a parchment containing the words of the Shema (שמע) prayer. Located on the front face of the mezuzah cover is the letter Shin, replete with its tagin. A Shin is also placed on the leather box holding the tefillin — the phylacteries; one is worn on the forehead and the other on the upper arm of the non-dominant arm. The leather straps are ceremoniously wrapped around the forearm and end in a specific wrapping pattern around the hand and fingers. The tefillin contains four Torah verses written on parchment that reference the reason for wearing tefillin and for placing a mezuzah on a doorpost. The verses include the opening sentences of the Shema prayer, which physically and spiritually links the two mitzvot by the letter Shin. 'Hear O Israel, the L-rd our G-d, the L-rd is One.'

One more understanding before returning to the matter of Joshua E. Katz. The letter Aleph meaning One (a capital letter reference to THE Big Guy) is not the only letter used to represent G-d. The letter Hey (ה) is often added to a name to denote a change in status such as when a higher level of spirituality is attained. Consider the following transformations, Abram (or Avram) to Abraham (or Avraham), changed with the addition of the letter ה to his Hebrew name, אברם to אברהם. Of note, G-d can also be referenced by using the letters ה/י in a name; other G-d references in names will not be *described here, except our own. The reflection of G-d in our name, the name by which we are known to Man/Woman, is found within us with the addition of the letters -el. My name Uri'el translates to: G-d is my Light. With but a few exceptions, angel names always end in the letter, -el. The pious do not casually speak the -el in Hebrew or the -hey when present in one of G-d's names; in these cases -kale and -kay are substituted, respectively.*

Another note of consequence. My name, Uri'el based on the spelling in English-speaking circles has been mutated over the millennia by some rocket scientist downstairs, probably by more than one who perpetuated the error. Names are important, and...

Uri'el heard the disgruntled, "A-hem." Reluctantly, he deleted his "by some rocket scientist downstairs" comment and was careful to not roll his many eyes before continuing.

My name Uri'el (אוריאל) begins with the letter א. The root of this name is found in the first chapter of the Torah, verse 3, 'And G-d said: 'Let there be light. And there was light.' I am part of the Light. אור meaning, light, and אורי meaning, my light. The simplest Gematria calculation of the word for light is 248, which is the number of positive Mitzvot (Commandments), as well as the number of human body parts, and also the same Gematria as the name Abraham (אברהם). Ari'el, my sister angel's name, translates to 'Lion of G-d' and should not be confused with Disney's 'Little Mermaid' character despite the sameness of their pronunciations. Our names vary by a single letter, the addition of the letter Vav (ו) after the Aleph (א) in my name. The numerical value of her name is 242, a difference of six between our names. She is often referred to as the Angel of Nature, as the root of her name, ארי (Ari) can be related to the word for lion, Aryeh (אריה). Though if strict gender rules are applied, she should rightfully be called a lioness, except pronoun nonsense is utterly irrelevant in these Heavenly realms. It should surprise no one that the numerical value of Ari'el's name 242 has the same numerical value as the word for 'roar' as in a lion's roar is reuma (ראומה), demonstrating the intrinsic relationship between the letters and words of Creation and that which is created.

Continuing. The lion is a symbol of strength and courage, the symbol of the tribe of Judah, carried on her flag and used on the city of Jerusalem's flag. The word, Ari'el, makes its first appearance as an intact whole word in Isaiah 29:1 and is repeated no less than four times in the chapter. According to most commentaries, Ari'el is the embodiment of Jerusalem, though it should be noted that there is a modern city in Israel called Ariel. Any confusion regarding the actual city referred to here can be settled by the fourth reference in Isaiah 29:7-8 which describes how the multitude of nations will war against her. While the Samarian city of Ariel has a University, a Medical School established in 2019, and several decent restaurants, Isaiah's Ari'el reference is to THE Mount Zion, undeniably located in Jerusalem, and most certainly not to any of the fifty-five places in nine countries around the world also named, Mount Zion.

Uri'el paused, pondering what point he had been trying to make. "No matter, what he wrote was a good enough introduction," acknowledging the breadth of information he had imparted to the aether. He drummed his wingtip on an invisible keyboard before continuing when his thought transfer was interrupted by the searing clang from Archangel Micha'el's swords in the plural. *When did he get a second sword?*

"Your boy is hitting the road again," Archangel Micha'el said, tapping his wing on Uri'el's shoulder more forcefully than was necessary to make his point.

"Thanks, but I might have to let this one ride," Uri'el said with an annoyed glance at the Guardian Angels he was ostensibly supervising.

"I don't think that's such a good idea," Micha'el responded, clearly intimating trouble on the horizon.

"Anything I should know about?" Uri'el asked, concern flashing across each of his faces.

"Nothing definite. Yet."

"Well, I can't exactly leave the rugrats on their own," he said with a sneer of his lion's lip, heavy on the teeth, and a slight shudder of his human head.

"I'll keep my eyes on the kiddies while you're gone."

"You sure?"

"No worries, I think I can manage. I can be pretty scary, you know." Archangel Micha'el offered the remark with a wink and a simultaneous glare at the GAs, who collectively cowered in a one-dimensional corner of Heaven.

Yessiree, Micha'el could be scary, part of his legend, Uri'el thought to himself (though his thoughts were never truly "to himself"). Micha'el, the Archangel of War wielded a powerful sword; served as Protector and champion of the Jewish people; defeated Satan (not alone, mind you); and, as a Messenger of the Almighty who claimed Moses' body for G-d.

For reference, Micha'el's given sword is sharper and longer than mine; but because of my current *Cherubic* attributes, my sword is fiery. My intention is not to sound competitive or to boast, since under the present circumstances, both of our swords will be needed to effect the desired end.

Waving demurely to Micha'el, Uri'el headed down to Reichman's University, using the Heavenly equivalent of Waze, hoping to avoid running into any other Unidentified Flying Beings, along the way.

"Please join me in welcoming our guest speaker, the CEO of Hazon Labs Joshua Katz," said Reichmann University's Chancellor, leading the group in a round of applause. At least four-hundred-fifty graduate and undergraduate students and twenty faculty members were sardine-packed, though not vacuum-sealed, in the University's Ivcher Auditorium. The guest seminar was always a popular event and marked the end of the summer term. The bonus lecture would not be graded nor was any note taking required, though many in the audience would hang on every word Hazon Labs' CEO said. If a vote were taken, Joshua Katz would have been inducted into the Start-up Hall of Fame, if there were one.

Joshua took the stage, waving to the crowd. The decibel level ratcheted upwards as the crowd offered their genuine appreciation with thunderous applause. No doubt, many in attendance also felt more than a twinge of wannabe jealousy about the handsome, twenty-eight-year-old entrepreneur on the 30-under-30 Rising Jewish Stars' list. Joshua came in at a respectable No. 10 and was No. 5 on Israel's hottest bachelor's list. Most however were curious about the person who'd had the balls to turn one of the most hotly contested piece of Israeli real estate, the Temple Mount in Jerusalem, into a gamer's paradise.

Uri'el heard the initial applause during his descent and arrived just as Hazon Labs' three-minute promotional video began playing. He found space against the auditorium's back wall, where the rest of the riff-raff, latecomers, and would-be disruptors were gathered. The University had moved the lecture from the smaller Alpern Hall to the larger Ivcher Auditorium as the early arrival numbers swelled. Unfortunately, there still wasn't enough room for everyone to sit, unless floors and stairs could be counted as seats. Uri'el's sensitive ears picked up every breathlessly whispered and oft-repeated, heavily accented "sorry" or Hebrew equivalent, *slicha*; a steady stream of whispered "ows" and ever-popular Israeli tsk-sounds. As the lights dimmed, people continued to crawl over one another, ostensibly searching for non-existent empty seats, all hoping to inch a millimeter closer to the already-famous, or infamous, Joshua E. Katz. Despite the rumblings, the video presentation proceeded with minimal disruption.

The crowd was comprised of an interesting mix of undergraduate students, BA and BS-level psychology, business, computer science, and communications studies, and many from the accelerated Executive MBA program. The latter would have gladly taken time away from work on any day of the week to hear Joshua E. Katz, the latest guru in the "oracle-of-the-month" club. He wasn't a graduate of Israel's top-ranking private research university, but Joshua was still considered a favorite son/grandson of serial inventor Jacob Katzenstein who'd endowed a chair in the School of Sustainability. While Joshua earned enough creds on his own to merit a guest lecturer invitation from the University, the Chancellor had leveraged his lineage to get him to agree for what was ostensibly billed as a Memorial lecture in honor of his late grandfather. Despite HaMikdash3.0 being in its final stages and the High Holidays about to cause every-other-day disruptions to the work week, there was no way Joshua could refuse Reichman's invitation.

As the auditorium lights dimmed, the crowd grew silent.

On the giant screen, the Hazon promotional video opened with a stark white screen and a large number zero prominently placed off-center.

Timed to coincide with the *Sefirat Omer*, the counting of the days between *Pesach*/Passover and *Shavuot*/Pentecost holidays, everyone in the audience knew about Hazon's mega enrollment drive. Many in the audience were also familiar with the *Kabbalistic Omer* counting calendar having joined the ranks of HaMikdash3.0 members themselves.

> *The calendar was a color-coded chart that used the colors associated with seven of the ten Sefirot comprising the mystical Tree of Life. These were arranged in a 7x7 grid for the 49-day count between the two holidays. Each of the seven weeks was depicted with a dominant Sefira color and each day with a secondary, colored Sefira attribute. The concept was usually represented by a smaller-colored circle, the day within the week, inside a relatively larger-colored circle, the number of the week.*

Hazon's marketing team built a colorful marketing campaign around the changing colors, running a spectrum of eye-catching hexadecimal colors to coincide with the advancement through the colorful *Omer* count. The group debated which of the 16 million available colors to use to represent the *Sefirot*, as each *Sefira* corresponds to one or more frequencies in the visible light spectrum. In the end, the campaign delivered a rainbow wash of colors, spanning the electromagnetic spectrum from reds, at approximately 405-480 Terahertz (THz), to the purple/violets in the 715-800 THz range.

While the Hazon Labs team did not specifically have LGBTQ++ groups in mind with the poly-color design, it earned them the group's goodwill and free publicity. By default, the rainbow flag endorsement also created a firestorm of bad press from the ultra-religious right that transcended any particular religion. Joshua casually added it to the burgeoning file of hate mail he received daily.

Heaven's Angelic watchdogs, who guarded the three *Upper Sefirot* of *Keter*/Kingship, *Binah*/Understanding, and *Chochmah*/Wisdom, were pleased by the Marketing team's restraint and only interceded when they occasionally chose design over function in portraying the other *Sefirot*. The elucidation of the *Sefirot* was profoundly complicated; it was one of the reasons why Uri'el preferred the simpler description that portrayed complementary color visuals. In the Celestial realms, the *Sefirot* conveyed a vibrational range spanning the entire visual spectrum with complementary vibrational frequencies that extended across the breadth of the known, and unknown, electromagnetic spectrum. The *Omeric* juxtapositions and nuanced interactions of the *Sefirot* on any given day could be applied to relationships between Man and G-d, Man and Man, and Man and himself/herself, and, of course, between the sparks of a given soul root.

Uri'el considered applying a simplified color-coded system to organize and train the Guardian Angels as part of an emergency Angel Response Alert System (ARAS). In his mind, ARAS could be similar to America's DEFCON — DEFense readiness CONdition — using a 1-5 scale with red alert status represented by fiery-red 1 up to a minty-green 5 for A-Okay. His ARAS thought proposal, however, was rejected when some of his peers on THE Committee noted the potential for confusion with another DEFCON — the premier hacker convention which inversely used green for "good to go" in causing red-alert type problems. He appealed the decision and won the opportunity to develop the system; implementation, however, would depend on THE Committee's final approval.

Unlike the *Sefirot HaOmer's* use of only seven of the ten *Sefirot* for the 49-day count in the 7x7 grid, it wouldn't do for Uri'el to exclude any of the *Sefirot* considering what Joshua E. Katz faced in the coming days. His ARAS would need the full complement; a 10x10 grid that would include all the *Sefirot*, assigning each level with a responsiveness rating and taskings. Uri'el was convinced it could work. The weeks' measure would extend for one hundred days to match the 10x10 format. For good or bad, he already knew that the label for his grid would define a significantly smaller period of time in Joshua E. Katz's life's cycle… one measured in fewer than one hundred days.

"Hmmm," thought Uri'el. "Maybe that was why THE Committee hadn't approved the 100-day planning chart." Were they privy to additional timeline information, or rather time-limited information? The latest circular from "End Times Events" laid odds on its start on the Jewish New Year, *Rosh Hashanah*, and continuing through *Chol HaMoed Sukkot*, the *Sukkot* holiday's intermediate days.

Knowledge of future events gave Uri'el pause. His wistful sigh, while barely audible, drew unwanted glares and shushed whispers from the gaggle of students around him, none of whom could pinpoint the source. While Uri'el pondered how best to implement his color-coded chart for Guardian Angel training, an actual DEFCON alert was happening at Hazon Labs. HaMikdash3.0's PICSSid — an advanced, image-based user authentication system that used a dynamic image database to link user profiles, avatars, and passwords — was under attack.

While only parts of the HaMikdash3.0 site were accessible, over 75% of their 1.5 million-plus users could be found online at any given point in time. Users could be found building their avatar personae portfolios; choosing avatar roles; reading storyline bibles; strategically identifying initial game scenarios; and, participating in chat groups. In addition, their online engagement helped build their "stock" supply of grain (*mincha*) and virtual burnt offering animal sacrifices of goats, sheep and turtle-doves for when the site went live. Eventually, Hazon's dynamic, multidimensional relational database would contain a comprehensive visual record of user interactions and purchases, including what sacrifices each user favored most.

Today's hacking target appeared to be the *Korban Olah* — the twice-daily offered burnt sacrifice.

The first incursion occurred at 10:07:01 AM, though it would take another seven seconds before it was detected and another five minutes before it was *supposedly* contained. The incursion triggered Hazon Labs' Checkpoint's Intrusion Alert (CIA) system, sending an alert to the phones of all Hazon employees, including those belonging to Joshua and Jay. For good or bad, Joshua was only vaguely aware of the trouble since his phone was with Jay who'd turned both phones to vibrate-only mode once Joshua's presentation started.

Uri'el was aware of the incursion and hoped his thinking about DEFCON, the hacking conference, hadn't inadvertently contributed to the occurrence. Prescience was a given, but Angelic interference was strictly forbidden; except for the influence exerted by the "Dark Forces" in the course of Human events — a necessary part of the soul rectification equation. Today, the "Dark Forces" were on the move. Uri'el couldn't help but wonder how the Hazon team was handling their first major crisis without J1 and J2's onsite oversight. Julia, J3, despite her persistent vegetative state, was aware of events in her plane of existence. Unfortunately, there was little she could do, at the moment, to help her friends.

"It will be what it will be," Uri'el thought, then quickly followed up with, *Baruch Shem K'vod Malchuso L'Olam Va'ed*, 'May His Name, the honor of His Kingdom be blessed forever and ever,' acknowledging the Holy One

Blessed Be He's ruling guidance. His words were answered by an express delivery "Amen" direct from the Heavenly Court which was elaborated beyond the acronym to a most proper *E-l Melech Ne'eman*. Uri'el turned his attention back to the fifty-foot screen filled with the colorful *Kabbalistic Omer* counting visuals.

> *Onscreen, the colorful date tearaways were removed, the running counter above it churned at breakneck speed, rapidly changing the rising number count across the ones, tens, hundreds, thousands, tens of thousands, hundreds of thousands place, quickly reaching and breaking the million-number mark in a little over a minute — one-hundred-forty-four seconds to be precise. At the thirty-three-day mark, Lag b'omer, HaMikdash3.0 members numbered 1,079,980; by the end of the forty-nine-day registration drive, the tally reached 1,144,000 members.*

A student standing below Uri'el shook his head back and forth, conveying both disbelief and respect, then whispered to no one in particular, "…brilliant," though he prefaced it with a colorful expletive. Uri'el couldn't disagree. Joshua's timing of HaMikdash3.0's early-bird registration to the *Omer* count was inspired, and a resounding success, except for the angel-generating 2.99-second-long *tekiah* blasts associated with signing up each new member plus each of the 15-second milestone toots.

Regardless, he'd deal, Uri'el thought and then punctuated the thought with an annoyed subsonic-level growl.

"And deal you will," came the reply.

The response thought surprised Uri'el. He usually talked to himself but in a much nicer manner. These words carried an ominous chill that swept over him, ruffling his eagle's feathers.

Uri'el ventured a tentative subsonic "Ugh, hello?" then surreptitiously scanned the faces of those around him and those to his side, casually looking for any vibrational or frequency aberrations. It was certainly within the realm of possibilities that representatives of the opposing team — be they of the fallen angel kind or generic evil human variety — might also be attending Joshua E. Katz's presentation. Evil had a distinctive vibrational signature, a frequency that could radiate an empty void or a DEFCON Level 1, red-alert twitching restlessness.

"Show yourself!" Uri'el demanded.

The response came quickly… a sinister, mocking laugh.

Uri'el again scanned the room, searching for the slightest disturbance. A sense of relief washed over him as he spied several Guardian Angels attached to other souls in the crowd. All but one of them respectfully nodded to him in deference to his superior position in the Angelic hierarchy. Uri'el tagged the offending GA's number. The seemingly intentional disrespect required an official angelic reprimand. Ignoring the rebuff for the moment, he turned his attention back to Hazon's promotional video.

The Membership Enrollment ticker ominously froze at 1,144,000, displaying the date June 11, 2024, 17:49 PM, marking the end of the HaMikdash3.0 early registration drive and the start of the Shavuot holiday and Jerusalem candle lighting time.

An interesting number, Uri'el thought at least according to Christian eschatology. The 144,000 represented the number of people expected to ascend to Heaven in the Rapture. If that were the case, the 144,000 would represent a highly competitive spot to secure. In reality, the 144,000 was attached to the number of souls, not individuals, making it possible for a far greater number of good Christian folks to qualify… a not-so-minor point in incentivizing a righteous life filled with good deeds.

The video drew Uri'el's attention again.

Onscreen, the number count faded out and was replaced with a street-level view of greater Jerusalem, filled with an array of three-dimensional structures popping up in identifiable places. The axis shifted and the scene panned out, switching to an aerial view from the perspective of a peace dove bearing an olive branch flying above the city. As the dove neared the Old City, the scene zoomed in to encompass the city walls, gates, and the surrounding areas which resembled the ancient Madaba map — an exquisite detailed mosaic of Jerusalem and the surrounding region.

The membership ticker then flew to the center of the screen, rolling forward until hitting that morning's 1.5M member enrollment milestone. The date 9/27/2024, 10:07AM is written above it, before receding to a lower right-hand corner position.

A clickable icon then appeared with the text, "Learn" and options to click on either the Madaba Map or the Cardo. Guided by an unseen hand, the mouse cursor moved across the screen, then clicked on the Madaba Map icon, engaging the audio file and companion text.

"The Madaba Map highlights the landscape of ancient Israel and its environs, extending from Lebanon in the north to the River Nile in the south, east beyond the Dead Sea to the Eastern Desert, and West to the Mediterranean. The Madaba Map, dating to the 6th century CE/AD, is one of the oldest surviving mosaic-tiled maps of the Holy Land. What remains of the actual map is part of the mosaic floor in what is now the Byzantine Church of Saint George in Madaba, Jordan. Notably, a portion of the southeastern area of the map, leading to the Dead Sea, is missing. Curiously, or perhaps not surprisingly, the city of Madaba lies in a direct line with the city of Jerusalem… mere minutes of difference on the longitude-latitude scale."

Onscreen, a second prompt appeared, offering users two options: "Return to the previous animation" or "Learn more about the Cardo." The "Learn" icon flashed red and a small countdown timer appeared above the "Learn" icon encouraging users to engage with the time-limited opportunity. While users could always click back to the primary animation, HaMikdash3.0 indirectly informed users that the information contained in the Cardo link may be valuable, be it for gameplay or general knowledge.

The mouse cursor then moved across the screen and clicked on the "Learn" icon, engaging an audio file and companion text about the Cardo linking it to the Madaba map.

"The Madaba map prominently features the walled city of Jerusalem, its gates, and the Cardo Maximus which extends from the city's north to the south, ending near the Zion Gate. The ancient Roman street, once a center for commercial activity, is captured in the Cardo today with art, jewelry, spice, and textiles shops extending along its entire length from the Jewish Quarter on the south into the Muslim Quarter in the north.

> "A small replica of the Madaba Map is on display in a stone passageway leading from the shops in the Jewish Quarter to an indoor archeological garden, located below the shop's street level. The excavations feature four intact twenty-six-foot-tall pillars and five partial shafts demarcating what would have been vendor stalls and hinting at the Cardo's former glory days. Additional excavations have extended the remains of the Cardo in the Byzantine era south to David Street."

> *A small map icon with a compass appears onscreen. The map automatically enlarges, showing the route from the Damascus Gate to David Street. The map then reduces to its icon form and moves to the upper right-hand corner before the audio continues.*

> "There is evidence of similar vendor stalls mirrored on the opposite side, but the pillars are missing, though a few plinths with supporting platforms (stylobates) are still evident; wall mosaics help visitors visualize what might have been sold in these other vendor stalls. Visitors to the Cardo should take note of the large, colorful mural painted on the wall. The mural conveys rich details of what this bustling marketplace might have looked like where its vendor stalls, separated by towering columns, stretch into the distance as far as the eye can see."

> *Onscreen, a Posh Vendor avatar, his robes neatly trimmed in purple velvet, emerges from the Cardo mural.*

Even without the benefit of special 3D glasses, the figure-ground illusion effectively conveys depth, prompting a chorus of well-deserved "wows" from the audience.

> *The Posh Vendor asks, "Would you like to purchase a copy of the Cardo Mural?" with the companion text prompt of "Yes/No" options. Onscreen, an exchange of ShekCoins is made with an unseen buyer; a balloon above the Vendor's head shows the number, 100SC.*

> *The Posh Vendor nods to the unseen buyer, "Yom Tov!" he says, wishing the user, "a good day" written in English above the Posh Vendor's head. He then turns around and walks back into the mural, pausing to give a ShekCoin to a Street Beggar avatar.*

Onscreen, the Street Beggar avatar says, "There's more to see," raising a bony finger pointing south.

The audio guide continues, "The Cardo continues south, leading to an open-air archaeological garden with five intact pillars and the excavated remnants of what are believed to be larger vendor stalls, perhaps for goats or sheep."

The image freezes on the outdoor Cardo excavation. Onscreen, a pop-up appears onscreen, labeled "MiYuchadim/Special Notes." The mouse cursor moves to the link, triggering a text and audio file. "Note #1: a reproduction of the Madaba map can also be found in the lobby of the YMCA on King David Street in Jerusalem."

Onscreen the image of the Madaba Map is presented before Special Note #2 is voiced. "Note #2: During construction work on Route 60, a street replete with towering pillars, running perpendicular to the Cardo below the Jaffa Gate, was discovered. This perpendicular street arrangement is known in Greek as the Decumanus and is visible on the Madaba Map. Thank you for your attention."

Onscreen, the "Special Notes" pop-up closes. The narration continues.

"There are many still unknowns yet to be discovered about the Cardo, which has only been partially excavated on its northern and southern ends, as well as what exists below the current excavations. Like much of Jerusalem's history, her story is hidden in her golden-hued stones, in the passageways and tunnels yet to be uncovered, perhaps by you.

"One can easily imagine other hidden gems secreted in the tunnels beneath the Old City, a real-world backdrop ideally suited for building an endless array of HaMikdash3.0 scenarios and virtual interactions.

Joshua developed the promo to visually highlight key HaMikdash3.0 features using the Cardo marketplace as a single point of reference to represent the range of possible virtual user interactions. The layered gameplay included missing puzzle piece rewards to sourcing out hidden objects or other knowledge-based interactives. The Cardo image was officially "borrowed" with permissions from the Jerusalem Municipality and coordinated with the local Jerusalem Development Authority and the Ministry of Tourism in a development deal designed to help promote Israeli tourism. By design special incentives were built into HaMikdash3.0 gameplay, allowing for a potential real-world scavenger hunt challenge for online to offline cross-over challenges, and *vice-versa*.

> *Onscreen, the video shows Hazon Labs' teams working intently but with a nice mix of playfulness, photographing the Cardo fresco from dozens of different angles and then digitizing it to create the animation sequence. The word, "INNOVATION" is boldly scripted in block letters and scrolls across the screen, along with key technology words: Enhanced Texture; Vibrant Graphics; 3D-like Enhancements; CGI; and, Motion Capture. As the words disappear, onscreen a motion capture wireframe of a person walks across the screen, entering from the left and exiting on the right. A first "skin" is applied: a young male walks across the screen, followed by a quick manipulation of the same wire-frame structure to a child's size form and a new "skin" applied as the two avatars then walk side-by-side with fluid, flawless human-like movements.*
>
> *A cartoonified avatar of Joshua then appears onscreen.*

His appearance prompts a round of tittering laughs from the audience, then hushed silence as it/he speaks.

> *"Our animation teams used a similar approach throughout HaMikdash3.0, transforming static, real-world images into dynamic scenes populated by Non-Playable Characters (NPCs), as well as avatars created by you, and me. Though telling the difference between the two can be challenging," the Joshua avatar says with a wink before continuing the tour.*
>
> *"The integration of real-world backdrops offers us the possibility of creating virtual to real-world crossover opportunities, and vice-versa." The companion video shows Hazon teams shooting scenes, working on motion capture sequences with leotard-clad actors/actresses, including Dov Luznick, the well-known, mostly*

androgynous, refusing-to-be-gender classified model, and then switches over to the heavy-duty lifting in the editing suite, with Tzion at the helm. A rapid sequence of scenes of HaMikdash3.0's virtual world come to life.

The next sequence was one of Joshua's favorites, shot as if looking over the animator's shoulder.

The camera zooms into the wall of monitors used for screening animation sequences, every detail fine-tuned and color-corrected to perfection. The camera zooms into the Cardo scene till it fills the entire screen as a static background image. A bird flies into the scene and lands on one of several brass lamp holders hanging in a vendor's stall. The lamps then begins to sway. In the blink of an eye, the static Cardo fresco transforms into a bustling marketplace with crowds of male and female avatars, young and old, moving in a mixed scene that blends the ancient with the modern.

Floating above the heads of a subset of the avatars are plus and minus symbols with differently scored points. A Spice Vendor, one of many user roleplay options, is surrounded by brass bowls filled with spices and smoking incense. To the side of the marketplace scene, a drop-down menu displays a list of different roles players can assume.

The Spice Vendor avatar has a balloon above his head showing points earned. The Spice Vendor offers a handful of crystallized incense to a robe-attired Customer avatar, who shakes his head no. The persistent Spice Vendor scoops up a handful of besamim, a potpourri of aromatic dried cloves and myrtle leaves, and pushes it toward the Customer avatar. The Customer avatar bends down and appreciatively sniffs the aromatics while reciting the blessing over the sweet spices… "Borei minei besamim."

The words, "Intuitive Gestures" and "Contextual Responses" scrolls across the screen. The letters A and I, written vertically, appear onscreen. The letters are then filled in, forming the words, "Avatar Intelligence." A transaction occurs, the Customer avatar nods, and the Spice Vendor avatar weighs out the handful of the spice mix and places it in a small burlap sack. The 3.0 brand is visible on the sack. The Spice Vendor hands the sack to the Customer avatar who drops a few ShekCoins into the Spice Vendor avatar's hand; points balloons float above both avatars. A Female avatar, adorned in gold jewelry and wearing regal, flowing robes trimmed in gold, walks past the Spice shop and passes a Street Beggar avatar. She then turns back, offering the Street Beggar avatar a handful of special TzadikShekCoins, double value ShekCoins; positive points are awarded to both avatars.

The animated sequence then zooms in on a tall avatar; the name Ari of Judah is displayed across the back of his tekhelet-colored T-shirt. He emerges from the crowd scene and walks toward a bank of single-person, walk-in kiosk pods; at either end of the row is a collection of five larger family-sized kiosk pods… Jay's T-osks.

Joshua, standing to the right of the auditorium's 50-foot projection screen, pauses the video, "Yeah, yeah, we know. It's a little too phallic. I assure you, our -osks are now gender neutral." His comment prompts a round of chuckles and hoots from the capacity-plus audience.

Onscreen, Ari of Judah steps into a pod. At once, the hustle and bustle of the marketplace is silenced in the private space. Ari of Judah reaches into a cubby, selects a knitted kippah from one of the bins, and places it on his head. He closes his eyes. His lips move in silent prayer. A hologram of a barefoot Kohen, a priest avatar, dressed in a long white robe appears in the space before him. The Kohen avatar performs the Priestly Blessing making the traditional sign of the double Shin letter with his hands.

The scene zooms out to show a long row of kiosk pods where other male and female avatars are seen entering the pods. In one, a Male avatar leads a smiling virtual sheep into a pod; while a Female avatar has two turtle doves perched on her shoulders as she enters a pod.

In the background, a Young Boy avatar wearing a black and white soccer jersey kicks a soccer ball between his legs. The scene follows the ball as it rolls into a dark corner behind one of the Cardo columns. The boy runs after the ball, peering into the dark space behind an ancient wall. From within the darkness, two eyes blink back at him. Frightened, the Young Boy backs away and bumps into the Ari of Judah.

The Young Boy timidly says, "My ball," then adds, "it rolled in there," pointing a trembling finger, his every word infused with fear. Ari of Judah pats the boy on the head, crouches down, and reaches into the crevice.

The screen shudders as Ari of Judah tumbles into the hidden space.

A booming voice says, "Surely you must help the boy, but it is more than his ball you will find. A stone is not a stone, nor a coin just a coin. A seal, a word, one for each of the twelve tribes, discover these and solve the Riddle of the Choshen... the jeweled breastplate belonging to the Kohen Gadol, the High Priest. The soccer ball rolls back into the Cardo, but the Young Boy is nowhere to be found. A sinister-looking black and white cat hisses at the audience. The screen fades to white with the words, "The End" written in black appears on screen, but the auditorium lights remain off.

The gathered students aren't sure if the video is over, or if perhaps it's a glitch. Some tentatively applaud, but which doesn't catch on. Then, the words and background color transform themselves, white letters written on black appear onscreen and the words, *HaMikdash3.0 — The Beginning*. The auditorium lights are brought up abruptly, painfully bright, eliciting a visceral reaction from the audience, and a collective murmur followed by unrestrained applause.

Joshua steps to the center of the stage wearing the VR/AR glasses to protect his brain from the harsh glare of the lights. He allows his eyes to adjust and then casually pushes the glasses onto his head. A thunderous applause fills the room, amplified to noise-pollution decibel levels reverberating off the walls in the acoustically unbalanced space.

Thankfully, Joshua's headache had simmered down from its high-heat levels to a slow simmer, as they pulled into the Reichman University parking lot. As the applause tapers off, the audio-visual tech comes up behind him, startling Joshua. He hands Joshua a hands-free microphone headset, then clips a new battery pack to his pants. As Joshua spins around to face the audience, he nearly trips over his feet, stepping backward as a strange face materializes out of nowhere just inches from his face. He hears himself inhale sharply in a staccato of sounds amplified by his mic which he tries to cover up by clearing his throat and a fake cough. His eyes remain transfixed on the face which seems to rapidly alternate between the face of a lion and a man's visage like some evil lenticular hologram. He coughs again, taking a swig from a water bottle, and then closes his eyes hoping the apparition will disappear. No doubt, numerous students were recording his talk, and it wouldn't do to have one of them tweet about Hazon Lab's CEO displaying Tourette Syndrome-like squawks.

His pulse continued to race, easily hitting eighty-five beats per minute, nearly two dozen beats above his usual sixty-three to sixty-five range. *What the hell was that?* he wondered. In his research for HaMikdash3.0, he delved into the esoteric, and occasionally nightmarish representations of current and former Heavenly creatures. If he didn't know better, he'd guess what he'd seen was a *Cherub*, an Archangel, or some unknown demon species. Still lost in thought, Joshua nearly jumped out of his skin again when the Reichman AV tech tapped him on the shoulder, giving him a thumbs-up sign for the mic.

Joshua nodded to the technician, but for whatever reason, he still can't shake the creepy crawly feeling of someone walking over his grave. Behind him onscreen, the membership count reappears, climbing up another 270,665 to 1,770,665. The live ticker takes only twenty seconds to register the new HaMikdash3.0 membership count, giving Joshua just enough time to slug down more water and pull his proverbial shit together. The vision, the image, or whatever the hell it was, had disappeared as quickly as it had manifested itself. And with any luck wouldn't be returning any time soon.

Joshua took an extra beat to glance over to Jay, who had been standing in the wings behind the auditorium's stage for much of the presentation. Visibly agitated, he had Joshua's phone tucked between his neck and shoulder while rapidly scrolling and swiping across his phone with its oversized 7.6" display. Joshua recognized Jay's familiar "loaded for bear" *Krav Maga* stance, eyes darting, brow furrowed, leaving little doubt in Joshua's mind that Jay was juggling a major Hazon Labs' 911 emergency. He'd passed his phone off to Jay, to minimize any distraction from any more of the annoying incoming blocked number calls. Whatever Jay was dealing with was clearly more serious than a simple blocked call.

The display screen behind Joshua should have continued scrolling any changes in HaMikdash3.0's membership numbers. On the way in, they'd daisy-chained Joshua's phone to a "secure" temporary sandbox between their two phones, isolating the enrollment count data to a mirror site and hot-spotting the running count to the auditorium's giant whiteboard screen with less than a microsecond delay in transmission. Their average was 123,000 new members per hour. On their worst day they recorded only 3,600 new sign-ins. But for some reason, the membership ticker was mysteriously frozen, flickering mid-change between 1,770,665 and 1,770,666… an indication that the feed had been interrupted. The numbers rapidly flipped between the two …665 and …666 as if the ticker was deciding which of the two numbers to display. Then a decision.

The membership count froze at 1,770,666… an unsettling set of numbers, if one were attuned to their diametrically opposed significance. Uri'el's tuning was on hyperdrive. He again scanned the room looking for the unearthly threat to HaMikdash3.0 and Joshua E. Katz, which had dared show itself in his presence.

Jay sensed Joshua looking at him and looked up. He blew out a huff of air, looking at the fiery Red Alert on the phone's screen. He turned it out for Joshua to see. In that turning moment, the fiery Red Alert went to a Day-Glo yellow… a temporary reprieve but which didn't last long. The screen was immediately upgraded to a higher alert status, filling the screen with a dark pumpkin orange color. HaMikdash3.0 was under attack. They were still in trouble… big trouble.

Chapter 7

Thirteen-year-old Effi Davidson sat at his gaming console in the ergonomic gamers' chair his Aunt Davi insisted he use, staring at the miserable message from Hazon Labs. The microphone headset he wore was looped around his neck, utterly useless to him at the moment. In retrospect, he wished that he'd turned on the auto-record function so he could have saved his expletive-filled rant to play back to Hazon Labs' chatbot, frying and frustrating it trying to decipher his unrepeatable spew. He still planned to give Hazon Labs a large piece of near-genius IQ mind for crashing unceremoniously as he was finishing work on his third avatar. He refreshed the screen, willing the message to change. It didn't, displaying the same obtusity as before.

"We apologize for any inconvenience. If you were on the site during the service interruption, rest assured that your work is safe and secure, and any data you entered in the last hour has been saved to your account. Please check back later — better yet, try tomorrow."

"My work better be there," Effi shouted at the screen, then reading the message in a whiny singsong, "Please check back later — better yet, try tomorrow. Attitude seasoned with a poor attempt at humor. Didiculous!" he shouted.

Effi shook his head at his overall bad timing. He'd skipped school by faking a terrible headache; a credible story since he did get migraines and now felt one coming on for real. Missing school wasn't the problem, especially on a Friday which was a short school day because of *Shabbat*. Besides, his classes weren't difficult or challenging. He did feel bad about lying to Aunt Davi — short for Davida. He'd been staying with her for the past two months, the usual setup whenever his dad Solomon "Sol" Davidowitch, who preferred using the family's original Eastern European name as his *nom de plume*, was off on another book tour. His publicist insisted the non-anglicized *-witch* made him sound mysterious. Currently, his father was in the United States, promoting *The Chladni Progression* trilogy. The newest release in the series, *The Power to Spin Time*, gave the story's lead character, Blaise Manning, multi-dimensional time travel-shifting abilities so he could reunite with his dead wife who was presumably alive in at least one parallel time-space continuum. Effi saw it for what it was… a desire to escape from their current reality where death meant death in exchange for time-warping alt-dead travels across the multiverse. Were it possible to breach death's barrier, Effi would be happy to see his mom again. But he was smart enough to know that indulging in the fantasy served no one, least of all him.

Besides, the book's physics wasn't exactly kosher, a comment Effi offered when he read an early draft of the third, and supposedly final installment, in the "Chladni Progression" trilogy. It wasn't that his dad's books were bad, objectively the Progression series was good, but the storylines hit a little too close to home for Effi's taste, especially the last one about the lead character's obsession, his father, with Effi's mother. His dad's truth, and by default his, was on display in the 354 pages of *The Power to Spin Time*, and of course in the soppy dedication, and would continue if Netflix optioned the book for a series. With any luck, Effi hoped his dad might finally be home again writing his next book, rather than disappearing every few months to meet his Publisher's "seen and be seen" press tour requirements. The first two books about sound energy and the translational power of a sequence of sounds to heal, Book One, or to destroy in Book Two, were rooted in solid science, building his father an impressive fan base that hung on every word that the former literature professor turned pop-culture icon offered on his twenty-city book tour and sci-fi convention appearances.

While Effi resented his father for being away all the time, he could separate his personal feelings from the attendant benefits of having a famous father. Usually, he would meet his father in one of his pit stops on the book tour, but not this time. The blacklisting of authors, academics, artists, and musicians for supporting Israel or for simply having Jewish characters or themes, let alone being Israeli, had escalated far beyond internet hazing and posting bad reviews. Those who dared to challenge the boycotts now faced open threats, canceled events, heckling, and protests from the *keffiyeh*-wearing watermelon mob. Thankfully, Effi's father traveled with a friend of Aunt Davi's as his personal bodyguard. Despite the anti-Israel boycotts, his dad's sales numbers continued to climb. Effi took it as a clear sign that sci-fi fans and technologically-oriented folks (admittedly a group of oddballs for which he was a proud card-carrying member), still had brains in their heads unlike the wokies who took their checkered *keffiyeh* cosplay literally, parroting diehard anti-Israel slogans and pro-Hamas chants.

Effi was more concerned that his dad's fans might turn on him because of the dubious scientific merit or accuracy of his latest story. He understood why the notion of being able to open a doorway to an alternate reality would capture people's imaginations. Escapism and utopian visions were a popular science fiction and fantasy topic, as was the zone, the flow, which referred to a waking mindfulness state, for the uninitiated. Here, or there, the "moment" was embraced by THE greater stream of consciousness. If you believed the alt-Flow crowd, the process could manifest transformative, evocative visual experiences to help one emerge as a kinder, gentler version of you, and of course in the process contribute to affecting world peace, if that was the chosen intention or other selected action one chose to manifest. Effi's general view toward the manifest(o) was, *whatever*, which he offered with the perfunctory eye roll. His "drug of choice" was gaming, an ADHD-defying immersion of total concentration, and his personal choice for holding reality at bey.

On par, his reality wasn't too bad compared to the many ills in the world… real long-standing problems, and not the angst of a thirteen-year-old who saw himself as 60% introvert:30% extrovert, and 10% unknown. His self-awareness meter fluctuated somewhat, mostly adding a few percentage points to the unknown category without a corresponding loss in the other categories, reassuring him that he was indeed greater than the sum of his parts. Effi's happy place was game theory and decision-making heuristics, the shortest distance between two points, or in this case between the problem and the solution. He'd built simple games and elaborated on some, and most recently, he'd gotten into dissecting other people's games to learn how others developed their UX (User eXperiences) and building a shortlist of dos and don'ts.

Still three years out from graduating high school, but two years younger than most of his classmates, Effi figured his computer skills would likely get him placed with 8200 where his quirks and borderline Asperger's traits would blend in with other computer geeks. His introvertedness had labeled him "different" early on, but among the cybergeeks and visual-spatial savants he'd fit right in. Effi didn't mind the label as it didn't define him, and overall, he considered himself fairly well-adjusted and high-functioning. In truth, Effi thought everyone was on the spectrum, recognizing traits in nearly everyone he'd ever met.

"What a waste," he said as it seemed that getting on the HaMikdash3.0 site today was a lost cause. And to think, he'd wasted a perfectly good headache fib. There were many mysteries in life, one particularly troubling one was why his Aunt Davi, a crack shot (literally) and co-owner of Magen Security Services, MAGSS, hadn't caught on to his frequent "illnesses" which left him miraculously cured after reporting in sick. He figured maybe she was a pushover, at least when it came to her favorite nephew... her only nephew. Hopefully, it wasn't because she just felt sorry for him. Too much reflective thinking, Effi thought.

This day was fast becoming a total bust... Unless! The epiphany struck him with 20/20 hindsight. The day needn't be a total loss. He did a double-handed finger snap and launched himself out of the gaming chair. He threw on a reasonably clean T-shirt and black jeans but opted for the only-worn-once socks lying on the floor. He got within a foot of the socks, caught a whiff of the Blundstone stink, and shrugged, but put them on anyway. Time for a new pair of boots, he thought. The socks he should probably burn.

If he hurried to the Old City, he could study the giant mural depicting the ancient Cardo. Most people only knew about the open-air archeological excavation of the Cardo, located below street level. The five, towering intact pillars are a popular backdrop for picture-taking, especially from a small outcrop on the stairs that connects *Habad Street* on the west to *HaYehudi Street* on the east. A staircase at the southern end, where the Cardo seemingly dead ends, can be accessed from stairs from *HaYehudi Street*. Effi's target was through a stone entrance into a continuation of the Cardo. The large space had more intact pillars and a colorful mural depicting the Cardo marketplace as it might have been in ancient times. Hazon Labs' used a similar, or maybe the same mural as a background image for its entry page. He'd have to compare them carefully, in person, rather than rely on the hundreds of photographs of the mural posted across the web.

With any luck, and a bit of time, he could check out a second, a lesser-known depiction of the busy Byzantine Cardo. He "discovered" the other mural, and the other Cardo, during a class trip to the Jerusalem Archeological Park, formerly the Davidson Archeological Center. The class stopped for coffee, tea, or what have you, at the Aroma coffee shop and sat for a bit in the partially excavated garden. He'd found an empty rock and sat facing the mural for ten minutes, puzzling out why the mural was placed to the East, a good half a mile (700 meters) from the main Cardo. The ice in his iced coffee had long ago melted as he spatially mapped the area until he recalled seeing a second smaller marketplace, running parallel to the main Cardo, on the replica of the Madaba Map. Formal education was apparently good for something.

"Sneaky sneaks," he sneered, already formulating a Plan B. He'd have to compare the two murals to the one on the HaMikdash3.0 site. He wondered if Hazon Labs had inadvertently given players in Israel an unfair advantage, or more likely tried to confuse the locals. Effi doubted the "Katzman" was stupid enough to leave HaMikdash3.0 open to allegations of unfair practices or other deceptives. According to a reverse image search he'd done on the *Tineye* site, there were nearly four hundred photos of the Cardo mural. The number was far fewer than Effi thought, but more than enough for any player, anywhere in the world, to access the images, eliminating what might be misconstrued as a home-team advantage for players living in Israel. In either case, Effi was convinced the colorful Cardo mural held secrets that could help his gameplay and was determined to find all the "Easter eggs" and other hidden gameplay clues. Besides, it had been a while since he'd done a walkabout in the Old City.

While he would have liked to go through the Mamilla Mall, the open-air, high-end shopping area, there wasn't time. He was less interested in the shops, but in recapturing the feeling of being there with both of his parents five years ago. They'd strolled, stopped, and ate, along the way. They marveled at a wall of stones, meticulously numbered before being removed during the Mall's construction so that each could be properly replaced in their original order. The attention to detail fascinated him even though he was only eight years old at the time. He remembered his mom… the way she looked, how her hair smelled and could almost hear her voice… almost, but not quite.

* * *

"Unlike some of the tools we have today, this was painstakingly slow work," she said.

"But why bother?" Effi asked. He directed the question to his mom, a tenured Professor of Biblical Archeology at Hebrew University. He wasn't being contrary; he was genuinely curious why the history of these particular stones should be maintained, and not all the others that had surely been displaced during the Mall's construction.

His mom respected his questioning mind, his father not so much. Effi's curiosity about everything seemed to bring out the worst in his father, who lived on this side of a short-temper's edge.

"There was a lot of destruction of the original structures here from the War of Independence and the intervening years of Jordanian occupation. Even then, shops and homes were built on the site. This particular wall was likely one of the few that remained nearly intact. Other stones are numbered too," she pointed to a few stones adjacent to a store further down, its location identified with the heavy black numbering. "Unique but not so much, plus it accomplishes what it did for you, making visitors stop, look, and ask why." His mom offered an answer that satisfied Effi's curiosity on the macro and micro scale, including knowledge tidbits which tempered the "why" of these particular stones. She smiled and shared more information about the Mamilla Mall project.

Effi tuned out the rest of the conversation between his mom and dad. He'd gotten the answer he needed and spent the balance of the walk to the Old City trying to discern the numbering pattern with the stones' spatial placement. He had committed the wall's numbering system to his memory and was juggling the numbers in his head trying to find the logic. There were some patterns, but there were obvious skips and incomplete patterns with stops and starts to multiple numbering systems. As they entered the Jaffa Gate, he left the Mamilla Mall numbering conundrum behind.

They continued across the main entrance past *Migdal David* and the *Kishle*, the police station, before turning left onto St. James Street, down the cobbled street before reaching *Habad Street* and the open-air Cardo. They paused and took pictures, a very touristy thing to do, even though his family had made *Aliyah* years before when he was 18-months old. They continued into the Old City's public square, dominated by the *Hurva Synagogue* and the golden Temple Menorah encased in bullet-proof glass in the foreground. He'd been so distracted in his mind's musings that he'd missed his mother speaking about the rebuilt *Hurva Synagogue* in contrast to the wasted *Tiferet Yisroel* Synagogue.

"The original *Hurva* had been built in the early 18th century on the site of a 15th-century synagogue. *Tiferet Yisroel* was built in the late 1800s.

Both domed, multi-storied structures dominated the Jerusalem skyline for years. After the War of Independence in 1948, both synagogues lay in ruins for years. The *Hurva's* resurrection began in earnest but became mired in controversy. Its rebirth was finally agreed upon and the reconstructed building was dedicated in 2010. Once again rising to become a dominant feature of Jerusalem's skyline."

"What happened to the other *Beit Knesset*?" Effi asked using the Hebrew word for a synagogue, which translates to a house of gathering.

"*Tiferet Yisroel* remained in ruins for another dozen years. The three-story, towering domed structure stood on hill, so it was higher than the *Hurva Synagogue*. It had been reduced to a pile of rubble, except for one part." She turned to point to the remains of the *Tiferet Yisroel Synagogue* further east. Only a west-facing wall with an arched facade was left standing, a testament to both endurance and its destruction. "In 2014, a new cornerstone was finally laid, with work expected to continue for the next several years," she said, then added, "except for the usual bureaucratic and financial delays."

The rest of the architectural tour, included backtracking a little to the ceremonial arch and Mosque of Omar located next to the *Hurva*, neither of which interested him. Instead, Effi decided to have a closer look at the golden Menorah. "Effi don't go too far," his father shouted after him.

It was a nice memory, Effi decided. He wondered what other parts of the Old City Hazon Labs would integrate into HaMikdash3.0's storylines. Effi could hardly wait for 3.0 to open its virtual Jaffa Gate on launch day. The $250K prize offered to early subscribers would go a long way towards delivering a steady diet of serotonin highs for the thirteen-year-old. Though Effi's ideas on how he would spend the money differed from what might be viewed as the typical indulgences for a thirteen-year-old when, not if, he won. Without question, he would splurge on a new state-of-the-art gaming setup which he considered to be a legitimate business expense. But of greater interest was the one-percent stake in Hazon Labs which he considered a long-term investment, well hopefully not that long-term, since he planned to parlay it into a coveted internship with the company.

With the naivety of youth and brilliance of mind beyond his years, Effi firmly believed winning the Hazon Labs' grand prize was well within his grasp. Why not him? Except with the soaring enrollment numbers, his odds of winning were dropping each day. Just before his computer crashed, the number of registered people at HaMikdash3.0 had topped 1,770,665 with an upward trending trajectory. While the launch wasn't till after *Sukkot*, early registration would close on Erev *Rosh Hashanah*, just six days away. To qualify for the Grand Prize, pre-registration was required. Effi wondered how many more people would become eligible for the Grand Prize between now and then?

If Effi got the chance, he would ask Joshua Katz (JK) why those dates. The reason might be practical or part of some wondrous algorithm JK had designed. Effi figured that Hazon Labs chose that deadline before the onslaught of Jewish holidays and the upcoming disruptions to work schedules. While people could still register after *Rosh Hashanah*, the prize packages and gameplay incentives were only open to the early registrants. The $25.00 investment, or, in his case, the seventy-five bucks he'd plunked down for three avatar personae, was a bargain when weighed against the potential quarter of a million-dollar payout.

Avatar development was an art form, and Effi considered himself a virtuoso which just happened to be the name of HaMikdash3.0's avatar generator. He took it as a good sign. Each avatar personae and role-play were strategically chosen, allowing him to craft concurrent long-term and short-term strategies for his multiple avatars. He realized a subset of HaMikdash3.0 gamers, the serious ones, would likely also use multiple avatars and divergent personalities to improve their gameplay odds. Translation, the number of unique users could be considerably less than the current 1.7 million-plus users, and the additional new users HaMikdash3.0 added between now and the *erev Rosh Hashanah* deadline.

While Hazon Labs provided few details on actual gameplay targets, the qualifying age cut-off of twelve was prominently displayed in the description and needed to be acknowledged by users clicking the *I agree* button in the rules section before processing the subscription fee payment. Of course, the under-18 crowd also required parental permission. There were other conditions, such as employees and family members of employees or contractors could not participate in the special promotion. The specifics of gameplay would be posted once the site launched officially, along with an iron-clad set of rules with the proper disclosures to avoid any legal entanglements or sore-loser lawsuits once the grand prize and other prize packages were awarded. Full disclosure. HaMikdash3.0, with its $25.00 annual subscription price tag, was by far the cheapest game out there, and one of the few that offered sizable, tangible prizes. Even in pre-release, 3.0, HaMikdash3.0's shorthand handle online, had already surpassed #4 on the Altar's site of Top 6 MMORPG of 2024. Effi sensed that 3.0 offered players more than the usual Massively Multiplayer Online Role-Playing Game in-the-zone highs at least based on reading about the site's online to offline (O+O) crossover activities. The question in Effi's mind was whether Hazon Labs' User Engagement strategy was by design or a default outcome of great role-play game design?

 Effi mapped his route to the Old City. Hopefully, the bus gods would be kind and he'd be back well before *Shabbat*, and before his aunt was any the wiser. A bus from *Katamonim*, then a change of buses for the Old City at First Station #38 or #83. Alternatively, he could walk from First Station, cutting around the *Valley of Hinnom*, past the southern end of the Sultan's Pool, and then either go right up the stepped path overlooking *Silwan*, a sprawling Arab village in East Jerusalem; or, follow the snake path overlooking the Sultan's Pool, and continue past the Armenian cemetery and on through *Sha'ar Tzion*. Once he got to First Station, he could decide whether to walk or take a bus from there, and, more importantly, how to avoid running into any of his classmates from the Shalom Hartman Boys High School. It wouldn't do for him to have a miraculous recovery and be seen out and about.

 He used to wonder if going to Himmelfarb wouldn't have been a better High School choice for him, but not so much anymore. October 7 hit everyone hard, schools throughout the country lost teachers and alumni, friends and family… but Himmelfarb especially so. While he wouldn't have minded the twenty to forty-minute commute, depending on traffic, to the Jerusalem suburb of *Bayit Ve'gan*, his father was adamantly against it, though he never explained the "why" of his objections other than to say going to Himmelfarb was not an option. As far as Effi was concerned, which school he attended didn't much matter. Making friends wasn't easy for him so he wasn't leaving any behind, and making new ones, well, time would tell. Being eighteen months younger than most of his classmates didn't help. Sometimes, Effi envied other people's friendships, but you could get hurt

STRANGE FIRE

caring for, and about, people. Especially now, where some things were especially hard to forget, and in his case… impossible.

For Effi, having a photographic memory was both a blessing and a curse. Useful at times, but not so much when he couldn't forget the 7th-grade picture of three Himmelfarb school classmates taken during *Shacharit*, morning prayers, years ago. He remembered every detail of the photo of Aner Shapira, Ben Zussman, and Hersh Goldberg-Polin, which was juxtaposed with individual images of the three as young men in their 20s. Only none of them would ever get any older.

Staff Sergeant Aner Shapira, age 22, and his best friend, Hersh Goldberg-Polin age 23 went to the Nova Music Festival on October 7. After the Hamas attack began, Aner, Hersh, and twenty-seven others sought refuge in a roadside bomb shelter roughly the size of a walk-in closet. Dashcam video showed Hamas terrorists peppering the entrance with machine gun fire and tossing grenade after grenade into the shelter. Aner, who was off duty at the time, stood by the doorway, defending the terrified group, tossing one grenade after another back out of the shelter. The talented musician's last song spoke volumes of his heroism and honor in standing in defense of others no matter the cost. Hamas terrorists threw seven grenades into the shelter, all were tossed back out by Aner… the eighth, however, found its hero target, killing Aner and severing Hersh's arm below his elbow. Of the twenty-nine young festival goers who'd gone into the shelter that day, only eight survived, many hid themselves under the dead bodies of their friends to avoid capture. Four of the festival-goers were kidnapped into Gaza, among them Hersh Goldberg-Polin… the rest, including Aner Elyakim Shapira, were murdered by Hamas on October 7th.

That day thousands of reserve soldier heroes didn't wait to be called up by their commanders or receive their orders. Young men, *giborim*, like Ben Zussman drafted themselves into service, racing to fight in defense of the people and the land of Israel. Day by day, the horrors of October 7 emerged, and were quickly denied or dismissed, swatted like an annoying fly, despite the overwhelming, indisputable evidence of evil. Video evidence broadcast around the world of twenty-two-year-old Shani Louk's twisted, half-naked body surrounded by RPG-wielding terrorists in the back of a white pickup truck, became emblematic of the violence, one of the hundreds, one of the thousands, brutally, callously murdered that day.

Were those kidnapped into Gaza still alive? How would they survive, if only as bargaining chips and ratcheting up fears for their lives and the suffering they were forced to endure in the Hamas terror dungeons. Days passed. More videos emerged. But still no word about those kidnapped into Gaza or outcry from the world demanding the release of the innocents, of the men, women, children, and elderly stolen from their lives on October 7. Painfully, slowly, videos of the hostages taken into Gaza emerged, gleefully posted by the monsters themselves. But for too many, the fate of their loved ones, living or dead, remained unknown while the International Red Cross shrugged their shoulders, impotent and silent. By a strange twist of fate, CNN's Anderson Cooper discovered video footage of Hersh being taken captive. He privately shared the video with the Goldberg-Polin family which showed Hersh (23), Or Levy (33), Eliya Cohen (26), and Alon Ohel (22) being dragged over to a white Toyota truck and taken into Gaza; all were bloodied by hate. Hersh's left arm had been traumatically severed below the elbow... his shattered bone clearly evident in the video footage and a makeshift tourniquet, he tied by himself, to try to stop the bleeding.

And then nothing. No word, no news about the hostages was forthcoming, only a number... 251 hostages, men, women, and children, even a nine-month-old baby, Kfir Bibas, and Ariel, his four-year-old brother, along with their mother Shiri and father Yarden. Families, cousins, relatives, old and young... people from twelve different countries taken from the festival or the nearby communities of *Kfar Aza, Nachal Oz, Kibbutz Be'eri, Nir Oz, Netiv Ha'Asara, Ofakim, Sderot*, and others. Whole communities along the Gaza border were decimated, entire families murdered, shot dozens of times, others burned alive in their homes and cars, and where safe rooms offered little protection from gunfire and RPGs. By week's end, the count stood at over twelve hundred people brutally murdered on October 7; and the fate of hostages remained unknown.

Hersh's parents, Jon and Rachel, knew nothing about the whereabouts of their son who needed immediate medical attention for his severed arm. In many ways, they became the voice and public face for the hostages and hostage families as the horrors of October 7 continued to be revealed. Joined by other hostage families, they waged a public war, traveling around the world, speaking to leaders and people of influence; a public campaign to raise awareness about all the hostages abducted by Hamas while advocating for their only son. A torn piece of masking tape marked the painful passage of time… the number of days the hostages had been held captive by Hamas since October 7th. Placed next to the heart, the number was updated day after day; the symbol, a rallying cry heard around the world: *Bring Them Home*. A first hostage deal was struck; 101 people were released between November 24th and November 30, 2023. Hersh was not among them. One-hundred-fifty-one hostages, living and dead, remained captive, starved, and abused in Hamas' terror dungeons. That much was known.

On December 3rd, days after Hamas broke the ceasefire deal, Sergeant Major (res.) Ben Zussman, age 22, was killed in combat in Northern Gaza. At the time, he became the fifth former Himmelfarb student to be killed since October 7th. His final letter to his parents crystalized Ben's character and strength… *I am writing this message to you on my way to the base. If you are reading this, something has probably happened to me. As you know, there's probably no one happier than me right now. I was just about to fulfill my dream soon. I am grateful for the privilege to defend our beautiful land and the people of Israel.*

Effi was struck by the words, "I was about to fulfill my dream…" which meant Ben hadn't gotten a chance to live his; though, in many other ways, he had. In the days following his death in combat, people learned more about Ben's character and its tangible translation as Ben drafted himself on October 7. Because he was about to start his training with Israel's internal security service, the *Shabak*, better known as the *Shin Bet*, he was exempt from Reserve Duty. Despite the exemption, Ben drafted himself on October 7, and only weeks later did his enlistment become official. His dedication to protecting the State and people of Israel was further evidenced when Ben's "just in case" letter was published. His loving words to his family paved the way for other families to share the last words of their loved ones online and on stickers placed in bus hutches, car windows, and lampposts.

Effi hoped he would live a life of purpose and meaning, a statement that spoke for him after he was gone. Maybe, that was why his father wrote books, to make a statement, to leave a mark on the world… Effi re-read Ben's letter in his mind. *That if I have to die, let it be in defense of others. Jerusalem, I have placed guards, and I will be one of them one day.*

While not an exact quote from the words of the prophet *Isaiah*, Ben's words captured their essence; words that resonated through time as Jerusalem had come under siege again and again through the ages…

I have set watchmen upon thy walls, O Jerusalem, they shall never hold their peace, day nor night: 'Ye that are the LORD'S remembrancers, take ye no rest, and give Him no rest, till He establish, and till He make Jerusalem a praise in the earth.'

Ben's mission would continue. Effi wondered if Ben (z"l) and all the young men and women who'd been killed fighting since October 7 were really standing on Jerusalem's walls, protecting her, protecting them all. Ironically, tomorrow's *Haftorah* reading for *Shabbat Shuva*, the *Shabbat* before *Rosh Hashanah*, would include *Isaiah Chapter 62*. Maybe he'd go to the *Beit Knesset* tomorrow for *Shabbat Shuva* to honor Ben (z"l) and all those who had fallen since October 7.

The *Haftorah* reading was the seventh and final *Haftorah of Comfort*, readings from the *Nevi'im* that began after *Tisha b'Av*. Effi hoped Ben's family would find comfort, as would those of Aner (z"l) and Hersh (z"l), along with all the other families. It was hard for Effi to let those feelings touch him, but denying the sadness meant also denying joy. He was smart enough to know that. He'd learned that when his mom died, it's all a part of you… the good and the bad. The idea was captured in the still-popular 1980s song by Naomi Shemer, *"Al Kol Eleh"* which translates to, "On All These Things," and which speaks of the sweet and the bitter, the honey and the bee sting. In other words, you can't have one without the other…

In Effi's mind, the iconic photo of Ben's mother, Sarit, reaching her hands to the heavens in a strangled, silent plea was nonetheless a source of strength… strength reflected in the clarity of her remarks in the face of such a profound loss… *We will prevail. We don't have any other option. We are a people that value life. Not like our vile and wretched enemy, cowards, Nazis, and their allies who sanctify death.*

Effi didn't know any of them, but he'd gone with Aunt Davi to a special prayer program, held mid-August, the day before the *Tisha b'Av* fast. The program was organized by Ben's parents Tzvi and Sarit in support of Hersh and all the hostages. Hersh's parents led a march from First Station to the plaza in front of the Great Synagogue where the program was held. There Effi first saw the picture of the three young boys juxtaposed with the photos of them as young men. He knew then that the image would never leave him. He could put it away, but the details were embedded in his brain. It was Sunday, August 11, 2024. All the names of the hostages held captive by Hamas were read, together with a special prayer composed by Ben's father asking G-d to grant special wisdom to the leaders during the negotiations to effect the release of the remaining hostages and bring about a just end to the war.

Twenty days later, Israel heard the horrific news that six hostage bodies were recovered from the tunnels beneath *Rafah*; the entry to the tunnel was secreted in a child's room. In a twisted bit of sick irony, the walls above the tunnel entrance were decorated with colorful Disney characters. The evidence was clear, Hamas had brutally executed six young people… Eden Yerushalmi (24), Carmel Gat (39), Ori Danino (24), Alex Lobanov (32), Almog Sarusi (26), and Hersh Goldberg-Polin (23). Effi couldn't reconcile how Hersh and the others had survived for so long only to be murdered when rescue was feasibly just a few relative moments away… a breath between life and death. They had been alive and survived for nearly a year, each day measured from October 7, 2023, and displayed on a frayed piece of tape… Day 327, Day 328… Day 329. On Day 328, Hersh's parents stood with other hostage families, calling through loudspeakers to their loved ones trapped in Gaza. Were they heard? By someone, anyone? Or was Hersh already dead?

How could they have been alive and then executed with only hours separating them from a possible rescue? There was no victory for Israel and a brutal, demoralizing reality for the IDF in a true zero-sum game. No winners. At least the families had bodies to bury; others were not so blessed. Hadar Goldin and Oron Shaul's families were still waiting for the remains of their sons to be returned after ten years. Effi didn't understand evil, and that was the only word he could think of to describe that kind of cruelty.

Aunt Davi asked if he wanted to go to the *Shiva*, the traditional seven-day mourning period, for Hersh. Every fiber in his being told him not to go, and every fiber in his being told him he needed to go. They went on the last morning for the *Shacharit* prayer service. A tent had been set up near the family's home to accommodate the thousands of people who came to pay their respects to the family and Hersh. Effi didn't go up to the family instead he stood by the food table, looking up at the printed death announcements for the other five hostages killed with Hersh. He took a cracker and made a *bracha*, a blessing in memory of Hersh and those who were killed with him. He waited and watched as Aunt Davi stood before Hersh's parents and said the traditional words of comfort, *May G-d comfort you among the rest of the mourners of Zion and Jerusalem.*

They stayed for the *Shacharit* prayers, the final morning service during the *Shiva* period. Traditionally, during the month of *Elul*, the month before *Rosh Hashanah*, the *shofar* is sounded — a call for people to do *teshuva*/repentance, before the Day of Judgement. At the end of the service, the *shofar* was sounded. Maybe because of the circumstances, it seemed to Effi to be more than just a call to repent, but also a call to action. On the walk home, Aunt Davi told him the person who blew the *shofar* was Aner Shapira's father. The eleven-month period for saying the *Kaddish* prayer for his son had just ended, while the eleven months for the Goldberg-Polin family had only just begun. Ben's family still had a few months to go before they would mark the one-year anniversary of his death.

Judaism gave structure to mourning rituals. Effi knew them all. The Zussman and Shapira families, like so many families since Oct7, and now the Goldberg-Polin family would mark the next "milestone" in mourning on the 30th day, counting from the funeral, known as *Shloshim*. The parents would then say the *Kaddish* prayer for the next eleven months, repeating the prayer multiple times during the morning, afternoon, and evening prayer services. They would also participate in communal prayers of remembrance called *Yizkor* on specific holidays.

The specifics of Hersh's murder slowly emerged, a more precise timeframe for when Hersh (z"l) was killed… sometime between Thursday, August 29th and August 30th, the 26th or the 27th of *Av* on the Hebrew calendar. The family could mark Hersh's *yahrzeit*, the anniversary of his death; though, without truly knowing when. In that cruel twist of fate, Hersh might already have been murdered when his parents stood outside the Gaza fence crying out to their son on Friday, August 30th. Effi imagined that Hersh heard them from Heaven, where he and all the other Holy Ones, the *Kedoshim*, were now. Effi imagined a different image of the three boys, the three young men only as angels together once again. The thought didn't make him sad. Instead, Effi felt a sudden gratefulness for how lucky he was. His father was usually around when he needed to go to synagogue on those special days, for his mom's *yahrzeit* and the *Yizkor* service. If not, Aunt Davi took him. He would also light a memorial candle for his mother. Effi was glad he went to the *Shiva* for Hersh, even if he didn't speak with his parents. He wasn't sure if Aunt Davi had a special connection to Hersh's family, none was necessary in a small country like Israel. You just showed up… just because.

Hersh seemed like a really good guy with a great attitude. He loved to travel, and everybody liked him. He was open to talking to everyone, to really listen. "A true light unto the nations," he heard someone say. The posters he'd seen described Hersh as a *yeled* of light, love, and peace. Effi thought it was pretty cool for someone so young, just 23-years-old, to have that kind of presence and effect on the world. His parents were heroes too, able to raise the hearts of people around the world, while theirs were breaking. Had he spoken to the family, he would have said, thank you… "Thank you for sharing Hersh's life and light with the world." Not surprisingly, Ben and Aner were like Hersh in that way. Good people, the best of us. Effi usually wasn't sentimental, but the words felt right.

When he was older, Effi planned to watch the video of his mom's funeral. He'd been there, but none of it seemed real at the time. Maybe everyone felt that way. With the New Year coming, Effi wondered how do you pick up the pieces? His mom had died years ago, and it was still hard, especially on the holidays, all the holidays. The *Shloshim* for Hersh would be the day before *Rosh Hashanah*, Effi had calculated it and realized how hard it would be to go from a memorial service to bringing in the New Year. Thankfully, Judaism's New Year wasn't marked like a secular one with alcohol-fueled parties. *Rosh Hashanah* was a solemn day. Still, he imagined it would be hard on the family, on all the families who'd lost people in the Hebrew calendar year of 5784. Hopefully, 5785 (תשפ"ה) would be a better one, though Effi was smart enough to know it could always be worse.

Effi shook away the strange feelings he'd been having of late. He no longer considered everything within a gamer's framework, where emotions could be packaged and compartmentalized and reality changed with a purposeful click or swipe of a screen. This kind of gloom and doom always made him uncomfortable. Strange, that he'd been able to yield to the thoughts for longer than usual. "Enough," he said, calling up Israel's much-vaunted resilience. He needed to get moving.

Jerusalem was a small city and running into people you knew was almost a given, especially on Fridays. Missing his classes didn't bother him; he aced most subjects without cracking open a book, and his accelerated "specials" were infinitely boring. Getting caught playing hooky, however, could spell disaster if his father, over-compensating for his absence, could decide to suspend his internet use, and restrict computer privileges to schoolwork only. Misery Maximus! Effi smiled, wondering if the Eastern Cardo, his "discovered" Cardo, also had a Greek name like the *Cardo Maximus*.

Maybe HaMikdash3.0 was up and running sooner than their vague notice indicated. He decided to check the site once more, just in case. *If* so, he could skip the Friday mad-dash hullabaloo before *Shabbat*, and the added complication of getting back to *Katamonim* before the buses stopped running, and without running into any of his classmates, or G-d forbid his teachers, let alone Aunt Davi.

This time, Effi critically studied the Hazon Labs' notice, unusual for what it didn't say including how long the site would be down. It was standard practice to try to avoid pissing off both current and future customers by stating a fixed date and time, along with apologies for the inconvenience of *computer interruptus*. He figured that even with using a distributed computer network, Hazon Labs's main servers had crashed due to a sudden influx of returning users and new registrants, none of which bode well for launch day when the volume of users would be somewhere in the *uber-maximus* range.

He mapped the best route from *Katamonim* to the *David Remez* stop when he'd have to make his next routing decision. The biggest unknown was when Aunt Davi would get home; if he miscalculated *Shabbat* would be anything but quiet, and certainly not restful. While Aunt Davi took a relaxed attitude to *Shabbat*, on time plus eighteen minutes, lighting candles was a ritual she enjoyed… Truth be told, so did Effi. They celebrated the day of rest with the traditional food rituals, including gefilte fish, chicken, and *cholent* as the palate demanded, light on the ge-filter fish, but heavy on chicken for Aunt Davi and vegetarian *cholent* for himself. The basic beans and barley were cooked overnight in a crock pot, with additional ingredients added to taste, chunks of carrot and potato, and a vegetarian hot dog to add a bit of savory and salty flavor. Except for *cholent*, the rest of their meals were always store-bought. They'd developed a color-coded system to rate the best takeout places and/or the *Shabbat* stores which opened on Fridays only… not all ge-filter fishes or kugels were created equal.

Sometimes, Effi missed the more traditional aspects of *Shabbat*, the quiet pace once the candles were lit, especially of going to Friday night services and singing *Lecha Dodi*, which welcomed the *Shabbat* Queen, and

Shalom Aleichem which welcomed the *Shabbat Malachim*, the Sabbath Angels. Some people sang each stanza of *Shalom Aleichem* three times, once for each of the three angels joining them for the 25-hour day of rest. He and Aunt Davi still said the *Kiddush*, the blessing over the wine, or in his case grape juice, and the *bracha* over the two *challah* loaves, rotating recitation duties between them in who said what, when. But it had been a long time since they, he'd, had the full *Shabbat* experience. Effi remembered the last time well enough. He was only eight at the time. They had gathered in his mom's hospital room to make *Shabbat*… it was the week before she died.

"Oh man," he said, blowing out his cheeks. Remembering that the good memories of his mom were always a trigger for one kind of migraine or another. He'd forgotten the golden rule, be careful what you manifest. Now, he *really* did have a migraine; an ocular migraine, unpleasant with the silver scissoring, but thankfully not painful *this* time. He donned the blue-light protective eyewear Aunt Davi bought him for his birthday and tried logging back onto the HaMikdash3.0 site. The same message appeared as before, "We apologize for any inconvenience. If you were on the site during the interruption in service, rest assured that your work is safe and secure, and any data you entered in the last hour has been saved to your account. Please check back later — better yet tomorrow."

Blah, blah, blah. He was done whimpering and shouted, "Screw it," and grabbed his phone. "Better hurry," mumbling to himself.

As the saying goes, Man plans and G-d laughs. Effi barely managed to cross the threshold out of his room when he heard the jangle of keys and the apartment door open. He silently screamed a slew of epithets.

"Ef, you awake? How are you feeling? I wanted to ask you something" his Aunt Davi called out from the hallway.

He dove for the bed, didn't bother with the covers, but forgot to take off his shoes. With practiced ease, which on any given day would have gone smoothly except when you need things to work. He quickly pushed one boot against the other to get them off. Usually, he whipped them up from a sitting or standing position, targeting the ceiling. This time, however, he was already lying down, and were an instant replay available, Effi would have immediately seen the trajectory error. His aim was off by a significant margin, meters to be sure, with a vector targeting the doorway just as his Aunt Davi stepped into the miscalculated convergence point between the

X, Y, and Z axes. Timing is everything, especially from a fourth-dimension perspective.

Without flinching Davi swatted away one flying tan-colored Blundstone and caught the other in her left hand.

"Yours I believe," she said then tossed the boot on the floor, wincing slightly at the stink.

"Nice moves, Aunt Davi," Effi said, hoping his usual "amuse, confuse, diffuse" tactic might work for him now.

She offered him one of her infamous fake smiles, a close-lipped, scrunchy face that wasn't very flattering but which she often used to convey, "I've got your number, mister and you are 100% busted" message. The no-nonsense, former IDF sharpshooter in the elite Givati Combat Unit was a walking study in contradictions for anyone who underestimated the petite 5'4" in her stocking feet with shoulder-length bouncy blonde curls. She usually went to work dressed in stretch pants and a T-shirt, except when she needed to meet with clients.

"You're home early?"

"Observant. Got a better question for you," she responded.

Getting busted and then trying to scam his unscammable aunt twice on the same day was a recipe for disaster. "Just so you know, I really *do* have a headache… Now that is."

"And?"

"In the interest of full disclosure, I was about to go to the Old City." The look of disbelief on her face was priceless. "*Meah achuz*," he added, using the Hebrew phrase for 100%.

"Dare I ask why?"

Effi paused, wondering whether the question was rhetorical. *Do I really want to know*, or did Aunt Davi *really* want to know? He opted for the latter. "See, there's this Israeli company which developed a new game called, HaMikdash3.0. They haven't launched it yet, but all the storylines are based in Israel. How's that for cool? If you think about it, it's educational too. I can learn some history and *Torah* stuff, and check out the latest game tech while playing, and learning. I did mention that didn't I?"

Curious, Effi wondered. When he usually ran on about this or that, his aunt would hold up a restraining hand which translated to *maspeek*, meaning enough, or when he really went on, she'd invoke a frustrated *dai*, meaning enough already. Instead, she listened intently to every word. He paused to take a breath.

"Go on," she said.

While suspicious, he wasn't about to look a gift horse in the mouth. "They've built this virtual world centered around the Temple; you know the Jewish one. Some people want to build it for real, but that's way-crazy problematic. So, this guy, Joshua Katz, who's like a real freaking genius, came up with this way beyond cool idea to make a virtual version of the third *Beit HaMikdash*. You get to create your avatars; you know what those are right?" Effi paused.

Aunt Davi nodded, raising her eyebrows at the gaming-101 question.

"Sorry. Anyway, avatars are no big deal. Except 3.0 uses an intelligent AI system that makes the avatar's behavior so much more realistic, responsive, and weirdly intuitive. It knows stuff, like how you would react or act, but not in a creepy way. Well, a little creepy." Effi debated whether or not to mention that he'd signed up three times which cost him some of his *Bar Mitzvah* money, only seventy-five bucks though. Less is more, he decided. "Anyway, what's super cool is the social thing for people to participate in, smart discussions, tasks to complete online and offline like in the real world, which is how you earn points, and actual prizes… like, we're talking serious prizes."

"Like what?"

"Like a quarter million dollars and a share in Hazon Labs. That's Joshua Katz's startup," Effi said, with a "duh" comment punctuating his statement.

Davi didn't break stride though "duh" should have warranted a reaction, but instead continued her interrogation. "So, you play this HaMikdash3.0 game for the prizes?" she asked.

"Yeah, sure. But that's not the only reason," he said.

"And…"

"I want to play because every new game is cool to check out."

"And you get this excited about every new game?" she asked.

"Yes, and no. This one is special since it's made here, but mostly because the storylines are fresh. Unknowns. Some games are based on books, TV shows, or movies, so you mostly already know where the story is going, who the bad guys are, the missions, and the ending. That makes it cool on one level, but also boring.

"With 3.0 it's different because you don't know what's coming at you. Unless…" Effi grimaced, "you get someone from Hazon Labs to drop the deets. Which is never going to happen." He grabbed his laptop, scooted over to the edge of the bed, and motioned his aunt over. The screen was open to the HaMikdash3.0 site which still displayed the "site down" apology message. He then clicked on a graphics file sitting on an open tab.

"Recognize it," he asked, pointing to a screenshot of the Cardo mural. Effi hoped his aunt didn't ask him about the second graphics file tab. She didn't miss much. He'd named the file for his new avatar, "EffU" the one with an attitude problem but which was contextually congruent with his character's character.

"So, you wanted to go to the Cardo in the Old City because…?"

"Oh yeah! I wanted to compare the screenshot here to the actual image, actually two, and see which mural they used or if they changed anything, maybe snuck a clue or two into their version."

"Interesting."

"Do you want to see my avatar?"

"No." She hadn't meant to sound so abrupt. "I mean, not right now. I have an appointment to get ready for."

"Can I please, please, please go to the Cardo? Please…" he asked, since miracles have been known to happen, though realistically he didn't expect Aunt Davi to say, yes.

"If you hurry, I can drop you off."

"Really?"

"One question, what's with the site-down message?"

"Not sure. It crashed on me when I was working up a new avatar."

"And his name wouldn't happen to be…"

"I can change that, no worries," he said, though he probably wouldn't.

"Be ready in ten," she said and disappeared down the hallway to get ready for her meeting with none other than Joshua E. Katz, Effi's so-called freaking genius.

Her company had been hired to provide protection for Katz, who'd attracted the unwanted attention of a bunch of religiously-inspired nutcases, one of whom might just be dangerous enough to act on his or her paranoid delusions. Other categories might fit too; stalkers obsessed with famous folk and fame. Then again, a bad actor could be motivated by something entirely different, an unknown with an endgame that was also unknown.

She doubted a gamer would push the "game" into the real world only to gain an advantage. But they were an odd bunch who sometimes grew up to be bad actors, desensitized and unable to differentiate between reality and fantasy. Still, it might be something as simple as the prize money that could tempt someone to do an end-around and maybe just kidnap Katz for ransom.

According to public disclosures, Josuha E. Katz's net worth was around $202.7M, mostly sourced from inherited wealth including an insurance settlement from his parent's estate and ongoing licensing revenue from his grandfather Jacob's patents. At this point Davi wasn't going to rule in or out one scenario over another, and certainly not before meeting the man himself to get a handle on how much hate he could inspire.

* * *

The saltwater rinse stung her new belly piercing, a twisted helix of silver and gold. The supersaturated salt concoction burned like hell. Pain *sans* the pleasure, what a waste other than to further support her alibi since she figured smelling like the sea couldn't hurt.

"How do I look, Ez?" she asked, standing at the foot of the bed opting in her re-dress for the mid-thigh length neoprene shorty. She draped the wetsuit around her hips and paired it with a skimpy sports bra. He was sitting in bed using the mini-Hookah, seeded with a mix of pot and tobacco.

Distracted, he barely looked at her. "Great, like always."

"You're such a charmer," she said, sneering and allowing her sarcasm to ring each word.

He sneered back at her. "Did you detonate already?"

"Done."

"Would love to watch the little shit squirm."

"Stay away, Ez. I mean it. You'll ruin everything."

"Yeah, yeah, I get it," he said, lighting up a fat joint.

"And make sure you stay off the computer. You can watch your porn later."

"No fun watching it alone, darlin.'"

"I'll be back." She smirked, then pulled down her top, flashing him one pierced nipple.

"You're killing me here."

She teased him, slipping her finger through her nipple ring and pulling it hard. "Hmmm," groaning slightly at the pleasure. "Keys?"

He nodded to the discarded black jeans lying on the floor. "Later," she said and blew him a middle-finger kiss.

Ez returned the middle finger salute when he heard the door slam closed behind her. He had no intention of being a casual bystander to Joshua Katz's downfall. Jackie would explode if she knew he was a registered HaMikdash3.0 user, a paid-in-full member using an anonymous and untraceable online bank account and email. He trusted Jackie only so far to not screw it all up. Unstable was a word that came to mind. She fit into his plan well enough.

Check. Check Mate.

Chapter 8

In Arabic, *Barak's* name meant blessed, except he'd never lived a blessed life. His father often "joked" that the doctors at the *Shaare Zedek Hospital* must have dropped him when he was born. It wasn't his fault, his mother was supposed to give birth at the St. Joseph Hospital, located in the *Al-Quds'* neighborhood of *Sheik Jarrah* where they'd lived since before the Occupation. But his mother had been visiting her family in *Sur Baher* when she went into labor, an apparent breech birth complication, an emergency, the Jew doctor claimed. Apparently, so much of an emergency that there was no time to get her to St. Joseph. Granted his mother had a difficult birth with *Barak's* older sister *Amina*, and had lost another baby ten years ago, so maybe there was some truth there and not another Jew lie. *Barak Abadi* came out of his mother's womb a dusky blue-gray, as foreboding as a winter sky before a storm, no thanks to the Jew doctor. Not enough oxygen to the brain, he said. Still, it wasn't his fault.

He wasn't stupid, but reading for him was hard. The letters got all jumbled together, flipping and changing to other letters. He didn't even bother trying to read text with fancy Arabic script with their exaggerated letter style, which were all but impossible for him to decipher. He attended the UNRWA school on Karl Netter Street in Jerusalem, not far from where his family lived. School was mandatory, even though he couldn't learn, and didn't learn much. Mostly, he took up space. His teachers didn't bother giving him special tutoring so he could read better, so he might succeed. Then again, he didn't need to read for what he was born to do, a great honor for *All-ah*, and a much better alternative than working in a restaurant cleaning up someone else's mess, stocking shelves with things he couldn't afford, or mindlessly moving boxes from one place to another. He was better than living a lowly future life rife with menial jobs that didn't require him to read anything except, maybe the tea leaves at the bottom of a dirty cup. Construction was his other choice, not a bad option. His uncle, *Faoud* was the runner for a construction company that worked in the Jewish parts of Jerusalem, building fancy homes for the Jews. His mother's brother found daily workers; extra help needed on work sites. He could do that, but it was usually hard work and following someone else's orders wasn't always easy; hard work didn't hold much appeal for *Barak* either.

His sister was a pharmacist with the *Clalit* Health Service with regular hours in an air-conditioned clinic. She was the smart one. Being different wasn't a good thing, unless you were destined for greatness. He'd show them… he'd show them all. Maybe they'd even name a street after him or a school. That made him laugh. His time was coming soon, they'd told him. *Barak* wished he'd been among the heroes who'd broken through the fence line on the 22nd of *Rabi' al-Awwal*, 1445 AH, October 7, 2023, but he'd never been to Gaza. He often fantasized about what role he might have played in that great victory. The *Yahudi* massacre was glorious, but he would bring even greater glory to his mission, to *All-ah*, and bigger than *Tufan al-Aqsa (al-Aqsa Flood)*. In 1446 AH, he would bring glory to *All-ah*.

"Patience *Barak*, your time will come," *Ismail el-Masri* reminded him. The others in their group, their terror cell, were all older than him, but only big-talkers. He would not be when the time came. They'd met after prayers on *Haram al-Sharif*, what the Jews called the Temple Mount, on the fifteenth day of *Ramadan*, last March. He'd followed a group of boys picking up stones and setting them into small seemingly innocent piles. They casually arranged them along the far eastern side path used by the Jews where they defiled *al-Aqsa* with their filthy feet. They'd be ready when the time came, striking the Jews with the stones and forcing them once and for all from *al-Aqsa* and then from all of *al-Quds*.

The long-anticipated follow-up to the *Tufan* unleashed on the 22nd of *Rabi' al-Awwal* didn't come. *Ismail* assured him that *al-Rahman*, The Beneficent One, would set an appointed time to slay the *Yahudis* that would leave them running for their lives, and out of *al-Quds* like dogs with their tails between their legs… out of all of Palestine.

Let them count their days. *Barak* was ready. The anniversary of the *al-Aqsa Flood* was coming soon for the *Yahudi*; but he would unleash a new flood before then. His strike against them would be greater; they promised him as much. Then he would be free. For seventeen-year-old *Barak*, freedom meant everything. His life was small, living in a small, twelve-square-meter bedroom in his parents' second floor apartment. Like other Arab families, they lived in a multi-story family house; his sister *Amina*, her husband *Asif*, and their three screaming brats lived on the floor above; while, his eighty-five-year-old *Jaddi*/Grandfather, *Khalid Abu Sayed* lived on the ground floor, which made it easier for his wheelchair to be rolled into the small garden at the front of the house.

Everyone in the family was always in his business; especially his grandfather watching and waiting for him. *Amina* was almost as bad as his grandfather, question after question. She thought she knew what was best for him, standing at the top of the stairs all high and mighty watching his comings and goings rather than looking after her children. She wasn't afraid to confront him or his choices, watching him like a hawk. A noble bird, but a predator, nonetheless. He was the predator, not her. He'd show them.

Barak wasn't book smart, but thankfully he was tall and broad across the chest, and which kept the bullies at school at bay. He tried to remember if he was ever a happy child. He didn't think so. He'd been left alone mostly since no one expected much from him. No matter, they would soon bless his name. He would be an instrument to help bring the *Madhi*, the bearer of true Justice to the world. *Ismail* was expecting him, waiting for him in the *Kidron Valley*, a fitting place among the long-dead *Yahudis* and their broken stone monuments. They met right under the very noses of their cameras and the watchers who were none the wiser to their true purpose. *Barak* chased down the stairs, knowing his grandfather would stop him for another one of his little chats.

Coming around the landing, he saw the discolored, swollen leg with the festering wound resting on the wheelchair's footplate. The bandage needed changing again and the rotting flesh beneath it smelled of decay. He'd have to take the old man to the clinic where they would clean it and re-bandage his diseased leg. For a moment, *Barak* wondered who would take the old man to his weekly clinic appointments after he fulfilled his destiny? Would they congratulate the old man? Would the old man finally be proud of him? Maybe regale the other old-timers at the community center with stories of his hero grandson *Barak*?

Barak the Blessed.

"You're late," his grandfather *Khalid* shouted from the ground-floor landing.

"And I'll only be later if we stand here talking," said *Barak*, as his grandfather maneuvered the wheelchair to block his way.

"You leave here every Friday. Same time, always. Not for prayers. You go to him."

"What do you know, old man?"

"I hear. I know," he said, then with a glance upward, "they know too."

"No matter. They are nothing and they will return to nothing."

The old man shook his head in disgust. "Where does your hate come from? What do you know of our struggle? You are but a child," he said, adding a dismissive wave of his hand.

"And yet old enough to know that your struggle has gone on long enough with little to show for the effort. The Occupiers still stand on our necks."

"You make noise with this talk. Buzzing like a bee with no stinger."

"Yes, but a noise that will be heard. So too a stinger as none before."

"Big talk. Big Talker, like your friend *Ismail*."

"Rest, old man. Leave the fight to me."

"Then surely we are doomed," the old man grunted. "You'll take me to the clinic Sunday, yes?"

"*Inshallah*," Barak said, meaning *All-ah Willing*, but all the while knowing that *All-ah* would be busy singing his praises before too long. If all went according to plan, someone else would be taking the old man to the clinic. And it would be anything but a happy new year for the *Yahudis*. Barak was suddenly overwhelmed by his purpose. *Amina* would take their grandfather to see the doctors. A proper woman's job, smirking at the burden he would leave his sister. Uncharacteristically, he bent and kissed his grandfather first on the right cheek, then the left, and again on the right. The weathered skin felt cool but rough against his lips, leaving him feeling cold inside. Or was it him that was cold, already dead inside?

The route by car to the Old City was different from the one Effi planned. Faster but also a bit scarier. With Aunt Davi in the driver's seat, they left their *Katamonim* neighborhood and headed to *Derech Hevron*. He hoped she'd continue onto Mamilla, but instead she cut through the Arab village of *Silwan*, racing through the narrow streets, past *Ir David*, the City of David. A few wrong turns and you could easily get lost in *Silwan*, and if you were Jewish you better hope someone found you, quick. He'd heard about a busload of first-year Gap Year *Yeshiva* students from *Torat Shraga* who'd been boxed in on one of the village's narrow streets when their driver made a couple of wrong turns. Thankfully, they'd "escaped" without incident. Effi hoped he'd survive his aunt's Mario Andretti driving style in one piece.

The intersection of *Ma'alot Ir David Street* and *Derech Ha'Ophel* was usually busy, doubly so on a Friday. They were about to cut across the intersection when city buses Numbers 1 and 3, came around the corner from *Derech Ha'Ophel*, one after the other. Unfortunately, both buses were stuck in traffic, waiting to turn from *Ma'ale HaShalom* into the Old City through the Dung Gate for a single pick up of people at the Western Wall stop. Not surprisingly, no one was willing to give an inch in the mini-gridlock.

"You can just let me off here, Aunt Davi," Effi suggested.

"Patience, young man." Seeing a hint of an opening, Davi floored it across the street, squeezing her black Jeep® Wrangler between the buses. "Now, you can get out," she said, sporting a satisfied grin.

Effi had closed one eye when she accelerated and only opened it, and started breathing again, once they'd crossed the great divide.

"I'll text you when I'm heading back this way. I'm not far away, so you'll have maybe ten minutes to get back here from wherever you are."

"Got it, Aunt Davi. Good luck getting out of here."

"Piece of cake… maybe."

"Thanks for, you know."

"Glad I could help, and thank you," she said without elaborating. Effi had provided her with a gamer's perspective on HaMikdash3.0 and its creator Joshua Katz. "Don't go wandering *too* far off," she added, unsure if the admonishment made its way from her mouth to Effi's ears, let alone his brain.

Effi nodded, still confused about his Aunt's thank you… no matter. He opened the car door, climbed out then turned back around saying, "No worries, I'll be safe and smart."

"See to it, Mister."

Effi had barely closed the door as Aunt Davi pulled away from the buses into the adjacent lane, none too elegantly, and headed up *Ma'ale HaShalom* Road toward *Har Zion*, Mount Zion.

He entered the Old City through the Dung Gate; a terrible name, especially if you wanted to make a good first impression. The name, however, reflected the historical entry/exit point as the main thoroughfare for disposing of waste and other refuse from the Temple Service, including ashes from the *Korbanot*, the Sacrifices. Having decided to start with the smaller Cardo mural, he took a sharp left into the Jerusalem Archeological Park plaza. He snapped off half a dozen images with his phone before deciding the mural was definitely not part of the HaMikdash3.0 playbook. Still, since this secondary Cardo was shown on the Madaba Map it was probably in play, but the mural itself was too obscure for anyone outside of Israel to know about. He picked up an iced coffee from the nearby Aroma Cafe so it wasn't a waste of time.

With only a week before *Rosh Hashanah* the Old City was thick with tourists, adding to the pre-*Shabbat* rush. Not surprisingly, it took him longer than expected getting to the main Cardo mural, but it was well worth the effort. Up the down staircase near the *Aish HaTorah* dorms, Effi cut across the plaza in front of *Hurva Synagogue* then took the steps down from *Habad Street* at the southern end of the open-air Cardo. He passed through a smaller stone passageway to the large interior Cardo and THE mural. Effi studied it with a new appreciation, committing every detail to memory, and automatically comparing it to the image of the Cardo mural provided by HaMikdash3.0 already permanently lodged in his memory.

"Wow," he said aloud, drawing the attention of a group of twenty tourists all wearing the same colorful (read that silly) caps; an easily recognized identifier in case they were accidentally separated from one another. The large Cardo mural was definitely in play. He'd previously screenshotted 3.0's Cardo mural but didn't need to reference it to discern nuanced qualitative and quantitative differences between 3.0's digital version and the real thing. The colors of garments and objects differed enough to draw Effi's attention, the number of sheep in a stall, the order of the hanging lantern/candle holders, or the variation in a capital adorning the top of a column's shaft, the 4th on the right was definitely different. There were big differences, obvious ones, as well. In HaMikdash3.0's version, the bowls of colorful spices smoldered with wisps of smoke while the actual Cardo mural didn't have any smoke. As he suspected, the Hazon Labs team embedded a "Hidden Objects" styled game mixed with "Find the Differences" like many other game Apps. He imagined there were probably other clues embedded in the mural and cryptic messages written in a stall or a clue that might be spoken by a Vendor avatar. The attention to detail was impressive, but not so much the gaming aspect. Finding hidden objects in the object-rich image would be tedious, and annoying, but no different than hundreds of other games... and really no big deal. Effi was positive the Hazon Labs development teams must have also developed more sophisticated HaMikdash3.0 storylines to enhance the gaming experience. Nonetheless, he took a dozen photos of the mural, carefully including closeup and establishing shots.

※ ※ ※

Tzion fixed the problem with the *cha-cha-cha-challenge* audio, dropped the "offending" cup in his backpack, then left Hazon Labs shortly before the first red-alert cyberattack alarm sounded. He planned to have another look at Zedekiah's Cave before revising the storyline. They couldn't afford any more mistakes... there wasn't enough time for any more mistakes. Tzion grabbed the box of *tekhelet* strings off his desk, stuffing it in his back pocket. He decided to walk to Zedekiah's Cave, planning to use the time to clear his head and nail down a shot list for the reshoot. If the shoot couldn't be scheduled for early next week, it would have to wait until after *Rosh Hashanah*, a three-day adventure this year, even in Israel.

There were quicker routes, in other words, less crowded routes for him to follow in getting from Point A to Point B but walking through the Old City was always enlightening. He never tired of breathing in the eclectic mix of people, from all walks of life and religious persuasions that defined Jerusalem — a dynamic spiritual blender of the ancient and the new, all draped in Jerusalem limestone. The golden hues were spectacular in the golden hours... the hour just before sunset or the one after sunrise which bathed scenes in warm tones and were amplified in Jerusalem as her limestone walls shone from within. There was always something new to discover, not only on a personal level, but many of his journeys around the city became part of HaMikdash3.0, enriching each scenario with nuanced details.

But today couldn't be about sightseeing. His goal was simple: grab a few shots of the cave, including new areas that could be included in the Motion Capture (MoCap) reshoot. While Motion Capture was technically challenging under the best of circumstances, shooting in Zedekiah's Cave presented more than a few problems, including slippery limestone and sweltering humidity which made the sensor suit less pliant, not to mention the obvious scene lighting challenges in capturing content inside a cave. From the beginning they decided not to shoot in front of a traditional green or blue screen, instead, HaMikdash3.0 used the onsite backgrounds to give the virtual world a more realistic, textural look and feel. By using multiple cameras and real-time auto-lighting and shadow algorithms, they could seamlessly blend the footage with the appropriate lighting adjustments. The high front-end production values saved them a ton of work and money in after-effects editing on the backend.

The biggest problem Tzion faced was dealing with Dov Luznick. The nth-degree prima donna had been less than pleased with the three days of dungeon shooting, as he called Zedekiah's Cave. Tzion could imagine his reaction in finding out a reshoot was necessary. Dreading it as he was, Tzion had to call Dov back for the reshoot. His ambiguous body type gave authenticity to his execution of both male and female movements, and he served as the stand-in for all the Avatar intros and how-to explainer videos. What mattered was getting the sequences and the visuals right. One positive aspect of the reshoot was that Tzion could take care of some background angles he wasn't too crazy about in the ZC introduction… a minor issue, but noticeable to him and likely also to Joshua.

He couldn't believe the cup fiasco had escaped him, forcing him to scramble up an alt-scenario for his boss. Hopefully, the rest of the team didn't know about the splish-splash cup. He'd told Jay, who'd given him a pep talk that helped him pivot the storyline. Thankfully, the creativity gods were smiling. Ironically, the new acid-base science twist improved the scenario, adding finesse and curiosity to the solutioning process. When Tzion first discovered the flipped cup, he consoled himself knowing everything happens for a reason whether the reason is readily apparent or not. The idea fell under the umbrella of Divine Providence, both for the individual under *Hashgacha Pratit* (HP) which translated to private supervision; and, to its companion concept of *Hashgacha Klalit* (HK), communal or universal supervision.

The big question was whether either *Hashgacha Pratit* or *Klalit* extended to bringing the HaMikdash3.0 project in on time. Under budget would also be nice, though unlikely. A rather mundane application of Divine Providence, he thought.

STRANGE FIRE 147

* * *

"Not so mundane, my young friend," Archangel Micha'el said aloud.

In the Heaven of Heavens Tzion and Effi's linked Providences were taking center stage with the Powers that Be. THE plan for the day also included redirecting Effi's path to effect a not-so-chance encounter carefully orchestrated by a tag team duo of Guardian Angels recruited from the HaMikdash3.0 legions. With their marching orders in hand, or "in wing" as the case may be, they would double-team their young charge to complete the mission-critical intercession.

"Your timing needs to be precise," Micha'el instructed them. Uri'el had yet to return from shadowing Joshua E. Katz, leaving Micha'el to deal with the unexpected development that accelerated the timeline even further. To avoid a "me too, I wanna go" whining riot among the Guardian Angels, all eager to test their wings on Earth, he wisely used a Bingo game's ball tumbler to select the four Guardians for the mission. Whether by chance or that confluence of unknowns often consigned to fate the selected GAs were ideally suited to the task. GA-697.4 and GA-696.0 had co-founded the GA Parkour club and handily took gold in that morning's tag-team relay; while GA-699.54 and GA-699.55 were ranked as the Parkour club's top rock wall climbers. In the revised scenario, all of their skills would be needed.

The group, lined up along Micha'el's dual-edged sword to study the mission portfolio, which included a map of Zedekiah's Cave and two holographic photos: 1) a relatively recent picture of 13-year-old red-haired, freckle-faced Effi Davidson copied from his student identification card, and 2) Tzion Beru Mengistu, mid-to-late-20s Ethiopian, relatively tall at 5'9" with short-cropped brown hair that was lighter at the tips from weekend cycling. Micha'el then presented the Parkour co-founding team with two knapsacks overflowing with provisions.

"Wait, I thought this was supposed to be a quick in-and-out gig," GA-696.0 asked, whispering so that Micha'el wouldn't hear him, but which was impossible.

"I reckon not," noted GA-697.4, peering at the survival equipment, overnight camping gear, and infrared goggles.

"Succeed," said Archangel Micha'el, tipping his massive wing in their direction.

"At least he didn't say, survive," GA-697.4 whispered.

"Yeah, but he also didn't say, see when you get back."

With a snap of his wing fingers, Micha'el sent the two Guardian Angels on an express drop to the Old City.

"What about us?" asked the GA-699s.

"Be ready," Micha'el said, adjusting their parachute jump lines.

Tentatively, they gave him a "thumbs-up" sign and waited for the green light. Micha'el hoped their quick reflexes were matched with strong arms for carrying extra wide loads. Initially, Micha'el debated whether to mix the GAs, leveraging the talents of each in a mixed pairing but in the Gestalt handbook on Guardian Angel Works, the multi-part mission that was part of a multi-part plan gave better odds of success if teams with longstanding working relationships continued to work together. Who was he to mess with what works? In truth, he was honored to be a part of the process whose ending was already known, if only to the Almighty.

Effi mapped out his planned route, continuing north through the Jewish Quarter's Cardo where it connected to the Arab *souk*. He planned to follow the street named, *Shuk ha-Besamim* (the Spice Shuk) through to the next street name change to the *Sha'ar Shechem*/Damascus Gate, and exit into Arab East Jerusalem. Throughout the route mapping, he'd unconsciously been holding his breath and heard himself sigh audibly as if relieved that by divining his endpoint and how he'd navigate his way through the crowds to get there he'd be safe.

Reality check, there were places he didn't go, wouldn't go, and where he knew he absolutely should NOT go. His trek north through the Arab Quarter was one of those times he should've known better but for whatever reason his actions and brain didn't properly analyze the risk-reward matrix. Fortunately, he was about to be helped by a couple of friendly Guardian Angels.

Effi stepped over the two-person-wide Cardo threshold into the Muslim Quarter, when he stopped suddenly. In a chain reaction, the crowd of shoppers and the tourist group he'd seen earlier, bumped into one another in a cascading domino effect of bruised shoulders and stepped on toes.

GA-697.4 and GA-696.0 turned a deeper shade of bluish-purple, a.k.a. indigo, and shrugged. "We didn't mean to pull him that hard," they said.

With a quick roll of their eyes, the GA-699s gently heaved the 95.3 kg (210 pounds) Polish woman from her back-leaning position to an upright one.

Effi stepped aside to let the group pass, awkwardly enduring their glares and stares. "*Slicha*," he repeated, apologizing as the troupe walked by. He ignored most of their multilingual complaints and whatever else the large woman said, but took note of her reference to Auschwitz, using the Polish word *Oświęcim*, which he recognized from the March of the Living trip he'd taken the year before. Disturbing! Effi couldn't help but wonder why he'd stopped?

Aunt Davi's warning, replayed with claxon clarity, don't wander too far off. Sound advice any day, but especially relevant on a Friday, the Muslim Holy day. Tensions were at an all-time high, bolstered by the ongoing war and the approaching first anniversary of October 7. Maybe his subconscious was warning him? That, or maybe, he had a Guardian Angel looking out for him.

Terrified, the two GAs turned to one another... if they'd blown this mission there would be hell to pay, in Hell, or wherever poor-performing Guardian Angels went in the afterlife. They waited for the hellfire and brimstone to strike. But none came.

"Okay," Effi said aloud, acknowledging the message. He spun on his heels, headed out of the Cardo, and backtracked to the *Kotel* Plaza. He still planned on going to *Sha'ar Shechem*/Damascus Gate, but he'd follow a different route that hopefully wouldn't give him the heebie-jeebies. Effi gave Joshua Katz props for devising a solid user engagement tool that allowed users to submit an interactive storyboard for a 3.0/3.1 game module. His yet-to-be-developed "most excellent" interactive would gain him the recognition needed to land a coveted internship with Hazon Labs; from there, the sky was the limit. If his plan succeeded, he could bypass the need for a first degree in computer science or math.

From a list of five, he'd narrowed his choices down to two possible storyline submissions. Each was intricately and strategically woven into existing HaMikdash3.0 scenarios, or at least the ones 3.0 was willing to reveal before the official launch, but he still couldn't decide between them. For seekers of any Faith, but especially those who prayed at the altar of the gaming gods, 3.0's storyline Bible was the go-to tool. Effi had memorized the first edition and set an alarm on his phone that would alert him to content updates.

Maybe, he should toss a coin on which scenario to submit and leave it to fate. The spelunking-themed cave adventure was good. It started in Zedekiah's Cave and included dizzying climbing challenges using matter-state phase transitions that transformed the composition of climbing gear and rock walls to adjust skill-level difficulty. The second storyline was a geocaching-type adventure that focused on an architectural anomaly Effi had discovered and his own quest to solve the mystery surrounding the stone. For the 3.0 storyline, players would collect puzzle pieces to build a part of the virtual *Beit HaMikdash*.

Either scenario would likely be good enough to pass the first review stage and land on the desk of HaMikdash3.0's certified genius creator. Odds were other developers and gamers would jump on the spelunking bandwagon. The storyline was good, but obvious considering the layers of history, underground passages, and deep caverns and cisterns in Jerusalem built up over time. But even if his "splunk" idea was good, he'd be competing with too many lump-summed others making it harder for him to stand out from the pack of wannabees. His architectural quest (code name: Archie) was truly unique, educational, and, quite possibly, even historic. "Archie" offered multiple online to offline (O-2-O) crossover opportunities, making it a boon for scholarly pursuits, tourism, and Hazon Labs' quarterly earnings statement.

Forget the coin toss, in that moment Effi decided "Archie" was the way to go and knew his historian mom would have been pleased by his decision. He half ran, half skipped through the square near the *Hurva Synagogue*. While tempted to grab a quick bite to eat, he didn't want to waste any more time and shielded his eyes from the tasty offerings at the dozen or more fast-food shops lining the narrow *Tiferet Yisroel Street*. He continued down the main stairs of the Jewish Quarter, *Rova HaYehudi*, the *Rova* for short. The main security entrance below the *Aish HaTorah Yeshiva*, renamed the *Aish* World Center, was closed. He followed the crowds to the *Kotel* Plaza security entrance on the east side, located adjacent to the security entrance to *Har HaBayit*, the Temple Mount.

Ironically, he'd made almost a complete circle back to the Dung Gate after his little Arab *shuk* misadventure. If he were smart, which he was, he'd take the "Dung Gate Revisited" scenario as a bugaboo sign of Aunt Davi's warning, "to not wander too far off," to be read, *stay in the Jewish Quarter*.

But smart isn't always enough to keep a thirteen-year-old from thinking himself invincible, besides the call of "Archie" was too strong for him to ignore.

His challenge now was to build the best storyline around the "Archie" anomaly, which, to date, had been confined to Effi's mind and scribbled on coded notes in his gaming notebook. Now he needed to see if it played out in the real world before putting everything onto the storyboard template Hazon Labs provided. He'd already decided to end the game sequence on *Har HaBayit*, with the recovery of the final architectural piece — the missing piece in an elaborate puzzle built out in each successive level of play to the perfect end goal and...

He was still thinking about the "and" part where a win would confer on the player the title rank of *Kohen*, priest. Except in the real world, not everyone could be a *Kohen*. He might have to re-think the points, power-ups, achievement trophies, and/or rewards. Over-complicating the storyline wouldn't win him any points, but he did need to include enough detail to demonstrate his command of gameplay.

Standing in the *Kotel* plaza, Effi took several establishing shots which he would complement with striking vista views of the Temple Mount from the East. During a break from the advanced computer programming class he'd taken in the summer, he'd discovered a narrow path south of the Hebrew University, Mount Scopus campus. The path skirted above *Emek HaTzurim*, the valley where the Temple Mount Sifting Project was started in 2004. The vantage point allowed Effi to capture the expansive backdrop of Jerusalem looking to the west and showcased the Temple Mount. He'd taken a picture of the view, blown it up to poster size, and hung it on his bedroom wall. There were other places where the view of the Temple Mount/Dome of the Rock could be captured, including from the Haas Promenade to the south or from the *HaMasu'ot* lookout at the top of the Mount of Olives Cemetery from the east. His view was from the northeast, an atypical view, which might make his submission stand out from the others, or at least garner him a second look and positive creativity points.

"*Slicha*," a young Ethiopian man in his 20s said after bumping into him.

"*Sababa*," Effi said, though the "no problem" reply never quite rolled off his tongue the way it did for most Israelis, and the guy was gone before he could get the words out.

As he turned, Effi saw one of the local reporters stopping people for a quick soundbite. He stood near the camera guy curious about the "question of the day." With only six days left until *Rosh Hashanah*, it had to be the topic of conversation. That, or the war.

The interviewer had a copy of the *Selichot* prayers, the Prayers for Forgiveness, sticking out of his back pocket. For Ashkenzi Jews, *Selichot* prayers would begin that Saturday night at midnight. It would also be the first time *Selichot* would be said with Jews of Sephardi and Mizrachi descent, who had already been saying *Selichot* for the entire month of *Elul*. Maybe he and Aunt Davi could go to *Selichot* too, though the *Kotel* would be packed. They could always go on another day since *Selichot* would be recited until *Yom Kippur*. Effi imagined at least 75,000 people would crowd the wall and plaza this year… probably more because of the hostages and the war. Maybe, they could go to the *Beit Knesset* tomorrow too since it was *Shabbat Shuva*. This year the 25th day of *Elul*, the first day of creation, fell on *Shabbat Shuva*. Cool.

"Down to business," he said to himself, though apparently a bit too loud.

"Did you say something, young man?" the reporter asked.

"Me? No," Effi said, trying to wave off any further conversation.

"Would you mind if I asked you a few questions?"

"Ugh, no. Can't," he croaked. "Sorry."

Effi then hightailed it from the *Kotel* Plaza to *Bar-Quq Street*, passing through security, which was just a guard at the turn style for people leaving the *Kotel* area. Coming in to the *Kotel* was a different story. People had to pass through a magnetometer and have their bags screened in an X-Ray machine. No biggie, security checks were everywhere including shopping malls, markets, airports, and bus stations… all considered to be high-value targets where large crowds gathered, and where security checkpoints were mandatory.

Effi's revised route through the Muslim Quarter to *Sha'ar Shechem* was well-traveled by religious Jews from the nearby *Musrara*, *Shimon HaTzadik*, and *Mea She'arim* neighborhoods who used it as a shortcut. He'd never ventured into the side markets with entrances leading to the numerous Muslim-only gate entrances to the Temple Mount. At the *Kotel*, people looked up to the Temple Mount; in the Arab Quarter, the Temple Mount was on street level. He'd previously visited the *Kotel HaKatan*, the *Little*

Kotel, located near the Iron Gate, *Sha'ar haBarzel/Bab al-Hadid* where at least two Border Police officers were always on duty. "No side trips today, Ef," he thought to himself. He needed to stay focused.

If the gods were smiling, he could follow a fellow Jew all the way to the Damascus Gate/*Sha'ar Shechem*. Despite being called streets, no cars were allowed in or on the narrow passageways, except for passenger golf carts or small carts with flat beds for moving garbage and goods from point to point in the Old City. If all went according to plan, once he made it out of *Sha'ar Shechem* he'd head over to the original "Archie" stone he'd discovered, and then "more or less" head straight back to the Jewish Quarter.

The "more or less" part was part of his "Archie" scenario. He needed to get *lost*, a necessity, since anyone playing his game scenario might also make a wrong turn and he needed to give them a way back into gameplay. By design, Effi planned to build the scenario with the necessary re-directs and alt-paths with corresponding penalty points. While players would be given an extra set of lives, he didn't plan on having any of them forfeit them because of a terror attack — an all-too-common occurrence along the Old City's routes. The vital next step in his combined real-world test/storyboarding draft meant taking more than a few risks.

"What the hell was he thinking," he thought to himself. He'd be better off asking his gun-toting, jiu-jitsu black-belt aunt to cover him on the escapade. Effi knew about several small Jewish enclaves that had taken up residence in what was traditionally known, and generally accepted, as the Muslim Quarter. The division of the Old City into Christian, Jewish, Muslim, and Armenian Quarters was both a physical and political reality, a relatively recent accommodation from the 20th century to address an increasingly religiously divided Jerusalem. Before the 1929 Arab riots, the now-designated Muslim Quarter was home to a mixed population of Jews, Muslims, and Christians. When he wasn't in school, Effi didn't normally wear a *kippah*; for all anyone knew, he could be a tourist from Connecticut.

He had a lot to accomplish, with an unknown time limit as to how long Aunt Davi's appointment would take. The last thing he wanted to do was to keep her waiting, or worse… go MIA. He liked being efficient, except today there were too many variables out of his control. He might have to forego the "getting lost" part of his research, at least for today.

Lost in thought, Effi smacked into the person walking ahead of him. Automatically, he said, "*Slicha*," the Hebrew word for an apology. He said it without thinking, even though he was already deep in the heart of the Muslim Quarter of Jerusalem where Hebrew was *not* the predominant, or most popular, language of choice.

"*Sababa*," the Ethiopian in his mid-20s said to him, then continued speaking softly, "*Achi, haKol b'sder?*" frowning noticeably.

Their minor collision occurred near the site of a *pigua*, a terrorist attack which was marked by a plaque in memory of *Elhanan Attali*, killed in 1992, and where a second attack occurred in 2018 killing Adiel Kolman. There were similar memorial plaques all over Jerusalem, and the rest of the country… too many to count. Effi rightly interpreted the question to mean, *what the hell are you doing here, kid?* or *are you out of your freakin' mind?*

"*B'seder*," Effi responded with a fairly certain nod, realizing it was the same fellow he'd bumped into in the Kotel Plaza.

"Okay, but…" Tzion said, leaving the question dangling after glimpsing the Google Maps program on the boy's smartphone. "English, yes?" he continued. Effi nodded. "Tzion Mengistu," he said, holding up his closed hand for a fist bump.

"Effi," introducing himself then lightly tapping Tzion's fist. In his usual ADHD mode, especially when meeting new people, his mind immediately went off on a contextually related tangent. Mengistu was the same name as a hostage held by Hamas for the past ten years. "Are you…" but he didn't get a chance to finish the thought.

"*Na'eem me'od*," Tzion said, offering the "nice to meet you" greeting in a whisper, before switching back to English. "Look, I'm going to Zedekiah's Cave, if you're heading that way, maybe we can stick together here," Tzion said, conveying his not-so-subtle concern.

"Well, a minute ago I would have said yes, but this day hasn't exactly gone to plan. I think I better call it a day. Too many starts and stops *baderech*."

"Happens to everyone," Tzion said with a genuine smile. "I think the light train's still running."

"No worries. I'm supposed to get picked up in a bit."

"Then it's probably a good idea to head back," he said, raising his eyebrows and adding an eye shift to his left at the older man with a cane, sitting in front of a spice shop.

"Yeah, I got a little carried away doing research. I'm working on this thing…" but before Effi had a chance to share his excitement over the HaMikdash3.0 storyline he was developing, Tzion interrupted him.

"Sorry, *achi*. I hate to run off. I've some work to finish before things start shutting down today."

"Sure, no problem… and thanks. I appreciate the save."

Tzion gave Effi a quick thumb-up then reached into his shirt pocket for a business card. "You might like to check out where I work," he said.

"Thanks," Effi said, absently slipping the card into his back pocket.

With a wave over his head, Tzion disappeared into the crowd.

GA-697.4 and GA-696.0 waited an extra moment to make sure Effi had made a 180 back to the Jewish Quarter. "He could have thanked us too," GA-697.4 said.

"Right, if he knew we were here. Come on, we better catch up," GA-696.0 said. "On your six."

Tzion looked back over his shoulder but couldn't see the *yeled*. Hopefully, he was smart enough to head back to the Jewish Quarter. He couldn't have been much older than his brother Zev. If he hurried, he could shoot a few minutes of video for the revised cave sequence and then be off to his parent's house in *Beit Shemesh* with time to spare before *Shabbat*. His mom was good about his schedule, making certain allowances for him… especially lately. She was probably already preparing excuses for the rest of the family in case he was late for *Kabbalat Shabbat*, the welcoming in of *Shabbat*. He was looking forward to the *Seudat Mitzvah*, the joyous meal in honor of Zev's *Bar Mitzvah*, and enjoying the 25-hour break. He planned to call his mom from the road, giving her a solid ETA. After *Shabbat*, putting in an appearance at the *Bar Mitzvah* party was mandatory, but then he would head to the office, work through the night, and with any luck, present everything to Joshua first thing Sunday morning.

With the benefit of 20/20 hindsight, it probably would have been better for him to drive to the Old City instead of going on foot. Unfortunately, now he'd have to backtrack to the office to get the car and lose precious time driving to *Beit Shemesh* before *Shabbat*. But the 15-minute walk to the Old City helped him clear his head enough to pare down the shot list. Plus, he'd been able to help the *yeled*. A couple of bonus *Chesed* (Kindness) points couldn't hurt before the *Chagim*.

* * *

The old man by the spice shop was giving Effi that jeepers-creepers feeling again. He stomped his cane on the ground, then pointed it towards him in a "shoo" type gesture. Effi turned to leave, then noticed the business card lying on the ground. It had completely missed his back pocket. The old man had tried to help him. He mouthed, *todah*. The old man nodded back in acknowledgment. Effi looked at the card for the first time since Tzion handed it to him, immediately recognizing the Hazon Labs logo.

"Holy Moses," Effi shouted a little too loud, drawing stares from several nearby shoppers and a *tsk* from the old man. He couldn't believe his good fortune and terrible luck; he'd just been talking to Hazon Labs' Chief Developer and had blown a primo opportunity. He was ready to chase after Tzion, but when he looked up again he'd disappeared into a sea of hijabs and shaved heads that flooded into *Haja'y Street*.

Chapter 9

Shortly after the early afternoon Muslim *Dhuhr* prayers ended, hundreds of people poured out from the western Temple Mount gates, flooding the multiple mini-Souks and streets in the Arab Quarter. Tzion's progress through the Friday afternoon crowds was unusually slow. History proved that attacks on Jews were often crimes of opportunity, or possibly in this case of proximity as people crowded in around him. He was still deep in the Arab Quarter when his phone sounded the ear-splitting klaxon — a cyber alert from Hazon Labs indicating another high-level security breach. The whop-whop sound immediately drew the unwanted attention of those around him as many scurried for cover not recognizing the alarm and not knowing what to expect.

Apologetically, Tzion raised his hands, quickly reaching into the backpack's side pocket to silence the offending noise. Rather than risk a repeat, he put the phone into vibrate-only mode. The previous week's news was filled with reports of the exploding "pager attacks" on Hezbollah operatives. Understandably, people were skittish. Tzion wondered what was behind Hazon Labs' four-alarm alert, and considered whether he should return to the office. But save for showing up to lend his support, there was little Tzion could do, except what he'd already done. He'd shut down his computer for the weekend and unplugged it from the network, an air gap precaution to protect HaMikdash3.0's servers. He could always get an update later when he picked up his car from the First Station parking lot.

The near-constant buzzing updates from the unfolding cybersecurity crisis were annoying, but at least they were silent. Unfortunately, turning off his phone entirely was not an option, though he would have a bit of peace and quiet once inside Zedekiah's Cave. Cell reception was spotty at best; a lesson he'd learned the hard way on their first day of shooting in the "dungeon."

"Incommunicado won't work, comprende?" Luznick shouted at Jay, officially the company's CTO but in reality, Vice President of Everything and Anything Joshua didn't want to deal with. Today, he was supervising the ZC shoot. Jay listened carefully, nodding thoughtfully in true Zen Master mode.

Tzion was thankful he wasn't the target of Luznick's latest rant. Less than an hour into the shoot all they'd heard were complaints about the lighting, the temperature, about this and that.

"I got you, Dov," Jay said. "I'll send an intern to wait outside with your phone." His voice remained calm and steady, despite Luznick's histrionics.

"Fine, but I better not miss any calls from my agent," he shouted, reasonably satisfied until realizing that *all* his precious contacts would be given over to some nobody intern. "Wait, who? Who are you giving my phone to? My whole life's in there!"

Jay motioned to a baby-faced eighteen-year-old intern, who'd stayed close enough to hear the exchange but far enough away to stay out of the direct line of fire… until now. "This is Matan," Jay said.

"Matan what," Luznick interrupted.

"Matan Glick. He's doing an internship with Hazon. He's from the Aardvark Israel gap-year program. He's shown himself to be very responsible." A bit of a stretch since the two Aardvark interns had only started that very morning.

Matan perfunctorily put out his hand to greet Dov, who apparently didn't have time for pleasantries including any meet-and-greets. Embarrassed, Matan withdrew it quickly.

"Fine," Luznick said, eyeing the baby-faced intern, who looked thirteen rather than of college age. He dug into his leather backpack for the phone, stretched out his hand but didn't give it up immediately. It looked like a full-on, tug-o-war with the phone as if Luznick was still debating the matter. He added a stern warning. "I'm holding you personally responsible. You got that?" and only then reluctantly released his phone.

"I'll guard it with my life."

"Hmmm, see to it." With that, Luznick raced through the shoot, anxious to finish and be rid of "this god-forsaken cave."

Once Luznick was out of earshot, Jay spoke with Matan. "Don't go too far, just far enough to get a signal. Give a shout when the call comes in," Jay told him, adding a reassuring nod and pat on the back.

"Got it."

"Hope he'll be okay," Tzion said, with some concern. He wasn't sure if he'd send either of his younger brothers to "just hang outside" the cave. They were deep in the heart of Arab East Jerusalem, a stone's throw from the Damascus Gate where bad things happened nearly every day.

"Me too. The last thing Hazon Labs needs to do is lose an intern from Colorado in East Jerusalem. No amount of insurance would cover that one," Jay noted.

Things finally lightened up, somewhat, once the long-anticipated call from Dov's agent came in an hour later and the *prima donna* returned to the set, all smiles.

"Got the part," he announced, strutting like a featherless peacock in the full-body leotard spotted with neon-green sensors.

The assembled production team politely congratulated him with little enthusiasm and as transparent as glass, but which went right over Dov's head. Tzion was sure he was disappointed that no one asked him what part he'd gotten. Thinking back, the stress of the shoot likely contributed to his having missed the now-obvious, splish-splash cup oversight. Ironically, he probably owed Dov a thank-you for his lemonade fix, since he liked the revised storyline considerably more than the original.

Crossing over the *Sha ar Shechem* threshold, Tzion breathed an audible sigh of relief… too many things could go wrong, and wearing a *kippah* in this neighborhood often invited trouble. He took the stairs to his right up to *Sultan Suleiman Street* and turned right for Zedekiah's Cave. Surprisingly, the gate was open, but no one was at the cave's entrance when he arrived. The cave was closed on Fridays, and a guard was generally present at the entrance to kindly, or rudely, turn away hapless tourists who had mistakenly shown up. Hazon Labs had been granted special permissions from PAMI, the Hebrew acronym for the *Pituach Mizrach Yerushalayim* (East Jerusalem Development, Ltd), and the Jerusalem Municipality to access multiple sites around the city that were otherwise closed to the public, including the excavations below the Jaffa Gate and the Pilgrimage Road, or when they needed to work outside of regular business hours.

The only known entrances to Zedekiah's Cave are on *Sultan Suleiman Street*, on the north side of the Old City. At the main gate, visitors to the cave can buy entry tickets and opt-in for the audio-visual show. The other access point is visible from the street in a fenced-off stone garden to the right of the main entrance, an emergency exit. It is generally closed, except when moving equipment, chairs, and a modular stage in and out of the cave for concerts and other events. Inside the cave, just past the ticket booth are stairs leading visitors deeper into the cave complex. To the left of the entrance, down a rocky slope are two sets of stairs, one ancient set of stone steps, and the other indicating the emergency exit. Tzion was always curious about the mysterious stone steps, degraded by Time and, no doubt, leading somewhere equally mysterious. Tzion suspected the stairs likely led to a space between the Old City walls, or maybe it just deadened, seemingly going to nowhere.

From the main entrance to Zedekiah's Cave, it is a mere four-tenths of a mile, a near-perfect straight line to the Temple Mount. But getting from point A to point B is anything but simple. The upper cave currently ended about 300 meters from the northern edge of the Temple Mount and was located under parts of the Arab and Christian Quarters, near the *Via Dolorosa*. To date, only 40% of the cave has been excavated. Above ground, the walking route would meander through the Arab Quarter before crossing over into the Christian Quarter. The limestone in Zedekiah's Cave is considered to be of the highest quality. *Meleke*, the Queen's stone; the same as is found in the Western Wall, and dates back to at least the second Temple period (516 BCE to 70 CE).

With the full extent of Zedekiah's Cave yet to be excavated, Tzion suspected one or more routes would lead directly to the Temple Mount. The ancient Cardo, which lies just west of Zedekiah's Cave, lies four to six meters (13 to 20 feet) below current street level, while the deepest part of the cave is 30 meters — 100 feet — underground. Where passages and tunnels intersect or cross over to connect this quarry to points closer to the Temple Mount is anyone's guess. Like any missing-link mystery, finding the connecting piece in this geolocation puzzle could be key to locating a long-theorized underground access point to the Temple Mount — one big enough to accommodate the hewn limestone building blocks of the *Beit HaMikdash* for both the First and Second Temples, versions 1.0 and 2.0, respectively.

"*Shalom*," Tzion called out. Save for the hollow echo of his voice, no one replied. No matter. With any luck, he'd get the shots he needed and be on his way to *Beit Shemesh* with time to spare. Rather than running in circles scouting additional locations for the reshoot, Tzion went directly to Zedekiah's Tears, located to the right, beyond the Hall of the Freemasons. The constructed paths took much of the fun out of discovering Zedekiah's Tears even via the circuitous route to the far end of the cave, the long way around by heading left out of the Hall. The "far-end" designation was relative; the cave was still being excavated, leaving the full extent of the cave's actual dimensions a very big open question.

Several years earlier, a lower cave dating back to the 12th century — the days of the Crusader Templar Knights — was discovered but kept mostly under wraps. A sneak peek at the cavern area under the cave's floor revealed multiple rooms with constructed walls, doorways, and windows. The discovery of the lower cavern lent credence to the idea that other hidden underground areas and passages were likely waiting to be discovered. For the time being, however, the Templar cavern area was off-limits, even to HaMikdash3.0 and Hazon Labs.

The cave's history and legends were perfect for a HaMikdash3.0 storyline — one that Tzion gladly crafted. Using the flashlight from his phone, he approached the hollowed-out opening in the cave's southwestern wall, Zedekiah's Tears. Water from an unknown source trickled in, filling the shallow pool. Rivulets overflowed Zedekiah's Tears, wearing the surrounding stones smooth. He carefully negotiated a path over the slick stones, then removed the limestone-hewn cup from his backpack. Carefully, he set the cup in the water and stepped back a bit to eye the cup from various angles. The clear plastic platform that would raise the bottom of the cup to the water's surface was still sitting on his desk. Truth be told, he liked the look of the partially submerged cup. He grabbed a few still shots and a short video of the cup, and the empty pool of water, before turning the cup upside down to get the *now-desired* splish-splash effect.

Satisfied, he put the wet cup into an outside pocket of his backpack to dry, then decided to spend a few minutes scoping out anything new in the cave. Their original shoot had taken place in early June. Since then, the Israel Antiquities Authority's ongoing excavations might have uncovered new areas of interest that they could easily include in the reshoot. Previously, they hadn't included anything about the Ancient Gate, located immediately adjacent to and below *Sha'ar Shechem*/Damascus Gate. For years, the long-ignored area had become a handy dump site for garbage flung over the railing from *Sha'ar Shechem*/Damascus Gate.

While the Ancient Gate has been uncovered in the 1930s and later explored in the 1960s and 1980s, it didn't debut as a historic attraction for another forty years. Its restoration was expertly handled by a team of archeologists from the Israel Antiquities Authority, working closely with a team from PAMI. The Ancient Gate temporarily opened to the public in mid-August 2024 for several weeks with an impressive multimedia show in the excavated Roman-era space. A highlight was a central square that included a towering 22-meter-high column which was likely used to provide travelers with information on the distance from Jerusalem to other cities. Tzion planned to propose the Ancient Gate be part of an expanded TZ module in HaMikdash3.1, due out in April/Pesach 2025 according to Joshua's master plan. The proximity of TZ and the Ancient Gate begged the question… was there a secret, or yet-to-be-discovered, tunnel or street connecting the two? The Ancient Gate would be a great addition to HaMikdash as a separate storyline, or connected to Zedekiah's Cave, if only by its relative proximity.

Tzion cut across a newly excavated portion of Zedekiah's Cave, pleased at having made a new discovery. The ceiling extended over 7.5 meters (approximately twenty-five feet) above his head with two recessed areas carved into the stone — both were enveloped in complete darkness. The cave within a cave on the right appeared smaller than the one on the left. The left cave had one large opening, measuring at least three meters high (ten feet) and of a similar width, but its darkened depth was impossible to discern from the ground. Degraded steps led up to the deeply recessed area on the left — *if* he were foolish enough to climb them. He stepped back a bit and shined the light from his cellphone into the recessed space but couldn't see much before loosing his footing and tumbling backward. Tzion caught himself on a large boulder, but his phone slipped from his hand, clattering to the ground. The flashlight shone upwards, illuminating the area and immediately drew the attention of two Arabic-speaking men. Their loud whispers echoed through the cave. Strange, Tzion thought; he hadn't seen or heard them before.

Instinctively, he grabbed his phone, turned off the flashlight App, and pressed the phone to his chest to hide any stray light from the screen. While he couldn't explain it, every fiber in his body told him to hide, and pray, so that they, whoever they were, wouldn't find him. He remained in a crouched position, straining to hear their hushed whispers. He'd taken Arabic as an elective in high school, but the cave's echo distorted their conversation. While he couldn't explain why the men and their whispered Arabic worried him; and, yet they did. Maybe, Joshua's Spidey sense was rubbing off on him. Erring on the side of caution was always the safer bet and Tzion knew he needed to notify the authorities. It wasn't unusual to report anything out of the ordinary, an unattended shopping bag or backpack left under a bus seat could be rigged with explosives, or a person acting odd, or a sudden change in direction when security personnel approached. Unfortunately, bad things happened all too often in Israel and suspicions ran toward being vigilant sprinkled with a healthy dose of situational awareness tempered by justified paranoia.

Another cyber alert buzzed him, lighting up his screen and the space around him, a bright blue beacon, screaming, "Hey, guys! I'm over here." Tzion said a silent prayer, hoping they hadn't noticed…

* * *

"Did you see that?" *Jibril* shouted excitedly.

"What?" asked his cousin *Ahmed*, the shorter of the two Arabs from East Jerusalem.

"I don't know, a light. There's someone else here."

"You worry too much. No one is here," *Ahmed* said, pausing before adding, "except maybe the *Jinns* coming to get you." Since they were children, *Ahmed* loved to tease *Jibril*.

The fabled *Jinns* were a touchy subject. *Jibril* had confided that he suspected they lived under his bed. At the time, he was only six, tall for his age, and his legs stuck out from the end of the bed. He was worried. *Ahmed* took full advantage of the confession to scare *Jibril* whenever the opportunity presented itself.

"That's not funny, *Ahmed*. You ever meet a *Jinn*?"

"No, and there's no one here." *Ahmed* knew better than to push his cousin too far. Besides, he needed him for the task at hand. *Ahmed*, stood at 5'5" and couldn't easily see over the top of the black containers to set the timers. *Jibril* would need to make sure each was in good working order. He could try to do it himself, but his permanently twisted neck, courtesy of a not-so-playful stranglehold, a parting gift from Arafat's *Fatah* thugs, sometimes made him see double.

"Come, we better finish before *Ismail* arrives."

"A *Jinn*," they said in near-perfect unison and laughed.

Tzion picked up enough of their conversation to know they were skulking around the cave, reasonably confident no one else was around. He felt his phone vibrate against his chest. Even in vibration mode, the sound found resonance in Zedekiah's Cave, reverberating off the limestone walls in the five-acre complex. He clamped his hand over the phone trying to stop the vibration, but a second too late. It had already been heard.

"There!" *Jibril* shouted.

"What? There's nothing, more *Jinns* or maybe a bat. Woo!"

Except someone else was in the cave with them and *Jibril's* instincts were 100% correct. The limestone under Tzion's feet was slick, slippery. Ironic, since limestone chalk was used by gymnasts and other athletes to dry their hands. He wasn't sure if the cave within the cave above his head would be deep enough to afford him any cover, but there was no place else nearby. He'd have to wait them out. While Tzion couldn't hear them anymore that didn't mean they weren't still around. He waited until the multiple flashlight beams skittering across the walls and floors of the cave disappeared in the distance before moving from his spot. The steps were barely there and he risked breaking his neck, but he didn't dare turn on the flashlight App. Tzion scrabbled across the open space, keeping low to the ground. There was no choice, he'd be exposed for a time, but there was no time to waste.

The flashlight beams suddenly cut across the path where he'd been just moments before. Tzion pressed himself against the wall, closing his eyes and holding his breath. They had laid a trap. He grabbed a loose rock and tossed it wildly into the distance, hoping to distract the intruders, who ironically, viewed *him* as the intruder. He followed the flashlight beams as they turned away and dove for the uneven stairs. With only seconds to spare, he crawled across the chalked dust into the overhead cave as multiple beams of light cut across the recessed area above his head.

"It's probably a bat. Satisfied?"

"I'm telling you, I saw a shadow move,"

"Yes, perhaps the demon has missed you. He is back to haunt you once again!"

"Not funny, cousin."

"Come on." *Ahmed* poked *Jibril* in the ribs, then awkwardly slung an arm around his taller cousin.

The two laughed together.

"Come, we must hurry."

Ahmed pulled a surgical mask from his pocket and handed it to *Jibril*. Confused, *Jibril* asked, "You sick, cousin?"

"For the last tank. It's different from the others."

"Different, how?"

"No matter, we'll be finished soon."

Jibril wished he'd known sooner that *Ahmed* had masks. He had a sensitive nose, which was good for his work at the Waldorf Astoria Hotel serving wine to its fancy guests. The sommelier sometimes asked him to describe the notes. That's what he called the different smells and tastes of the wine. Truth was he'd much rather be surrounded by the hotel's extensive wine collection, smelling corks than stuck in this hellhole wreaking of diesel oil and mold. Except he couldn't say no to *Ahmed*; his cousin had gotten him the job at the Waldorf in the first place.

Still trapped in the upper cave, Tzion knew he'd be cornered, trapped up here with nowhere to run or hide. He needed to find a better hiding place where he could wait them out. GA-697.4 reinforced the idea with a whisper in Tzion's ear, knowing *Jibril* and *Ahmed* would be back soon enough.

GA696.0 went ahead to scout out the Templar cavern; a much better hiding place and set up camp. Tzion "remembered" the Templar cavern, a closed area, below the cave's current ground level. The place wasn't ideal. There were no solid walls, but sections of randomly extracted limestone created numerous, tall freestanding pillars for him to hide behind. What, or from whom he still wasn't sure but this shadow game of hide and seek might become a deadly game of cat and mouse where he was the mouse.

Once they left, the gate would be locked behind them. He could call the police, assuming he could get a signal. The *Mishtara* wasn't far away. If he made enough noise, someone would probably hear him. Alternatively, he could use the alarm on the emergency exit. It would sound and bring the *Mishtara* running. Better to be embarrassed at needing to be rescued, than to be stuck in the cave complex until Sunday when it would reopen to the public. The police could investigate if anything was amiss in the cave. In the worst-case scenario, he might be stuck here over *Shabbat* which meant missing his brother's *Bar Mitzvah*… his *ima* would not be pleased. However he managed to escape, he would need to report whatever these guys were doing. A search of the cave might turn up nothing more than a new septic or water tank. His instincts, however, told him there was nothing innocent about what these two were up to.

Instead of risking his neck on the steps again, Tzion shimmied to the ledge, hung off the side, and dropped down. He didn't dare use his flashlight. If he had, it would have led him to choose a different drop point. Unfortunately, he landed awkwardly on a slick stone, twisting his right ankle. The men were returning, their voices carried through the cave making it difficult to determine how much time he had. The beams from their flashlights were pointed low, illuminating the space immediately around them. There was no time to waste, he hobbled off to a roped-off area that blocked the entrance to the underground Templar cavern. Blindly, he dropped into the hole and slipped, knocking his head on the stepping stone's jagged edge. Dazed and bleeding from a deep gash on his head, Tzion stumbled deeper into the lower cavern beyond where the walls, doorways, and windowed structures had been excavated by the Antiquities Authority. He stumbled forward, bending to avoid the low ceiling. At least, he was out of harm's way, or so he hoped.

Chapter 10

The Reichman University audience applauded enthusiastically, giving Joshua the chance to steal a glance at Jay who held up the phone for him to see. The alert was back down to yellow with a tinge of orange around the edges, but neither Joshua nor Jay was ready to relax. In the last few minutes, the intruder alert rating system had fluctuated between yellow and orange, but thankfully had not risen back up to a red-level threat. The flip-flop between yellow and orange, however, was perhaps more troubling since it meant the intrusion, while detected, had not yet been resolved. In other words, it was still an active threat. Every minute, every second mattered, and the longer the event went on, the greater the potential damage to the HaMikdash3.0 servers, data, or whatever else the hacker had targeted.

The warning system they'd developed automatically ranked the risk level of an intrusion event using multiple weighted variables with end-to-end event tracking. The challenge was identifying an event's true starting point. Containment also included defining the context — the minutes of data before the detection to identify missed opportunities and rolling back the server clock to identify other early/earlier warning signs of an imminent intrusion. The approach not only recognized the likelihood that the intruder had previously tested the system's defenses, knocking on the proverbial door, and possibly, though rarely, leaving behind a signature of sorts. Most importantly, the approach accepted the fact that another intrusion, or attempted intrusion, had a 100% probability, posing the realistic question of when, not if. Countermeasures notwithstanding, the pervasiveness of hacking also recognized one's inability to stop an attack 100% of the time.

Joshua planned on keeping the Q&A session short. Very short. But the last thing he wanted was to set off any alarm bells with any official press who might be in attendance, along with social media bloggers and internet butterflies who could speculate *ad nauseam* in tweets and posts about the abrupt departure of Hazon Labs' CEO Joshua Katz and CTO Jay Sofer from the lecture hall.

With a calming breath, he began. "Thank you. I'm honored to be the last talk of the summer session, the grand finale to your studies. I wanted to touch on a couple of points and maybe have a brief Q&A. I'll try to keep it interesting, or at least not too boring. As you might've figured out, the number behind me is the total number of member-players HaMikdash3.0 has signed on to date, as of an hour ago."

Joshua turned to the freeze-framed number 1,770,666 onscreen. "That total includes our *Sefirat Omer* early-bird registration drive which closed *Erev Chag Shavuot*, the day before the *Shavuot* holiday, and was then re-opened again after *Tisha b'Av*, the ninth of the Hebrew month of *Av*.

"This morning, we hit 1.5M users, a significant milestone, and in just over an hour we've added 270,666 new member-players. Many are working on developing their HaMikdash3.0 experience using our advanced *Virtuoso* profile-building program to develop their avatar's online personas and user experience." Joshua's matter-of-fact statement drew another round of applause. He didn't skip a beat at the minor lie he'd just told. None of the new, or existing member-players, were doing anything within the system at the moment; once the intrusion had been discovered; every last one had been unceremoniously and immediately locked out, except the intruder. It was a Yin-Yang balancing act, deciding between engaging the black hat in a live battle of wills; or, containing the intrusion and protecting user privacy on HaMikdash3.0's distributed network. Their approach hopefully accomplished both tasks, and hopefully, no one in the crowd had opted to sign on to the site in the last hour.

The portable mic allowed Joshua to roam across the stage, which kept his nervous energy in check. His graduate school advisor once told him he paced like a caged lion. It was the one piece of advice he'd accepted from "he who shall remain nameless." He'd since learned how to command the stage, remaining at center stage much of the time, but deliberately looking left and right to engage the wider audience.

"I'm often asked, how would you describe HaMikdash3.0? A popular question with VCs, plus the caveat, tell me about HaMikdash3.0 in thirty seconds, or worse a short fifteen-second elevator ride pitch." The comment brought another round of laughter. "A good lesson here for anyone planning on embarking on the start-up rollercoaster. Just curious, anyone here planning a start-up?" Joshua jokingly asked. Not surprisingly, nearly every hand in the room shot up; some with double-handed *Hallelujah* waves.

"So how did you answer the question?" a male voice shouted from the back of the room.

Joshua deliberately ignored the query's unmistakable snide tone and sought to diffuse it with a bit of amusement. "Funny you should ask." His response garnered the appropriate titters and chuckles. He tried to track the question's source, but with the glare of the stage lights in his eyes, he couldn't see much beyond the first few rows.

"At first, I had a tough time separating what I wanted Hazon Labs to be from the reality of what it was, or for that matter what HaMikdash3.0 could be, or what would attract potential investors. Our first challenge was the name, *Hazon*. The company originally filed paperwork as *Chazon* Labs," he said, emphasizing the *CHHHH* sound. "As with most plans of mice and men, we were persuaded to change it within weeks, when the 'CHHHH' proved too difficult to pronounce in branding tests. Not here mind you, but in the US and elsewhere. That stumble was very costly, as we had to toss out all our printed materials, from business cards to promotional materials, get a new domain name, re-register the company, and add DBAs to the bank accounts. And our tradeshow booth and banner had to go too; a costly business expense that went straight into the crapper. It was a valuable, but expensive lesson to learn. So, lesson number one you have to be willing to go all in with your start-up, just not too soon, and not on every front. Test the waters. Do the market research. That's lesson number two."

Uri'el smiled as he listened to Joshua; the kid chose his words carefully. The Hebrew word, *chazon* translated to vision and HaMikdash3.0 was indeed Joshua's vision, one built around the activities of a virtual Third Jewish Temple, and which had become concretized in the last days of his grandfather Jacob's life. HaMikdash3.0 and Hazon Labs, even with the name change, were indeed another homage to Joshua's grandfather, an ardent follower of the *Chabad* movement and the *Rebbe*, Rabbi Menachem Mendel Schneerson, who some believed was the *Moshiach/Messiah*, the Anointed One, or that the *Rebbe* would be, returning when the time was right.

From the corner of his eye, Joshua saw Jay intensely focused on the two-phone juggle, swiping across screens, and angrily speaking into his phone. Joshua felt his stomach do a couple of somersaults, and the acid burn at the back of his throat, ratcheting up his blood pressure. He tried to get Jay's attention but to no avail. He'd have to wrap this up quickly and was about to continue his remarks, when someone called out, "So how much did that little branding misstep cost you?"

Joshua sighed. "Let's say it ran upwards of 125K. That's dollars, not *shekels*, with a goodly chunk of it going to legal fees. We took a big hit and not just financially. Perhaps more importantly emotionally. We/I had become so vested in HaMikdash3.0 that any failure meant I was a failure, a reflection of my self-worth, a personal valuation but which isn't true. So, what do you do? Simple, you pick yourself up again and realize it's a stumble on your path, a bump in the road. You haven't fallen off a cliff, at least not yet. Plus, I still hadn't solved my pitch problem trying to explain HaMikdash3.0 in an elevator pitch.

"So, I tried using a Hollywood technique, the high concept way of describing HaMikdash3.0 relative to known quantities, it's this meets this; or this on steroids. Well, that didn't work either. Hazon Labs was fortunate in that we had a fair amount of runway with revenue from licensing our IP, and my grandfather Jacob Katzenstein's invention brilliance from which we've all benefited from his generosity."

Joshua made a not-so-subtle reference to the innovation chair his grandfather endowed, prompting a round of grateful applause led by Reichman's Chancellor, who buoyed the applause by timing several definitive head bobs while encouraging the audience to join in. During the pause, Joshua re-formulated his off-the-cuff remarks, on the go/no-go launch on *Tisha b'Av* — a useful case study on lessons learned for the Reichman students on how the best-laid plans can go awry and how to pivot gracefully or at least with as little egg on one's face as possible.

"So, I still needed a pitch. My revelation came when I gave up trying to fit into everyone else's mold. Instead, I simply described HaMikdash3.0 for what it is: part Monopoly, with its property and wealth-building stratagem; a hybrid quest of discovery and action, where engagement in the site's storylines and missions can earn member/players both virtual as well as real-world prizes, while also driving change; and a participatory religious and spiritual consciousness-raising experience. HaMikdash3.0 is a richly layered community centered around Temple life experiences, including the opportunity to bring virtual *korbanot* — sacrifices and offerings. But most importantly, HaMikdash3.0 is a place for uplifting spirituality and even existential ponderings, *sans* all the political machinations and pundit pontificating. For me, HaMikdash3.0 was, and is, a way to inspire, to bring knowledge, and raise *Moshiach* consciousness levels."

Joshua paused, shocked by the words which had recklessly tumbled out of his mouth. He hadn't intended to bring *Moshiach* into his presentation, and quite literally bit his tongue to keep from mentioning *Techiyat HaMei'tim*, the Resurrection of the Dead… his true endgame.

Across the stage, Jay had stopped mid-rant and stared bug-eyed at his best friend, not quite believing Joshua had shared the well-guarded truth — his Truth — about HaMikdash3.0 and the impetus behind its development. Not everyone appreciated *Moshiach*-talk, and any press in the audience would have a field day about the remark, at Joshua's expense.

Uri'el also couldn't hide his surprise. His *heads* shuddered discontinuously, causing the lights in the auditorium to flicker ominously, giving agency to Joshua's words. Hazon Labs' CEO used the distraction to get his remarks back on track. He took the VR glasses from his head and ceremoniously wiped the lens to buy himself some time.

But before he could say anything, the same voice that spoke up earlier asked, "Not exactly an elevator pitch, is it?"

"No, sometimes you have to throw the rules out the window. People listened, not everyone, but the right ones did. I should add that our technology certainly helped. We have some killer predictive analytics and visualization tools, a true-to-life virtual world, and new wearable and hardware components to give the user an out-of-this-world experience."

Joshua glanced offstage at Jay. The unspoken command was to find out who the questioner was. Hazon Labs was always on the lookout for smart interns. Holding a phone in each hand, Jay threw his hands up in the air, and for good measure, stuck his tongue out the side of his mouth to complete the comical portrait.

The mystery questioner spoke up once again. "Speaking of rules, shouldn't you leave it to your users to decide, define, and review your 'out of this world' product and not you?" A barbed comment, delivered with more than a spoonful of contempt.

Unfazed, Joshua responded calmly to the mixed comment and question, and which bordered on heckling. "An excellent point, but in a pitch to your prospective investors a little swagger can't hurt, as long as you can back it up," Joshua said with a smile. "Any chance you can stand up so I can see who I'm having this conversation with?"

"Not today, but with any luck in the not-too-distant future." With that the door at the back of the room opened, letting in a burst of light until closing loudly.

Uri'el felt an immediate release, a pressure emanating from the dark energy as it/she/he left the auditorium. He would have liked to pursue the "it" but leaving Joshua was not an option. Instead, he looked at GAs, "Sleepy" and "Dopey" perched on his shoulders who'd clung on to his wings when he descended to Reichman. He thought-transferred the "Go" command to Dopey, who sped away toward the door and promptly tumbled backward as if he'd been slugged by a powerful swing from Babe Ruth's baseball bat. His little head halo was askew as he plopped back down on Uri'el's shoulder. With the ministering help from GA-730.71, a.k.a. Sleepy, who fanned him with a handy Kleenex®, GA-755.23 stood unsteadily and properly straightened his halo then offered a slight shrug, simulating a mock punch in the face.

Curious, Uri'el thought. Micha'el had been right to insist on his presence. But who, or more likely what, had been here he couldn't say? G-d was omnipotent, angels and even archangels not so much. More importantly, was that the source of the gauntlet challenge and cackling laughter that mocked him earlier? And why hadn't he detected the presence himself? Not many creatures could mask their signature frequencies. Over the eons, Uri'el had become one of the more adept at detection.

Joshua couldn't help but wonder about the odd encounter. MBAs generally relished the opportunity to be seen… to stand out in a crowd. The interaction was unsettling in ways Joshua couldn't put into words. The mystery questioner had been correct on one point. The major reviews of HaMikdash3.0 were still out and would be until the actual release date. The gaming community could be Hazon Labs' best ally, helping to identify bugs up to a point, championing the advanced VR/AR interactivity, and touting HaMikdash3.0's wow-factor multiplier to their peers. They'd leveraged the positive reviews from their one hundred Beta testers and reaped the rewards with hundreds of thousands of member-players signing on when they reopened registration. Joshua hoped the winds would continue to blow favorably in their direction, earning HaMikdash3.0 a Triple-A, five-star rating.

Unfortunately, gamers were notoriously fickle and could just as easily, and mercilessly, pan HaMikdash3.0 on blogs, user groups, forums, and other online hangouts. The gaming community could breathe life into 3.0, and in the next breath deliver a kiss-of-death — dooming Joshua's work to the annals of outrageously expensive, failed MMOs (Massive Multiplayer Online) games. From a gamer's perspective, HaMikdash3.0 was first and foremost a Virtual World with Role-Playing Games and Real-Time Strategy game-based interactions. Unlike free-to-play MMOs, HaMikdash3.0 adopted a non-freemium approach, charging a modest, non-refundable $25 annual subscription fee instead of relying on a subscription plus a recurring monthly payment. By disrupting the freemium model, HaMikdash3.0 planned to offer members additional incentives, including the 3D wrap-around VR/AR glasses, exclusive access to proprietary products from Hazon Labs, such as the Hand TUI (Tangible User Interface) device, and other unique rewards. It was difficult to say which was the greater draw: the technology or the financial tangibles, including a single share in Hazon Labs and a potential $250K prize package. The substantial prize money was perhaps the greatest game-changer that HaMikdash3.0 brought to online/offline gaming. If someone could not or refused to pay the annual subscription fee, it was waived without argument or questions, which didn't make the folks at Price Waterhouse, the company's accounting firm, happy. Surprisingly, over 85% of their subscribers paid the upfront fee for the right to be part of the HaMikdash3.0 community. Paying members did have the barest of additional access advantages compared to non-paying subscribers, but not when it came to the Grand Prize offering.

It was all legal, but change is never easy. Joshua E. Katz had changed the rules of MMO gaming, especially with the quarter-of-a-million-dollar prize offer, outside of tournament play. To avoid any hint of impropriety or pyramid-scheme lookalikes that used subscriber monies to fund prize monies, said HaMikdash3.0 monies were already set aside in an escrow account for the lucky grand prize winner who would be algorithmically chosen — a righteous approach based on user profiles and gameplay, but which had little, if anything, to do with chance.

"As most of you know, our original plan was for a *Tisha b'Av* release date, but we canceled that in part because of the looming threat of an attack by Iran at the time. Can't exactly go online if someone turns off the *chashmal*," Joshua said, using the Hebrew word for electricity but which hinted at the mysterious form of Divine energy in *Kabbalistic terms* also known as *Chashmal*.

"So, now, we faced our next hurdle. When do we launch? Naturally, we didn't want to lose momentum by delaying the launch for much longer. We knew/I knew that linking HaMikdash3.0 to a Jewish holiday was important. And Judaism has *a lot* of holidays to choose from." Joshua's comment drew a round of snickers and modest laughter. He was stating a fact and hadn't intended it to come off quite as sarcastic as it did.

"Each major calendar event offered Hazon Labs an embedded marketing opportunity. I set my sights on the *Shalosh Regalim*, the three Holidays during the year when Jews are required to visit Jerusalem during Temple times to offer one or more sacrifices. A marketer's dream right? In many ways, it was even better than the original *Tisha b'Av* plan. The *Sukkot* holiday, the Feast of Tabernacles, is the first of the *Shalosh Regalim* festivals on the Jewish calendar after the Jewish New Year, but the last of the three on the Gregorian calendar. Not surprisingly, the upcoming first anniversary of Oct7, gave me, us, pause. Could we… or even, should we?" Joshua paused respectfully, no explanation was given or needed.

"We're a resilient bunch, but the temporal proximity of our fantasy land to Oct7 might push the bounds of acceptable just a bit too far. My team tried to dissuade me from targeting *Sukkot* for the launch. We/I gambled that people would not be offended by the HaMikdash3.0 product launch so close to the first anniversary of last year's *Simchat Torah* horror show and the ongoing unresolved nightmare of the war, the dead and the injured, the displaced families, and, of course, the hostages still in captivity and their families."

Joshua decided not to share the special project initiated by Rabbi Doron Perez, head of World Mizrachi, and his wife Shira, to honor the memory of their son Daniel, an officer and tank commander at the *Nahal Oz* Army Base. The 22-year-old had been killed in Gaza on October 7, though his death was not confirmed until March 17, 2024… five months later. His tank crewmates Itay Chen and Tomer Livovich were also killed on the 7th and their bodies kidnapped and taken hostage by Hamas. The lone survivor of their tank crew, Matan Angrest, was kidnapped alive and was still being held hostage in Gaza.

The family's project, *A Bayit in Every Bayit*, aimed to bring the most important *Bayit*/House, the *Beit HaMikdash*, into every home. The *Bayit* project was inspired by a Facebook post by the mother of another soldier, who asked her son what he wanted to do when he came home. The young man said he wanted to get a picture of the *Beit HaMikdash*, the Holy Temple, to hang on the wall of his room. His answer surprised her; she asked, why? His response revealed a simple truth and delivered a powerful message of purpose: in every home in Gaza, in every child's room, and in every school classroom, there is a picture of the Dome of the Rock prominently displayed. Rabbi Doron and Shira Perez chose to honor their son by creating a woodblock printed with the image of what the *Beit HaMikdash* might look like atop *Har HaBayit*, and also delivering a singular message of hope to restore G-d's Home, His *Bayit*, on the Temple Mount.

"I won't go into the details of what convinced me of my decision, but I'll just say that I hope HaMikdash3.0 serves a higher purpose." Then to lighten the mood, Joshua added, "Besides, I'm a stubborn sonofabitch, and putting 'all eyes on Jerusalem, on the Temple Mount' has its appeal. It's still a gamble, with many unknowns. Time will tell.

"I will say that any concerns about the accountants or our investors were, at best, an afterthought. Besides, they couldn't argue with our results to date. Based on all projections, we'd close out 2024 on a HaMikdash3.0 high. And with that, we had an absolute, firm release date, a drop-dead deadline, and an absolute statement of resilience. HaMikdash3.0 will go live two days after *Simchat Torah/Shemini Atzeret* 5785."

The remark prompted an enthusiastic round of applause and fist-pumping woofs from the audience, but a reflective moment for Uri'el at the mention of a "drop-dead deadline." His charge was hurtling to a reckoning deadline and where Death would figure prominently.

Jay gave Joshua a head nod and a finger twirl. They needed to wrap this up and head back to Jerusalem ASAP to deal with the crisis that was still sending out Red Alerts. He nodded to Jay, but Joshua knew he needed to be careful not to end the historicals too abruptly.

"Pre-registration to qualify for the $250K promotion ends before Rosh Hashanah, in just a few more days, in case any of you still haven't signed up," Joshua said, with a warm smile.

"General registration is set to reopen during the *Aseret Yemei Teshuvah* — the 10 days of Repentance between *Rosh Hashanah* and *Yom Kippur*. The period is traditionally given to three activities: repentance, prayer, and charity. Gaming, not so much. But I figured since I'm already going to hell, what's one more foul play in G-d's playbook?" Joshua's irreverent quip prompted another round of applause. "To be honest, I could have argued in favor of 'using' the *Aseret Yemei Teshuva* as a marketing tool, but thankfully my team pulled me back from the edge of the abyss for which I, and my soul, are forever grateful," he said with a shrug to the whiteboard still displaying their current number of registered users. "I'd say, we're still doing okay."

Ironically, HaMikdash3.0 would have partly fulfilled the *Aseret Yemei Teshuva* mandate of repentance and charity, though not so much on the prayer front. HaMikdash3.0's balance sheet was healthy, though it would have been significantly healthier were it not for HaMikdash3.0's revenue usage. Only $10.00, 40% of the $25.00 member subscription fee, went directly into the company's profit column, another $10.00 for operating expenses, and $5.00 was immediately banked for players' use as HaMikdash3.0 *ShekCoins*. Since 85% of their 1,770,666 worldwide subscribers paid the full subscription price and 40% went into the profit column, they came in at just over $14.7M in revenue. HaMikdash3.0 was a money-maker, an upstart start-up to watch.

Hazon Labs offered an extremely generous HaMikdash3.0's bitcoin exchange rate, one significantly better than the actual dollar-to-*shekel* exchange rate, at a whopping 1:10,000 exchange. *ShekCoins* could be used for in-app purchases in one of HaMikdash3.0's planned shops, restaurants, entertainment, and learning centers scattered throughout Jerusalem's New/Old City and exchanged for premium *TzaddikShekCoins* for giving charity. Member-players were required to *tithe*, giving 10% of their total starting bank to charitable causes of their choice; actual organizations with a presence in the virtual world or to perform acts of charity within the various storylines. Acts of kindness, *gemilut chasadim,* yielded benefits in both the real world and virtual space, life lessons that earned members points and which directly helped people in need… real people with real needs. Another 10% of a member-player's bank was automatically pledged to Temple activities, which could be accessed online or through Temple kiosks, Jay's augmented virtual reality kiosks that would offered both members and curious non-members opportunities to interact with the site, receive a blessing and the pièce de résistance offer up a range of virtual sacrifices.

The schedule of *korbanot* followed what was prescribed in the *Torah* for the daily and holiday offerings, *sans* the actual killing of animals. The marketing team's swag bundles included T-shirts, hoodies, and coffee mugs emblazoned with the phrase, "No animals were harmed in the making of HaMikdash3.0" which quickly became one of the company's more popular slogans. The statement resonated with vegetarians and vegans alike. HaMikdash3.0 proudly displayed multiple stamps of approval and endorsements on the Hazon Labs' website from dozens of animal rights organizations and vegan/vegetarian activists.

On Sunday, Joshua would receive an award from Jerusalem's Society for the Protection of Animals (J-SPCA) at their annual event. It was an event he could easily do without, but it would provide HaMikdash3.0 with an opportunity to engage a dedicated network of like-minded users: advocates for a gentler, meatless world. Hazon Labs was a Gold-level co-sponsor of Sunday's J-SPCA event, despite Joshua's avowed carnivore status. As a connoisseur of *Shabbat cholent* — a stew made from meat, barley, beans, and potatoes, left to simmer overnight on a *plata* (a heated metal sheet used to keep food warm on the *Shabbat*, since cooking is not allowed) — it was hard to imagine that his favorite meaty *cholent* might become an early casualty if all went according to plan. According to several Rabbinic scholars, when the *Moshiach*/Messiah came everyone would be a vegetarian; other commentators suggested that eating meat would be optional, an "if you want" menu item. Only Time would tell, and hopefully soon. Oddly enough, the J-SPCA's Executive Director, Tani Bennet, didn't seem to care about Joshua's meat-eating habits, though some on the fundraising committee questioned the organization's choice of honorees.

But being a meat eater didn't mean Joshua didn't love animals... especially dogs. A day didn't go by that he didn't miss Boomer, his labrador retriever pal. Fifteen years gone... it was a long time, ninety-three in dog years. As an homage to Boomer, Hazon Labs was a dog-friendly company, even though Joshua had never gotten another dog of his own. Boomer had been killed in the same plane crash which took his parents' lives... the week before his *Bar Mitzvah*. The El Al plane that brought his parents' bodies to Israel, also carried a small coffin with Boomer. He was buried in the Daniel's Farm pet cemetery called "The Rest of Animals" in English on *Moshav Magshimim* near *Petah Tikva*. The translation of *magshimim*, which means "dream fulfillers" loses a great deal of its meaning from the Hebrew.

Joshua kept Boomer's favorite throw ball in his office space, often bouncing it against the wall during brainstorming and decision-making sessions. Boomer's Ball, as it became fondly known around Hazon Labs, became their oracle, akin to a magic eight ball, helping Joshua and the team resolve an impasse or seemingly divergent solution options. In one of the more critical decisions, Boomer's Ball helped them decide on what percentage of membership fees the company should allocate to the profit column on its balance sheet.

Joshua took a deep breath before continuing. "On a practical level, missing the upcoming post-*Sukkot* holiday launch is not an option, since it means waiting for *Pesach*/Passover — the next in the *Shalosh Regalim* cycle. While our prime marketing opportunity launch window lacks the precision requirements of a NASA moonshot, it is no less important. My team argued for *Hanukkah*, which don't get me wrong, was a great option and also very much contextually congruent with the Temple.

"I listened patiently to Arik Anders, Hazon's Chief Marketing Officer. He offered a great pitch, a rough and tumble first-person, role-playing gaming scenario with the triumphant Maccabees battling the Assyrian Greeks and culminating with the rededication of the Temple with obvious allusions to contemporary times. Without question, *Hanukkah* would be a golden opportunity with endless tie-ins. Arik didn't get any arguments from me, except for one… we'd be competing with winter vacation travel and already well-established activities. The discussion was good, great even, and Arik offered to script the elaborate storyline, incorporating suggestions from the discussion including collateral art contests for children, and a vibrant *Chanukah* Boutique where artists could sell their creations. In the end, we decided not to delay the launch but to incorporate Arik's suggestions into a special *Chanukkah* Holiday module for this year complete with gilded gelt and dreidels, oil quests for lighting the *Chanukiah*, and a few other surprises that you'll have to wait for until later this year. Arik also took charge of the Christmas extravaganza with a family-styled hide and seek game for ornaments to decorate the family tree. In 2025, we plan to host a live-action game tournament to keep things interesting."

The applause started with his "gilded gelt" remark, rose with "surprises" and reached a crescendo with the mention of the "2025 live-action game tournament." Joshua realized he was probably over-compensating trying to make sure Hazon Labs didn't come across as being *too* opportunistic and, by default, fulfilling the all-too-familiar anti-Semitic, money-grubbing tropes or risk being immortalized in a derogatory meme as the face of greed as his slightly, disproportionately-sized nose would make his caricature fit the bill to a tee. While the majority of the audience was Jewish, tropes were tropes, and to be avoided even among one's own kind.

HaMikdash3.0 was about religion and spirituality and not being a *chazer*, a pig, in the money-making department. Drawing the comparison between a Jewish person and a pig was particularly insulting. Pigs were decidedly not kosher and often associated with negative human traits, a.k.a. flaws, such as greed and gluttony, which ran counter to Hazon Labs' foundational ethics, and most of the world's too as the two piggish behaviors ranked among the seven deadly sins. Ironically, or perhaps in that confluence of thought and actions, pigs had taken center stage in the ongoing cyberattack on HaMikdash3.0 by one or more bad actors.

During the thunderous applause, Joshua looked again over to Jay. This time his *sgan* was staring at him head-on and turned the phone to Joshua. The screen was flashing black and red, which in Hazon Labs' security parlance meant that the initial event had been re-evaluated and escalated from an orange to yellow status back up to red, that or a second attack had occurred. It was not unusual for a first assault to be part of a decoy strategy, designed to create a distraction, diverting resources away from a second more serious intrusion. Within seconds the screen color changed again back to solid orange. Joshua made a subtle downward motion with two fingers to Jay, indicating the threat level had just been downgraded. Jay signaled back his frustration with an Edvard Munch-styled scream, this time pressing the phones against his cheeks.

"I'd like to close with a comment about risk-taking. Hazon Labs has taken several significant risks in its short history. The first, we released HaMikdash3.0 to Beta testers, extracting an iron-clad, "cone of silence" clause in the non-disclosure agreement the testers signed, but which helped us organically spread positive head nods to rally the gaming community. Our gamble was that if the Beta version of HaMikdash3.0 fell flat on its proverbial face, too buggy to be bothered with, or too clumsy to make the game worthwhile, we'd lose before leaving the gate. We gambled on it, and, fortunately, won.

"Gamble number two: Perception. We took a hot potato issue and presented a logical solution. The third Temple could be virtual, hyphenating the religious and political tinderbox associated with the Temple Mount by moving the experience to an online 'reality' and eliminating the need to bring actual animal sacrifices, among other virtues in keeping up with our technology times. Not everyone agrees with that view. Others feel HaMikdash3.0 is an anathema, running contrary to everything Holy associated with Judaism, a usurper, and improperly drawing attention away from the actual Temple Mount. HaMikdash3.0 is both a great divider and a great unifier among people, resonating across diverse religious and spiritual views. HaMikdash3.0 has also earned the distinction as a lightning rod for political and religious arguments and has proudly joined the ranks of topics that should not be discussed at the dinner table or in polite company.

"I'm sure all of you can appreciate the ongoing challenges of the war and Oct7 moving forward. One point I'd like to convey is to remember that you can't do it all. You can try, but you've got to trust your people, which means ensuring you have good people in your corner. On that note, thank you."

The audience was on their feet, offering a thunderous applause. Jay caught the Chancellor's eye, and without hinting at the ongoing brewed and stewed crisis at Hazon Labs, tapped the non-existent watch on his left wrist and held up a single finger firmly in the air to signal to the Chancellor that there would be time for only one question. The Chancellor, himself a serial entrepreneur, understood the demanding needs of the start-up world and nodded to Jay. With practiced ease, the sixty-something Chancellor joined Joshua on stage for that all-important photo op of them together.

"We don't want to impose on our guest's time any more than we already have, but perhaps we have time for one question?" the Chancellor said, turning to Joshua with a slight deferential bow to confirm.

Joshua figured his appearance was probably good for another fifty grand, an overt play to continue the Katzenstein-Katz donation legacy with its next-generation scion. "I think I can manage one question, but then I do have to head out," Joshua said with a perfunctory nod. Without waiting for the Chancellor to select a questioner from the dozens of eager hands that enthusiastically shot up, Joshua pointed to the young man wearing a barely-there crocheted *kippah* perched on his head who'd been standing at the microphone, placed in the center aisle throughout his talk. Joshua liked to reward persistence, though standing in the aisle throughout his presentation could be just as easily construed as consummately rude. The answer came soon enough.

"Elisha Hoffman. I'm working on my doctoral thesis on Religion and Society at TAU," referring to Tel Aviv University.

"Okay, nice to meet you." Though Joshua got the distinct impression the young man had attended more as a reporter troll than a graduate student by offering up his credentials before launching into an assault. The internet had democratized and decentralized content distribution, allowing anyone with a modicum of technological know-how to present themselves as an authority, regurgitating and recycling news feeds regardless of their accuracy, across social media channels. The jury was out on Mr. Hoffman.

"I appreciate you calling on me. My question is, what's your response to Pastor Jeremiah Vine's claim that… and I quote," pausing briefly to read from his notes and applying a good old boy Southern twang, "you're the 'gosh darned anti-Christ!'"

A few people in the room snickered, a couple tried to stifle their laughs which turned a few faces bright red, while the remaining conspicuously cleared their throats. Joshua distinctly heard one or two boos also filter through the crowd. All waited expectantly for Joshua Katz's response. Most had been following the running diatribe of fire and brimstone condemnations leveled at HaMikdash3.0 in general and at Joshua in particular. Pastor Vine, the reformed and saved televangelist, was a good ole' boy who'd once claimed to have been possessed by the Devil himself, even proclaiming to have been to hell and back. He had offered all of this as part of a non-Catholic *mea culpa* to his followers to excuse a string of financial and marital infidelities dating back to the early 2000s. His sins and confessions lived on in perpetuity on his YouTube channel and in assorted mocking memes.

As "luck" would have it, the question was precisely what Joshua hoped someone would ask. Pastor Vine was annoying, but his ongoing rants helped boost HaMikdash3.0's enrollment every time he opened his mouth. While Vine's bluster was mostly hot air, there was always the real risk that someone in his flock might take his words to heart and take it upon him, or herself, to slay the Demon, a.k.a. Joshua. In the grand scheme of things, Pastor Vine was a minor concern. Joshua had real threats to worry about, the hardcore anti-Semites who believed Jews wanted to take over the world. The truly paranoid bunch of sociopaths who, like Hitler, would love to see the world Judenrein, cleansed of Jews, and who might just be willing to revive the *Endlösung der Judenfrage*... Final Solution to the Jewish Question.

Since Oct7, Jew-hatred was no longer closeted or couched by thinly veiled innuendo. Hate had been unmasked with violent marches of conflated causes all linked by their shared anti-Semitism, anti-Israel, anti-Jewish, anti-Zionist vitriol, paraded unchallenged down Main Street in countries around the world. Many of their ilk had already accused Joshua of seeking world domination by building the Third Jewish Temple, even if it was just a virtual one. They claimed it would "enslave" non-Jews, forcing them to adhere to the seven Noahide Laws, relegating them to second-class citizens in a Jewish-run world *sans* Jesus as the Messiah or the *Mahdi* from Islamic theology. While that notion couldn't have been further from Joshua's truth or mindset in creating HaMikdash3.0, he was helpless to convince the brainwashed that what they accused him of wasn't part of his endgame.

By and large, Pastor Vine was a bit of a lightweight when compared to the "Deep State" nutjobs; a profoundly scary bunch. The room grew silent as Joshua seemed to be considering his response to the "Pastor Vine" question. The irony was that Pastor Vine, and a goodly number of his flock, were also paid-in-full Jubilee members of HaMikdash3.0. Their lifetime membership came with residential parking permits in J-NOC, Jerusalem's New/Old City. His people assumed avatar roles that ran the gamut from sheep farmers to incense sellers, farmers, fishermen, priests and even rabbinical students, street beggars, artists, and an array of penitents eager to bring an offering to the Temple, albeit a virtual sacrifice in a virtual Temple.

HaMikdash3.0 already had hundreds of merchant shops and seventy-five Houses of Worship which had sprung up in the waning days of the pre-registration period, Pastor Vine among them. He opened a storefront ministry in the New/Old City, around the corner from the virtual *Hurva Synagogue*. In the real world, Christians, Muslims, and people of all faiths, were free to practice their religions throughout Israel, and specifically in Jerusalem... at least in the parts under Israel's governance. Ironically, freedom of religion excluded the Temple Mount where only Muslims were technically allowed to pray. Proselytizing, however, was a no-go and, in the real world the good Pastor and his flock would have been run out of

Jerusalem on a rail as missionaries. Missionaries of any faith, Judaism included, were not welcome in public spaces. In a real-world to virtual crossover example, *Yad l'Achim*, a counter-missionary group, set up an information booth directly across from Pastor Jeremiah's online operations. Once the site went live, it would be interesting to see how the two groups interacted. HaMikdash3.0 had already put AI and human "monitors" in place to keep an eye on things and, of course, to keep the peace, if necessary. From Joshua's perspective, HaMikdash3.0 would evolve as events in the real world unfolded, a mirror between reality and the virtual, and as he hoped between Heaven and Earth, but with an eye to helping to support peace on Earth and goodwill towards man and womankind.

Joshua took issue with the claim that "There was no such thing as bad publicity." He preferred to keep *Shalom Bais* — peace in the house — for as long as possible. He'd have to remember to send a note to graphics to create a nice-looking wall ornament with the *Birkat HaBayit*, Blessing for the House, and to send one to all HaMikdash3.0 subscribers. Better yet, note to self, announce an open call to artists to create *Shalom Bais* plaques.

Lost in thought, he almost forgot to answer Hoffman's question. "The anti-Christ? Really? I hadn't heard that one," Joshua joked, prompting a round of laughter from the audience. He'd heard Pastor Vine's latest, and more from others which were even worse. "Well," he continued in a sarcastic tone, "I think being the anti-Christ is certainly a step up from being the Devil incarnate which is who I was last week, at least according to Pastor Vine," Joshua said with a grin. More laughter filled the room. "But seriously, I am not the anti-Christ, nor have I ever been, or the Devil for that matter. Though, I can't say what might happen tomorrow or next week. Just curious, how many of you have already signed up for HaMikdash3.0?"

Nearly every hand in the room went up. Even Uri'el put up his human hand. "I guess, we must be doing something right," Joshua said with a wink and a smile.

But Elisha Hoffman wasn't done with his question. He chose the one he hoped would leave its mark, "Joshua, do you believe in G-d?" he shouted, but his voice was drowned out by the rousing applause and standing ovation.

Joshua, however, heard him loud and clear, though he had no real answer to offer, not for himself, Elisha Hoffman, or for G-d.

* * *

Uri'el joined the throngs of eager students making their way down the center aisle towards the stage, except the crowd on their way out of the hall continued to impede his forward progress. Uri'el needed a face-to-face with the man of the hour to ensure Joshua would recognize Uri'el's human face the next time they met. In another minute, his charge would be exiting stage left to handle the 911 emergency alert from Hazon Labs' white hats, the good guys relative to the black hats, i.e., the bad guys. There'd been a breach, which appeared to be a prank, at least on the surface. Only it wasn't and those behind the attack were running a covert search, not unlike Joshua's own. So far, neither program had come up with the answer Joshua E. Katz so desperately sought.

> *Joshua believed with perfect faith that the results of his Dimensional Torah Codes (DTC) search program were the only way, the one chance he had, to reunite his family again. At least, that's what Joshua E. Katz of the Katzenstein Kohanic lineage believed was possible. He was correct, but confirmation was still pending, and he'd gotten one not-so-minor detail wrong. The true power to bring about the resurrection of the dead was innately embedded in building the Third Beis HaMikdash... even a virtual one. HaMikdash3.0 in the virtual realm was always meant to be paired with the realm of souls in the Heavens above and the steady march towards the coming of the Messiah and fulfilling Joshua's ultimate mission in this life.*

> *The timing? Joshua thought that detail was in his power to control, except he couldn't have been more wrong. Whether one embraced a non-Abrahamic perspective of a repeating cycle of decay, renewal, and rebirth; or, whether one saw it as the "Day of Judgement" with the coming of the Mahdi according to Islam, the "End Times" with the second coming of Jesus according to Christianity, or the "End of Days" (קץ הימים) with the arrival of Moshiach Ben David, in the end, for the Abrahamic religions, and to quote the words of the immortal Duncan MacLeod of the clan MacLeod, late of the 1992-1998 television series, Highlander, "There can be only One." Consistently though, all interested parties seemed to define a time*

limit on the happenings, creating a palpable tremor as the "Signs of the Times" became clearer every day, both with the positive transformations in the world, and the near-constant turmoil and upheaval. All were viewed as the fulfillment of prophecy, its bona fides. Even avowed atheists and agnostics were drawn into the fray, an uncomfortable awakening that forced a re-examination of their positions on G-d many with a default mode citing Pascal's Wager. Their position was based on the philosophical argument proposed by the 17th-century French philosopher and mathematician Blaise Pascal on the question of G-d. Pascal posited that given the unknowns one must make a "wager" betting on either the payoff or a punishment. As such, is it "better" and/or more reasonable to believe in G-d and be proved wrong with a worst-case outcome of being called a fool, versus not believing in G-d and being proved wrong and doomed to suffer the hell fires of damnation for all eternity with the other fools and useful idiots.

Joshua E. Katz believed, more or less, that his salvation would indeed come through HaMikdash3.0, only it wouldn't be in the way he thought. Taking a cue from HaMikdash3.0's promotional video... So, it ends or begins, the story within a story, the one Joshua E. Katz had a hand in orchestrating, and the other story: when Providence would meet destiny and where the past, present, and future would become confluent in a single moment of self-sacrifice.

"OMG, that was excellent," Uri'el thought, hoping the recent sunspot activity had finally cleared enough for his thought-transmitted chronicle entry to be recorded. His companion Guardian Angels gave him two solid thumbs-ups, then bowed their heads solemnly at the profundity of his entry.

Joshua E. Katz probably wished he could zip-zap dematerialize and rematerialize in a snap at Hazon Labs where he needed to be. But that was not to be. Reichman's summer calendar, the Chancellor's invitation to Joshua to give a talk in memory of Jacob Katzenstein, the timing of the presentation which took both him and Jay out of the office and out of Jerusalem on a busy Friday, and the Waze-defying slow commute back to Hazon Labs... all recent events, and the many before these, were part of THE plan that gave the bad guys a temporary lead. Time enough for a malicious code, stegnographically hidden in a graphics file, to activate a devastating worm. Given enough time, the worm would insinuate and assimilate itself like a virus into Hazon Labs' mainframe, initiating a necessary final step in this particular End Times' game.

For He will give His angels charge over thee, to keep thee in all thy ways.

— Psalms 91:11

Chapter 11

On the wings of eagles, or as if being chased by a pack of jackals Jay tore out of the Reichman University parking lot. Hopefully, the traffic gods and Waze would get them back to their *Derech Hevron* offices in record time. Traveling on Highway 1, Jay's foot never left the gas pedal, keeping them at a cruising speed of 120 kilometers per hour, just a "tad" over the posted 100 km/hour speed limit. While they weren't breaking any land speed records, they were getting a little help from a legion of ten Guardian Angels, among the first Guardian Angels made during HaMikdash3.0's membership drive. The group was riding in the backseat during the daredevil chase back to Jerusalem. Correction, nine Guardian Angels, one had already prevented a near-catastrophic collision with a refrigerated *Tnuva* truck, a behemoth of a beast loaded with dairy products, and which would have sent the Land Rover careening into the highway's guardrail and disabling the car. GA-690.45 managed to distract the *Tnuva* truck's driver with a simple tap on his shoulder, causing him to swerve towards the highway's shoulder rather than into the black bullet tearing up the roadway.

Jay filled Joshua in on some of the details of the hack, at least what he knew about the incursion. Throughout Jay's description, which was already out-of-date and growing more so by the minute, Joshua resisted directly calling the white-hat team. They still had their hands full and didn't need any distractions, let alone the added pressure of the Big Kahuna breathing down their necks with a frustrated, unrestrained rant.

"Did you call in another team?" Joshua asked, referring to a second white-hat team, ensuring that the under-fire team had enough resources, and relief, if necessary.

"Both teams were already on their way in when I called," Jay responded. Hazon had three white-hat teams, a *pluga* (squad) of five 8200-unit graduates each. The other two had mobilized after receiving the alert. While half lived outside of Jerusalem, all were already at Hazon Labs or *baderech* (on their way).

The Threat Level (TL) had been holding at a disconcerting yellow-orange for the past thirty-plus minutes. Joshua anxiously waited for the TL to drop to a solid yellow or even a yellow-green swirl, which would signal the start of the system's diagnostics and reconciliation report that would determine the full extent of the breach. As if willing the TL to change (which he did), the screen color on his phone shifted to a yellow-pale green swirl. While they weren't out of the woods yet, Joshua felt unrestrained relief.

"Yes!" he shouted, offering a triple-staccato fist pump to the air, and then a fist bump to Jay, who gladly joined in. "We've got some green. Finally," Joshua said, breathing a temporary sigh of relief. Containing the threat was step one, assessing the extent of the damage would be the next hurdle.

"Hallelujah, thank you, G-d!" Jay said, then continued with the Hebrew version, saying, "*Baruch Ha-Shem*."

"Ugh, I'm happy too, but '*Baruch Ha-Shem*' that's got to be a first?" Joshua asked, air writing a *Beis-Hei*, the phrase's acronym.

"Actually, not. The HaMikdash3.0 bug is pretty contagious."

"I better be careful then. Now could you please drive a little faster?" Joshua said, trying to remember the last time he'd said, *Baruch Ha-Shem*, blessed be His name, in a show of gratitude.

*   *   *

"Did he really say faster?" the legion of squeaky-voiced Guardian Angels shouted in a single terror-filled chorus in near-perfect unison.

"Oh, this can't end well," one GA said.

They locked their wings together for added support and held on for dear life… that is if angels were alive in the human sense of the word.

The most daredevil GA among them noted, "Let's all try to relax here. This could be fun, you know." The others looked at him cross-eyed.

Picking up on the theme, the oldest of the GAs, GA-690.0, tried reassuring the others, "A nice cleansing breath might help." He then added, "Let's sit back and enjoy the ride. Think of it like Disneyland."

Unfortunately, none of them had ever been to the Magic Kingdom and eight of the nine remaining GAs imagined the "happiest place on Earth" was one of the scariest places ever.

"Here we go, ready in 3, 2..." They all joined in on the countdown, but never made it to one, jumping instead directly to blast off as they were G-forced back into their seats as if Jay had given the Range Rover engine a hit of nitrous oxide to turbo-charge the air-to-fuel engine ratio. In truth, Jay's extra speed was due in no small part to two new Guardian Angels, GA-695.2 and GA-695.3, who busily blew enriched air into the engine manifold to optimize the 14.7 parts air to 1 part fuel ratio. The tag team worked with restraint to keep the backseats from lagging behind the chassis, leaving either Joshua and Jay or their fellow Guardian Angels, in the proverbial dust.

Like clockwork, Joshua felt the now familiar pensiveness overtake him, an uncontrollable visceral response that seemed to be happening more and more often lately. Jay looked across to his friend and understood the "why" of Joshua's contemplative silence and the welling of tears at the corner of his eyes. Yesterday's ghosts had once again invaded the present. Isolating the specific trigger for the unwelcome intrusion wasn't rocket science. It always seemed to start as they passed the *HaMeshuryanim*, the seven iconic armored vehicles, skeletons of the convoy that had battled for the road to Jerusalem in 1948. The heaviness hit its zenith around *Lifta* and lasted until they passed the Chords Bridge. The challenge, however, was getting to the Chords Bridge whose design was intended to resemble a harp with its long cables as the strings. At night, the Bridge was often lit up, filling the sky with thematically varied colors as a warm welcome to Jerusalem, but not for Joshua. For him, the Chords Bridge only offered him a mournful tune. Jerusalem filleted him every time; and, yet he couldn't imagine living in any other city.

Despite the usual Friday madness, they made good time, flying through the traffic from Herzliya to Jerusalem. Unfortunately, they hit the predictable snarl of cars and buses on the notorious, wide-sweeping turn along *Sderot Ben-Gurion* above *Lifta*.

There were still miles to go before reaching their offices near First Station at the Jerusalem Venture Partners (JVP) office complex, established by entrepreneur Erel Margalit. Joshua often questioned his choice of office locations. On paper, the incentives were good; the environment well-suited to the size of their startup, but for him the real selling point was the view from his second-floor office window. *Har HaZei'tim*, the Mount of Olives Cemetery, rose dramatically to dominate the Old City's eastern vista. So many memories and tragedies that punctuated his life were all linked to his family's final resting place. That's why he couldn't leave Jerusalem… he couldn't leave them.

"I'll turn onto *Sderot Rabin*, once we clear this mess," Jay said, referring to the roadway that would take them past *Gan Sacher* and which would hopefully bypass at least some of the traffic heading into the *Mercaz*, the City Center.

Joshua nodded absently but continued to stare out the window at *Lifta's* mostly abandoned buildings, which, though overrun by wild weeds and rife with colorful graffiti, still hinted at the village's former prestige with its multi-storied hillside structures and uneven paths leading to arched entryways. A popular hiking spot, *Lifta* boasted two freshwater pools fed by natural underground springs. The pools were frequented by trekkers looking for a brief respite from the heat, as well as students from the nearby *Yeshivot* who used the southern pool as a *mikveh* for ceremonial immersions before *Shabbat*.

The memories were still painfully fresh. Joshua had stared out the window back then too. It had also been a Friday with only a few hours to go before the start of *Shabbat*. Despite the intervening fifteen years, the memory of the long drive from *Ben Gurion Airport* lived just below the surface. His grandfather's regular driver, Yonatan Levy, cautiously drove behind the *Chevra Kadisha* (Jewish Burial Society) van carrying the bodies of his parents and the smaller casket of his beloved dog, Boomer. It was a miracle they made it out of the airport as the long-bearded men from the *Chevra Kadisha* had flatly refused to take Boomer's casket in the same van as Joshua's parents. "Humans and dogs, not good, not right," one said in broken English. The other repeated the statement in Hebrew, adding a disgusted grunt and a hallmark Israeli *tsk*.

Jacob Katzenstein was having none of it, noting that all *Ha-Shem's* creatures have souls, and they had no right to deny Boomer's soul an eternal rest. For good measure, Jacob added, "Who do you think you have to thank for the parchment scrolls used in writing a *Torah*?" That ended the discussion as the learned men knew that animal excrement, including dung from a dog or cow, was used to tan hides in preparing parchments for various Holy writings.

Joshua's *Bar Mitzvah*, the coming-of-age ceremony at age thirteen for boys, should have been a celebration with *shofar* blasts and candies thrown at him as he read from the *Torah*, his parents joyously *kvelling* nearby. That's how it was supposed to be... how it should have been. Instead, he spent the week sitting *shiva* for them. Joshua's parents were buried in the family plot on *Har HaZei'tim* near Oma Rachel.

Joshua's final "resting place" was secure, a spot next to the rest of his family. For many Jews, the choice of burial on/in *Har HaZei'tim* was a simple matter of logistics. Those interned there hoped for a short tunnel approach to the famed Golden Gate, also known as *Sha'ar HaRachamim*, the Gate of Mercy, believing it would give them a first-in-line, front-row seat, so to speak, to the arrival of the *Moshiach*, a subject of much controversy and hostility among the Abrahamic faithful. After East Jerusalem was recaptured from the Jordanians in the 1967 Six-Day War, Jacob, along with a group of Holocaust survivor friends, took on the responsibility of helping to rebuild a portion of the cemetery destroyed by the Jordanians. The survivors of Hitler's genocidal reign had no bodies to bury or places to memorialize their lost families. The restoration of *Har HaZei'tim* was an act of rectification, restoring what the Jordanians tried to erase — smashing headstones and denying the identities of the dead to obliterate any semblance of a Jewish connection to the Land.

Already a successful entrepreneur, Jacob Katzenstein had the foresight to purchase a large family plot in 1972, on the second tier of the *Har HaZei'tim* cemetery. If home is where one's family is, then the cemetery was home for Joshua. His first official visit to the cemetery had been on his fifth trip to Israel.

Joshua E. Katz was six years old when his Oma Rachel, his paternal grandmother, passed away. The family had already planned the trip to celebrate the *Pesach* holiday together, one of his Oma's favorite holidays, and based on her doctor's prognosis more than likely her last *Seder*. The doctors gave her around six months, maybe more with the latest round of chemotherapy and the experimental biologics treatment using antibodies to treat the HER2-positive breast cancer. But during a routine blood draw from the access port in her chest, her condition, already terminal, took an unexpected turn for the worse when she developed septicemia, a raging blood infection. Joshua and his parents caught an earlier flight, three days before they were scheduled to leave Colorado for Israel. Flights were overbooked and the circuitous route they were forced to take included a lengthy layover in Russia. The delay was several hours too long as Joshua's Oma died while they were still *en route*. In the plane's first-class cabin, Joshua sat next to his mother Shoshana, while his father David, the only son of Jacob and Rachel (nee Koehler) Katzenstein, sat across the aisle from them. The funeral was delayed long enough for them to arrive in Israel and travel from Ben Gurion Airport to the *Har HaZei'tim* cemetery.

Oma Rachel's burial plot was near the *Path of the Kohanim*, just outside of the cemetery since members of the Jewish priesthood, *Kohanim*, are forbidden from contact with the dead with but a few exceptions. Joshua's father David stood just inside the cemetery, near the short wall separating the cemetery from the *Path of the Kohanim*. Joshua's father held him steady on the uneven rock wall to keep his feet from touching the ground. Jacob stood a few steps away, watching as the body of his beloved wife of thirty-five years was lowered into the ground. She was wrapped in Jacob's white and blue-dyed wool prayer shawl. Jacob could see no further use for it since he would only take it out of its embroidered velvet bag and dust it off for the High Holidays to please Rachel; or, six years prior when he was the *sandek* at Joshua's *Brit Milah*. He sat in Elijah's Chair holding Joshua on a pillow as the *mohel* performed the ritual circumcision. The family album had several photographs of Jacob covering his eyes and wiping away tears with his *tallit* as Joshua's Hebrew name was read aloud. He was named after Jacob Katzenstein's younger brother Yehoshua murdered by the Nazis at age 10.

Rachel had bought the *tallit* for Jacob and fittingly, it would be laid to rest with her. Jacob looked at the *tallit* as a relic of another time when prayer came naturally to him. But he was tired of praying to a G-d who never heard him, never listened. Where was G-d in 1938 when Nazi thugs broke into his parents' home on Kristallnacht? He'd only been seven at the time, but carried the rage of someone twice his age, as he watched his father being dragged off to the Buchenwald concentration camp. David Katzenstein was released two weeks later, beaten and bloodied, and more determined than ever to save his family. But fate intervened as the family waited and waited for their visa number to come up… it never did. Instead, in a bureaucratic snafu, Esther Malka and Jacob's five siblings were deported to the Theresienstadt ghetto in 1942. Jacob and his father were deemed healthy enough for slave labor and were sent directly to Auschwitz. Against all odds, he and his father survived together, until two years later when Jacob thought he caught a glimpse of his mother and siblings as trains arrived at the Auschwitz platform on October 4, 1944, during the *Sukkot* holiday. Jacob only knew the date because some of the new arrivals insisted on holding onto some semblance of normalcy, keeping track of Jewish time to mark *Shabbat* and the holidays.

Jacob's father soon joined the rest of his family, collapsing during one of the roll calls. The *appels* provided cruel sport for the guards as the half-starved prisoners were forced to stand in the freezing rain for hours. After standing for three hours, Jacob's father finally fell to the ground. Deemed too weak to be of any further use to the Nazi death machine, David Katzenstein was reclassified, and like his wife and other children, was consumed by the fires of the crematoria. Jacob managed to survive, avoiding the last death march out of the camp, until Auschwitz was liberated on January 27, 1945, by the Soviet Red Army.

Jacob looked over to the headstone he'd erected bearing the names of his family. There were no bodies he could bury, only the memories of them. Hopefully, his mother Esther Malka would welcome Rachel. She could be a difficult woman. Almost immediately, he regretted the unkind thought. Oh, how his sweet Rachel suffered these last years. What kind of "merciful" G-d did that? Jacob Katzenstein had asked the question too many times. He inhaled sharply at the thought of his wife trying to hide her pain from him. She rarely complained, not with the surgeries, radiation, and chemotherapy treatments she'd endured. She'd lived to see a dream or two fulfilled, long enough, and then some, to see David finally married off to Shoshana, and then becoming Oma Rachel to Joshua, a little less than nine months later.

The breast cancer treatments left her weak; she tired easily. The partial mastectomy left her right arm edematous and permanently swollen from the lack of lymphatic drainage. She could hardly lift Joshua even when he weighed a mere 3.4 kilograms (7 pounds 8 ounces). For the better part of ten years, the cancer had been kept in check until it finally metastasized to her spine. Hers was a ten-year struggle punctuated by joyous family celebrations. Some said it was why she fought so hard, for so long, even hoping to see Joshua reach his 13th birthday to celebrate his *Bar Mitzvah*. Her dream fell short by seven years. A woman of unselfish grace, always more concerned about those she would leave behind, Oma Rachel prepared a special gift for Joshua; a velvet bag embroidered with the pattern of a colorful, geometrically fractured Star of David, a pattern by noted artist, Yaacov Agam. One day, it would hold Joshua's *tallit*.

Finally freed from her suffering, Rachel Katzenstein, age 67, blessedly died in her sleep, less than a week before the Passover 2002 holiday. The family had planned to celebrate the holiday by the sea, staying for the week at the Park Hotel in Netanya. Since Rachel Katzenstein had gotten sick, all of the *Chagim*, the holidays, were a gift and a time to be spent with family, a time to gather while otherwise living over eleven thousand kilometers apart. Passover would be as normal as possible; celebrated with a traditional *Seder*, readings from the *Haggadah*, and the retelling the story of the Jewish people's escape from Egypt with Joshua asking the *Ma Nishtana* four questions which looked at how the Passover seder night differed from all other nights. That was the plan. Instead, the family sat an abbreviated *shiva*, for only three days instead of the usual seven, preempted by the Passover holiday. Instead of going to *Netanya*, they spent a relatively quiet holiday in Jerusalem with *Pesach,* a much-subdued affair.

Joshua climbed down off the wall, while his father openly wept for his mother, clinging to Joshua's mother who he called Shosh, short for Shoshana. They stood together as bags of dry, dusty earth mixed with fine gravel filled the grave holding the body of *Rachel bat Reuven HaKohen*. Joshua slipped away, joining his Opa near the small headstone inscribed with the names of Jacob Katzenstein's parents and siblings. He took hold of his grandfather's hand and looked up, his eyes brimming with tears. "Opa, Oma's up in heaven, right?" though it was more of a statement, a pronouncement no one would dare argue with.

Jacob nodded, words escaped him, even comforting ones. He had none for himself nor any he could offer his grandson.

"Opa, do you think everyone will like Oma?" The innocence of the question gripped Jacob's soul, his eyes brimming with tears and turning his guts inside out. Words continued to elude him, leaving room for Joshua to supply his own answer to the question.

"I think so. Bubbe's waited a long time to meet Oma," Joshua confidently said, using the *Yiddish* word to refer to his great-grandmother, then quickly added, "I bet, they'll play Rummikub® together too."

Jacob wiped a single tear trailing down his cheek.

"Don't be sad, Opa. You'll see them both one day."

For this, Jacob found the surety of voice. "Yes, let's hope it's still while I'm in this world. But if not, then in the next."

Jacob Katzenstein had expressed the longing for the resurrection of the dead in this world, an event foretold by the Prophets with the coming of the *Moshiach*. Always one to hedge his bets, Jacob Katzenstein left room for the possibility he would not live to see that day and accepted an alternate hope of joining his loved ones in the World To Come, the afterlife in *Olam HaBah*. It was a heady topic on any day, and certainly one for a six-year-old to consider, even a boy as precocious as Joshua.

Joshua was about to ask Jacob another question when his parents joined them near the small headstone. Together, they said the *Kaddish* prayer for Jacob Katzenstein's parents and siblings and all the others killed in the Holocaust.

Once they concluded the prayers, Joshua looked to his father and said, "Oma and Bubbe can play Rummikub® together, can't they?"

"That's a nice thought, Joshie."

"You know, Oma always let me play with her. Can I be on your team now?"

"Sure, son. Whenever we play the next time. How does that sound?"

"When?" shouted Joshua, a little too loud for the reserved decorum of a cemetery. But all around him, his family couldn't help but smile at the unbounded innocence of youth.

The next Rummikub® game was held on the first night of Passover. It was long past Joshua's bedtime, but he insisted on playing a game in honor of Oma. No one could argue with that. They opted for an early *Seder* with the traditional readings and rituals. They even sang the last half of the service; the part with the *Hallel*, prayers of praise, and other songs celebrating G-d. Singing songs of praise would seem inappropriate in light of their loss, but not so in Judaism where Jews honor G-d even while mourning the death of a loved one. Their singing was, however, notably subdued, punctuated by sniffles and deep sighs, but they tried to carry on for Joshua's sake.

With childlike glee, Joshua ran to open the door for *Eliyahu HaNavi*, Elijah the Prophet, who supposedly visits each home as a welcomed guest during the *Seder*.

According to tradition, Elijah is given a place of honor at the Passover table with a separate cup of wine, the 5th cup of wine, symbolizing the Final Redemption since he is charged with announcing the coming of the *Moshiach*. Joshua closed the balcony door and raced to the table to see if the "Messiah's advance man" had drunk from the special cup of wine, prominently placed in the center of the table. He'd secretly marked the cup to be able to detect any change in the wine's meniscus level. While checking the levels though, he accidentally touched the surface of the wine then absently licked his finger, tasting the delicate Malbec blend for the first time, but which evoked a distant memory he couldn't place. Not surprising. He was only eight days old when the *mohel* for his *Brit Mila*, his circumcision ceremony, dipped a cloth napkin into the cup of wine for him to suckle on. With a sigh, Joshua shrugged, then added, "Maybe next year!" For the first time that evening, his family truly smiled.

They sang 'Who Knows One' a counting number-associated song, and then concluded with the *Chad Gadya*, which translates to *one little goat*. A not-so-simple lyrical narrative, a mashup of Hebrew and Aramaic verses symbolically representing historical conquests by the nations over the Jewish people, but whose ultimate Salvation rests in G-d's hands when He kills the Angel of Death in the last verse.

Ironically, or perhaps not, Salvation also came that evening for the Katzenstein/Katz family. At 7:30 PM on the evening of March 27, 2002, a suicide bomber detonated an explosive device in the Park Hotel in Netanya. Of the 250 guests attending the Passover seder, twenty-eight were killed, and one-hundred-twenty attendees injured, twenty severely. The Katz/Katzenstein party was a no-show at the *Seder*, though their table was still reserved and the blood-drenched placard bearing their name lay scattered among the dead… or rather what was left of the dead. Amidst the tumult of Rachel's death and the *shiva*, no one had bothered to cancel their hotel reservations. It wasn't the first time, or even the second time, that fate had intervened, nor would it be the last.

At the time, no one could have, or would have, conceived that seven years later, during the week they were supposed to celebrate Joshua's *Bar*

Mitzvah, he and his grandfather would stand on the hilltop rise looking towards the Temple Mount on the *Har HaZei'tim* cemetery as the empty plots next to Rachel Katzenstein's own grave would stand open, ready to accept the remains of Joshua's parents, David and Shoshana Katz.

Again, fate stepped in. This time, it spared Joshua from meeting the same end as his parents, and Boomer. Next time, Salvation wasn't assured, since the outcome would depend entirely on Joshua.

Chapter 12

The modern city of Jerusalem is built on layers; layers of history burned into its stones telling the story of its repeated destruction and conquerings. Destruction after destruction with tens, sometimes hundreds of years separating each conquest. With the founding of the State of Israel in 1948, the battle cry against Jerusalem rose to fever pitch as the recently founded country of Jordan tried to erase every last trace, the last evidence, of any Jewish presence in the city. From its graves on the Mount of Olives to systematically destroying every synagogue and home in the Jewish Quarter, its precious stones were broken into pieces and pulverized to dust or repurposed as paving stones for streets and walkways on the Temple Mount.

For the next nineteen years, Jerusalem was once again occupied, a painful modern conquest until its liberation in the 1967 Six-Day War, a bloody victory won in just six days. While the battle for the Holy City would continue year after year and into the new millennium, her hidden archeological treasures came under the watchful aegis of the Israel Antiquities Authority. Discoveries layered over by time, secreted beneath the floors of houses and shops, or casually discarded in rubble piles from unauthorized excavations on the Temple Mount were recovered. The warren of disconnected tunnels beneath the city sloped and slanted, converging then stopping suddenly as if a hand were holding up a stop sign that said, do not enter. For hundreds and thousands of years, her secrets remained locked away, until ready to be reclaimed.

In 715 BCE, in the 14th year of King Hezekiah's reign, *Sennacherib's* Assyrian armies threatened to conquer Jerusalem. To build up the city's defenses, Hezekiah dug a 533-meter-long winding tunnel stretching from the *Gihon Spring*, the city's main water supply, to the *Pool of Siloam*. Several hundred years later, Zedekiah, the last King of Judah, would use these same tunnels beneath Jerusalem to flee from a different enemy.

> And it came to pass, that when Zedekiah the king of Judah and all the men of war saw them, then they fled, and went forth out of the city by night, by way of the king's garden, by the gate

betwixt the two walls, and he went out the way of the Arabah. But the army of the Chaldeans pursued after them and overtook Zedekiah in the plains of Jericho; and when they had taken him, they brought him up to Nebuchadrezzar king of Babylon to Riblah in the land of Hamath, and he gave judgment upon him.
— Jeremiah 39:4-5

As discoveries go, even building a parking lot or repairing a burst sewage pipe can unlock Jerusalem's secrets. In 2004, the 2,000-year-old Pilgrimage Road was discovered when a sewage pipe burst in the Arab village of *Silwan*. Repairs uncovered an ancient Roman Era road extending from the *Pool of Siloam* to the foot of the Temple Mount at its southwest corner. From there, pilgrims might bathe in one of the dozens of *mikvaot*, ritual baths, before ascending the Temple Mount.

It is not beyond simple imaginings that one tunnel connects to another coursing through deeper layers under the city, intersecting, merging, or diverging over Time. Historically, biblically, the "king's garden" was located in the *al-Bustan* neighborhood in the East Jerusalem village of *Silwan*, also known as *Siloam*. So then, how or why would a cave located over a kilometer away become associated with King Zedekiah? Was there once a passage connecting the southern end of Old City to its northern end as it was described by Jeremiah?

If such a passage were ever found, it would crisscross the city through a network of interconnected tunnels and caves. Such a breach would certainly be more than adequate for one person or even a small army to pass through, even a raiding party, or be used as an escape route such as one theoretically used by King Zedekiah to evade Nebuchadnezzar's soldiers as he fled to the plains of Jericho and where he was eventually caught.

If found, such a breach would be the perfect place to plant a small suitcase nuke, if one existed; or, just a regular bomb that would forever change the *status quo*. Such an explosion would follow the path of least resistance, collapsing the unseen array of underground tunnels, taking out whole city blocks, killing hundreds, maybe thousands.

Perhaps, that passage has already been found, hidden behind a seemingly seamless wall where a real-life demon, a *Jinn*, might be found. Maybe...

* * *

Ismail al-Masri's instructions were clear. *Ahmed* and *Jibril* were told to wait for him in the lower Templar Era chamber before moving the explosive tanks into Zedekiah's Cave. Instead, they moved the tanks into the cave; three of which contained diesel fuel mixed with fertilizer and distributed them throughout Zedekiah's Cave using the map Ismail had given them. The placement would yield the desired effect… one which the man known as *Ismail al-Masri* had meticulously planned. The fourth tank would deliver the pièce de résistance, chlorine gas.

Neither of the cousins understood why they needed to meet first, and "then and only then" place the tanks as *al-Masri* instructed. What difference would it make? To them, there was no difference, besides *Ahmed* knew *Jibril* needed to get to work, and the diesel oil tanker was only on loan. Filled with ammonium nitrate, the tanks were especially heavy to move until the clever *Jibril* rigged a wonderful pulley system to lower the tanks down to the Freemason's Hall and then move the tanks into position throughout the cave.

al-Masri only saw the big picture and had no clue how long these preparations could take. *Ahmed* was a detail man. Practically speaking, it was the limit of the flexible corrugated fuel hose, even with its extension hose, for pumping the diesel oil into the tanks, which took the most time. Once done, positioning second and third tanks deep inside Zedekiah's Cave was relatively easy and quick, though they needed to be careful when replacing the cap with the timers. Again, thanks to *Jibril* who was tall enough to place and preset the timers.

G-d only knew how the Jews brought the stones they quarried here up to the *Haram al-Sharif* for their Temple. Probably more of their devil magic, *Ahmed* thought. He felt confident in being able to explain to *al-Masri* why they had moved the tanks before their meeting. It would be a rush job otherwise and a single spark could make them all go, kaboom… *al-Masri* would definitely not be happy about that. *Ahmed* decided that if *al-Masri* planned any more such momentous operations, then he would ask for funds to invest in a diesel oil tanker of their own, and a larger team to handle the heavy tanks. His twisted neck made physical labor doubly painful. *Ahmed* put all of his arguments in order, thinking perhaps he should start with the obvious and most important for a devout Muslim. Friday was a Holy day, and if they waited as *al-Masri* instructed, they could very well miss the last time for *Asr*, the third prayer, before sunset.

Despite his appearance as a devout Muslim, *al-Masri* could care less about prayer times or anything else to do with Islam. Al-Masri was a practical fellow, and having told *Ahmed* to wait until after regular closing hours, even though the cave was technically closed on Fridays, he expected his orders would be followed. The cave's proximity to the Damascus Gate and the permanent Border Police presence in the two Guard Towers meant their actions could be easily observed, and any unusual activity might call unwanted attention to the plan. After-hours maintenance work in the cave was typical, and would not be immediately suspect. *Ahmed* was told to precisely follow *Ismail's* instructions. He'd been warned. Only, he wasn't a very good listener.

After positioning the last of the tanks, the one which irritated *Jibril's* nose despite the mask he wore, *Ahmed* and *Jibril* dropped down into the Templar Era cavern, located under Zedekiah's Cave. Neither heard nor saw any more *Jinns*. *Jibril*, for one, was grateful. The lower chamber was considerably cooler, almost cold, as compared to the rest of the cave.

"He's late," said *Jibril*. While taller than his cousin, he was two years younger and nervously shifted from one foot to the other foot, trying to warm up. He wore a short-sleeved tee shirt which afforded him little warmth or protection from the lower cavern's cooler air.

"He'll be here," *Ahmed* said, picking at a stray cuticle on his thumb until it bled.

"How long are we supposed to wait? I hate this cave, even more so down here."

"What's to worry? You'll only find Christian ghosts down here, cousin. Long dead. Not so scary. Conquered by *Suleiman the Magnificent*." *Ahmed* laughed then tapped his cousin on the shoulder and laughed. "Woo!"

Jibril nearly jumped out of his skin, brushing aside the offending touch, then shoved *Ahmed* into a moss or maybe it was a fungus-covered wall. *Serves him right*, he thought.

Behind them, they heard a shuffling noise and froze immediately. They had remained near the entry hole to the lower chamber, but no one dropped down from the cave above them.

"Yes, woo," said a new voice, growling as he spoke. Angry, but eerily calm. "You were told to wait until after regular closing hours. Someone might have seen you. Heard you."

The sandaled feet kicked up tufts of dirt and tailings of the quarried stone that settled in the enclosed space. The sudden movement startled the two young men who quickly aimed their knives at the noise as the lone figure of *Ismail al-Masri* emerged from the shadows behind them like a *Jinn*.

"*Ismail*," Ahmed said, deferentially dipping his head. "We did not know you were here." Fearful of the price Ismail might extract from him for showing disrespect. It could be high. He wondered if *al-Masri* had been here all this time? If not, then where did he come from?

"Apparently," *Ismail* said, his word choice and tone betrayed his proper British education but not much else about the man who'd assumed a leadership role in their cabal of wannabe terrorists. The thick scar traced a jagged line down the left side of his face, pulling on his eye and leaving it half-closed while lifting his lip up into a permanent sneer.

"We wanted to finish before you arrived," *Jibril* said, eager to leave this place quickly. It made him nervous, as if death could touch him in this underground tomb.

"And yet those weren't your instructions," *Ismail* said, keeping his voice even but inwardly seething at their unmitigated incompetence.

"Yes, but…" *Jibril* started to say, but the words were cut off by a strangled cry.

With the swiftness of a tiger, *Ismail* struck, dropping into a crouch and sweeping his leg at the back of the tall Arab's knees. With a brief, pain-filled scream that lasted only a second, *Jibril* fell to the ground as the man known as *Ismail al-Masri* brought his sandaled foot across the young man's throat and crushed his windpipe.

"*Jibril*! You killed him."

"Yes, and if you don't wish to end up like him, *Ahmed*, you'll never again disobey my instructions. Follow each word that I say to the letter. Is that understood?"

"Yes *Ismail*, my apologies. I intended no disrespect."

"This one, he is your best, *Ahmed*?" *al-Masri* asked with a disdainful look at the shorter man, pudgy around the middle. *Ismail* hated insolence almost as much as he despised incompetence.

"My cousin. I valued trust over common sense. A thousand apologies, *Ismail*," bowing his head deferentially. "He knows, knew, nothing of the plan."

"You're only saving grace, *achi*," *Ismail* said, adding a light chuckle which seemed wholly inappropriate considering he'd just killed a man. In the short term, *Ismail* needed *Ahmed*. But soon, he too would be dispensable. They all were. *His* plan to see Israel and its Jews vilified for the atrocity to follow would be a glorious day. Hallelujah! The true identity of the perpetrators would take days to discover and by then the blood lust would be at a fever pitch and no amount of truth would be able to restrain their vengeance.

The man called *Ismail al-Masri* only needed to make sure no trace of him, or his fingerprints could ever be linked to any of it. They would emerge as the saviors of the Savior, wresting control of all of Jerusalem. Hallelujah, Praise the Lord

Ahmed was surprised that *Ismail* referred to him as, "my brother," using the Hebrew term *achi* (אחי). They were neither brothers nor friends, and the *Jinn* had just killed his poor cousin. Granted, the greeting was part of their behavioral training exercises, watching endless hours of published videos of Israeli soldiers posted on social media sites. They watched to learn how the soldiers acted, their casual interactions, how they stood, carried their weapons, chanted, laughed, and greeted one another with the simple word, *achi*.

"What about…" *Ahmed* asked, pointing to the body of his dead cousin. The dead eyes stared back at him wide in terror, accusingly even in death.

"Him? You can claim him as a martyr, if you wish?" *Ismail* said, nudging the body with his sandal.

"Thank you, *Ismail*," *Ahmed* said, grateful his voice hadn't cracked or betrayed his heightened emotions. *Ahmed* hoped for a glorious death, honoring *All-ah* with his own sacrifice rather than being dispatched in a G-d forsaken cave beneath the Arab quarter. It would be good to honor his cousin, claiming he'd died an honorable death as a *shahid*, a martyr. In the confusion of the attack, no one would know the difference. A good death. What was one more body?

There was little left to do, save for recording a video of young *Barak*, though *Ahmed* wondered if *Ismail* might then dispatch with him as well. He understood the plan, but still found it difficult to reconcile the deaths of so many of his *actual* brothers, though *Ismail* made a compelling argument. "They will die only if *All-ah* wills it. This you must know. All is with *All-ah*." Who was he to argue the point?

"Come, show me what you have done," said *Ismail*, brushing the limestone dust from his foot with the back of his hands, before casually stepping over *Jibril's* body. *Ahmed* climbed out of the entrance hole to the upper cavern first, giving the man known as *Ismail al-Masri* a moment with his long-dead Templar brothers. He inhaled deeply, breathing in the history of his predecessors. He would finish what the Knights started centuries before, a legacy passed on through the generations, under Rome's watchful eyes and quiet blessings. Soon, he would be rid of this place, of these people. With a last look around the cavern, he imagined the flickering candlelight as the Knights Templar gathered inside the city's tunnels, strategizing and planning how to crush *Saladin's* Muslim hordes.

But in 1187 AD, it wasn't to be. He, would avenge their mortal souls and end the obscenity of their false gods. The time would once again be for Him to rise and reign over Jerusalem.

Non nobis Domine, non nobis, sed Nomini tuo da gloriam… Not to us L-rd, not to us, but to your Name give the Glory.

* * *

The voices sounded more distant, echoing down from the cave above.

"Come my brother, let us make ourselves a *shahid*," al-Masri said.

"Rest well, cousin," *Ahmed* said, with a last look at his cousin's broken body, and rolled the heavy stone across the entrance to the lower cavern.

Tzion heard the sound of scraping and labored breathing, then a loud thud. He waited another five minutes before crawling out from his hiding place in the Templar cavern, which was now noticeably darker than when he'd first taken shelter there. He was sure the intruders had left as he could no longer hear their voices or the soft shuffle of their feet on the dirt floor. Still, he didn't dare use the flashlight App on his phone. Carefully, he made his way in the dark toward the opening to the cave above where he expected to see a glimmer of light reaching down from the upper cave, but there was none. Slowly, he shuffled across the floor, his arms extended out in front of him when his foot clipped the edge of *Jibril's* leg. In the next instant, Tzion went flying forward. His right temple slammed into the edge of the steppingstone, knocking him unconscious.

As head wounds do, Tzion's bled profusely. Guardian Angels 696.0 and 697.4 sprang into action, checking their backpacks for anything to stem the bleeding. To their surprise, they found a First-Aid kit and an abundance of transparent gauze pads which they used to pack the site, then wound an entire roll around Tzion's head. Both GAs would swear the First-Aid kit wasn't there earlier when they'd unloaded their supplies. But at least now they understood the overnight camping gear and the task ahead. They were charged with watching over Tzion and would sit with him until…

The dizzying, Waze-defined route across Jerusalem helped them bypass the worst of Friday's usual traffic jams. Jay nudged his best friend as the navigation system estimated another seven minutes before they'd arrive at JVP's back parking lot which also served the First Station.

"I'm awake," Joshua said in a clear voice. "Better yet maybe just 'wake me when September ends,'" quoting lyrics from the popular Green Day song.

"You and me both," Jay replied, half-wishing they could skip all the preliminaries and get to HaMikdash3.0's launch at the end of October.

"I hope we'll be saying one of your *Baruch Ha-Shems* once we see the extent of the damage," Joshua said.

"Always a good thing to say, no matter what," Jay noted, shrugging his shoulders. Publicly wearing his newfound spiritual self, even around his best friend, still took some getting used to. "Speaking of which, what was with all that *Moshiach*-talk back at Reichman. I mean I'm fine with it, but just a little surprised."

"Me too. It sort of just came out," Joshua said, shaking his head wondering how his mouth got ahead of his brain. He popped down the visor to check his reflection in the mirror and adjust the bedhead effects of sleeping with his head against the window. For a brief second, he glimpsed a man's face in the mirror, a stranger he'd never seen before, but whose face was nonetheless familiar. Joshua closed his eyes, trying to shake away what could only be a hallucination. Cautiously, he opened his eyes and looked again in the mirror. It/He was still there. The face seemed to be offering him the wisp of a smile; a thin close-lipped smirk that slightly turned up at the corners of his mouth. Friendly even. He quickly looked over his shoulder into the backseat in a logic-defying query to see if someone was actually there. Technically speaking, no one was.

The helpful host of Guardian Angels that had stayed with them from Herzliya until the Chords Bridge vibrated near the upper limits of Man's visual sense. Even if Joshua could see them; or, sense them with his Spidey sense, Uri'el had already sent them back to Heaven for safekeeping. After Jay's daredevil race back to Jerusalem, the GAs' collective nerves were understandably frazzled. They'd done their part, as did Uri'el by making himself known to Joshua E. Katz in a mere blink of an eye and which was banked for the future.

"Hope you're ready for your close-up?" Jay said jokingly.

"What?" Joshua asked, still distracted by the fleeting image he'd seen in the mirror.

"Arik orchestrated a little distraction," Jay said.

"Dare I ask?"

"Just a bunch of balloons and congratulatory signs."

"A little like Nero fiddling while Rome burned?"

"At least you, we, won't be alone. According to Arik, the alert brought in the troops. He figured we would need a good cover story about why we're all assembled here today," Jay said.

"Piece of cake… it's my birthday," Joshua said, smirking.

"Really?" Jay asked, though he immediately questioned the logic of Joshua's statement.

Joshua nodded enthusiastically, keeping up the ruse and wondering how long it would take for Jay to figure it out. Jay knew perfectly well when his best friend's birthday was, except the usually sharp-as-a-tack *sgan* must be almost as exhausted as he was to forget the obvious.

"How did I not know this? Sorry, happy… hey, wait a minute," Jay said, doing an immediate one-eighty for missing Joshua's birthday. "Your birthday's in April, like mine!"

"No kidding, genius."

"We could probably get away with it since nobody fact-checks anything anymore."

"True that. Except I'm partial to my *Bar Mitzvah parsha*," Joshua said, referring to the *Torah* portion associated with one's Hebrew birthday.

He and Jay shared the same *Bar Mitzvah parsha,* though Joshua's birthday was in mid-April, April 13th, while Jay's was March 25th. Despite being born a year apart, Joshua in 1996 and Jay in 1995, their *Bar Mitzvah parsha* was *Shemini*.

"I can't say I ever liked that *Parsha* too much," Jay admitted. "The Kosher laws and all. It made no sense to me considering my family never kept Kosher when I was growing up. I do now, but not then."

"I got stuck on the strange fire episode with Aaron's sons, Nadav and Abihu. The whole *Kohen* thing speaks to me."

"You do remember they died in that story," Jay noted, realizing Joshua needed no reminders.

"Ironically, death was contextually congruent to my *Bar Mitzvah*. Fire too, I guess," Joshua said, hiding a heavy sigh by blowing out his cheeks.

A world of memories were inextricably tied to Joshua's *Bar Mitzvah* and the celebration that never was… April was a rough month in general. *Smachot*/celebrations and the *Chagim* weren't in the cards for Joshua not when his Oma died, not for his *Bar Mitzvah* when his parents were killed, and not for any of the Passovers since then… In a word, Nisan/April wasn't Joshua's favorite month by any means.

* * *

Joshua came to live with Jacob when his parents, Shoshana and David, Jacob's only son, were killed when their private plane slammed into the side of a Colorado mountain. A freak April snowstorm with wind gusts of 75 mph. Joshua had narrowly escaped their fate by chance, or so everyone believed, since he was supposed to be on the plane with them. While his parents closed their winter home in Aspen, Joshua decided to head to Israel early to spend some extra time with his grandfather.

His mom and dad, and Boomer were supposed to arrive a couple of days before his Oma's *Yahrzeit*. They'd make *Pesach* at the Laromme Hotel and Joshua would then have his *Bar Mitzvah* ceremony at the *Kotel*, reading from the *Torah* on the *Shabbat* immediately following Passover. That was the plan. News of the plane crash hit the Colorado airwaves when Joshua and his grandfather were in Tel Aviv at the Carmel Market. Official word came about four minutes later through the Israeli Ambassador to the United States, Eliahu Ben-Elissar, a close family friend. It took several days for the recovery, but eventually his parents' remains — or what little could be recovered from the Colorado mountainside — were flown to Israel and buried in the family plot on *Har HaZei'tim*, next to Oma Rachel.

Once again, a time limit was placed on the length of the *shiva*. This time, the traditional seven-day *shiva* period was hyphenated to less than a day with the start of the Passover holiday which began at sundown on the day his parents were buried. Much of the *shiva, such* as it was, was spent sitting in the back of a taxi heading back to Netanya to "celebrate" the holiday. Once again, the official commemoration of the Exodus from Egypt was tempered by loss, just as it had been in 2002 when his Oma died, now compounded further. Passover would forever be a time of mourning and not of freedom, and more fittingly linked to *Yom HaShoah*, Holocaust Remembrance Day, which came five days after the last day of Passover on the 27th of the Hebrew month of *Nissan*. Joshua and his grandfather went through the motions… reading from the *Haggadah*, having their first taste of *Matzah*, the traditional flatbread, and more or less welcoming *Elijah the Prophet* into Jacob Katzenstein's 20th-floor duplex apartment overlooking the beach in Netanya.

With some prompting from his grandfather, Joshua reluctantly rose from the table, but instead of opening the apartment door, he slid open the balcony door. He figured Elijah should have to work for it, fly in, or wait for the *Shabbat* elevator to ascend the twenty floors, just like everyone else. As Joshua closed the balcony door, Jacob Katzenstein allowed himself to cry.

"*Saba…*" Joshua said, calling his grandfather by the Hebrew version of grandfather. He'd rarely seen his grandfather cry, not even at the funeral. Now his entire body shook silently screaming until finally inhaling sharply and wailing uncontrollably. The sound ripped through Joshua, shaking his soul and threatening to tear him apart. He was only centimeters away from breaking down himself. He came over to his grandfather and stood next to him, stroking his cheek, then took his grandfather's head to his chest and held him silently.

Jacob cried for the barely healed wounds ripped open, for his son and daughter-in-law, for his wife Rachel who'd passed from breast cancer seven years earlier, and for his family killed in the Holocaust. And for Joshua, who would one day have to go on alone. Between the heaving sobs, Jacob Katzenstein looked into his grandson's eyes and shared his hope, his vision.

"One day, Joshie. One day," Jacob said as he trudged off for a short nap on the couch, "just five minutes." Joshua let him sleep through the night, covering him with one of *Savta* Rachel's knitted throws; a colorful patchwork quilt pieced together from hundreds of mismatched yarns that surprisingly all worked together.

By week's end, Joshua became an Israeli citizen as there was no question about where or with whom he would live… there was no one else. He would live in Israel with Jacob. Israel would be his home. And as befitting the generations following the Holocaust, and as the grandson of Jacob Katzenstein, winner of the Israel prize, Joshua soldiered on with his *Bar Mitzvah* as planned at the *Kotel HaMa'aravi*. These parts of Joshua Katz's biography were public knowledge, part of the official company lore. The blank spaces in Joshua's history were notable, ostensibly designed to protect the privacy of a minor during his tumultuous high school years, ages 13-17. Ostensibly. His official biography focused on his exemplary IDF service in the 8200 Unit and not on his brushes with the law.

The specific triggers for his mental journey back in time, the emptiness seizing his heart, didn't much matter. In this particular moment, everything in his world was about the confluence of time — past, present, and future embodied in the hopeful promise of HaMikdash3.0. In an epiphany of sorts, Joshua realized that everything in his life, the good and the bad, what he'd planned for and the unexpected, the missing years of his youth, and even the friends and family he'd lost along the way, had all conspired to bring him to the here, the now, and to whatever he was moving towards in the future.

With gratitude, he whispered a prayer of thanks for having reached this time in his life, a *She'hechiyanu*, "Blessed are You, Ado-nai our G-d, King of the Universe, for giving us life, for sustaining us and for enabling us to reach this time." Amen.

Half a Celestial world away, Joshua's impromptu prayer, long overdue in its arrival, was well-received across Heaven's realms. Uri'el smiled and offered a single, *Amein* as the pre-*Shabbat* choir of Guardian Angels offered a mixed chorus of Ameins, Hallelujahs, and Blessed Bes, heralding Joshua's return. Truth be told, his song had been sorely missed.

The next time fate intervened, G-d's salvation would be helped by more than a million Guardians Angels, joining forces with His Ministering angels and a host of Archangels led by Uri'el. Each had played a role in the evolution of the Katzenstein/Katz soul root, or more precisely in one Joshua E. Katz's becoming.

*   *   *

Jay negotiated the final roundabout on *David Remez Street* to *Derech Hevron* before pulling into the JVP parking lot. Joshua was at once surprised and relieved to see a full contingent of cars, together with an assortment of regular bicycles and motorbikes, the Hazon Labs' crew. The all-hands-on-deck red alert, even on a Friday, had brought the team together. Joshua knew he tended to inspire diametrically opposed emotions, love or hate, and rarely anything in between. Apparently, a new one had been added to his repertoire, loyalty. He understood they had come to show their support. They'd all worked too hard to let a hacker bring the company down, not when they were so close to launching HaMikdash3.0.

The full parking lot, however, had also drawn the attention of the company's resident protestors, who snapped off dozens of photos as the Range Rover pulled into the one remaining empty spot near JVP's rear entrance.

"Let's try to be as casual as possible with a twist of triumph," Jay said, nodding to the encampment across the fence line. The Hazon Labs team had assembled at the back entrance with an odd mix of balloons and signs. Hazon Labs' Executive Vice President of Marketing Eric "Arik" Anders was surrounded by about two dozen Hazon Labs employees who'd shown up in response to the red alert. Anders juggled an armful of colorful balloons that conveyed a mad mix of messages, "Happy Birthday" "Congratulations" "Mazal Tov" in Hebrew and English, and a few clearly celebrating the birth of babies, in the plural with baby bottles and color-coded ribbons that stretched the ruse's credibility. The group clapped and cheered to beat the band. It took Joshua a moment to process the scene before smiling appreciatively, though he found his attention drawn to the petite blonde, standing to Anders' right.

"Let's try not to disappoint anyone," Joshua said as both he and Jay climbed out of the Range Rover.

With ameboid fluidity, they were immediately engulfed by the staged welcoming committee. *En masse,* they passed through the building's security checkpoint and headed to Hazon Labs' headquarters. The petite blonde, with fiery green eyes, casually walked in with the group as if she belonged.

Joshua turned slightly to Anders, a tall, blonde-haired, blue-eyed German, Jewish on his father's side, and who preferred to be called Arik, was known to have a reputation with the ladies, lots of ladies, who were infinitely attracted to his boyish/goyish good looks. For the most part, Arik kept his personal life separate from the office, except apparently for today, and in the middle of a damn crisis. "Great job on the diversion," Joshua said with a certain head bob.

"I had a lot of help. Everyone was worried. Besides, the party is a good decompressor, a boost for morale, and we actually did hit a milestone before the shit hit the fan. I'll post a few pics on FB and Twitter just for appearance's sake. Should be enough to satisfy the newshounds," Anders said with the confidence of a veteran marketer. Formerly with Google's Madrid office, he'd left the cushy position to work with the fledgling startup.

"You've outdone yourself. Hopefully, it should do the trick too. If, we manage to get out of here before *Shabbat*."

"I had a lot of help, plus the printer was mostly agreeable today," he said, referring to their always fickle printer. "I had to use the one in your office too. Hope that was, okay?"

"Sure," Joshua said, wondering if he'd locked away everything before he left. "I gotta ask you though, since when do we hand out security passes to every Tom, Dick, or Jane as the case may be? Did I miss the memo about today being bring your girlfriends to work in the middle of a damn crisis day?" Despite Arik's stellar PR save, Joshua couldn't hide his annoyance.

"Um, she's not my girlfriend…" Anders said, followed by a pregnant pause, "she's *your* girlfriend, boss. Remind me to introduce you two later!" Anders winked then broke away, escorting the pretty blonde wearing form-fitting beige pants, and a black tee shirt into a conference room down the hall.

The brief parking lot deception, staged for the curious eyeballs ever alert to HaMikdash3.0 happenings, had hopefully covered up the day's sine wave-like rollercoaster intrusion event and remained clueless to the drama still unfolding inside. Despite the system's analysis, indicating a reduction in the Threat Level, the real threat was in fact not contained; its footprint, however, remained undetected by the White Hat team.

Joshua and Jay made a beeline to the secure lab to the right of the entrance, offering appreciative, corkscrew-tight nods to the Hazon employees lining the hallway. They flashed their company ID badges to the card reader and entered the air-gapped room, or at least what was supposed to be an air-gapped room. Hopefully, by now the White Hatters had pinpointed the breach site and assessed the extent of the damage.

J1 and J2 stepped into the cybersecurity war room like generals stepping into battle. They looked at the wall-mounted digital display, showing a deep aquamarine "go" level signal. Distracted for a fraction of a second, Joshua realized the alert status traffic light's green-blue color was a near match to *his* new girlfriend's eyes.

"Okay, let's hear it," he said.

But before the white-hat team could respond, a young woman with Day-Glo® blue and pink-tipped highlights at the ends of her thick blonde curls rushed into the room, exhaling an apology for being late. The wetsuit she wore hung casually around her waist, giving everyone an eyeful of her multiple tattoos, including a hissing snake that coiled around her barely-there bikini top. "My bad, boss. I was at the beach."

"Clearly," Joshua said.

"Didn't want to waste any time changing," she said, feeling the rush of blood racing to her cheeks. He could always make her feel small. But not today. Today was her day to make him feel small.

"No problem, we just got here."

"Almost beat you then," she said, offering him a toothy grin which carried nothing but malice.

"Better get on with it then. I want us all out of here before *Shabbat* starts."

"No problem, I'll map all user actions before and since the incident. New login attempts as well. No worries, boss. Jackie be quick, Jackie be nimble but always quick," she delivered her retort with a third-person finish, punctuating the statement with a sharp double snap of her fingers, then headed to her workstation.

She didn't get far. "Jackie, here," Anders shouted and tossed her a teal blue Hazon Labs T-shirt. "Matches your hair. Some of it."

"Thanks," giving him one of her best sneers. Gay-boy couldn't appreciate girl beauty.

Leaning into Anders, Joshua whispered, "Thanks." He generally tolerated the cyber teams' quirks and odd behaviors, actually from all of the software teams which could vary from Tourette Syndrome-like clucks, whistles, or a running stream of epithets to on-the-spectrum avoidance of all eye contact. But the team didn't need any unnecessary distractions.

Blessedly, Joshua landed on this side of normal. He couldn't begrudge their unique expression patterns. Jackie, however, took odd to another level. He'd been surprised when she approached him for a job. They'd never gotten along when they were in the 8200 Unit… oil and water was a better description. He never understood the "why" of that either. They'd grabbed a lunch or two, coffee once, and maybe even drinks, pleasant enough. She claimed they had a one-night stand, for which he had only vague recollections of her or the entire night. It was awkward and over before it began, at least as far as he was concerned. Then she turned snarky, outwardly hostile less so to him, but to Julia. He guessed it made sense. He, Jérémie, and Julia were a team, and despite having the right letter in her name, she hadn't been invited to join their little circle as J4.

Old news. She did good work since joining Hazon Labs, and he couldn't complain, except for her talking in the third person. He knew it bothered others at Hazon.

"Okay then, let's try this again. Let's hear it," he said.

Chapter 13

Hazon Labs' didn't attempt to hide the intrusive practices of its parallel processing and recursive neural network. Each HaMikdash3.0 member had authorized Hazon's all-access pass to user data with a simple check mark in the box next to paragraph 15 subparagraph 10.3 of the user agreement. To further ensure no one could later claim, "I didn't know" each member was also required to install the proprietary security package including a firewall that allowed for secure bi-directional information flow, remote updating, and advanced filters to keep bad actors at bey. The elaborated multi-path builder helped inform dynamic user interactions with presented scenarios and "go-to" options matched to user responses. The technology teaser not only tapped the interests of the gaming community but also others eager to sample the latest and greatest innovations in customer acquisition and user experiences.

Security considerations were ongoing, every minute of every day as users brought new content into their computer's cache. Hazon Labs recognized that not all of HaMikdash3.0's netizens were fastidious in maintaining cybersecurity when not on the site. Cookies, spiders, and other creepy crawlers resident on a customer's computer system might infiltrate Hazon's network, even when users were not actively engaged in 3.0's spiritual business. The number of potential access points was at a minimum equal to the number of HaMikdash3.0 members, a growing number that stood for the last two-plus hours at 1,770,666 — the number when the site shut itself down. The number of vulnerable access points was magnified as users/members on average had 2.4 connected devices. At the same time, the number was also somewhat reduced since the member count didn't distinguish between users with only one avatar or those who had purchased multiple avatars, averaging out to 1.78 avatars/member.

Technically, Joshua could be included in the "Bad Actors" category since his Dimensional Torah Codes search program siphoned information from the data gathered for building HaMikdash3.0's extensive user profiles and adaptive AI user-specific responsivity. It was a vigilance versus privacy versus all-access trade-off that Joshua was willing to risk in the hopes of finding what he needed to mine from the petabytes of gathered data.

Hopefully, it would be enough, and he wouldn't have to sift through exabytes of data, or G-d forbid probe data anywhere near the zettabyte range.

HaMikdash3.0 served many masters. For Joshua, it was a means to an end, multiple ends, all involving his DTC search program. Directly or indirectly, the *Dimensional Torah Codes* program was already enhancing user experiences by grinding through a wonderland of algorithmic layers to help profile and then build secondary profiles for its members to elevate user experiences with "you must be reading my mind" content offerings. The dynamic, multi-dimensional user profiles were further informed by answers from an extensive questionnaire users completed at registration. The additional data points were then used to identify, authenticate, and validate a member's encoded *Torah* address, the cluster of letter groupings in the Hebrew Bible that told their life story... and that of the entire world.

Today's Red-Level threat only applied to critical backbone and infrastructure issues, as well as to any unauthorized access, an intrusion, into the system. They'd put in the usual safeguards and checkpoints and then added a proprietary image-based user authentication system. They'd managed to fend off a near-constant wave of baby assaults, but Black Hats were a relentless bunch, and without fail, could nearly always find a way to outsmart the White Hat guardians at the gates. Joshua could only imagine what the problem might be and prayed his *Dimensional Torah Codes* subroutine had not been affected by the intrusion, or worse had been the actual target of the attack. It seemed unlikely that DTC could be the target since only he and Jay actually knew how he'd evolved his graduate school thesis into the dimensional imaging program.

With today's incursion, Joshua couldn't help but wonder if he shouldn't add another category of watchers: "minders" who would watch the watchers. Not everyone joining the HaMikdash3.0 rank and file was what, or who, they appeared to be. Call it a wolf in sheep's clothing, a chameleon, a poseur, and in the worst-case scenario a traitor in their ranks — their own in-house Judas. Joshua's mind always landed on the worst-case scenario, which at times bordered on the paranoid but with cause. He'd once operated on the Black Hat side of the aisle which his very expensive attorney argued was a matter of "youthful indiscretion, your Honor." He knew and understood tactics, and the plethora of motivations ranging from the playfully benign to the maliciously destructive. He braced himself against whatever the White Hat team had discovered and hopefully crushed.

"Sorry for the 3-alarm, boss," Shai Rosen said. Then, nodding to the Alpha team, "We contained the infiltration almost immediately after the first event." His lead White Hatter had come in to support the White Hat Alpha crew. He quickly assumed a leadership role, which, by default, also put his head on the chopping block.

"The operative words being, 'almost' and 'first event,'" Joshua noted. "Can we maybe skip the preamble of excuses?"

Shai called up a computer screen. "We think it came in as a trojan tagging onto a user avatar that subbed all the little Lamb sacrifice purchases with *Miss Piggy* heads."

Joshua examined the chimeric graphics, noting the seamless editing, replete with Miss Piggy's iconic pearl necklace, transplanted onto a lamb body with its little lamb legs.

"We had 2,743 users stocking up on the discounted *keves*, an *Erev Shabbat* special, when Miss Piggy showed up," Shai said, using the Hebrew word *keves* for lamb. "Thankfully, it was only a small number of users. The message boards blew up almost immediately," he said, then with a hint of embarrassment, "actually, that's how we caught it."

"That 'actually' doesn't make me happy. I'm glad 3.0's members are on top of things, but why didn't the chimeric graphic automatically trip the system's intrusion sensors? Whoever did this replaced our graphics at the root directory."

"Or on the fly," Jay commented.

"That's a scary thought," Joshua said.

"Our graphics identification and analysis system are better than anything else out there, bar none. The problem is players can upload their own graphics file with the user-defined avatar creation option."

"And giving players the option to personalize their avatars is *not* the problem. The filters should have detected something that wasn't kosher… literally!"

The unintended joke drew a few light chuckles, which were silenced with one look from Joshua. "Till we can screen user-defined avatars better, all accounts can only use stock avatar images."

"Got it."

"So, who did Miss Piggy track back to?" Joshua asked, hoping they could nail the specific user with any luck, and set an example. Maybe include a public flogging or shaming for good measure *ala* Game of Thrones.

"We're trying, but that's proving to be a little more challenging than we thought. We're running the system's virtual memory backward. We should be able to tag its entry and identify the user."

"Right, and there's always the chance that the user is the black hat and not just an unwitting carrier," Joshua said, considering the implications. "How are we dealing with customers?"

"Bashir and I issued a blanket apology to their registered email addresses for the mix-up," said Max Feldstein, one of the newer white hats. He'd graduated MIT and came to Israel as a lone soldier serving in Golani, and one of the few non-8200 alumni working at Hazon. He and *Bashir Aboud* made a great team, respecting one another's deeply held religious convictions. *Aboud* had gotten a Master of Science degree from Caltech and done a stint at CERN in developing secure systems for transferring Electronic Health Records, specifically large file imaging data. While Fridays didn't carry the same restrictions as *Shabbat* for Muslims, Joshua was nonetheless impressed that *Bashir* had come in.

"We're also monitoring the chatter. These guys like to boast," *Bashir* said.

"Don't I know it. Whoever it is has been locked out. They'll be looking for congrats somewhere. Keep me posted on anything suspicious," Joshua said, then with a shake of his head, "the pig head is a bit concerning."

"At least they have a sense of humor," Shai said, adding a breathy chuckle.

Joshua let the chuckle pass, but only just barely. Substituting a pig for a Temple sacrifice, even a virtual one, was unacceptable on more levels than Joshua cared to count. He'd made every effort to make HaMikdash3.0 conform to the religious rules governing sacrifices, Temple design, clothing, and *kelim* (vessels) to lend authenticity to the virtual world and to also engage a wider user base — Jewish, non-Jewish, religious, and non-religious alike, beyond those with pure gaming interests. Genetically engineered hybrids and chimeras probably fell into a separate category in Kosher versus non-Kosher. Immediately, he thought of posting a question to HaMikdash3.0's Council/*Vaad* forum — a lively and popular discussion group on contemporary *Halachic* questions in Jewish practices.

The forum was open to all HaMikdash users and was already popular with non-gaming members, including Rabbinical, Yeshiva, and Divinity students. The forum used a debate-style format, allowing HaMikdash3.0

members to opine (*paskaning*) on contemporary, real-world issues by choosing either a *Beit Hillel* perspective, emphasizing broader context and practical applications, or a *Beit Shammai* approach focusing on stricter adherence to core principles. Topics were approved and AI-moderated as they hoped to maintain some semblance of civility in an arena where religious views could all-too-quickly devolve into shouting fests and where participants would type in all caps, hit ctrl B, use red font colors, and punctuate freely with multiple exclamation points. They embedded a dissension filter not to co-opt the discussions, but to provide preventative mediation and hopefully steer topics towards more productive discourse using civil tone and text netiquette. The topic of genetic engineering of people, animals, and crops for food and medical/health applications, along with a dozen other seminal issues was the theme for their sponsored "Debatable/*Machloket*" Conference, a "hybrid" offline/in-person conference, tentatively scheduled for November 2025.

Joshua envisioned HaMikdash3.0 living in its virtual home, but with abundant crossover opportunities into the real world with brick-and-mortar engagements and interactions, with commensurate additional revenue streams. He didn't doubt that pre-launch enrollment might take a hit with the PR fallout from the Miss Piggy affair, and the site remaining down for the foreseeable future. The big question was how to mitigate the damage to the system, and also from a PR perspective.

"Arik, let's start tracking, and hopefully plugging, any leaks about Miss Piggy," Jay said, knowing the team could quickly configure an App alert to search for any memes or text-based posts about the incident, searching for relevant keywords in primary posts, shares, and comments.

"On it," Arik said with a definitive head nod.

"How many people got booted off the site?"

"Since hitting our milestone at 9:07 this morning, we added 270,666 new users. When we shut down, eighty-six percent were still online. So, we're looking at 232,772, plus existing customers 49,035 with active logins at the time," said Hila Segal. She'd been crunching numbers as soon as she raced back to Hazon Labs from her home in *Mevaseret Tzion*, a Jerusalem suburb, located 11.7 kilometers to the west.

"Did any of our newest members buy the mutant lamb?" Joshua asked.

"No, but thirteen were on the forums, though none on the specific *keves* discussion thread," Hila responded.

"Any other numbers we need to worry about?"

"I'm running a log file on chats to get a read on comments from our angrier members. Numbers too."

"Make sure Arik gets those numbers and copies of the texts too," Joshua paused to consider how best to compensate members for the inconvenience. "Let's try to keep our customers happy. Credit every account with 100 *ShekCoins*. Double that for anyone online when we went dark, and triple that for users who had the misfortune of buying that creature."

"For all 2,743 users?" Shai asked incredulously.

"What? Is it coming out of your pocket?" Joshua's tone was sharp, more so than he intended.

"It's just that it seems pretty generous for something that wasn't even our fault in the first place."

"Everything, and I repeat everything affecting HaMikdash is under our *Hashgacha*," Joshua said, using the Hebrew term for supervision or providence, though the term was more commonly used in terms of *Kashrut*, Kosher food matters. "Do you have any idea how sacrilegious pigs are in Judaism? How many times a pig-this or a pig-that was used to defile a synagogue or for that matter the actual Temple?"

He hadn't intended to raise his voice, but like many *Kohanim* his temper could flare without much provocation. Over the years, he'd mostly learned how to keep it in check thanks to weekly yoga and daily mindfulness meditation. Joshua only realized how loud he'd been when Jay tapped him on the arm and threw him a stern "cool it" look. The matter was deeply personal. Joshua had been weaned on Jacob's Holocaust experiences. During the 1938 Kristallnacht pogroms of November 9-10, synagogues throughout Germany were destroyed and burnt to the ground. Jacob's synagogue suffered the added abuse of being draped in pig entrails, and the lintel of the Rabbi's house swiped with pig's blood, and only then was it torched. It was a memory never to be forgotten. Except that as two-plus generations had passed since the Holocaust, many millennials were often ignorant of the vile acts and atrocities of both the flesh and spirit perpetrated by the Nazis and their accomplices.

"Apologies, Shai. It's a touchy subject. Just take care of it. More importantly, I want you to backtrack to the first user who encountered Miss Piggy, then back further to user uploads for the last week, maybe we'll get lucky and find out who piggybacked the graphic into our system. Literally."

"Will do," Shai said, then added, "they might have stegged something else in with it too."

Elana Berg, a *Betzalel-trained* artist, and now Hazon Labs resident graphic artist, leaned into the computer screen to have a closer look at the graphic, "If we isolate the head, we can compare attributes to official and unofficial Miss Piggy headshot graphics formats. We might get lucky picking up the image's digital trail and be able to track it back to an online image source. I'll dig."

"Do it. Let me know what other image forensics we can tag up, including a pixel-by-pixel analysis. I don't want any more stegged surprises."

Joshua turned to leave, with Anders on his heels. "Have legal shoot a memo off to the Muppet folks so they know we're not interested in infringing. Also, put out a feeler and see if they want to partner with any of their *other* characters. Maybe they can act as helper guides or run the companion under-8 educational site."

"What if they want us to license?"

Joshua opened his eyes wide, communicating a long-standing answer in his silence… no licensing. Partners are partners, not customers, and share in the profits or losses.

They reached the short corridor leading to Joshua's double-wide corner cubicle. "Your lunch date is in *Meleke*. Her name's Davida." *Meleke* was one of two interior, secure conference rooms and the name of the highest-grade limestone used in the building of the *Beit HaMikdash*… the actual one.

Joshua rounded the corner, literally running into his girlfriend. "Davida, I presume?"

"My friends call me Davi. You are happy to see me, no?" she said, greeting him with a casual, double-cheek air kiss.

"It's been way too long," Joshua said, trying to play along.

"You have no idea who I am or what I'm doing here, do you?"

"Lunch, right?'

She leaned in suggestively and whispered into his ear, "Magen David Security Services," then pulled back far enough to see his reaction, hoping he'd been warned to expect her.

"Cute, only you're not exactly what or rather who I expected," Joshua said, surprised that the corners of his mouth turned up in a genuine smile.

"My partner David is out slaying giants. We thought this might be a great way of hiding me in plain sight," she said, offering him a well-practiced wink, one she'd used dozens of times on similar "girlfriend" assignments.

Joshua Katz wasn't a player, though he had many offers as one of Israel's most eligible bachelor millionaires. Matchmakers the world over, both the professional ones plus every Jewish mother and grandmother, viewed his impressive status as an open-door invitation to find him a *shidduch*, a match. Joshua didn't have time to spare for casual dating, or for a more serious relationship for that matter either. For now, it would only complicate his already intensely over-scheduled days and nights.

Davida, or whatever her name was, slung her leather bag over her shoulder, then in one smooth continuous motion, she spun on her heels, hooking Joshua by the crook of his elbow.

"We're kind of busy right now. No offense, but this isn't a great time."

"And exactly the right time."

"Did Anders call you in?"

"No, and I'm not psychic either. We've been monitoring some of your com channels. When the incursion alert went out, I thought it would be a good time to see your team under stress conditions," Davida stated matter-of-factly.

"And how exactly were you alerted?" Joshua asked, more than a little concerned about who authorized an outside company, even a highly respected security firm, like MAGSS, to access Hazon Labs' inner workings.

"Don't look so worried. We only have access to your outer rings," Davi said, hoping to reassure her new and, apparently, skittish client. "A necessity, if we're to understand the threats, especially if they turn out to be internal."

"I'm not sure they are," Joshua said.

"We'll see. I know this is not the best time, but bad apples tend to show their hands, especially if they're dirty. Also, anyone, not here?" she asked.

"Tzion Mengistu, my lead developer. It's his brother's *Bar Mitzvah* this weekend. He's cool though."

"I'm sure everyone's sparkly, but I'm still going to check them all out."

Joshua couldn't disagree with the approach. Crises tend to bring out the best and the worst in people. While Joshua highly doubted that the worst of the threats he received were sourced internally, they still needed to rule out all of the possibilities. Hiring MAGSS was a concession he'd been forced to satisfy Hazon's Board of Directors. Right after they took out a two-million-dollar life insurance policy on him… just in case.

"You do know that I'm only going along with this whole personal security thing because I have to and…" Joshua started to explain when she cut him off.

"What, am I such a hardship to be with?" she said with pouty pink lips.

"No," Joshua said, shaking his head. She certainly was a charmer.

"I have been briefed, thoroughly and I also know you're busy so I'll only trouble you for a short while, fair?" she asked, smiling disarmingly. "Besides, I brought lunch from Eucalyptus, and you should eat," she said, sounding a little too much like a Jewish mother. She affected a decent broken English which was an advantage for eavesdropping on conversations.

Normally, she'd never consider speaking about any of MAGSS clients, confidentiality breaches were frowned upon in her line of work, except Effi would get a kick out of knowing she was having lunch with his hero! She was looking forward to seeing the look on her nephew's face and maybe pumping him for more information about this HaMikdash3.0 game.

"Eucalyptus? Nice," he said, playing along with whatever charade she'd concocted. At least, it promised to be tasty and a welcome break from the fast-food he usually picked up. In the land of milk and honey, deconstructed gefilte fish, hummus, and Yerushalmi *kugel*, actual cuisine was a wonderful treat.

"I was going to order from *Shila*, but their lobster isn't exactly what you call, Kosher."

"Not even close," he said with a smile. "On behalf of Hazon Labs, we thank you for respecting the company's Kosher/*Kashrut* rules. I have been known to be tempted though…"

"Josh," she said in a seductive voice, adding a subtle pout to her blush pink lips, and the ever-popular Israeli tsk which could convey a dozen different meanings.

Despite himself, Joshua smiled. Very few people called him Josh. Jay for one. Julia for two. It sounded good coming from Davi. Her accent hinted to Eastern Europe, a lilt within Israeli-accented English, but that too could be a cultivated affect.

"You should know, this whole bodyguard thing doesn't sit right with me."

"Yes, I was told you might be," she paused, choosing her words carefully, "none too pleased." then, thinking about it, "difficult was also mentioned."

Joshua reacted with a genuine smile that surprised even him.

"We eat, we talk, you go back to work. Deal?" she said, but didn't wait for him to answer. Instead, she led him down the hallway to the *Meleke* conference room. "And yes, we will also laugh a lot, then you'll close your parabolic mike-dampening blinds and the exterior shutters. On Sunday morning you have the Jerusalem SPCA brunch, I will go as your date. I need for people to see us as a couple. Sunday night is your quarterly investor meeting, 17:00 start time. I'll drive you to Tel Aviv and hang around the hotel until it's over. Also being seen."

Joshua nodded, clearly arguing with her was pointless. He swiped his keycard to open the conference room and held the door open for her.

They sat opposite one another in the large conference room, which also served as a safe room, a *ma'amad*, when needed. She'd ordered every appetizer, a mix of vegetable, fish, and meat dishes on Chef Moshe Basson's menu — a feast that ensured leftovers for the Hazon team.

He helped himself to a yummy-looking, short-rib *Qatayef*, a decidedly non-dessert version of the Egyptian pancake, when Davida asked, "So tell me about the threats you've been receiving?"

He nearly choked on the lemon zhug condiment and coughed once to clear his throat. He was still trying to be clever with her, though he wasn't 100% sure why. "Do you want them in chronological or alphabetical order?"

"How 'bout starting with the ones which actually scare the shit out of you."

"What happened to your accent?"

"When it suits me. No one's listening now. My question, please."

They spent the next hour going over the cranks, crackpots, and crazies that put HaMikdash3.0, and by extension Joshua E. Katz, in their gunsights — a rather long list that cut across religious, ethnic, and cultural affiliations. As he spoke about HaMikdash, Joshua couldn't hide his disappointment at how it had become a lightning rod, a polarizing one, that divided people into two distinct camps but which, by default, and ironically also acted as a substantive unifier. He'd said as much during the Reichman lecture. All eyes were focused on Joshua E. Katz, half wishing him well, and the other half wishing him dead, or at least gone.

Joshua was anything but naive. He took the death threats leveled against him seriously, more than he let on. If Davi was there to protect him then he welcomed the assist. If she were fishing for motivations, he'd give them to her, but he wasn't about to let anyone know his true reason for creating HaMikdash3.0… that truth would remain between him and the good L-rd.

Joshua texted Anders, asking him to bring a copy of the file with all the active threats, a voluminous collection of eclectic emails and voice messages, and which included pictures of the protestors camped out in the parking lot. He also requested an inactive "mood ring" prototype.

The conference room door buzzer sounded, and Joshua unlocked the door. Anders handed over the file, "Had it ready," he said, smiling at Davida, then passed Joshua a sealed plastic bag with a finger-sized grey silicone ring inside.

"Thought you might need this too," Arik said, passing Joshua a laptop. "Anything else?"

"We're good, and thanks," Joshua said, tapping the laptop lid.

"I'm sticking around for a bit. I've got some work to do on the kiosks. Maybe, when, if, you get a chance?"

"Sure thing."

Davida smiled at Anders, looking for any tells in his mannerisms. The guy was as cool as a cucumber… maybe too cool. Practiced.

She waited until the door closed once again before opening the thick file. "Looks like I have my work cut out for me."

"You should probably add the unknown party who hacked us this morning to your list. I can't explain why, but the attack felt personal."

"Your Spidey sense thing?" she suggested.

"You get a feel for this kind of thing. This morning, I also got three calls, all from blocked numbers. My number isn't exactly in the directory. I didn't answer any of them."

"Could be connected, maybe they were giving you a warning, an ultimatum."

"What are you saying, if I had answered the calls none of this would have happened today? That we wouldn't have been attacked?"

"Whoa, slow down there. I didn't mean to imply anything of the sort. The psychopathology of these guys varies, but one aspect is interesting: timing and the personal aspects you mentioned."

"How so? And my apologies.."

She nodded, accepting the outburst for what it was… over and forgotten. "For one thing, it's a Friday, so minimum staff on hand. You weren't just out of the office, you were out of the city. You and Jay both. How many people knew your schedule, specifically during the hack?

"Way too many suspects on that front. Everyone at Reichman, for one. The lecture has been on the books for the last couple of months or more. A few hundred people attended. I'd have to check with Arik to see if he posted anything about Reichman online. My guess is yes. Plus, our parking lot groupies saw Jay and I leave. Besides, my work calendar is open to anyone in the company."

"Safe to say lots of people knew your schedule for today, at least the morning part."

Joshua nodded, not sure where this line of thinking was going. He was about to point that out when Davida asked, "What about old enemies?"

"I've kept my nose fairly clean."

She tipped her head to the side, questioning his response. With her contacts, she more than likely had access to his juvenile record. "You're in business, successful, smart, rich by most standards, handsome too, by most standards, that's enough to piss off a few folks who feel they've been wronged or slighted by you."

"And thanks, I think," he paused, taking a deep breath, "honestly, I can think of only one person who hates me enough to want to see me fail, even wish me dead."

"I'm listening."

"He's my former thesis advisor…"

"Ah, yes. The intellectual property lawsuit."

Joshua nodded. If she already knew the details, then he had no interest in rehashing that episode in his life.

"You haven't heard from him directly though?"

"No. Last I heard he left the University. I don't care, don't want to know where he is, or what he's doing."

"Okay, got it. But I'll look into it."

"We about done?" he asked abruptly, his tone brusque.

"Not quite, I was hoping you might give me a mini-tour of HaMikdash3.0, if that's okay? It would be helpful."

"You haven't been inside HaMikdash yet?" he asked, a little surprised. He would have considered it part of her due diligence.

"Honestly, no. My nephew tried to explain it to me, but he's thirteen so we don't exactly speak the same language. Why don't you tell me about HaMikdash."

"What do you want to know?"

"What would draw me to the game? Why would I want to play?"

With the gauntlet thrown, Joshua took up the challenge. "Our age demographics of registered users span ages 10-92, with a good representation across all age groups. First off, it's more than just a game. But that being said, from a gamer's perspective it's about points, acquisitions, the leader board so it has attracted a significant number of players who are in it for the prizes, the win."

"$250,000, right?"

Joshua nodded, then added, "Among other things, stock options, discounts, merch, and certainly bragging rights on becoming the *Kohen Gadol*... for those who qualify."

"Qualify?"

"There are multiple tracks which player-members can choose or be selected to fulfill. It goes along with the 'chosen people' theme. Males interested in pursuing a Priestly track must consent to give a DNA sample for analysis to see if they carry the associated markers on their Y chromosome.

"In the real world or virtual?"

"Real. It's free and non-invasive."

"Yes, but still intrusive."

"A choice."

"But not for women. Your Y-chromosome screening selectively eliminates women candidates from your Big Kahuna search?" she said, sounding slightly miffed. The disparity between male and female roles in Judaism, in most religions, always got her fired up. Things were changing, albeit at glacier-melting pace.

"Actually, not."

"Explain."

"*Kohanic* lineage is patrilineal, defined by markers, a haplotype of clustered polymorphisms on the Y-chromosome," he paused to see if she was following.

"My first degree is in criminal justice. Coursework in Forensics was a given, plus my family are all *Kohanim*. The men at least are."

"Not only the men. As you know it's not enough to have a father who is a *Kohen*, you still need to be Jewish, which is matrilineal. Our research partners have identified mitochondrial DNA markers that validate Jewishness, a Jewish gene. They're looking at women whose family tree also includes *Kohanim* on both the mother's and father's side to compare *non-Kohanic* and *Kohanic* mitochondrial DNA to identify new markers. A comparison might prove interesting. Ashkenazi women appear to descend from one of four maternal ancestors. So, there's likely something else hidden, another unique difference, that can distinguish between *Kohanic* and *non-Kohanic* women."

"Interesting," she said between bites of a fish shawarma profiterole. "These are good," she said, pushing the container over to Joshua, then wiping her hands. When the napkin came away from her face, she was smirking. "Without getting too sidetracked here, I imagine looking for a *Kohen* component in women has pissed off a few folks in the *Rabbanut*?"

"In their words, we, I, am undermining the very foundations of Judaism."

"Then, I'd call that definite progress," she said, smiling.

"One of the beautiful things about HaMikdash3.0 is we have an active community of scholars, researchers, scientists, and entrepreneurs among our members. They've pushed the frontiers on many fronts. Like the discovery of a potential mtDNA marker."

"We've spun off a genetics testing lab and grabbed a patent on the mtDNA screening process."

"Clearly, more than your run-of-the-mill video game."

"We've had seventy people go through the process, including three women. You're welcome to throw your DNA hat in the ring."

"Thanks, but no. I'm already in one too many databases."

"For the record, we have a testing lab at *Har Hotzvim* if you're interested," he said, referring to the sprawling hi-tech campus in the Jerusalem suburb of *Ramot*.

"I think I'll keep my DNA to myself," she said with a quick wink.

"The track isn't for everyone since there is a warning about bringing so-called 'strange fire' which could get you killed off."

"Again, in the virtual world or the real one?"

"Only virtual, as far as we're concerned," Joshua smiled. "I'll show you."

He handed her his VR/AR headset, a lightweight version that looked like wraparound sunglasses rather than the bulky clunkers.

"The site's down, but we have a sandboxed version for demonstrations."

"I forgot my shovel and pail, I'm afraid."

"No worries, you've got everything you need. Ready?" he asked.

"As I'll ever be…" she said, as he clicked on the sandboxed HaMikdash site narrating the scene for her. The laptop screen was linked to the touch-screen whiteboard at the front of the conference room.

"In this scenario, we take the story of Moses' brother Aaron and how Aaron's sons, *Nadav* and *Abihu* were killed when they offered up a strange fire to G-d. We then apply the theme to a storyline in HaMikdash3.0. We don't kill off a player entirely. But you can end up losing whatever 'wealth' you've accumulated such as property, businesses, *shekel* bitcoins, rights to perform certain ritual tasks and special tools, or worse-case scenario be sent to *Gehinnom*, Hell, for any transgressions. That's the game part. It takes a mixture of *chutzpah* and guts to take the Priestly track. We haven't had a lot of takers yet, just the seventy members I mentioned."

"Getting bumped off might not appeal to everyone, even virtually."

"There are plenty of other roles people can assume and tasks to perform which is how you earn points, credits, and opportunities." Joshua pulled up a registration screen with mini-movies highlighting the different jobs/roles.

"We have shopkeepers in the New/Old City Cardo, musicians and minstrels, ranchers and farmers who raise sheep and goats, fishermen in the Galilee feeding the hungry, winemakers who make both sacramental and dinner wines, including a lovely Riesling, weavers who make prayer shawls, scribes who can write *Torah* Scrolls and *Mezuzot*, as well as a few other specialized roles."

Joshua chose not to elaborate on the defenders, a serious game within HaMikdash3.0. The defenders were troubleshooters, watchers, and analysts, a role that heavy-duty gamers usually gravitated to, as did their counterparts, the sociopaths and marginal personalities with delusions of grandeur more interested in destroying worlds than building them. The would-be saviors standing against the would-be destroyers had evolved such that similar role-playing could be used to identify behavioral biometrics for psychological screenings of suitable candidates for security and military-related jobs. HuScreen was one of their latest spin-off startups.

"With HaMikdash3.0, people can simply enjoy the site for the social component with a gaming edge, earning points for picking olives then pressing oil for the Temple, visiting a gravesite and placing a stone to honor someone's memory, giving charity to a person in need, getting a blessing, bringing a sacrifice to the Temple, getting sprinkled with the ashes of the Red Heifer. It's about being a part of the *Third Beit HaMikdash* experience, even a virtual one."

"So that's why it's more than just a game," she said, removing the VR/AR glasses.

"Yes," he said, then paused wondering how much he should tell her about *his* HaMikdash3.0. More troubling though, was why he was even considering it?

She seemed to sense his hesitation. "The more I know, the easier it will be for me to keep you safe."

He switched gears to a plausible segue. "3.0 has both detractors and champions in the religious camps, plus outreach appeal to the unaffiliated or marginalized. The whole idea behind HaMikdash3.0 is controversial, but as long as we keep our 24-karat gilded doors of HaMikdash open our investors are happy."

"Sorry, but that doesn't ring true."

"Excuse me."

"This can't just be about the money. Or is it?" Davida asked, surprised that she sounded more judgmental than she intended, or maybe even a little disappointed at his bottom-line answer.

"You're right. For me, it's never been about the money," Joshua answered without offering any further explanation, just a vague distant look that brought the barest of smiles to his face. Joshua wasn't sure anyone could protect him, especially not from himself, but he wasn't about to dwell on that.

Davi was smart enough to know when to push and when to stop, but not before she noticed Joshua's eyes misting, betraying the emotional baggage he carried. He seemed to be biting back the tears, which he tried to cover, though not very well, by clearing his throat. She decided to change the subject, but only just barely. To be continued…

"Back to the Priestly track screening, what happens if someone doesn't pass the screening test? I imagine they'd get pretty pissed off to be booted out of the running for the top spot."

"Gamers are a serious bunch. But separate from that, the genetics screening is information for them and their family in discovering their past and possible future. If you don't pass, you can always request a re-screening, free of charge, and then take your chances at the Temple if you insist on pursuing the *Kohen* track. Let's face it, not everyone can be the *Kohen Gadol*. To quote Gavin McLeod of *Highlander* fame, "there can be only one," he said, then quickly added, "same with the *Moshiach*. In the end, there can be only one."

Davi didn't say it out loud, but the religious angle jumped to the head of the line. People were pretty protective of their beliefs, especially if they felt threatened, and it wouldn't take much to push a zealot over the edge. There were enough groups that took their religious supremacy a little too seriously, and which, by default, denied all other comers' rights.

"If we ever get back up and running, I'll set you up with an account so you can monitor the site for any barometer changes as people set up their personae when they register. You'd be surprised how open people are when they think they are operating with a modicum of anonymity. We flag 'em and try to diffuse any potential problems or conflicts before they happen."

"You're a regular United Nations."

"We're certainly a helluva lot more pro-Israel than the UN will ever be."

For the next fifteen minutes, in between nibbling on a chicken liver pâté Macaron and the "Jerusalem Mix" platter with *amba*, a type of pickled mango, Joshua showed Davida around HaMikdash3.0, using the VR/AR tools. She seemed to be genuinely impressed by the technology underlying the experience.

Joshua checked his watch and was surprised at how long they'd been talking. She was developing a cipher to solve an intermediate-level *Gematria* number puzzle for back engineering to the word and/or words contextually congruent to the Zedekiah's Cave storyline, when Joshua asked, "What's his name? Your nephew."

"His full name is Yehuda Ephraim Davidson. He prefers…"

"Let me guess, Effi," Joshua said without betraying the hint of a smile or any hint of recognition of this particular *Ben David*. "I'll set him up with a few extra *ShekCoin* credits."

Davida stared at him blankly.

"It's a good thing. You'll be his favorite aunt."

"His only aunt."

Joshua smiled; a bit envious of Davida's nephew. He'd grown up without any extended family. No aunts or uncles, cousins, or other long-lost relatives.

"There's also this," he said, handing her the plastic-wrapped package. Surreptitiously, Joshua activated the sensor with a gentle squeeze of the collar. It emitted a pale blue-purple, leaning more toward purple, detecting his emitted *Kohanic* energy signature. He handed the bag to Davi, careful to only touch the plastic bag and not the ring itself. "We're developing a sensory-enhanced wearable based on human frequencies. Still in the testing stages. Your nephew should get a kick out of it."

She opened the plastic bag and dropped the ring into the palm of her hand. Joshua immediately saw the not-so-subtle shift to red-brown hues mixed with darker brown streaks, the color of the jasper stone associated with the tribe of *Levi* on the *Kohen Gadol's choshen,* the gem-encrusted breastplate.

He tried to hide his surprise at the unexpected color change. *That's different*, he thought. The device's sensors were primed to pick up *Kohanic* lineage energy signatures among other frequency signatures. The frequency range associated with the *Davidic* line was still under development, but all signs put it in the 750-1200 Hz range: the beryl gemstone's frequency. Maybe women and men differed in their frequency expressions… which would make sense. While still experimental, the demonstration Davida had just supplied might be the key to unlocking another aspect of the *Davidic* lineage. The wearable was a new area of research for HaMikdash3.0 based on marketing tools that captured galvanic skin responses to assess mood and customer/shopper/user engagement. The frequency detector was an updated version of the 70s mood ring craze but which only used body temperature to effect a color change.

"Thanks, I'm sure he'll love it. I should warn you, Ef is going to want to meet you. Check that, he absolutely will want to meet you. He couldn't stop talking about you and of course HaMikdash."

"Anytime, I look forward to meeting him."

"Why don't we pick this up on Sunday or you're welcome to join us for Friday night dinner?" The invitation was out of her mouth before she knew what was happening.

To Joshua's surprise, he said, "Sure, that would be great. I'll bring the wine."

Rather than trying to backpedal, she extended the invitation further. "We're in *Katamonim*," she said, writing her address on the back of her business card, then handing it to him. Her hand lingered on his for an extra moment.

Joshua was on his feet, escorting her to the conference room door. She turned to face him; the two stood uncomfortably close together in the doorway, but neither made an effort to move away from one another.

"What time?" he asked, aware that her hair smelled of sunflowers.

"Maybe come by before *Shabbat*, you can go to *shul* with my nephew, or after. No pressure."

"Great," he said, genuinely looking forward to dinner with Davida, and meeting her nephew, Effi Davidson, one of HaMikdash3.0's multi-avatar-personae members. Small world, he thought.

"I hope you're prepared. He's gonna go totally apeshit when he meets you."

"Red or white?"

"I'd love a Gewürztraminer, if you have time to pick one up."

"No problem." He'd bring the Cape Verde Gewurtz he found hidden on a back shelf at *Basher*, the neighborhood cheese shop on *Emek Refa'im*. "See you tonight. And Effi," he casually added, smirking.

She tipped her head to the side, still surprised he had used Effi's preferred name. Momentarily distracted, she was surprised when Joshua leaned down and kissed her cheek.

"For appearance's sake," he said.

"Indeed," she said, spinning on her heels before disappearing around the corner.

"Glad to see you two getting along so well," Anders said, coming around the corner.

"She seems very competent."

"And very attractive. Could be trouble, boss?"

"Drop it." Though Joshua couldn't disagree. Except distractions were the last thing he needed. "How's the '*Korbanot*' kiosk testing going?"

Anders responded with a sigh of his own, punctuated by "Oy."

"That bad?"

"We could use your help."

"No problem. I can give you about a half hour. That lunch just about did me in. Just give me a second," Joshua said, re-entering the conference room. With a quick surreptitious look over his shoulder, he grabbed a napkin from the table, then carefully picked up Davida's glass from the base, noting the pink lipstick on the rim.

"Pink? Not the best color for you, boss," Anders said, coming up behind him.

Startled by Anders, Joshua nearly dropped the glass.

"Thought I'd clean up some. A lot of leftovers."

"The White Hats might like some of the good stuff."

"Good idea. Any chance we can put off the kiosk issues till Sunday?"

"Sure, early afternoon work for you?"

"Should work. Check my Outlook."

"No problem. *Shabbat Shalom!*"

"To you too," Joshua said even though Anders technically wasn't Jewish. Yet. The greeting had become universal, especially in Jerusalem. If he remembered correctly, Anders was looking into officially converting to Judaism to address his paternal-only Jewish lineage.

Joshua wrapped the glass in a padded envelope and locked it in his filing cabinet. He'd swab it later and send it to the lab for DNA analysis. Effi Davidson had yet to sign up for DNA testing. This wouldn't be the same, but perhaps still informative. Maybe, he'd bring up the testing over dinner. The kid would probably go apeshit with him asking and offer up a sample then and there. He grabbed his backpack from the floor and headed down the hall.

There were only a few stragglers from the cybersecurity team still around. Jay left while he was lunching with Davida. He texted, apologizing for heading out without saying goodbye, and wished Joshua a *Shabbat Shalom*. Joshua responded with a *Shabbat Shalom* and thanked him again for today, for everything from start to finish, using an A2Z signoff.

Hopefully, Jay wouldn't hit too much traffic getting out to *Giv'at Shmuel* before *Shabbat*.

Joshua poked his head into the cyber war room. "I'm heading out. Get your reports in as soon as they're ready."

"No problem, boss."

He poked his head into Arik's office, but he'd already left. He grabbed one of the pre-loaded swag backpacks, Arik always kept handy by the door.

Effi Davidson would love the bag of HaMikdah3.0 branded goodies. He buzzed himself out and groaned, "Oy…" remembering he'd biked over that morning. Even the short ride would do him in. He crossed the First Station parking lot to where he'd chained his bike. Bone-tired, Joshua leaned over the bike rack. He didn't relish biking even the short distance to *Rehavia*. He fiddled with the lock, keying in the right code but it wouldn't release. He tried it a second time but with the same result.

This is ridiculous, he thought. His fingers came away with a gummy sticky feel. Out of the corner of his eye, Joshua saw her coming towards him. The tee shirt cover-up had long since been abandoned and once again she wore the wetsuit draped around her waist. If at all possible, Jackie had pushed it even lower on her hips, exposing herself even more than before.

"Open, open, you piece of …" Joshua said.

"Looks like you could use some help," she said.

"Locks gummed up with something. There, got it!"

Jackie touched the rear tire, "*Ichsa*," she said rubbing her fingers together and in a sing-song, five-year-old childish way added, "someone doesn't like you."

He managed to contain the glare and turned his attention to the rear tire.

"Oh, man. Just not my day." No way was he going to be able to bike home now. At least, they hadn't slashed the tire. Hopefully, the grease or whatever it was would come off, though he wasn't sure what kind of solvent to use that wouldn't damage the tire. Best to bring it to the *Ofanim* bike shop on *Pierre Koenig Street*. They always did good work. "This day's just been a winner all around," he said, hearing the fatigue punctuating every word.

"I've got my car here. I'm happy to give you a ride."

"You sure? I can always call a cab."

"Puhlease, I'm right here. You can rack your bike in the back."

"I appreciate it."

"NP. You're in Rehavia, right?"

Joshua nodded, then hefted the bike onto his shoulder, careful to avoid the sticky mess.

"The car's just a little way down," she said, leading him through the nearly full First Station parking lot. "Nice bike. Carbon fiber?"

"Yeah, you know your bikes. Pricey, but a good all-around choice. I didn't know you were into cycling?"

"Not and not. A friend of mine can't shut up about it. About the only thing that gets him up and out of bed." Shut up, shut up, her mind screamed. Jackie wasn't sure why she alluded to the Professor. Stupid, stupid, Jackie. What... were you trying to impress the self-centered egotistical bastard that you have a boyfriend? Like he cares that you're seeing someone. Except, he sure as hell would if he knew who, she thought, and laughed to herself or so she thought.

"Something funny?" Joshua asked.

"I was just thinking how comical this must look, you with a bike, me in a wetsuit." She slowed coming alongside a midnight blue MINI Cooper with a long boogie board strapped to the hood.

"This is me. I'll get the A/C going. There's a rack in the back."

Joshua circled to the back of the car. The rack was familiar; an older version with a simple latch and straps. Biking was the only good thing to have come out of his graduate school days, though it was always a competition in the lab or on the cycle trails with his former advisor. Piece of shit, creep. He shook away the unpleasant memory which had already started churning up his stomach acid. The sticker for the LeTour Biking Club on the rear bumper caught his attention. Casting his eyes to the Mini's rear license plate, he memorized the plate number, dreading a suspicion already taking root.

He'd ask Davi to check it out. In her line of work, she probably had more than a few connections to one of Israel's multiple security services.

"You got it?" Jackie shouted out the window.

"Be right there," he said, pretending to pull on one of the straps. If pressed, he couldn't say exactly what was niggling at the back of his mind, but there was no denying it... something wasn't right.

He opened the door and peered into the small car. A tight fit for anyone over six feet. Thankfully, it would be a short ride. He'd manage. The thought of Jay trying to squeeze in brought a smile to Joshua's face, and along with it a great memory that had once played out with Jay driving a tiny European car with his head sticking out of the sunroof. He slid in across the seat and nearly jumped out when Jackie's arm shot out between his legs, grabbing the release bar to adjust the seat. The seat jolted backward, giving him more than enough legroom.

"That's better. Where to, boss?"

Joshua hesitated with a reply. "You okay turning onto *Ramban*? Prima Kings has a place where you can stop out front."

"I can take you all the way home. I don't mind."

"I still have some shopping to do."

"The seat can go back a bit further if you need it. No one to crush in the back seat," she said.

Instinctively, Joshua turned around. He'd already had two close encounters that morning and wasn't sure his mind or heart could take another. "I'm good, thanks."

"Then away we go," she shouted gleefully, spinning the wheel.

Jackie was only half right. Four Guardian Angels, on standby duty, were seated comfortably in the back seat, a "just in case" precaution. Uri'el was riding shotgun, leaving nothing to chance while Joshua was in close quarters with Jezebel, THE Jezebel. Some *gilgulim* (reincarnations), should be put on permanent hold.

* * *

Across the parking lot, the cyclist climbed off the expensive racing bike. He kept his helmet and sunglasses on, partly to conceal his identity though he doubted anyone was paying any attention to him. She'd gone to the car, but then turned back around. *What was she up to?* He wondered. Then *he* stood up; the bike hoisted on his shoulder, and together they crossed the parking lot to the MINI Cooper. Her boogie board was strapped to the roof, probably scratching the hell out of the paint. *What was she thinking?*

Damn it, the little shit was using *his* bike rack and getting into *his* car. He'd have to fumigate it afterward to get rid of the little shit's stink. *What was she up to?* Oh, he'd make her pay this time. It was bad enough that the plan required her to work with *him*, for *him*. He'd swallowed his pride for the bigger picture, the greater good. But Professor Ezra Noiman had never quite swallowed the whole pill. Jackie was still hung up on the little shit, despite wanting to be part of his sweet revenge plan. But could he truly trust her? NO!

There was nothing more for him to do but get back to the apartment and make her pay. And oh, would she ever. Noiman was about to climb back on his bike when he decided to check out one of Hazon Labs' soon-to-be-famous — NOT — kiosks. It was placed just off the *mesila*, not two feet from where he stood. Too bad he didn't have a baseball bat, or a sledgehammer to take to the thing. He made sure to keep his back to the *mesila* security cameras. Too cheap to install a front-facing cam in the unit, he figured. Easy enough to siphon off the city's feed.

Hazon Labs expected people to stop and look at the pod emblazoned with the words HaMikdash3.0 scrolling across the screen along with the tease "COMING SOON," in bold caps. They looked slick. He'd give Katz that, but also vulnerable. Perhaps a late-night excursion might be in order, and smiled at the thought. But all that could wait, until after his *shamir* cut through the rest of Hazon's defenses, infiltrated its servers, and destroyed Joshua Katz's little project.

The *shamir*… a sweet bit of irony in the name choice. According to *Talmudic* sources, the *shamir* was a worm capable of disintegrating or cutting through stone, iron, and diamond. Diamond seemed to defy all logic unless King Solomon had been using laser technology over 2,200 years ago. That would be cool, though he doubted the whole fanciful story that the *shamir* was the agent responsible for cutting the stones for Solomon's Temple… the first Temple. The sweet irony was that his digital *shamir* would sow the seeds of destruction for HaMikdash3.0 — say goodbye, chump. Noiman climbed on his bike and headed to the apartment, thinking about all the wonderful ways he'd make Jackie-girl pay. Though he'd make a special effort to not ruin a perfectly-good wetsuit.

She was a terrible driver, talking to herself the entire time and narrating the harrowing 1.4 km distance as if she were both an Indy 500 race car driver *and* the race announcer. Thankfully, it was a short ride with little traffic for her to test her skills on. The small car made it easier to weave between the buses as she pulled into the cab/bus stand in front of the Prima Kings Hotel. Joshua finally opened his eyes as the car jerked to a stop and quickly jumped out. He leaned back in through the open door.

"Thanks, Jackie. I appreciate the ride. Have a *Shabbat Shalom*."

"Thanks," she said.

"Hang on till I get my bike," he said, slamming the door closed.

"Guaranteed, a *Shabbat Shalom* it will not be," she smirked.

"Did you say something?" he asked, leaning back in through the open window.

"Nope, not I," Jackie said, realizing she was being a little too cocky. They weren't in the clear yet.

Joshua tapped the back of the car, signaling he had unhitched the bike.

She found an opening in the line of traffic and zoomed out, with a wave out of the MINI Cooper's sunroof and a gleeful double-tap toot of her horn.

Chapter 14

The camera lens extended then retracted, a repeating cycle as the seventeen-year-old nervously shifted from one foot to the other, making both back-and-forth and side-to-side motions and confounding the camera's autofocus. The well-lit room contrasted sharply with the somber shadows surrounding *Barak*, his face wrapped in a black and white *keffiyeh* and a green Hamas headband boldly placed over it, "evidencing" his affiliation. The trappings of *Jihad* helped hide the sweat pouring down the boy's face but did little to conceal the sheer terror in his eyes.

The setup differed little from hundreds of suicide videos made by *shahids* throughout the world, a final message to advance the cause. A green Hamas flag hung on the wall behind him, a backdrop printed with the *Shahada*, the Declaration of Faith, emblazoned in white calligraphy, bearing witness to the serious business of a death cult. *Barak's* green headband bore the group's official logo — an image of the Dome of the Rock framed by two crossed scimitars, drawing absolute attention to their goal: the liberation of *al-Quds*, Jerusalem, from the infidels, but most especially to cleanse it from the filthy feet of the Jews and every other part of them. The multi-camouflaged army fatigues he wore hung off his shoulders, two sizes too big. Freshly removed from the plastic packaging, the uniform looked too new to make *Barak* into a believable soldier.

Ahmed tried his best to calm the young recruit but to no avail, as *al-Masri* looked on, arms folded in front of him, his jaw set firmly, and a permanent scowl on his face. This was their fifth attempt at getting the would-be, wannabe *shahid's* suicide video ready for publication. They were in an empty room, in the sub-sub-basement below the *Ras al-Amud Mosque*, in the East Jerusalem neighborhood of the same name in the *Kidron Valley*. The man known as *al-Masri* had no intention of letting this nonsense continue much longer. It was already 3:37 PM and their limited recording window was fast closing if they were to avoid the prayer time between *Asr* at 4:00 PM till sunset when *Maghrib* prayer times begin at 6:37 PM. Soon they would have to contend with the recorded voice of the *muezzin* issuing the call to prayer, over-shouting anything and everything for three-plus minutes of crooning. The sound was actually pleasant, but that wasn't the point. As it was Friday, the Holy day for Muslims, more of their people would attend prayers, significantly increasing the noise level with their scuffling, shuffling feet, moving in and out of the Mosque.

al-Masri's deadline was before sunset at 6:37 PM. His prayers religiously followed the seven sacred times, beginning at 6AM and continuing throughout the day at three-hour intervals until 6:00 PM. He would need to hurry this nonsense up and get out of this rat hole as *Ahmed* called it. While the Mosque's sub-sub-basement helped them avoid detection by the Israeli police, the room lacked soundproofing, a longstanding problem since one could actually hear rats scurrying behind the walls.

"We've used this place many times, with great success to honor *Allah*, *Ahmed* insisted. To cover the ambient scratching, a pre-recorded soundtrack, an Islamic marching tune favored by ISIS (Daesh), was looped in and could be edited to crescendo-on-demand, timed to the *shahid's Allahu Akbar* shouts, repeated at least three times, to complement the attendant visuals… a triumphant pumping of an AK-47 raised over his (or her) head with each *Alla-hu*.

The "*Shahid* template" was applied to all comers, delivering a consistent *Jihadist* message; other templates were available for beheadings with the same high production values perfected by Daesh. More recently the videos of hostages used a refined template where hostages were starved for at least three weeks, dressed in drab clothes, pajamas, or sweatpants, and presented either in pairs or individually. Off-camera, another hostage sat with a gun pointed at his or her head, an inducement to elicit an all-too-believable rant aimed at the Israeli government for failing to rescue them or to effect their release through negotiations or outright surrender.

The hostage was required to hit all the high points in the scripted charade but was allowed to authentically express, mostly their extemporaneous rage, outrage, pain, and anger which only added to the perverted theater intended to inflict as much psychological damage on hostage families and a war-weary nation. While never intended to serve as proof-of-life testimonies, the library of pre-recorded videos was cynically released to inflict the desired emotional trauma and psychological terror while at the same time fueling the terrorists' cause in the face of failed negotiations and pointing an accusing finger squarely at Israel. Emotional blackmail and a win-win for the terrorists on all fronts in manipulatively deflecting responsibility back onto back onto a ham-strung government coerced into making near-suicidal concessions. *al-Masri* had to admit they'd gotten their production values down to a science and only hoped *Ahmed* had remembered to unload the weapon before giving it to the boy. The report of gunfire was sure to bring the authorities down on their heads… something the man known as *al-Masri* couldn't afford.

Read the card, you moron, *al-Masri* wanted to shout.

Ahmed could see the rage building in *al-Masri*, a slow-boiling aggression, unlike the explosive fury that erupted in the cavern that ended his dear cousin's life. May *All-ah* have mercy on poor *Jibril*. If *Barak* continued with the disappointing reading, one of the few remaining tasks to be completed before Sunday, this failure would be his and he might be seeing his cousin that much sooner. He offered only the barest of excuses, bowing his head deferentially while keeping one eye on *al-Masri's* feet which had swiftly cut down poor *Jibril*.

"A truth," he explained, "the young man has dyslexia and can barely read."

The man they called *al-Masri* nodded his head as if understanding the dilemma. It was so hard to find good help, especially among this crowd whose hate-filled death wish made them an unpredictable lot, he sneered. *Ahmed* was a fixer; all the good terror cells had at least one; a detail man with relationships and trust built over time. At least for now, he couldn't afford to appear too harsh as he still needed these fools. *Ahmed* followed his orders like a trained puppy dog, despite knowing that the death knell would ring for weeks, maybe even months, as the battered and burned bodies of his Arab brothers were dug out of the rubble, and the stench of death filled the Arab Quarter.

The fallout would be spectacular with false flag accusations flying around the world, this one blaming the other, but where all good blood libels always landed on the backs of the Jews. This one, he thought, looking at the young man so eager to prove himself. A fool of a different kind. Dupes, the lot of them. Pawns in the geopolitical machinations of their Arab brothers who would no sooner welcome a Palestinian State than most Israelis. Ever ready to die for the struggle, the honor of martyrdom, they were so easily manipulated. The pattern all too easy to discern as the promise of statehood was dangled in front of them like a carrot on a stick, only to be used to beat them down again and again, undermined by their own arrogance believing themselves able to destroy Israel and its Jews.

When the dust finally settled, hopefully weeks later, their murderous cause would be put to an end, no sympathy for murdering their own people even from their most ardent defenders. These so-called martyrs knew nothing of sacrifice. If so, they wouldn't be so ready to bargain for their bounties, with pay-for-slay incentives commensurate with the level of the atrocity, or to lay claim to seventy-two virgins. Virgin goats, perhaps. What did these animals know of sacrifice, of a noble death?

Soon, his hellish masquerade would be over and he could rid himself of this ridiculous *keffiyeh* and filthy *dishdasha* robe. He had only one more of their prayer services to attend before day's end. One more bloody kneeling, back-breaking lie before this charade would be finished in one spectacular true *Glory Be Hallelujah* moment. Lost in the reverie of the glories of the Knights, he was shocked back to the here and now as the boy miraculously found his voice, unleashing a blood-curdling call to action that invariably preceded all of radical Islam's bloody chaos.

Ahmed could barely contain his excitement. "We got it! Difficult, but done."

"Excellent, my friend. Let me hear it all, from the beginning."

Al-Masri's lapdog tapped the touchscreen to replay the digital recording from the beginning while he motioned to *Barak* to join them. The fool, still holding the weapon, loped towards him. "The gun."

"Forgive me," the boy said and leaned it against the nearest wall.

They gathered around the video camera's small screen. *al-Masri* was impressed. The boy finally made it through an entire take without faltering. As instructed, he looked directly into the lens, his face a mask of calm determination. But the true transformation was in Barak's eyes; they no longer radiated fear but burned with fierce purpose.

"In the name of G-d, the Most Merciful, the Most Compassionate," his voice steady and grave. "Today, I am blessed to become a *shahid* in our struggle against the Occupiers. The infidels have desecrated our lands, defiled our people, and mocked our Faith. They, and the Great Satan their ally, will face the fury they have brought upon themselves."

Barak paused, his gaze unwavering, as if he could see the *Mahdi's* arrival on the horizon. "The world is awakening, and the time is near. The *Mahdi* shall vanquish the darkness and lead us to victory over those who trample the righteous path. I go now, knowing our cause is just, my purpose complete."

Barak then took a deep breath before a final affirmation of his just path. "My brothers and sisters, this is our calling. Prepare yourselves. The signs are clear. The hour draws near when the *Mahdi* will rise to restore the world to righteousness and establish his Caliphate. Each of us has a role to play in his glory. Let today be a message to the world: the righteous will prevail, and the armies of the *Mahdi* will soon march upon the enemies in the name of the one and only true Faith."

"That wasn't in the original script," *al-Masri* noted, surprised at the young man's passionate call to action.

"I know. This surprised me too. It is good though, yes?"

"Yes," he said. "Very good." Maybe he would release the recording, after all. Let it surface a few weeks later. He'd have to weigh the pros and cons, and the timing. He was counting on confusion reigning during the first days and weeks after the Arab quarter went kaboom, before choking itself to death.

"The memory card, if you will," *al-Masri* said, holding open his hand.

"But…" *Ahmed* began to protest. He always released the *shahid* videos. But *al-Masri's* steely gaze silenced any protest.

"I will speak with him now. A word or two of encouragement for our hero. You have done well, *Ahmed*," he said, gripping his willing sycophant's shoulder. *al-Masri* couldn't risk either the boy or *Ahmed* having a last-minute change of heart and running to authorities exposing all he/they had worked for. "You will not leave his side until this is done."

Ahmed nodded, knowing better than to argue the point. While he hadn't planned on babysitting *Barak* till Sunday, *al-Masri's* instructions made sense. The young fool might be tempted to shoot off his mouth, boasting of his coming mission. A most unusual mission, delayed for two days. Usually, *Ahmed* would send a *shahid* off on the same day to his glory and then upload the video to social media platforms and television networks. The neatly stacked flyers and posters announcing *Barak's* sacrifice were still boxed in the corner of the room, ready for distribution on Sunday. With speed and efficiency, he'd dispatch his runners to schools and mosques throughout Jerusalem and distribute digital copies electronically to their ever-growing network of followers in Palestine and abroad.

Ahmed didn't hear *al-Masri's* last words to the boy, nor did he need to.

"*Salaam Alaikum*," al-Masri said, then spun on his heels, almost tripping himself up on the bloody cheap sandals he'd gladly throw in the trash.

"*Wa-Alaikum-Salaam*," he and *Barak* responded together.

Trained monkeys, he thought. They couldn't even come up with an original greeting of their own, instead, they'd co-opted one from the Jews… *Shalom Aleichem* and meaning the same thing "Peace be upon you (plural)." Derivative nonsense.

"Let us give thanks to *All-ah*," al-Masri said.

Ahmed ran to the corner to retrieve three rectangular prayer rugs, their woven threads a colorful mix of blues, reds, and gold. He set them in a row, spaced eight inches apart, facing south to the *Kaaba* in Mecca. The two men and the boy removed their shoes, then washed their hands pouring water over them from a pitcher into a bowl. As usual, the man known as *Ismail al-Masri* instructed *Ahmed* to lead them in prayer… a great honor. He had no choice but to join in the heathen prayers, but he'd be damned before he'd lead them in praising their false god. He had to admit, *Ahmed* had a nice voice; not hymnal choir-ready, but still nice in that Middle Eastern way.

* * *

"Ez, I'm home," Jackie called from the living room. "You wouldn't believe what I did. I gave your favorite little shit a ride."

"Did you? Did you also make goo-goo eyes at him?"

"What? What are you talking about? Goo-goo eyes, spare me!"

"I can smell him on you?"

"You're being ridiculous!"

He rushed her suddenly, pushing her face against the wall.

"Well, why didn't you just say you were horny?" she said, looking over her shoulder, smiling.

Without saying a word, he grabbed her arms, looping a plastic band around her hands.

"This should be interesting," she said, still thinking this was just a new game Ez had cooked up. They were always experimenting, pushing the boundaries between pain and pleasure. She could count on one hand, the fetish taboos they wouldn't cross.

Jackie was still wearing the wetsuit, and the skimpy bra-type top. "Shall we move this into the bedroom," she suggested.

"Great idea. I have everything all set up for you," he said, grabbing hold of her arm by the elbow and roughly pushing her forward to the bedroom.

This should be..." she started to say but swallowed her words as she stared wide-eyed at the picture he'd taped on the wall to heighten her fear. It was the one fetish she absolutely refused to consider. Too dangerous.

"Don't you trust me?" he asked.

She struggled against him. "Ez, this isn't funny."

"It's not supposed to be."

She'd be bruised for a week by the time he was done.

"Shall we?" though he wasn't asking and secured the ball gag in her mouth. That would at least keep her quiet. No screams, just a whole lot of whimpering. "Might as well get this party started," he sneered, pulling the straps of her sports bra down, exposing her pert, size B/C breasts. Her nipples were already hard, he didn't need to work them at all as he clamped two clawed clamps on her unpierced nipple. The little things were small but had a nasty bite; these were only the first two of the more than a dozen clothespins, pincers, and clamps he'd adorn her lovely body with over the next few hours. She'd protest at first, as she had in the past, but then give in as the line between pain and pleasure became infinitely blurred. Though, this time he planned to make the pain last for a good long while.

Soon, Jerusalem's Old City would be filled with the sounds of that bloody song as the killers of Christ welcomed their Sabbath along with their visiting angels. Hopefully, he'd be able to avoid the bloody concert that could start as much as seventy-five minutes before the appointed candle-lighting times and continue in round-robin, live streams right through today's 5:49 PM official start to the Sabbath. The man known as *al-Masri* was acutely aware of the Jews and their customs, and the position of every one of their security cameras as he made his way back to his side of the Old City... to the Christian Quarter.

On Sunday, many of his fellow believers would also die, doubling the outrage of an attack perpetrated on Christianity's Holy Day. He held no illusions... some would question his decision. His choice of the day was also deliberate, delivering a fulminating punch to implicate the wretched Jews in the heinous crime that would leave scores dead or missing. With any luck, or the good L-rd's blessing, one or more groups of tourists would be thrown into the mix to spark international shock and outrage. Indeed, he chuckled to himself.

He felt a modicum of remorse over the death of innocents, but then who among the living were truly innocent. The Planners could only estimate the radius of the concussive blasts and the spread of the gas since many of the maps of the underground passages, tunnels, and caves had been lost to Time. While the placements would help confine the damage, these old buildings and underground passages would also likely yield to the heat. Neither he nor the Group of Seventy, the Septuāgintā, relished in the deaths of their own people, but there was no avoiding the possibility… the certainty. The Group only hoped their little corner of the Christian Quarter might be spared.

Hope, quoting Peter, a fisherman and fisher of men, Chapter 3, verse 15: "… Always be prepared to give an answer to everyone who asks you to give the reason for the hope that you have." His was hope for a new beginning.

The man known as *al-Masri* followed one of five circuitous routes he mapped out to Lion's Gate. The fastest still took him fifteen minutes to complete, the longest forty-five minutes to shed his Arab skin, the *dishdasha* and *keffiyeh*, and the cellphone which captured his movements thanks to Google Maps. Secured by friends, his change of clothes would be exactly where they were supposed to be; and, the Arab disguise, freshly laundered for when needed to reprise his role as *Ismail al-Masri*. He didn't anticipate needing to do so, at least not before Sunday… if then. There was still a bit of unfinished business requiring his attention. *Ahmed*.

In a moment of uncharacteristic goodwill, he might let the little fixer live. The prosthetic burn scar on the left side of his face and the grotesque effect on his eye and lip altered his appearance sufficiently that he doubted *Ahmed* would recognize him even if they stood right next to one another on a street corner. They'd tested the disguise with multiple facial recognition programs which only offered an accuracy match of 30%, an acceptable margin good enough to fool the Israeli Police should they take an interest in the man formerly known as *Ismail al-Masri*.

Once he reached Lion's Gate Road, northwest of the Temple Mount, and turned into the Pilgrim's House, he was fully transformed into the humble Father Lorencio Castellnou, Defender of Christ and Standard Bearer of the Knights Templar. He entered his Spartan quarters and stripped off his clothes, eager to wash himself of the day's foul stink. Fifteen minutes later, he wrapped the *cilice*, a spiked chain, around his left thigh. He tightened it enough so that it would remain secure while he walked down the steep steps to follow the path of Jesus, drawing blood with every step in this simplest form of self-mortification. Penance for his sins. There would be more to follow for having killed a man, whose name he had already forgotten, and the faceless and nameless others that would die on Sunday.

Father Lorencio donned a simple, brown muslin robe already stippled with his blood, a badge of contrition and honor, both well hidden within the robe's dark folds. He closed the robe with an off-white braided cord, adding a beaded rosary onto the rope then slipped his feet into handcrafted leather-soled sandals. He lifted the lid of a small wooden box, staring at the silver ring bearing the insignia of the Knights Templar. The red cross patée, with its bold, curving arms flaring out from the narrowed center, was set against white enamel. Father Lorencio could almost see his brother Knights riding triumphantly into Jerusalem astride their warhorses, the cross patée emblazoned on their surcoats, and the Beauséant, their sacred standard, billowing in the wind. After a long moment, the Grand Master of the Septuāgintā placed the ring on his index finger and bowed his head in deference to the past. While he may have looked like any other visiting monk or priest on a mission to the Holy Land, Father Lorencio was on an eight-hundred-year-old mission sanctioned on high to restore the Brotherhood.

He closed the door to the room behind him, walking with his palms pressed together in front of him as if in prayer. His destination was the *Lithostrotos*, the underground Roman-era street beneath the Convent of the Sisters of Zion. Its polished paving stones date back to the time of Jesus as his L-rd walked to his crucifixion; this is where His trial began. Here, too, Father Lorencio would renew his faith in blood just as he had every day. Father Enrique Andrés waited for Father Lorencio on the wooden bench near the private entrance to the *Lithostrotos*. He fingered the rosary beads, rolling them between his thumb and forefinger, contemplating the days' past and the days yet ahead. His charade would soon be over as well. He, too, wore a convincing mask, denying his true faith and betraying his brothers in Faith with blasphemous words but never in deeds. Here, he too could shed the sinful falsehood, the pretense of wanting to become one of *them*.

Only a few minutes had passed since Father Andrés left his quarters at 5:00 PM and sat, waiting. He heard the distinctive shuffle, the slow drag of one foot behind the other, the sound of Father Lorencio approaching. He rose from the bench, falling in step beside his mentor. No words were spoken, careful not to disrupt their thoughts; supplication from one, contemplation from the other. They walked side by side, passing beneath the elaborate cross set into an enamel gold-domed before unlocking the door to the chamber below. Later, they would descend to the lower levels to follow in the footsteps of Jesus, but first they would enter the Sanctuary to begin their penance. No tourists were ever allowed into the darkened space, a sacred space behind the ancient stone steps. After performing their penance, they would descend to the lower reaches and crawl along the paving stones, exalting in the Passion — the pure suffering of their L-rd before the crucifixion.

As *Seneschal*, deputy to the Grand Master, Father Andrés lit the eight candles in the corner of the room, a nave set aside for icons lost to Time. He lifted the ornate lid to the reliquary box, removing the tray of salves and balms; later, he would apply these to soothe the Grand Master's wounds. Inside were three different tools, a progression through time and pain. He turned and stared at the still weeping wounds and scars laid bare on Father Lorencio's back. In the footsteps of Jesus, he would confess his sins and accept punishment. Father Andrés chose the simple discipline whip made of knotted rope attached to a wooden haft. He handed it to the Grand Master who miraculously remained standing throughout the ritual. The robe pooled around his feet, Father Lorencio stood naked in the dim light.

"Forgive me, Father, for I have sinned. My soul is heavy with the blood I have spilled. One man, his life extinguished by my hand. But he was not innocent, no lamb led astray. Yet still, a man of flesh and bone, as am I. His face is in the shadows of my mind, his final breath an echo in my ears, his eyes reaching into my soul. In blood, do I atone."

By now, Father Andrés should have been accustomed to the sound of the whip slapping into the Grand Master's back, but the purifying ritual continued to shock his senses while stirring his soul. He kept his head bowed, watching as the *cilice* dug into the Grand Master's thigh as the muscle clenched with each taste of the lash, sending rivulets of blood dripping onto the robe. He didn't bother counting the lashes, but only watched as Father Lorencio's hand dropped to his side, prepared to accept the next Suffering. The confession would continue, this time the punishment meted out by the Medieval *scourge*, a multi-tailed whip, its leather haft securing the five braided thongs with knotted ends. He presented Father Lorencio with the *scourge*, taking the bloodied rope whip from his hand, ever mindful of keeping the dripping blood from sullying the white enamel of his own silver Templar signet ring.

"The days ahead hold more death. I know this. It is not one life but many that will cease in the chaos. I confess these thoughts not for absolution, for I do not deserve Your forgiveness. Nor do I seek release from my burden, it is mine to carry in your Name. As your humble servant, I speak these words because I must and ask that my soul will remain with me to bear witness to the Glorification of Your Name."

The Grand Master pounded the lash across his ribs, the knotted ends biting into the delicate skin. Father Andrés forced himself to watch, to bear witness to the Grand Master's valor in fulfilling the penance, but ready, if need be, to challenge him. There had never been a need. Father Lorencio's hand was true. He had fulfilled the Call.

Again, Father Andrés took the whip from his Master's hand, replacing it with the final flagrum. Gone were the simple knotted ends; the flagrum's leather thongs were tipped with sharpened bone recovered from the holy ossuary of Saint James, patron of Spain, pilgrims, and Intercessor of the Knights Templar.

Father Lorencio raised the flagrum above his head. "I stand before you, Father, bearing the weight of my sins. I do not ask for your forgiveness but only for the courage to endure what is yet to come. My penance, I ask for the lash. Let it tear the flesh just as my actions have torn the world. Let the pain remind me of the price of this life, of the sacredness I have forsaken. By the lash, I am judged for the sins of the flesh, but it is Your judgment I fear most of all."

Judgment Day would arrive soon enough, igniting a world war… a war to end all wars. The Jews would be blamed, the Arabs would be blamed, and tens of thousands would die before the cries of restraint would be heard. Christian groups would be up in arms. But the Church would survive. The sanctity of His supremacy would be preserved in a city of usurpers. Jerusalem would be theirs once again, guarded by Christ's Vicar on Earth, the Holy Church, operating under the protection of their Heavenly Intercessors, and ushering in the new Order of the Knights of the Templar as her ever-mindful, ever-faithful watchers.

A cold wind passed through the chamber, extinguishing the light from the candles and plunging the chamber into near-total darkness. The sign, since it surely was, gave them a moment's pause to consider its significance, to fathom its meaning, but which became lost in the need to complete the ritual as Father Andrés took the flagrum from Father Lorencio's hand and swung it across his mentor's exposed buttocks and genitals.

※ ※ ※

Sandalphon raced from one end of the Heavens to the other, searching each realm for answers, but always returning to the question of this so-called prayer from this so-called human. "I won't. I cannot," he shouted. His tasking demanded that he carry *their* prayers to the Almighty, but how could he be expected to raise this monster's words? How could these mortals of flesh and blood, he/they have been allowed to pervert the Word, to stray so far from the Truth… from what He asked of them in prayer?

"This is not the way," Sandalphon cried aloud. "G-d does not demand this of you," he said, directing his words at the cretin below. "You have perverted His way and sealed your fate." Sandalphon stood at the edge of *Aravot*, the seventh of the Heavens, knocking on the door of the uppermost reaches seeking answers from *–Yah*. Throughout time, he had survived listening to the tortured cries and calls for help of all G-d's children, enduring their painful pleas for forgiveness, and final release from the ravages of disease, poverty, and the ills suffered at the hands of their own kind.

But this… this creature brought evil with each breath, each lie, each deceitful thought that he encased with a lash offering, only no amount of suffering could repair the light he had shattered by causing others to fall into darkness. Like so many others who believed in such abominations, offering up their deaths and the deaths of others as so-called Sacrifices of Honor he only defiled G-d's ultimate gift. Life. He had distorted the Word, its meaning, the promise and hope. The One did not demand a sacrifice born in evil, drenched in blood not now, not ever, nor would it ever find favor in the eyes of the Most High.

Sandolphon stood before the Clouds of Glory resolute. "I will not carry this cursed monster's prayer forward. He is an abomination," Sandalphon shouted, shaking the spheres of the upper Heavens.

Then the Word came to him. "By denying him you deny Me. Are you to decide what prayers are Mine and which are not?"

"My G-d in Heaven, I have faithfully carried the words of these humans for the past 5,785 Earth years. I have cherished the love and light of your children who call upon your Names in faith, across all beliefs. But I have also listened to those who dwell in darkness, bringing their pleas and inane wishes to fulfill their selfish wants and desires, but only because there was always yet time for every shape-shifting darkling to be destroyed or be able to find redemption. But now? Now, there is no more Time. His words stand without hope for rectification. Have we waited only to witness this vile becoming?" Sandalphon had dared to speak his true mind, all the while knowing the words could be his last.

The Word did not come immediately, but after thoughtful consideration for this Archangel whose essence sheltered another's highest soul part. "Do not presume to know My ways. So many have died or been killed, without apparent rhyme or reason, seemingly before their time? But as my beloved Solomon spoke poetic words, wisdom for the ages in the book of *Kohelet*, 'To everything, there is a season, and a time for every purpose under the Heavens: A time to be born, and a time to die; A time to plant, and a time to pluck up that which is planted; A time to kill, and a time to heal; A time to break down, and a time to build up; A time to weep, and a time to laugh; A time to mourn, and a time to dance; A time to throw away stones, and a time to gather stones together; A time to embrace, and a time to refrain from embracing; A time to seek, and a time to lose; A time to keep, and a time to cast away. A time to rend, and a time to sew; A time to keep silent, and a time to speak; A time to love, and a time to hate; A time of war, and a time of peace.'

"Nothing is by chance or outside of My purview. Even this man with all the darkness his soul carries, the banality of his evil and cruelty in his heart, even he and the darkness in his soul have their own time… a time given to affect the time of others. The way is prepared as it is and as it was in the beginning. The end is known but given up to the path of free will. You, too, must prepare the way. Trust not in man, but in Me."

Sandalphon accepted the rebuke, given to him in love and punctuated by kindness and mercy despite his insolence.

And it was done just as it had been known from the beginning, hidden for 3,337 years in the 79,976 words and 304,805 letters of the *Torah* when Moses received the Word of G-d on Mount Sinai.

Chapter 15

Friday, Erev Shabbat. Jerusalem Candle Lighting Time 17:49

"Eff, I'm throwing in a load of wash before *Shabbat*. Have you anything else that needs to go in?" Davi called from the small alcove, off the kitchen. Absently, she checked his pants pockets to see what goodies he'd left her this time. She'd learned the hard way to always check his pockets for stray tissues, candy, and crumpled money to keep from having to clean out the drum or dryer. This time, she found a business card, one of her more unusual finds, but then her nephew was full of surprises.

"Eff, last call."

"I'm good," he responded after only a twenty-second delay.

As she set the card down on the shelf above the front-loading washing machine, Davi recognized the Hazon Labs logo: a simple, white horizontal hand, its fingers splayed as in the Priestly blessing set against a blue-purple background. She'd always been able to splay her fingers *Kohen* style which had been popularized as the Vulcan greeting by Mr. Spock in the original Star Trek series. She turned the card over and saw the name of the company's lead content developer, Tzion Mengistu.

As a matter of routine, she would run background checks on all Hazon's employees, Joshua included, and made a mental note of who was missing from the Hazon Labs roster that morning. Tzion Mengistu was on that list, though, apparently Effi had run into him somewhere in the Old City. She'd have to remember to ask him about the card using a wide-angle approach to ferret the information from her intuitive, too-smart-for-his-own-good nephew.

"Eff, I'm jumping in the shower. I forgot to tell you. We're having company tonight."

He ran out of his room, "I have that *Bnei Akiva* thing tonight," referring to one of several youth group programs with weekly gatherings he started to get involved with after Oct7. The groups usually met later in the evening, after dinner, only tonight's program also included a big pre-*Rosh Hashanah* dinner.

"I forgot about that. Is it for davening too?"

"Yeah, but I wasn't planning on going that early. Too much togetherness time."

"Sounds good. I…"

But then he was gone again before she could ask him about Tzion's card or tell him who their dinner guest would be.

* * *

Milk. Wine? *Challot*. Joshua ran through the mental shopping list as he crossed *Ramban Street*, dodging between stopped cars to the Paris Square *makolet*. The convenience store stayed open, till right before *Shabbat*, that, however, didn't mean he'd still find any *challot* for *Shabbat*. Milk was sometimes iffy too, wine never; the place had a selection to rival any dedicated wine store. He left his bike sitting outside the store, not worried about anyone stealing it. With the Prime Minister's residence around the corner on *Balfour Street*, the area was one of the most heavily monitored in the city with surveillance cameras capturing the streets, sidewalk, and any aboveground vantage points.

The shop was still crowded with mostly English and French speakers, likely from the Prima Kings Hotel in a mad dash to stock up their minifridges. Milk check. *Challot*, just two pitiful-looking rolls, semi-check. The wine he had in the house was perfect. He didn't bother with the offered bag for his purchases and dropped the items into his backpack.

What Joshua needed most was sleep. He hefted the bike on his shoulder, then headed to his apartment around the block on *Ben Maimon Street*. The building's entrance was secure; a keyless code for the outer security door. He left the bike in the outer entryway; the greasy mess on the tire should be enough to deter any would-be thief, not that he expected any takers. While he usually took the stairs to his top-floor apartment, the five-story building's elevator was too inviting to pass up.

He unlocked his apartment door and made it only as far as the living room couch, dropping the bags and himself onto it. Falling asleep would be so easy, too easy. The thought of moving prompted a long groan as he reluctantly propelled himself off the couch to put the milk in the fridge and the Gewürztraminer, which should be chilled enough by the time he left for Davi's. He shot off a quick text to her with the license plate off of Jackie's car.

"Can you run it?"
"Sure. Why?"
"Hunch."
"Fair enough."
"Have to skip *Tefilla* with Effi. K? Beyond wiped."
"NP. Dinner still?"
"With bells on." He smiled, adding a smile emoticon, hoping she was smiling at the exchange.

"6:30/18:30ish." Then after a brief pause, she added, "BTW, Ef doesn't know ur on the menu!"

Joshua texted back a smile emoticon, then added, "Swag bag for him. Gewurtz for us." *Us?* It was odd for him to use the term, but surprisingly, strangely comfortable. There was no denying his attraction to Davi but crossing that line would compromise both of them. Maybe once all the hoopla and controversy around HaMikdash died down. Then again, it could all be in his head, wishful thinking on his part, and she was playing her part as his attentive girlfriend following a well-rehearsed script.

Regardless, he was looking forward to meeting Effi. The thirteen-year-old had already left a mark on HaMikdash3.0 offering several helpful comments on improving the user interface, along with his pre-application, a statement of intent to submit a full interactive scenario for a future version of HaMikdash.

His last name Davidson was sufficient to ping HaMikdash's profile screening algorithm, which it did. The combination moved him up in the rankings of player-members to watch. Joshua had already dropped Effi's name and the information he supplied on the background questionnaire into the *Dimensional Torah Codes* search program. But extracting additional information about a minor was tricky, so hopefully the thirteen-year-old computer whiz would volunteer a few nuggets to improve the correlation between his biographical details and a particular section in the *Torah* containing the *Life and Times of Yehuda Efraim Davidson*.

4:52 PM. If he set his phone alarm to 5:30 PM he could rest for a bit and still have time to shower, light candles, and tackle the brisk thirty-minute walk to Davi's place in *Katamonim*. According to Google Maps, the 3.1 km walk would take forty minutes and change. He was a fast walker and should get there on time, plus/minus 5 minutes. For a brief moment, he considered skipping the mad dash by foot and just cabbing it to her place. But *Shabbat* was *Shabbat*, and was one of the few *mitzvot* he religiously tried keeping every week to honor his parents and grandparents. While he would take his phone, Joshua wouldn't use it except for emergencies. With the country at war, many of the country's Rabbis had issued exemptions about the emergency use of televisions, radios, and even phones in case of a *Tzeva Adom*, a red alert warning of any incoming rockets, missiles, or drones; though, the latter remained difficult to detect, leaving people little time to find shelter.

Jerusalem had been largely spared from the daily rocket barrages that plagued the coastal, Northern, and Southern regions of Israel. For many, there was no respite from the blaring warning sirens or the fifth column's "random" attacks falsely labeled lone wolves in order to quell fears by denying an overarching pattern. Holidays and *Shabbat* were prime target times for launching attacks. Israel had never known a true day of rest, a separation from the mundane and distractions of everyday life in what was supposed to be a preview of the World to Come, *Olam HaBah*. But since October 7th, a *Shabbat* for someone, somewhere in the country had always been marked, and marred, by parents grabbing their children, and adult children holding onto their elderly parents, and running for public bomb shelters and safe rooms.

Of all the many Jewish practices, Joshua liked *Shabbat* best and tried to guard its sanctity as much as possible. He was grateful for *Shabbat*… when both Time and Space slowed for twenty-five hours and his mind was able to truly rest. In many homes, windowsills held dozens of candles lit in honor of family or in memory of loved ones. Joshua only lit two *Shabbat* candles every Friday night to welcome the Angels and the extra soul given over for a time. While his grandfather was still healthy and able to walk, they went to *Kabbalat Shabbat* services together nearly every Friday night. The service could last thirty, even forty minutes, a reset button transitioning time from the fevered frenetic rush of the work week to the quiet surrender to *Shabbat* in song.

Joshua could listen to the words and melody of *Ana Be'Koach* forever — the haunting seven-verse, six-line, forty-two-word *Kabbalistic* song. The first letters of each word made up the *mem-bet*, the forty-two-letter name of G-d. The words were said to be embedded with profound mystical powers, able to suspend negativity and bring down the Primordial Light from

Above — a step closer to spiritual fulfillment, even redemption. He often listened to the various renditions on YouTube during the rest of the week. The prayer asks for G-d's mercy and guidance, but it's the song's first line that carries a singular message… the hope of the Nation to set free the remaining hostages — the living and the dead — still held captive by Hamas.

> *Please, by the great power of thy right hand, O set the captive free;*
> *Revered G-d, accept thy people's prayer; strengthen us, cleanse us;*
> *Almighty G-d, guard us as the apple of the eye of those who seek thee;*
> *Bless them, cleanse them, pity them; ever grant them thy truth;*
> *Mighty, holy G-d, in thy abundant grace, guide thy people;*
> *Accept our prayer, hear our cry, thou who knowest secret thoughts;*

Joshua set the alarm on his phone, then closed his eyes, quieting his mind to speak with G-d. That "talk" was also always part of his Friday ritual, and occasionally during the week when he could find the time. Sometimes, he was in the forest biking and would stop to sit on the ground surrounded by the trees or next to a stream. It was his version of *hitbodedut*, a mindfulness practice. Originated by Rabbi Nachman of Breslov, though not exclusive to his followers, *hitbodedut* included setting aside quiet time to commune with G-d. For as long as Joshua could remember, he'd been talking to G-d; he just wasn't sure G-d was always listening, or maybe he wasn't paying close enough attention to G-d's nuanced ways of communicating. He'd begun the formal practice at home, setting aside time, less about talking to G-d, and more of a silent meditation, though he often fell asleep in the middle of the conversation.

He tried to stay conscious long enough to finish the thought, though it wasn't always possible. Maybe that was okay. More often than not, he found himself challenging G-d to finally bring the *Moshiach*; raise the dead; and change the world into the utopian vision he'd promised the world in the Garden of Eden. The time had come to say enough, to end the pain and suffering of millions around the world; to stop the anti-Semitic horror show and neo-Marxist Progressive Left mind-boggling lunacy that was destroying civilization under the guise of progress. Except in that awakening moment, Joshua realized he'd neglected to ask for permission. *Funny*, he thought aloud. Wasn't that the point of a challenge? *Ugh, excuse Mr. G-d, just a heads up. Wanted you to know, I'm about to rock the boat some down here. Sure, hope you don't mind.*

No, permission wasn't the right word. He wanted G-d to grant him the fortitude to play a part in the grand Cosmic scheme of things and the wisdom to effect a change for the good. But he should've asked at the beginning when he'd first conceived of HaMikdash. He wasn't sure what now gave him clarity of thought, but Joshua knew the next step. He began the silent prayer with an apology, apologizing for his hubris; for the challenge gauntlet he'd thrown down as loudly as Thor's fabled hammer aimed squarely at G-d to bring on the *Moshiach*, or else… or else he'd digitally conjure one up on his own. He fell asleep with the words, "I hope HaMikdash3.0 will be an acceptable offering. We're really hurting down here, trying to fight the good fight. We're trying, but we're tired." Then, after a pause, he added, "You know, I've been tired for a really long time."

The alarm sounded at 5:30 PM, but Joshua had been awake since 5:20 PM, ten minutes earlier than he'd planned. His catnap lasted for a little less than thirty minutes. When he woke up, every detail of the remarkable dream was fresh in his mind though its meaning remained fuzzy around the edges. He spent the last ten minutes wondering if there was any significance to the numbers 520 or 1720 in military time, or if waking up ten minutes before his alarm went off might carry some meaning. Numbers were his thing and by default so was *Gematria*. Joshua was sure the images he'd seen were an answer of sorts… though he still had questions in a "Man's Search for Meaning" à la the author, psychologist, philosopher, Holocaust survivor, and witness to History, Viktor Frankl, sort of way. After waking up "early" he quickly pulled up the *Gematrix* website on his phone and keyed in the number, 520. It was always a crapshoot approach since inputting any number or word yielded pages of results, of single words and constructed phrases with an identical numerical value. The process was less than scientific, picking and choosing from the list of seemingly divergent, often contradictory, results or landing on a phrase that resonated with the "why" behind the input. The question. While decidedly biased, more often than not, the results were at least interesting.

The second result made him smile. אהיה שלחני אליכם Translation: "I will be the one who sent me to you," or alternatively, "I am the one who sent me to you." A circular statement with either translation, but still interesting. A message, a messenger, and the verb, "sent" (שלח). Interesting. The storyboard formatting of his dream didn't surprise him. He'd lived every hour of

STRANGE FIRE 259

every day for the last year in storyboard form, developing HaMikdash3.0's interwoven storylines.

First, he saw a relentless rain, pouring down with no breaks within its defined space. A sheet of rain. A heavy downpour. There were many ways to interpret the rain. On *Succot*, specifically on *Shemini Atzeret/Simchat Torah*, they would offer a Prayer for Rain. The closing lines for the prayer always included a qualifier. "For a blessing and not for a curse; for life and not for death; for abundance and not for famine." Since *Simchat Torah* 2023 the associations were dark.... one of the darkest of times for Israel and the Jewish people since the Holocaust. Maybe the downpour in his dream symbolized his request and hope for HaMikdash and which also came with the same qualifier that his actions, his hope would be for a blessing, for life, and for abundance, and not invoking their counterpoints.

In the second scene, he saw a bright, clear blue sky. Sunny, although the sun wasn't visible in a corner shining down. There was just light, and no rainbow refracting any lingering raindrops into a myriad of rainbow arcs. Rainbows could be interpreted in two ways, and not all good. Many religious people wouldn't look, talk, or even discuss the *keshet*, the bow, even though it was placed in the sky after the flood as a symbol of the Covenant, a promise that G-d would never again wholly destroy the Earth. A clear blue sky with the sun shining implied a new day, a new beginning, but nothing inherently bad. Artists had long used the sun to infer G-d in works of art where the heads of Archangels and Saints were depicted with a golden sun disk halo. Joshua thought, there might be something there to his sunny skies' scene, inferring the second scene as perhaps a Messianic symbol or maybe it was just a bright punctuation mark... clear skies after the rain. But there was no sun in the scene, just a day in the light. Maybe even THE Light.

Israel's 2024 Eurovision song entry was titled *October Rain*. Joshua enjoyed the original lyrics rather than the edited version, which had been deemed too political for public consumption. He was pleased to see the *Haredi* artist Shulem Lemmer perform the song whose words conveyed the gut-wrenching trauma Israel and the Jewish people suffered on October 7th, and the still unbelievable denials that dismissed the horrors by a world gone silent. Then, and still. Shulem's version made it accessible to the ultra-Orthodox *Haredi* world who would otherwise never hear it, since listening to a female singer was considered taboo. Both versions were moving, but he preferred Shulem's arrangement more. Maybe the first two scenes were supposed to go together, linked to October 7 and every day since. But his first insights about HaMikdash came well before that fateful day, though he was hard-pressed to attribute a specific date to its genesis.

The third scene in the sequence shifted time or space, maybe both. It contained a strange, light mist with a horizontal stream of light pulsing across the panel. This third scene wasn't the kind of lightning seen in a storm. There were no distinct clouds *per se*, only the mist. Lightning happens in regular clouds when there is a separation of charges. Positive charges that build up at the top of the cloud while negative ones cluster at the bottom, creating an electric field between the cloud's lower edge and the ground. But this mist carried an electrically-charged output, a single, continuous discharge pulsing within the haze, different from lightning. Joshua saw it as something Celestial, not unlike what he'd always imagined what "the spirit of G-d hovering over the face of the waters" might have looked like as it was described in the Book of Genesis. The word "spirit" was *ruach* and which was also the word for wind. But here *Ruach* was surely one of the levels of the soul and there was light in his vision of *Ruach*. Light which differed from the sun as its source, but rather a kind of Primordial Light.

But then the final scene shifted to an Earthly one, a foreboding cloudy, gray-filled sky and a spidery electricity-filled bolt scissoring to the ground below in a traditional lightning strike. The symbolism of the last scene was ominous, at least in his initial interpretation of it... as in striking one dead. Himself. But if scenes 3 and 4 were linked he could put a more positive spin on the interpretation, namely that he was part of bringing part of the Light from scene 3 down to Earth, albeit transformed into the familiar.

While Joshua couldn't say why, he was sure none of the scenes were a bad sign. But that didn't mean any of it was a "good sign" either.

5:31. He couldn't spend any more time dissecting the dream. He had been ten minutes ahead of schedule, but now a minute behind. He stripped off his clothes and jumped in the shower. He could still smell Jackie's patchouli oil air freshener and poured the Moroccan Rituals liquid soap over his head, replacing the stink with an aromatic spice blend of cardamom, cinnamon, and tangerine. As he rinsed off, the four-scene storyboard sequence played again in his mind. Without question, each part conveyed a message on its own. But was there a Gestalt where the parts were part of a greater, larger message, and where the sum was greater than its individual parts.

At 5:52 PM, Joshua lit *Shabbat* candles. Three minutes after the official Jerusalem start time of 5:49 PM, which was always eighteen minutes earlier than much of the rest of the country. Thankfully, he was still safely within the 18-minute "grace" window, before heading out the door.

* * *

"Come on, Joshua," Uri'el sighed. "You're so close to knowing." His sigh drew the attention of the entire HaMikdash3.0 team of Guardian Angels still in Heaven's realms. They gathered around Uri'el in a giant bear hug, comforting each of his faces.

Uri'el thought-transferred his thanks, adding a verbalized, "I'm okay." All but two Guardian Angels dispersed, GAs 730.71 and 755.23 lingering behind. Neither of them knew how to comfort him. GA-730.71 stood on his right shoulder, hoping to reinforce him with the *Sefira* of *Netzach*, supporting him with confidence, endurance, and victory of purpose; while GA-755.23 stood to his left concentrating on the *Sefira* of *Hod*, of splendor, glory, and humility in fulfilling the Will of G-d.

"Just frustrated, guys. I'm okay. Really," he said.

The sign was right there for Joshua to see. He'd correctly focused on the time disparity between waking from the vision he'd been granted and the sounding of his alarm. But he'd missed the recurring number 52, which had been put there for him to discern. Fifty-two. The number was in the time he set his alarm at 4:52 and also in the time when he woke up early at 5:20. Fifty-two. He searched for the number 520 and found the first message. But in simple *Gematria* manipulations, he could, should've, ignored the 0 to see the number 52, and its summing to 7. The message was in the time, but also in the nuances of time, and in a name with the *Gematria* value of 52.

Uri'el gathered HaMikdash3.0's Guardian Angels to welcome in *Shabbat*. Micha'el assured him GAs 696.0 and 697.4 wouldn't miss *Shabbat* while they continued keeping a watchful eye on Tzion in Zedekiah's Cave.

* * *

"I, we, have some concerns," GA-696.0 said, raising his angel eyes to the Heavens. GA-697.4 stood ready to throw in his two cents if needed. "I'm assuming you can hear me, us, I'm here with GA-697.4 as you know. It's Friday, and it's really dark here. Bottom line, we have no idea when *Shabbat* starts," GA-696.0 said, harshly tapping his winged wrist.

GA-697.4 then stepped up. "That's priority one, but then as you know we're part of your "Holy, Holy, Holy" choir and it seems like we're missing out being stuck here…"

GA-696.0 shot his brother Guardian Angel a warning look, quickly chiming in, "Not that we're complaining, or anything like that. Happy to be here, helping Tzion. We're taking really good care of him. As his chart says, he's still unconscious but his respiratory rate is good, and breath sounds are clear. But back on point. Basically, we could use a little help. That's if you're not too busy with everything else that's going on with *Shabbat*."

The instant the request was made, a little bell started ringing which thankfully had nothing to do the Hemingway novel, "For Whom the Bell Tolls" which GA-697.4 was reading. The GAs stared at one another, pleased that their prayers had been answered in what had to be record time and sourced the sound to their backpacks. They looked at one another, then cautiously lifted the flap just in case their prayers had been answered by the other side who were especially fond of things that went boom.

"On three," GA-696.0 said, stretching his wing out as far as it would go to lift the flap.

"We should have faith," 697.4 interrupted the count.

"I'm sorry, you're right."

"Let's do this," they said and confidently flipped open the knapsacks' flaps. Inside, they each found a small timer. 697.4's clock had the numbers 1-12; while 696.0 had the numbers 13-24. The little ringing bell showed a *Shabbat* start time of 17:49.

"Phew, that was close," GA-696.0 said, pleased that they were still on time for the upcoming "Holy, Holy, Holy" chorus.

They bowed their heads and greeted one another with a simple *Shabbat Shalom*. They flitted over to Tzion and wished him a *Shabbat Shalom*, assuring him he would be okay, adding *B'Ezrat Ha-Shem*, with G-d's help. The cavern was suddenly filled with a warm light.

"Thank you. It was getting kind of chilly in here," GA-696.0 said. There was a definite draft coming in from somewhere though neither could pinpoint the source.

The little timer bell sounded again. This time the GAs knew exactly what to do. They stood, turned to one another, and sang, *Kadosh, Kadosh, Kadosh…* "Holy, Holy, Holy is the Lord Almighty. The whole earth is full of His Glory" in perfect sync with their fellow Angelics in Heaven.

* * *

Like most Jerusalem neighborhoods, *Katamonim* was a maze of intersecting side streets and alley shortcuts, which weren't always easy to find. The street names were populated by an assortment of notable Rabbis — *Yochanan Ben-Zakai, Tarfoun, Yossi Ben-Yoezer, Yehuda ha-Nasi, Bnei Betera,* and *Rashbag*, an acronym for *Rabbi Shimon Ben Gamliel*. To confuse matters more, several streets had Greek names, including Hyrcanus, Antigonus, and Alexandrion. Thankfully, Davi's apartment was on a main street, *Yehuda ha-Nasi,* Judah the Prince. While not royalty, the second-century Rabbi was responsible for breaking with tradition by writing down the Oral Law, the *Mishnah*. He foresaw a time when the Jewish people would be dispersed around the world and feared the Oral Law might be lost or forgotten. His codification of it earned him the revered, single word title by which he was more commonly known, Rabbi. His work allowed the laws to be shared by scholars, but also more easily among the people and be passed with fidelity from generation to generation, until today.

In school, Joshua had learned the *Mishnah*, which included the lengthy volume of Moed, describing the laws of *Shabbat*, the Holidays and Fast Days. Unfortunately, he was about to break one of those laws. He'd forgotten to set his phone to silent *Shabbat* mode before candle lighting and did so now at 6:29 PM. He slipped the phone into the side pocket of the swag bag he'd brought for Effi. For some god-awful reason, it felt like he was showing up for a first date and and seriously thought of hightailing it out of there. Instead, he took in a deep breath, then knocked on the door.

* * *

"Ef, can you get the door?"

"Yeah, yeah. But I have to leave right after dinner."

"We'll see," she whispered, adding a smirk only the kitchen cabinets could see. If it weren't *Shabbat*, she'd love to snap a picture of Effi's reaction. She'd have to get the instant replay from Joshua, which made her smile. "Oy," she said, knowing this, whatever this was, could get complicated.

He'd texted that he wouldn't be able to make it in time for davening but asked if they were still on for dinner, essentially asking if she hadn't changed her mind. She thought it was cute that he seemed nervous or maybe he was doing a bit of fishing of his own. Surprisingly, Davi didn't mind it either way. Her reply had been just this side of flirty, which wasn't the smartest move she'd ever made but which suited her mood.

Effi raced to the door intending to make a decent show of hello since he'd have to sit through dinner with said guest. He was in the middle of "The Book Thief" for his advanced English class; the report was due Tuesday, erev-erev *Rosh Hashanah*, the last day of school. Aunt Davi could entertain what's her or his name was till they were ready to eat.

He flung open the door and wasn't sure if he'd stepped through a dimensional portal as he stared at Joshua E. Katz, in the flesh, on his doorstep. He felt his mouth drop open, but couldn't find any words or will his muscles to move.

"Can I come in?"

Effi still hadn't found his voice. Instead, he used wild hand gestures and head nods to usher in his hero until finally hearing words coming out of his mouth. "Aunt Davi didn't tell me it was you!"

"I'm guessing she wanted me to be a surprise."

"Oh man, is it ever! This is great, I have so much I want to ask you."

"First things first, *Shabbat Shalom*."

"*U'Mevorach*," Effi added, blessing *Shabbat*.

"I'm 100% sure that isn't what *Ha-Shem* intended with the added blessing."

"True, but I'm feeling mighty blessed."

"You should know, I generally don't like talking business or about work on *Shabbat*."

"Really?" Effi asked, genuinely surprised as well as disappointed. "How do you turn it off?"

They hadn't made it much further than the hallway when Davi popped her head in from the kitchen. "I see you two are getting along. I'm just finishing up. Wine already chilled?"

Joshua nodded.

"No hurry, Aunt Davi. Take your time, we're good," Effi said, leading Joshua out to the *mirpeset*.

"You said, generally, but there are exceptions?" If given the chance, Effi would pump Joshua for information all night.

"To what?"

"Talking about work, about 3.0."

"Not tonight, Ef."

Effi smiled as Joshua used his shorthand nickname.

"If I recall, you're interested in submitting a scenario, correct?"

"Oh yeah. I've pretty much decided to forget the Zedekiah's Cave one."

"That's good. Since we've got one already lined up for the launch. That's not to say it wouldn't be good for an expanded module."

Effi got his first nugget of the night, which he filed away for safekeeping. "Then I definitely won't burn my notes. The other one is pretty cool. I found…"

Joshua held up a restraining finger. "Let me stop you right there."

"But…"

"No, seriously. If you tell me and we've got something in the works that's even remotely similar you might think we stole your idea."

"There's no way you've got this one. No way," Effi said with an air of confidence that bordered on rude.

"Then all the more the reason. Besides, I think we may already have a problem."

"And this was going so well," he said sarcastically. "Why do I have a feeling I'm not going to like this?"

"Most problems have solutions, a turn of events that may be better than the original. I learned that one today."

"How?" Effi asked, shifting the subject away from the problem.

Davi joined them on the *mirpeset*.

"Great view," Joshua said.

"Close to open space, even in Jerusalem," she smiled.

Effi watched the exchange between Joshua and Aunt Davi. *Curious*, he thought. How had Aunt Davi made Joshua's acquaintance? It wasn't like they ran in the same circles, though he wasn't exactly sure what circles his mysterious Aunt ran in…

"I almost forgot," Joshua said, swinging the backpack off his shoulder. He unzipped the backpack and removed the Gewurtz from an interior cooling pouch. "This is for you," passing the long-necked bottle to Davi, then handing over the black backpack to Effi. "A bit of merch from HaMikdash."

"No way!" Effi peered inside. "Thank you!" he shouted, then raced inside. He emptied the backpack's contents on the coffee table. "The backpack too?" he asked, hoping the answer would be, yes. Emblazoned on the backpack was the Hazon Labs logo and the catchphrase, *The End is the Beginning*.

"The backpack also has a rain cover."

"Wow, this is amazing! Thank you so much."

Davi and Joshua stood in the *mirpeset* doorway, watching Effi tear through the Hazon Labs merch. She hadn't seen her nephew this happy in a long time. His father's extended absences had taken a toll on her nephew… especially, of late. Her errant brother, Sol had been away longer than usual this time since he'd be on an enforced travel hiatus during much of October for the Jewish Holidays.

Joshua noticed she was still wearing the silicon ring on her finger. It was still infused with the reddish-brown hue. She noticed him looking at the band and shifted her eyes to Effi.

"Fine," she said and rolled her eyes. "Hey Ef, here's another present for you," casually tossing the $1200 sensor to her nephew. Joshua held his breath as Effi caught it one-handed with barely a glance in their direction.

"I taught the kid everything he knows," she winked.

Joshua watched as Effi slipped the ring on his finger. The color band instantly changed colors to a vibrant green with red swirls. His mind raced, considering the implications of the color transformation. Davi's energy had turned the sensor a deep brown-red, like jasper. But Effi's was surprising. A dominant green mixed with traces of red where green was the color of the emerald gemstone associated with the tribe of Levi and the red perhaps like the garnet gemstone also associated with the tribe of Judah. Could the two together be a simple color/frequency merge spanning the 750-1200 Hz range. A man from the tribe of Judah, green; the woman, red. Could it really be that simple? Did people match up through complementary colors or frequencies that wouldn't cancel one another out in a successful union, but would rather strengthen the connection? Was that the hidden ground truth underlying the "Law of Attraction" of tuning into the right frequencies? He'd never put much stock in it, but was willing to consider the possibilities. After *Shabbat*, he'd have ChatGPT generate a comprehensive list of gemstone colors and their associated frequencies, which would be faster than sourcing out original datasheets himself. In yet another uncharacteristic digression, Joshua wondered whether Davi's reddish-brown hue would complement his blue-purple color scheme. Together, what might their frequencies be able to accomplish, unlocking something new, something powerful? The idea felt like, he was finding the missing piece to a puzzle he didn't even realize he was solving.

"Where'd you go?" she asked, touching his sleeve.

"Not exactly sure, but no place bad which is refreshing," he said.

"I could use some help in the kitchen," Davi said, touching the top of his hand.

"At your service."

※ ※ ※

"Do you mind grabbing the *challot* from the oven? Ovens off, but use a towel, they should still be.."

"Hot!" Joshua screamed.

"I tried to tell you," she shrugged.

He noted the time on the oven door as 6:52, realizing he'd seen the number 52 multiple times in the last couple of hours. *Strange*, he thought.

"We sing each three times," Davi said, referring to each stanza of the *Shalom Aleichem* song which welcomed the *Shabbat Malachim*, the special *Shabbat* angels.

"What? Yeah, sure. So do I," Joshua said.

She started singing as they approached the table, and Effi and Joshua joined in, then in a perfect kumbaya moment, all of HaMikdash3.0's Guardian Angels in the Upper Realms joined them, locking wings together and swaying from side to side with the first verse: *Peace unto you, ministering angels, messengers of the Most High, of the supreme King of kings, the Holy One, blessed be He.* The words of the verse could alternatively be translated to, "Welcome to you…" Both worked.

Joshua half-said, half-sang the *Kiddush*, the blessings over the wine, while Davi said the *bracha* over the bread, gingerly handling the two hot loaves, which blew off a head of steam as she unwrapped the baking paper.

The meal was an elaboration on the Eucalyptus treats from that afternoon's lunch, with the addition of vegetarian and meat-loving entrées to the menu: eggplant steak, wild mushroom risotto, salmon steak, and grilled ribeye. Davi set up a buffet service on the kitchen counter to keep the table uncluttered.

"Something I just whipped up," she quipped, glancing over at the Eucalyptus bags, waiting to be recycled.

Between bites, Effi lobbed questions at Joshua… how he came up with the idea, where he was when inspiration struck, and most importantly asking Joshua about the "why" of HaMikdash. Joshua steered clear of any "why" details since explaining that he wanted to raise the dead fell outside the bounds of polite dinner conversation. Besides, Joshua knew Effi's mother had passed away only a few years back and had no idea how sensitive the topic might be.

"I'm dying to tell you my storyline idea," Effi said.

"Yeah, about that," Joshua started to say.

"Oh, I'm definitely not going to like this."

"Once you get over the shock, you should be fine."

"Easy for you to say."

"It's one of those bad news things, but leaning more to the pretty good news side of things," Joshua hesitated.

"So rather than being depressed for the rest of my life, you think I'll land on the happy side of life?"

Davi looked on. She had no clue what the problem might be and dealing with an angst-ridden teen was definitely not her happy place. "Best to put my nephew out of his misery," Davi suggested, fearing Effi might be on the verge of launching into full-on histrionics.

"It's just that I don't think you're eligible to apply because…"

"No way, I got everything signed. I don't believe this. This can't be happening!"

"Relax," Joshua said, hoping to reassure him. He wanted to steer clear of citing MAGSS' security contract with Hazon Labs as the primary problem; which it was. To avoid any hint of impropriety, contractors, their employees, and their families were automatically disqualified from entering. Joshua didn't want Effi to blame Davi for the technicality. He decided to focus more on the second issue, namely that he felt he could no longer be impartial in judging Effi's entry as good, or amazing, as it might well be, having met him.

Cutting to the chase, "The good news is Hazon Labs has an internship program."

Effi looked at Joshua disbelievingly. "You wouldn't lie to me, would you?"

"Truth."

"Jeez, I just wanted you to notice me. To get the internship. 'Archie' was ever only meant to be a means to an end."

"Archie?"

"You're gonna love it! It's a code name," Effi said, grinning from ear to ear.

"Not another word. Once we get the paperwork out of the way, non-disclosures, permissions from a parent, or guardian," with a nod to Davi, "you can present your idea to the team at one of our Thursday 'show and tell' sessions. If you want to?"

"Is that even a question!" Effi shouted.

Davi cleared her throat and looked at Effi wide-eyed with a subtle head nod in Joshua's direction. Hopefully, her nephew would get the mental transmission to thank Joshua.

Effi got the hint, though he didn't need it. "Thank you, Joshua. This is beyond amazing! So, when can I start?"

Joshua laughed. So did Davi.

"No, seriously, when can I start?"

"Paperwork first. Tell you what, let's meet on Sunday at Zedekiah's Cave, I'll give you the executive tour so you can see how we construct storylines. It will help you craft your Archie storyboards."

"Man, this just keeps getting better and better."

Hopefully, the Hazon Labs' team, but most especially Joshua, would find the unusual stone, set in the Old City's Northern-facing wall, just down the street from Zedekiah's Cave, just as intriguing as he did. Come Sunday, Effi would be able to show Joshua the "Archie" stone. Man, he couldn't have planned this any better if he tried.

"Ef, your *Bnei Akiva* program," Davi said, tapping the non-existent watch on her wrist.

"Yeah, but…"

"No buts. People are counting on you showing up."

"Fine," he said, adding an exaggerated eye roll and heaving an exasperated sigh.

"Better finish up or you'll be late."

Without any further prompting, Effi began clearing the table of plates and glasses.

"You gotta train them early," Davi whispered, adding a wink and a smile.

Effi grabbed a jacket and the HaMikdash keychain, unscrewing the closure and slipping his key onto the carabiner-styled ring.

"Thanks again, Joshua. For everything!" He fist-bumped Joshua and kissed Aunt Davi, before chasing out the door. "*Shabbat Shalom* and a happy New Year!"

Reluctantly, Effi left for his pre-*Rosh Hashanah Bnei Akiva* gathering, the last official one for his youth group with the approaching *Yamim Nora'im*, the High Holidays, and the near-weekly disruptions to their regular meeting schedule. He'd been gone less than a minute when he raced back through the apartment door, his key proudly jangling from his HaMikdash keyring.

"Is this a paid internship or slave labor? A guy has needs, you know."

"Paid, but an intern's salary." Joshua smiled, then added, "and not even close to a quarter of a million dollars. *Shekels* maybe, one day, for a Junior Developer position."

"Sweet!" he shouted, spun around, none too gracefully, then headed out the door.

Joshua and Davi stared at the closed door, expecting Hurricane Effi to spin in again. They smiled at one another, their unspoken attraction undeniable, a moment full of possibilities, but which dissolved instantly, overshadowed by the license plate number he'd texted her earlier.

Without further preamble, she said, "The car doesn't belong to Jackie."

"Dare I ask?"

She scooped vegan vanilla bean ice cream into a bowl and topped it with macerated strawberries. "I imagine you already know. Or, you wouldn't have asked me to run the plates."

"So, he and she are likely behind the Miss Piggy hack?" He asked the question knowing it was more of a statement.

"A logic leap, but also a fair bet. Plus, whatever else they might've gotten into."

Joshua considered the implications. *If* they were behind the Miss Piggy attack, there was no way of knowing the full extent of the damage the pair had already done before today's episode, or what they still planned to do. Jackie had full access to the system, leaving HaMikdash insanely vulnerable. Jackie was all about the show. Ezra Noiman, on the other hand, could lie to your face while reaching around to stab you in the back in a sneak attack. Together, he was almost too afraid to consider the possibilities. Except he had to...

The implications were enormous, not only for the company, but also for the 1.7 million plus users whose systems could have been infected by whatever worm, virus, or other digital demon Noiman and Jackie had unleashed on HaMikdash3.0... on Hazon Labs, or more precisely on him. They made daily backup copies of 3.0 and kept each for seven days. But without a full forensic workup, there was no way to know when the pair had first started destroying HaMikdash from within, and maybe not even then. He could understand Noiman's motivations. But why did Jackie hate him enough to want to destroy him along with HaMikdash?

He dipped his spoon into the ice cream, but then set it aside. "Seems I've lost my appetite," Joshua said, acutely aware of the pressure building behind his eyes.

She topped off his glass with the Cape Verde Gewürztraminer he brought.

"I'm 100% sure that won't help," Joshua said, but then took the offered glass. "But it can't hurt either." Though he knew it would.

"Look, I'm here to help in whatever way I can. I don't want you to worry."

His eyes bugged out wide as he looked at her.

"Fine, worry if you want, but we're planning on having a peek at their computers. If they're behind this latest hack, which is likely, then we'll get him and her. I don't imagine she'd be stupid enough to upload anything at the office."

"You'd be surprised. We hackers are an arrogant bunch. I can help, you know."

"I know, but no. I don't want any of your mad Ninja skills taking over. My team and I are good at what we do. Trust me."

Surprisingly, he did.

"Right now, it's all speculation. Granted the connection between the two and then to you makes for a compelling case against them. Quick thinking on the license plate too."

"Yay, I cracked the case," Joshua said with little enthusiasm.

"Can I just say that you're amazingly calm, considering," she said.

"Ninja calm. Years of practice." There was a quiet resignation in his words as if he'd always suspected, even known, that HaMikdash3.0 was only a bit player in the great Cosmic plan of events. For Joshua, 3.0 was always intended to be a means to an end. The End. Maybe it wasn't in his aegis, his right to challenge the nuanced, inner workings of G-d's plan.

For now, if only for tonight, he wanted to forget. Tomorrow's worries would be here soon enough.

The next moment was a defining one as they once again looked at one another. Professionalism be damned, she wanted, needed, to comfort him as if that had always been her purpose, her reason for being.

For the moment, he wanted to forget about HaMikdash3.0, Hazon Labs… about everything. Tomorrow, and the next tomorrow, would be a day of reckoning, of decisions to be made, on how to move forward… or not.

For now, it was *Shabbat*, maybe his last one, and the five-alarm fire of burning questions needed to be quenched. He took this woman he barely knew in his arms and held her close. She reached up to him, a breach of every ethical protocol, but which held no sway over her heart. Joshua's world was imploding. No words passed between them. The next moment erupted in an explosion of color and fragmented scenes, lifetimes together but always left unfinished, leaving them to find one another again across Time.

He lifted her easily onto his hips and carried her through the apartment, eventually finding her bedroom after first opening the door to the bathroom, then Effi's room before finally opening door #3 and collapsing on her bed laughing. There was no frantic rush, ripping away at one another's clothes. They rolled to opposite sides of the bed and slowly began removing each piece of clothing, drinking in one another, savoring each moment as if it were their last.

SHABBAT/ SATURDAY

Chapter 16

Shabbat Morning, September 28, 2024
Giv'at Shmuel Neighborhood, Near Ramat Gan

On his way home from the *Beit Knesset*, Jay did what he always did… he stopped at the Sheba Medical Center, Brain Care Rehabilitation Unit to visit Julia Morgenthau. The staff no longer wondered if he was family, a former lover, or just a friend, they were just grateful that a long-term patient hadn't been forgotten.

He entered the claustrophobically small room which in reality wasn't all that small, except most spaces felt relatively small against his 6'5" frame. As far as hospital rooms go Julia's was large enough to accommodate her hospital bed, an air mattress compressor to minimize decubitus ulcers, i.e. bedsores, a night table, a straight-back chair, and a recliner. The small wristwatch on Julia's arm measured her temperature, respiratory and heart rates, and blood pressure, reducing the clutter of monitors and other equipment. It also told the time. The semi-permanent shunt introduced in the top of her head siphoned off just enough cerebrospinal fluid to keep her intracranial pressure in check. Her room had a large picture that overlooked the well-manicured gardens below. In early May, Jay took her down to the garden, a short-lived excursion when she was stung by a bee and had a profound anaphylactic reaction. Thankfully, the garden was equipped with a complete *United Hatzalah* First-Aid station just for those kinds of emergencies. He jammed the EPIPEN® into her thigh with such force he'd left a bruise that took weeks to resorb, turning all shades of blue and purple before fading to green and then finally yellow. He'd held her, while the doctors checked her thoroughly. Only afterward did he feel the wet spot on his shoulder where her head had rested. He looked deeply into her eyes, wondering if she was still in there. The last thing he wanted to do was inflict more pain on her already wrecked body. If pressed, he would swear that her tears had been purposeful; intentional in response to the painful stimulus. He'd considered the possibilities then of her recovering. Was it even possible? Was she still conscious, aware on some level?

From that day on, he spoke to her with greater confidence, talking *with* her as if she understood every word.

"Hey, Jules. Sorry, I'm late. They couldn't get a *minyan* again. No surprise there." He would have liked to change shuls, but he liked the 6:30 start time. Besides, if he abandoned them, he doubted the neighborhood's alter-cocker *Beit Knesset* would survive. As it was, he was often only the 9th man as the *gabbai* then became the town crier trying to rustle up a quorum of ten. Jay also tried to visit Julia on Fridays on his way home from work, whenever possible. But yesterday, he was wiped and could only make his usual *Shabbat* morning visit.

"Major crisis yesterday and wouldn't you know it, Josh and I were out of the office. He gave a lecture at Reichman. You know, IDC. Anyway, the timing of the hack makes me wonder. The whole thing stinks, there's something not quite right, though I can't put my finger on it. But, hey, you don't want to hear about my paranoia. Maybe I'm developing a bit of Joshua's Spidey sense." He paused, wondering, as always, if it was okay to bring up Joshua.

You look so tired, Jay. Thank you for always coming to see me. I like the updates. Go on. I want to know.

"The teams managed to get a handle on it, even without the J1-J2 dynamic duo on hand. Still, it was weird. I might as well tell you. They transposed a Miss Piggy head onto our lamb *korbanot*. You know, for one of HaMikdash's sacrifices. I told you about those. Anyway, it came off like a prank, made to look like it was some punk kid hacker behind it. Except we both know that pranks aren't always pranks." He paused again, wondering if she ever really heard him or if he used these visits more as an opportunity to think out loud. He was careful to never say anything that might hurt her feelings, inchoate as they may be. "We sure could have used your help, J-girl."

He dropped his head down to her hand. It was cool to the touch as always, but smooth against his skin.

✻ ✻ ✻

I would have been happy to help, but I know you and Joshua can handle it without me...

Even her doctors were clueless about Julia's newfound awareness. She could hear everything; understand most of it; and, desperately, wished she could speak or communicate in some way. She had to find a way to warn them. But how? Or was she already too late?

Her blinks were now purposeful, she'd mastered them, though the movement might be misconstrued as involuntary or worse, a seizure sending the staff running for the nearest drug cart to dope her up into a semi-comatose state far worse than the quasi-vegetative state she was in.

Oink, oink, and that horrid cackle. Something Jay said... hidden in a seemingly innocent prank, she realized.

Think Julia, think. A binary code message would take too long. Or would it? She ran the binary: 01001010 00110100 00100000 00111001 00110001 00110001 Doable but too difficult to distinguish the 0s from the 1s. It would appear too random, despite her intention.

Could she remember Morse Code's dits-dahs code for what she needed to tell him? Keep it simple. Would he recognize the cipher identifier their team added at the beginning of the training sessions to verify user idents? She had to try.

Look up Jay, look up. I need to warn you. You're both in terrible danger.

She crafted a careful message to convey danger and its source.

Jay! Her mind screamed.

He looked up and smiled, then stood to leave. He bent to kiss her gently on her cheek and looked lovingly, longingly, into her fiery green eyes.

With his face only inches from hers, she began the message –..–

She repeated it. –..– Closing her eyes for the dahs and blinking rapidly for the dits.

Jay, come on!

He looked at her quizzically. "Julia?" She repeated her call sign, J3, before continuing with the message.

.– – – ...– – then she paused, closing her eyes then opening them for the new signal sequence. – – – – .. – – – .– – –

She repeated the short message only fluently this time. Her message could be read with the second string first or second, the message, J4 911 or 911 J4.

Jackie had never been part of their group, a wannabe who resented Julia for usurping her place. Or at least what she presumed to be her place in her warped mind. She'd only become more obsessed during their time in 8200. *How long ago was that?*

Julia recognized her immediately. The different hair colors, and the new piercings. It had to be what, at least five years. No, five years since the accident, longer since they'd served together. Jackie came a while back, but Julia couldn't say how long ago that was.

There was a calendar on the wall that said what day of the week it was, but months and years were deemed too depressing measures to mark the passage of time to be used or of any use.

No jacket, only a T-shirt. If she were to guess, it was probably early spring. The black iris bloomed briefly, a depressingly beautiful flower. Jackie carried it in a bud vase with no water, set it on the window sill, and then came to sit next to Julia. Offensively close.

"Hey there, girl. Remember me? It's Jackie. What do you think? I'm looking pretty good these days. Your Joshua seems to think so. Oh, I'm working with your two boys."

Julia seethed. Her monitors captured a minor spike in her blood pressure and heart rate, but which grew exponentially with each passing minute in the presence of the she-devil.

"I must say, you're really not looking very good there. Bet you're not feeling so good either. Must be a bitch stuck in bed with no one to play with. Any who, just wanted to stop by, and catch you up on a few things."

Jackie went on for a while about the plan she and the Professor had cooked up. She gleefully took credit for most of the plan to destroy Joshua. Jay would go down too, though he wasn't her primary target.

"Oh, how the high and mighty will fall," she shouted so loud that the nurse down the hall came running.

"Guess that's my cue to leave. You take care now," she said, adding a wicked smile borne of perceived wrongs infused with delusions of grandeur. "Bye, bye, bitch," Jackie sneered, then weirdly added, "Oink, oink! I'll be seeing you. NOT!"

During their 8200 days, Julia had correctly diagnosed her with at least one psychopathy and several other borderline tendencies; all spot on. She'd warned Joshua and Jay to steer clear. She needed to warn them again but then she'd had a minor stroke, major in her case after her intracranial pressure spiked. She'd only just recently recovered enough of her faculties to attempt communicating.

What did Jay say... something pink, Miss Piggy!

She was getting tired, but she needed to warn him. *Come on, Jay. See it.* .– – – …– – then she paused, closing her eyes then opening them for the new signal sequence. – – – – . . – – – . – – – but he'd only picked up the last two numbers 1, 1 . – – – .– – –

"One, one," he said.

She began again. .– – – …– – pausing and closing her eyes.

"J4," he said.

Yes! She wanted to shout, but there wasn't much time left. She needed to finish the critical message – – – – then a pause. – – – before pausing again for the last sequence. – – – and then Julia closed her eyes to punctuate the message.

"911," he said, deciphering her blinks. "J4 Jackie, 911 emergency." Julia stared at him wide-eyed. He paused, interpreting the message, understanding dawning. "911, danger?" he asked.

Julia closed her eyes, keeping them closed for what she perceived was a two-count, then opened them again. A single tear skittered down her cheek as her eyes misted into a blank stare and the veil of death that had shadowed her for five long years finally fell over her. The effort had taken all she had left, a sacrifice worth giving. She loved them both. Now it was up to them to stop her. Her wrist monitor alarm beeped loudly, triggering a louder alarm, joined by the overhead Code-Blue announcement as Julia's heart stopped and every other signal dropped below life-sustaining thresholds.

The nurses rushed into the room, followed by the doctors, and another nurse pushed a crash cart.

"She's a DNR," Jay said. "Thank you, Julia," he said, moving to the doorway.

He waited until they pronounced her death at 7:52 AM.

The funeral would likely not be until Monday. Most of Julia's family was scattered around Europe or lived in the States. Sunday evening at the earliest, he figured. He'd let Joshua know after *Shabbat*. He remained in the doorway to her room as the medical team scattered. "*Baruch Dayan HaEmet*," he said. *Blessed is the Judge of Truth.*

※ ※ ※

At eight-fifteen *Shabbat* morning, Davi sent Joshua off with a 16-ounce go-cup of coffee and a sweet kiss on his cheek. "I'll keep you posted."

"I know," he said, punctuating the simple statement with a drawn-out sigh. "What's done is done," he added.

"If it's okay, I'll meet you at the J-SPCA event?" she asked.

"No problem. I better get going."

"Joshua, is HaMikdash salvageable?"

"An interesting question. We can always start over, or maybe just wait for the real thing to come down from Heaven with any luck."

"Not from under the Temple Mount?" she asked, genuinely curious and wondering if she'd caught the HaMikdash3.0 bug.

"I don't think so," Joshua said, then added, "but what do I know."

"Try and get some rest. You look tired," she said with an afterglow smile that lit up her face.

"Yeah, and who's fault is that?" he said, with a self-satisfied smirk.

"I don't want you to worry. We're going after the evidence. We've got a plan. I have someone getting into their apartment on Sunday morning." She didn't mention that part of the plan would begin shortly after *Shabbat* ended when residents of the *Nachlaot* apartment on *Hakarmel Street* would experience glitchy problems with their electricity.

"Then I look forward to Sunday."

"I'll let you know if anything comes up before then." A small fib on her part. Joshua didn't need to know the operational details of their sting operation to nail Jackie Allon and Ezra Noiman.

"Sounds good. Tell Effi, I'll bring the NDA and contract for him to sign Sunday so he can feel safe telling me his ideas."

"You have made my nephew very happy."

"De nada," he said, then added, "thanks… for everything."

They hugged at the door. He kissed the hand-crafted *mezuzah* on the right doorpost; a once-clear, stoppered test tube decorated with a precisely patterned patchwork of colored tissue paper. The parchment with the *Shema* was visible between the colored papers giving the piece a stained-glass effect.

"Effi's handiwork, age 5."

"Impressive. Talented."

"Runs in the family," she said smiling, then stood on her tiptoes and kissed him again softly on his lips.

✳ ✳ ✳

Joshua began the 30-minute walk from *Katamonim* to *Rehavia*. People were already on the street rushing to *Shacharit* prayers, soldiers carrying their weapons on leave for a few days, but always on duty. Fathers pushing a stroller or walking hand-in-hand with their children. He/they greeted one another with a simple, "*Shabbat Shalom*," and a few answered him back, adding the word, *U'Mevorach*, turning the phrase into "*A Peaceful and Blessed Shabbat.*" It should only be.

While Jerusalem hadn't been hit like much of the north or coastal cities, but the escalation in rocket and drone attacks from Yemen, Lebanon, and Iran put all of Israel in the target zone. He took a shortcut through *San Simone* Park, passing the dog area on his right. He could imagine Boomer chasing around the open space, while he worked. The park had Wi-Fi and a coffee truck. Sunday's J-SPCA brunch was a dog-friendly event. Fortunately, he was only required to say a few remarks, hand over a check, and stay long enough for the mandatory photo op. The Director was gushing about the puppies and older dogs that would be on hand and available for adoption. Joshua was sure Boomer would approve. He stood there awhile and finished the still-warm coffee, thinking but not thinking. The moment of reflection bled into another as the dream sequence again rushed forward. What did it all mean? What did any of it mean? Neither the parts nor the whole made any sense in the Gestalt of Joshua E. Katz's life. The book, the movie…

He slowed his approach to the *Shtiblach*, the neighborhood *Beit Knesset* at the top of *Ha'Khish Street*. At least three or four times a week, mostly in the mornings, he'd gone there to say the Mourner's *Kaddish* prayers for his Opa Jacob. There was always a *minyan*, a quorum of 10 men, to be found. He wasn't in the mood to chat with anyone and sped up, continuing on *HaPalmach Street* for another ten minutes, past the Islamic Museum at the top of the hill before veering to the left onto *Beit HaNassi*. He offered a simple wave of acknowledgment to the guards patrolling the President's House, before taking a shortcut down *Radak Street* to *Derech Aza*. He continued past his apartment, allowing his feet to guide him toward the Old City, mindlessly crossing the intersection of *Keren HaYesod Street* where it turned into *King George Street*.

Hopefully, he'd waited for the lights and remembered to check both ways. Though he couldn't be sure. Traffic was light on *Shabbat*; no buses tearing down the center lanes, mostly foot traffic of people, religious and otherwise, walking to and from the early *minyanim* when prayers started at seven-thirty or eight in the morning and finished by ten or 10:30 at the latest. A part of him envied the people sitting on the ground in Independence Park chatting and laughing seemingly without a care in the world… this world. That's what *Shabbat* was supposed to be like, a taste of *Olam HaBah*, the World to Come.

Across the street from the park, a high-security presence still paced the sidewalk outside the former U.S. Consulate. Mostly used as a satellite office, its official duties became secondary to the opening of the new U.S. Embassy on May 14, 2018, by then-President Trump. The uproar began on December 6, 2017, when the President rectified the hemming and hawing excuses and repeated six-month waivers, invoked by his predecessors for over 23 years, to finally and officially recognize Jerusalem as Israel's eternal and undivided capital. He acknowledged that fact by moving the U.S. Embassy to Israel's capital city… an official recognition that came 70 years after the founding of the State of Israel. If the rumors were to be believed, the old Consulate facilities were being maintained as the future embassy for a Palestinian state.

Continuing down *Gershon Agron Street*, named after the founding editor of the Jerusalem Post newspaper, Joshua paid little attention to the machine-gun-slinging guard, who paused just long enough from chatting with his partner, to scrutinize Joshua as he passed. The questions about his dream had been temporarily put on hold while at Davi's, but they had come back full force as he walked toward home. Home… Which home was that? The one on *Ben Maimon Street* or his other home on *Har HaZei'tim*.

Be careful what you ask for you just might get it. He'd asked and gotten an answer, of sorts. Satisfying and disturbing at the same time. The timing of the dream was troubling, contemporaneous with his suspicions about Jackie and her partner-in-crime, Ezra Noiman. Joshua couldn't help but wonder if the dream was less about him and more about HaMikdash3.0? Could he salvage it from whatever damage the pair had wreaked on what he viewed as his life's work? There were still too many unknowns and more questions still to be asked.

*　*　*

The social hall in the Ethiopian Center in *Beit Shemesh* overflowed with family and friends. Yafa Mengistu joined the women dancing around her youngest son and smiled warmly at each *Mazal Tov*. A few of her relatives asked after Tzion. She didn't know what to tell them and didn't want to lie, especially not on *Shabbat*... not on Zevie's *Bar Mitzvah*. His *Torah* reading, a double *parsha* of *Nitzavim-Vayeilech* from the book of *Devarim* (Deuteronomy), was pitch-perfect from start to finish. His accomplished reading of his *Bar Mitzvah parsha* was all the more impressive after overcoming the challenges of dyslexia which had sidelined his academic progress during his grade school years. Reading was particularly challenging. The reading difficulties were wrongly attributed to cultural differences until he was finally and properly diagnosed in 5th Grade. The combined *parshiot* were especially beautiful, and blessedly short, as *Moshe Rabbeinu* instructed the people to gather and read the entire *Torah* publicly every seven years. The reading ends with the Song of Moses, *Shir shel Moshe*, which G-d commanded Moshe to write down as testimony to His everlasting covenant with the Jewish people. Zev's voice sang the words as if an angelic choir had entered his soul. He stopped and cried a few times during the reading, which most people attributed to the moment. Yafa knew differently. Tzion had helped Zev practice this portion of the *Torah* reading, and her eldest son's absence today was most acutely felt by her youngest.

The youngest and the oldest of her seven children were not only brothers but also good friends, sharing interests in biking and computers. Yafa tried her best to hide her grave concern over Tzion, but after she'd been unable to reach him by phone Friday afternoon a feeling of dread overwhelmed the joy she should have felt at the festive Friday night dinner. Tzion had assured her he would leave Jerusalem in time to arrive in *Beit Shemesh* well before *Shabbat*.

"*Ima*, I wouldn't miss Zev's *Bar Mitzvah* for anything in the world."

"Better you're a little late, than rush driving here."

"Yes, *Ima*. You know I'm always careful." Which he was, Yafa knew. She'd tried calling him right up until candle lighting, believing he'd walk through the door, kiss her on the cheek, and join the *Bar Mitzvah* festivities.

Her sleep had been restless, fear punctuating the brief moments of rest she found. She'd left her phone on, mandatory with the war, but also feared a call from the *Mishtara* or one of Jerusalem's trauma hospitals with news of Tzion. Her frustration mounted with each passing hour, knowing she would have to wait until after *Shabbat* to try and track him down. She forced herself to think of simpler, more benign reasons for his absence. Maybe he had car trouble, a simple matter. Or his phone was lost. The battery died. Yafa hoped her eldest was safe in his apartment.

While walking to *Beit Shemesh* was doable, only a seven-plus-hour trek along the Israel National Trail, and far shorter than their journey on foot in Ethiopia, she doubted Tzion would undertake the route, especially after sundown. She prayed he wouldn't and certainly not in the middle of a war or after dark. Yafa knew Zev tried his best not to show his disappointment at first, but then even his feelings shifted to concern over Tzion mirroring her own worries.

"I'm sure Tzion is okay, *Ima*. *Ha-Shem* will watch over him. You'll see. Everything will be okay."

"Oh Zevie, I'm so proud of you," she said, hugging her youngest who'd become a man according to Jewish tradition on his *Bar Mitzvah*.

Asef looked on as his youngest son comforted his mother. His gentle soul had brought great pride and joy to his family. All his children did, especially Tzion… his firstborn. His eldest was often late, or absent from family gatherings, but knowing how close the brothers were Asef knew this was one day Tzion would never miss. Weaned on their family's journey from Gondar to Addis Ababa, walking hundreds of miles across the barren landscape, save for marauding criminal gangs harassing them even as the Ethiopian Jewish community was leaving, Asef knew that if his son were able he would have walked proudly from Jerusalem to *Beit Shemesh* to be a part of his brother's *simcha*. He didn't want to think about the possibilities, which were too numerous to count. While Asef tried not to worry Yafa, in his heart of hearts he knew something terrible had happened to his son. Shielding his fears from Yafa, he asked *Ha-Shem* to send watchful angels to guard over Tzion.

Little did Asef know, at least two very capable Guardian Angels were already on the job.

Protect him I beg you, Asef's heart whispered. He then came up behind Zev, hugging him with both arms. His eyes met Yafa's knowing the next few hours would be the hardest, and the longest to endure. Waiting. Wondering. Hoping.

"Today will bring what will be. Come, let's dance. You too, my love," he said to his wife, her eyes brimming with tears of joy and fear.

The Waldorf Astoria Hotel came up quickly on his right; his final destination was no longer in question, only how to get there safely. The intersection at the bottom of *Agron* was one of the busiest, offering a vista of the Old City walls on one side, and a poorly maintained Muslim cemetery across the street. He opted to cut through the Jewish Quarter rather than circling the Old City walls, walking along *Sultan Suleiman Street* on the north, past Zedekiah's Cave to reach the Eastern side of the Old City. Instead, he crossed the street to the Mamilla Mall. The shops were all closed for *Shabbat*, teasingly offering their goods in view-only mode, enticing any strolling window shoppers. He walked past the stores, ignoring the latest fashions from Diesel, Renuar, Zara, and Mango. Not even the numbered stones or the latest *plein air* installation of sculptures from two dozen artists gave him pause.

The steps to the Jaffa Gate lay just beyond the mall. But the last sculpture gave him pause. He looked at it from both sides, trying to understand the artist's construct. The majority of the sculptures in the mall depicted people, imagined in fanciful ways, but this sculpture showed the Western Wall. At least, part of Wall. An entire section had been hollowed out with a gaping hole cut into it. The sculpture conveyed a portal of sort leading into the wall, through the wall, and to a place, a *makom*, beyond the wall. The open space was filled with a shimmer visible from both the front and back of the portal opening. Perhaps, the artist saw the Western Wall in transition, a transformation representing a future time, or maybe the portal was from a different space-time dimension contemporaneous with their own in a confluence of past, present, and future across a multiplexed multidimensional array but which otherwise remained hidden, existing beyond the five senses' capacity to sense it? *Welcome to the Matrix*, Joshua thought.

He took note of the artist's name and gallery affiliation, a to-do after *Shabbat*. Normally, he'd jot a note to himself on his cellphone. Not on *Shabbat*, mind you, but in the association Joshua realized he didn't have his phone. He recalled slipping it into the swag backpack's side pocket. No doubt, it was still there silently vibrating for his attention.

Today, he welcomed "leaving behind" the distraction that kept him tied to everyday matters. The mundane. The inane pursuits. The follies of Man. He'd email Davi after *Shabbat* and ask her to extract it from the backpack's side pocket and get it from her Sunday morning. It could wait till the J-SPCA brunch, though it would be nice to see Davi before then.

Joshua realized she'd probably smartly, rightly, put any further romantic involvement between them on hold until after MAGSS' assignment with Hazon Labs was over. Maybe then, they could see. Or not. There was something intangible about their connection he couldn't explain. A sense of unfinished business, even though they'd only just met… or had they? Had they met before, or possibly known one another in another life? He often joked about "another life" maybe there was something to it. For now, though, he put the past-lives question on hold.

The Old City was already teeming with locals and clusters of tourists who'd braved the war and outrageous airfares to visit Israel during the upcoming holidays. Jews, Christians, and Muslims rushed across the open plaza leading from the Jaffa Gate, past Migdal David to one of four side streets. While tempted to cut through the *Arab Souk* following a dizzying number of side paths that would eventually take him along the Way of the Cross, the Via Dolorosa, the Lion's Gate, and out of the Old City, he was distracted enough to get himself into trouble. Instead, he veered and followed along the Armenian Patriarch's Way, an actual street where cars were allowed. He could decide his next move from there. If he continued straight circling around the Armenian Quarter, the route would certainly be less crowded than going through the Jewish Quarter. He'd be treated to an additional reward, a magnificent vista winding its way to *Habad Street* and down the *Batei HaMaseh* Road. He would still be within the Old City's walls, but on the outermost periphery following the ramparts' path but at ground level.

Any of the paths would do, since any and all would bring him to where he needed to be… *Har HaZei'tim*. Some routes were longer, some shorter, and some to be avoided, especially in his current distracted state of mind trapped somewhere between here and there, though exactly where there was he couldn't say for sure. Joshua decided on the sure route through the Jewish Quarter, veering left onto St. James Way — an ironic name for a path leading into the Jewish Quarter, the *Rova HaYehudi*. The sign attesting to the Saint's name had been repeatedly inked out with a marker and the name, *Derech HaKotel*, the *Path of the Kotel*, written on the plaque.

The Old City streets were familiar to him, like someone who'd lived there all of their life. He'd made friends with each of the Old City's Gates in constructing HaMikdash3.0. The plazas on any given day were filled with old men and children playing in the streets, their peels of laughter and soccer balls rolling in the streets, fulfilling the prophecy from the Zechariah, Chapter 8, Verses 4-5.

> 'There shall yet old men and old women sit in the broad places of Jerusalem, every man with his staff in his hand for very age. And the broad places of the city shall be full of boys and girls playing in the broad places thereof.'

And so it was, just as the prophecy foretold.

The crowds grew thicker, pouring in from the narrow streets that led from one named street to another, honoring a former Chief Rabbi or *Torah* scholar, others named for benefactors. Men, women, and children dressed in their finery, off to *Shabbat* morning prayers at the *Kotel*, soon to be swaying from side-to-side or forward and backward, bending deeply in supplication or thanks… a discontinuous continuum of prayers all striving for ascendency to Heaven's Gates.

His way from here was clear as he exited through the Dung Gate, turning left onto *Ma'ale HaShalom Road*, the Peaceful Ascent, which was anything but on most days, perpetually clogged with city and tour buses. Today, the tour buses were parked along the sidewalk and on it, having discharged hundreds of visitors on prayer missions, eager to pay their respects at Christian and Jewish holy sites. Joshua followed the curving road past the UNRWA school next to *Ir David*, the City of David, and then crossed to the eastern side of *Derech HaOphel*. Around the corner, further up the road, was a popular site for the annual *Ramadan* rock-throwing festival, targeting the #1 and #3 public buses. But today there were only a few people nearby, and a fox or two playing on the Old City's southern wall and fulfilling yet another prophecy, albeit in a convoluted explanation.

From here, Joshua could look into the *Kidron Valley* with its ancient towering monuments, Absalom's Tomb and Zechariah Tomb, separated by the *Bene Hazir Tomb*, belonging to a priestly family during the Hasmonean period, dating back to the 2nd century BCE. What Joshua always found difficult to reconcile in this lower portion of *Har HaZei'tim* was its utter disrepair, of the barely-there graves and headstones destroyed by the ravages of time and scorched by the evil of men. Tzion had incorporated a special interactive into HaMikdash3.0 for cleaning up the *Kidron Valley*; one Joshua hoped would transfer into the real world and bring honor to those buried here.

So many dead people. To his left, the *Bab al-Rahma Muslim Cemetery* sat at the foot of the Old City's walls strategically placed to prevent the *Moshiach/Messiah* from entering through the sealed Golden Gates; and the Catholic Cemetery at the southern end of the *Kidron Valley*, home to the nuns and priests of generations past; and, all the souls buried on *Har HaZei'tim*. He was almost home as he turned right following *Derech Yericho's* eastern ascent. The normally busy street skirted below the Eastern Orthodox Christian Church of Mary Magdalene with its iconic golden, onion-shaped domes towering on the hillside to the north of the multi-tiered levels of *Har HaZei'tim*.

Joshua E. Katz turned onto the Path of Priests, *Derech HaKohanim*, which ran parallel to *Har HaZei'tim* along its northern edge. He only needed to walk a few steps up the path to the plot of Earth belonging to his family. The depth of the question, the weight of the answer had brought him here. Or was it the weight of the question, and the depth of the answer that left him with no other recourse? The collection of five stone monuments were his family; four covered the Earthly remains of his loved ones. He stared at the empty space, his place, next to his parents. He'd be nestled between his mother on the right and the farthest of the *matzevas*, which held no bodies beneath its stone cover. The granite bore the names of Opa Jacob's family who'd been murdered in the *Shoah*.

These were the generations of the Katzenstein/Katz family dating back only three generations but with space left for one of their own from the fourth generation. By some form of prophetic insight or prescience, Joshua's end was given a space among them, already defined, predestined some fifty-two years ago when Jacob purchased the family plot.

Here were all the answers to all the questions, and the most recent one which he prefaced with an apology. The answers were all here, his for the taking but which, nonetheless, remained just beyond reach... He stretched his arms out wide, tipping his head backward, raising his face to the Heavens. This time the questions passing his lips reached back over time, to the very beginning, and were given voice in a silent scream. *Why G-d, why am I here? What more do you want from me? Please, help me! Help me fulfill my purpose.*

The first drop of rain, a tiny tear from Heaven fell across Joshua's face as he recited the *Birkat HaKohanim*, the Priestly blessing. He splayed the fingers of both hands in a split *Shin* formation, touching his thumbs together; the right and left hand, Kindness and Judgement, *Chesed* and *Gevurah*, joined together with G-d's name *Sha-ddai* represented by the letter *Shin*. The offering... a blessing to his family, to the thousands of dead surrounding him, and for himself. How much time had passed since he'd last uttered the words meant little in the grand Cosmic clock that kept Time for this world. Today, he stood, like generations of *Kohanim* before him, spanning across time from Aaron, Moses' brother, the first *Kohen*, to him, the last hope for his lineage.

Traditionally, the blessings are spoken from beneath a *tallit*, the covering creating a sacred space, its solemnity matched as the congregation bowed their heads or closed their eyes in humility, ready to receive the blessings as a gift. G-d's Divine Presence on Earth, the *Shekinah*, is said to enter this holy space, where the *tallit* further serves to respect the boundaries between earthly dwellings and the Divine realms. But there were no eyes to watch him, or *tallit* to cover him as he recited the blessings from the book of *Numbers*, Chapter 6 verses 24-26.

"The L-rd Bless thee and keep thee; The L-rd make His face to shine upon thee, and be gracious to thee; The L-rd lift up His countenance upon thee, and give thee peace."

The tears from Heaven continued to flow as Joshua's legs trembled and he dropped to his knees. He wasn't sure what power had taken possession of his body, but his soul called out to him as he brought his chest to the ground. The crown of his head faced the Temple Mount; his forehead pressed to the ground and hands stretched out in front of him, prostrating himself in full submission to G-d's will. Joshua recited the words of the *Shema* prayer.

Spoken throughout the generations in daily prayers and as the last words of G-d's holy martyrs. Today, Joshua offered the six words with a pure heart completed in humility and devotion. He inhaled through his nose, speaking a word with each breath, a testimony to the Unity of G-d, accepting His sovereignty, proclaiming Him King over all Creation, and declaring his willingness to sacrifice his life for His sake. With each breath, he drew the Light down from the Heavens. *Shema Yisroel, Ha-Shem Elokeinu,* and concluding the affirmation with the conjoined words, *Ha-Shem Echad…* G-d is One. The Light grew in intensity, exponentially diminishing the darkness plaguing the Earth. In a hushed whisper, Joshua continued with the words *Blessed be the Name of His Kingdom's Glory forever and ever.* His words reverberated across the Heavens as a chorus of Angels proclaimed to the generations of the World, *Holy, Holy, Holy* as the last soul spark destined to be born finally fell from the Tree of Souls, carried on an unseen wind into the Treasury of Souls, the *Guf,* before descending to Earth.

SUNDAY

Chapter 17

Sunday, September 29, 2024, 08:00
MAGSS Team Meeting.
Jerusalem Technology Park

By 08:03, the Hazon Labs financial forensics and cybersecurity team had their fill of coffee and the breakfast treats Davi delivered at 07:00 that morning. It was a modest show of appreciation on her part for their having worked through the night. With the connection between Jackie Allon and Ezra Noiman established, Davi set in motion a plan to gather the evidence against the pair.

The plan — an electrical ruse — would gain them entry into the *Nachlaot* apartment the two shared. They went operational two hours after *Shabbat* ended. Before proceeding, they checked with the Municipality if there were any special-needs residents in the building who depended on any life-saving electrical equipment, ventilators, chair lifts, or the like before hitting the building with a series of minor, though annoying, power outages. Then it would only be a matter of gaining remote access to their computer network; a piece of cake, relatively speaking.

The convergence between the Hazon Labs' security assignment, J-SPCA event, and Friday's cyberattack crystalized with the *Mishtara's* recent efforts to shut down dark web-based cybercrimes, targeting both criminal and financial offenders. Davi had been given the equivalent of a no-knock warrant, a *carte blanche* mandate to pursue Allon and Noiman.

"With pleasure," she smiled and gladly accepted help from the Australian A-team: identical twins, Avner and Avigdor, powerhouses of brains and brawn weighing in at a muscle-packed 100 kilos (225 pounds) at 1.89 meters tall (6'2") with matching long blonde ponytails. She welcomed the assist.

The MAGSS team had previously worked with the Australian twins on special assignments where confusion could be leveraged into an operational plan, and most definitely when an arrest, or two, was expected. After completing their required Army service as lone soldiers, the *Shabak*, more popularly known outside of Israel as *Shin-Bet*, tried to recruit them. But the fair-skinned blondes opted to join the Israel Police Force instead, working undercover for a time as *mista'arvim* — a special forces unit of the Israeli Police Force practiced in undercover and infiltration operations.

Davi kept the details only to the essentials her team needed, including not mentioning Allon's employee status with Hazon Labs as the inside "man."

"Once we established Allon's connection to forty-four-year-old Ezra Noiman, former Professor of Computer Science at Technion we initiated the sting operation. The timing was a godsend when Allon's name showed up on the J-SPCA guest list, a last-minute addition late Friday, and we scrambled to take them down today. The two live together at an apartment owned by Noiman on *Hakarmel Street* in Jerusalem's *Nachlaot* neighborhood, near *Machane Yehuda*.

From the back of the room, she heard Avner gag at the mention of the apartment. She understood. The techs were cataloguing the recovered video clips which even made her blush.

"Despite Allon's claim to be bodysurfing in Tel Aviv on Friday during the cyberattack at Hazon Labs her phone was pinged in *Nachlaot*."

Davi nodded to one of the techs who'd collected psych profiles on the two.

"While Allon's psych profile is dated to her 8200 service, even then she was identified with a borderline personality disorder and sociopathic tendencies. Given the general unpredictability and volatility of sociopaths, the natural sequelae we should be prepared for is an escalation at some point. She's potentially dangerous."

"A profile to be given due consideration, folks. Our Sunday walk in the park, may not be quite so pleasant."

"What about the Professor," asked Genia Silberman, who'd be working the J-SPCA event registration desk. While she wouldn't have any direct contact with him, Genia was interested in his psychopathy profile. He might be a good candidate for her post-doctoral research project.

"Ah, the 'good' professor is a beast of a different kind," Davi said, picking up the question. "His psychological profile, also an old one was developed prior to his dismissal from Technion. It painted Noiman as a sadistic narcissist with borderline psychopathic tendencies, but which had been mostly kept in check by his academic successes. His disciplinary file, however, contained complaints of alleged sexual harassment by half a dozen students, both male and female. After losing his lawsuit against Joshua, he went off the rails, hurling a series of online attacks at the University for not supporting him in what should have been an airtight case over the disputed IP. Intellectual Property," she said, clarifying the term. Her team was top-notch, but not everyone was cued in to academia or start-up world assets. "Months later, his tenure was quietly rescinded, when a second psychological evaluation labeled him 'a danger to himself and others.'"

"Danger to the world they are," Avner added. "I can tell ya that's a fact. Those two are working the dark side."

The tech who'd watched one too many hours of their films had tagged the content back to a highly-rated, XXX-rated *OnlyFans* account. "That's putting it mildly. Both Noiman and Allon enjoy the darker side of BDSM and were likely drawn together by their predilections and mutual interest in Joshua Katz. While Noiman's motives are straightforward; Allon's are still muddled in the gray zone."

"Has Avner checked in yet?" Davi asked Avner, hoping she hadn't mixed up the identical twins with one another. She had, but Avner didn't bother correcting her.

"Not yet, but busy stirring up trouble with the electricals," he said. Avigdor, the slightly wiser and older by one minute than his brother often said, *What's the point, mate? Jes gonna happen again. Waste of air.* Avner couldn't disagree, though once brother Aaron finished his medical school studies and made *Aliyah* they might want revive their "Who's on first" Abbott and Costello-styled routine. The triplets drove their mom bonkers with their schoolboy antics, perfected as adults.

While Avigdor won the coin toss, fair and square, and could have insisted Avner take the *Nachlaot* part of the assignment, A1 took pity on A2 after Avner patently refused to go back to what he described as the "den of iniquity."

A2 brother was quick to remind him, "Ya owe me one. Big time," before heading out the door to get on with tinkering with the electricals at the apartment building on *Hakarmel Street*. According to the plan, later that morning Avigdor would give a knock on Ezra Noiman and Jackie Allon's apartment door, playing the role of the ever-helpful electrician there to solve the root cause of a recent spate of "very" mysterious power surges and outages plaguing the older, 3-story apartment building. The first part of the day's assignment was to give Davi a heads-up when Allon left the apartment for the J-SPCA event, and secondly, to arrest the hell out of Noiman.

The *Nachlaot* apartment was within easy running distance of *Gan Sacher* in case either of the brothers needed a helpful assist. They didn't expect any trouble, at least not from the Professor. Avner had been able to assess the physical risks after returning from the *Hakarmel Street* love nest of horrors a.k.a. torture chamber and reported his observations in excruciating detail. While Noiman was in reasonably good physical shape, his gait listed to the left, and he seemed to be perpetually high on something, all of which Avigdor could use to his advantage in a fight, if it came to that.

Avner hoped his brother would fare better than he did during, and after, his encounter with the pair. After leaving the *Nachlaot* apartment Avner rushed into the *Mekor Haim* apartment the brothers shared and turned on the *Dud Shemesh* to heat up the water for a much-needed shower.

"*Ha-Shem Yishmor*," he shouted. "The place reeks of pot, skanks, and aye so much evil," nearly gagging as the stink trailed him into the bathroom.

Twenty minutes later, he emerged from the steaming shower, begging his brother to take over the apartment assignment before proceeding to give Avigdor a blow-by-blow of the of the encounter, a.k.a. Avner's Misadventures in Skankdom.

* * *

At 9:45 PM, Saturday night, Avner pounded on the door to Apartment 2 and announced himself, "*Chashmal*." He knew they were home. Avner had knocked on the other six apartments in the building, apologizing to the other residents that they may experience intermittent power outages over the next twelve to twenty-four hours. He didn't add that said power *problemas* were of his doing. Most were just happy the internet was still up and running and they wouldn't experience a cascade of Murphy's Law issues.

He then proceeded to Apartment #2, banging his fist on the door again when it swung open.

"It's about time," Noiman shouted.

The MAGSS' brief included photos of the subjects. The shirtless man, wearing a pair of black boxers and sporting a heavy five o'clock shadow, was former Technion Professor Ezra Noiman. Forty-four-years-old and his body remained ripped. Avner made the threat assessment to determine whether by strength alone Noiman might be a problem. Stoned and drunk as he was at the moment, he could be handled, but below the legal limit, he couldn't say for sure.

"Hey, mate, no need gettin yourself in a snit. You're might lucky, I'm getting to you all sooner than later," Avner began explaining, only he didn't get far.

"What the hell took you people so long?"

"Hey mate, these old buildings have lots of cark outs."

"Well, I'm having a damn cark out, a serious electrical issue in the bedroom. I need that power back on, man."

"Hey, you don't want the firies and ambos comin, waken you out of the sack in the middle of the night? We're just checking in for now. Tomorrow, morning time I'll be back to fix you right again. I see you have a laptop. Any others?"

"Just the one."

"Ez, I could really use a little help in here," the female voice called from the other room. Jackie Allon.

"I'll just get on with it, if you don't mind. Need to check your powe-points."

"My what?" Noiman snickered, barely able to decipher the Australian's heavy accent.

"Ya plugs," Avner said, nodding to the outlet behind the desk.

"Fine, but don't mess with anything else."

"Is the lappy on?"

"Always."

"Ez, seriously. You've got to get this thing fixed. Oh wait, I got it out, but it keeps zapping me," Jackie said, stepping into the living room, wearing an oversized, mid-thigh-length T-shirt and carrying a device with a giant dildo attachment that even made the burly Australian blush.

"Blame him," Noiman said, sneering at Avner.

Avner shrugged his shoulders and then couldn't believe the next words out of his mouth. "Um, does that thing plug into a powe-point too?"

"Oh yeah," Jackie said, adding a breathy exhale.

Avner held his revulsion in check. "Any chance you can get that turned on?"

"With pleasure," she said, leering at him. It would have been nice if Davi had given him a heads-up on the hyper-sexed Jezebel.

"Just get on with it," Ez angrily said, grabbing Jackie by the arm and leading her back into the bedroom.

They planned to tap the laptop on Sunday but this was even better. If he could keep them busy the forensics guys would be able to gain access tonight, twelve hours ahead of schedule. With that "just in case" mode in mind, Avner came prepared with the micro-sized thumb drive that could be fitted into one of the laptop's USB open ports or interfaced directly with an existing USB cable. Once deployed, the not-so-friendly payload would give them remote access to the laptop, monitor keystrokes, and virtually collect files implicating Noiman and Allon. With any luck, they'd finish this gig way sooner than later... though not soon enough for Avner.

"Let me know when you want me to turn her on," Noiman shouted from the other room.

"Good onya." Avner continued fiddling with the electrical outlet, removing the cover and pulling out an array of wires, mostly for show, but keeping the impedance meter nearby in case Noiman unexpectedly poked his head out of the bedroom. The groaning and grunting began almost immediately.

He needed to give the USB adjunct another sixty seconds to reboot the laptop; a non-trivial problem with suspects getting it on in the next room. Most laptops favored a series of "welcome" tones when rebooting, he needed to cover the ding-a-ling with an alarm on his phone to ring in test mode.

Avner swallowed hard, bracing himself against his next shout-out, a little extra insurance to keep them busy in the other room. They seemed the type to video their kink adventures. He rolled his eyes before brokering the next question. "You have any other equipment tapping the building's electricals?"

"Hold on," Noiman said, annoyed at the interruption. He was just getting into it, watching Jackie perform less for his benefit and more for the guy in the next room. Noiman fed all of her appetites, but he was still twenty years older than her and looking at turning forty-five soon enough. He held no illusions about his ability to meet all her sexual needs. He flipped on the video camera, making a minor adjustment to the tripod to get the best angle.

Their homemade BDSM films provided them with a nice revenue stream on their dark web's Torrid Channel. He toyed with the idea of putting their vids on the surface web's porn platforms, indexed and ready for on-demand use, to fully monetize their exploits. Jackie couldn't care less if all the world saw her. Noiman, however, couldn't imagine the nuclear fallout from his ex-wife if his sixteen-year-old daughter ever came across one of their videos; the damage to their relationship would be irreversible. Though how his daughter might come across his "Professor of Porn" and "Doctor Kink," the stage names he favored, was a question she'd better be able to answer. They were a popular duo, and an even more popular trio when a third party joined in the fun. He briefly considered asking the Australian hunk, but he had a job to do, an important one.

"All set, here," Noiman shouted.

"Okay then," he said, but hesitated before asking, "does that have a higher shifter, you know a higher setting?"

This time, Jackie answered. "Oh yeah, oh yeah!"

Avner then heard Allor yelp.

The laptop finished rebooting. He covered the ting-tong tones, shouting, "Reckon yous got some high spikers. Pretty dodgy," he said, hoping he sounded professionally serious in Australian speak. He picked up his tools, and made his way to the bedroom door, careful to keep his back to them and eyes averted to the floor.

"All set here. I'll be back with yous tomorrow. Your wiring needs a fix, spike suppressor too. Say 10:30ish?"

"Whatever," Noiman grunted.

"You folks get on with what… I'll leave you to it then."

This time Jackie answered, "Come again, anytime." The whimper that followed made him wince, imagining Noiman going to town on her with that device of his.

Avner closed the apartment door behind him and gagged. "Skanks," but then felt bad about linking these creepers with the popular Reggae stylings of *Reserve Skank of Australia*.

*   *   *

Avigdor listened, laughing at Avner's deets about the pair's rooting, as in rooting like pigs.

"I can't go back there. I just can't. I'm going to have nightmares for a week."

"Come on, it's a quick in and out," Avigdor chuckled, then broke out in a full laugh at the deliberate double entendre.

"Very funny," Avner said, shaking his head. "Seriously, please. I gotta take another shower."

"Fine. I'll go. But don't forget you're bringing Luna with you tomorrow. She loves *Gan Sacher*."

"Good luck," Avner said, knowing he'd have to deal with Allon in a crowd, but at least it wouldn't be one-on-one. A part of him was looking forward to hearing Avigdor's play-by-play.

※ ※ ※

Avigdor approached the door to apartment #2, wondering how Avner had talked him into switching places. The J-SPCA event started at 11:00AM. With any luck, Allon would be out of the apartment in short order. He'd staked out the place since 9:00 AM to report if she or Noiman left the apartment earlier than expected. Neither had.

At 10:45, he pounded on the door, and announced, "*Chashmal*." He heard muffled sounds through the door, then rapped on it again with his fist.

"Coming," a female voice said from behind the door.

He rolled his eyes, sneered, and put on his best smiley face just as Jackie Allon opened the door. After Avner's description of the skank, he was happy to see she was mostly dressed. A mini frou-frou dress, though it barely covered her ass. Most folks put leggings underneath short dresses which were really only tops. Based on Avner's report and what they siphoned from their computer overnight, he guessed there might not be anything under the flowered print.

"Well, it's about time," Noiman said, coming into view as Avigdor crossed the "gateway to hell" threshold. "You're late. 10:30 has come and gone."

"Busy morning, mate. -Ish is 10:30ish."

"Just get on with it."

"Maybe, I'll stick around," Allon said, leering at Avigdor hoping for one of those infamous butt-crack scenes you always see in the movies when the handyman, or, in this case, the electrician, bends over. Damn, she forgot to mention to tell Ez to try and get the Aussie into bed. She could do with a little two-on-one action, a ménage à trois in her favor. Better not on second thought. Ez was in a shitty mood.

Avigdor was beginning to understand his brother's discomfort. Full-on skankeroos.

"Don't you have a thing this morning to get to?" Noiman reminded her with a sneer.

"But I can be a little late."

"Think again. Get dressed," Noiman said, manhandling her towards the bedroom, then let go of her arm pushing her through the doorway. She flashed Avigdor, flipping up her dress and giving Avigdor an eyeful of her bare ass and a tat that read, "your ass is mine" in fancy script. He'd already seen the tattoo hanging in the air in one of their homemade videos. Noiman closed the bedroom door loudly behind her.

Muttering the word, "Bitch" under his breath. Then seeing Avigdor still standing facing their bedroom door.

"Seen enough?"

"Hey," holding up his hands in surrender. "No drama here, mate. Have you right and ready in no time."

"Do that," Noiman said sharply, deciding against letting this Aussie anywhere near Jackie.

Avigdor unloaded his equipment. He'd make his move once Allon left the apartment. He'd brought along backup; H and T were having coffee around the corner at the Natural Choice Cafe on *Agripas*, waiting for his signal to take down Noiman.

Noiman got a text or video that held his attention. He smirked to himself. Ten minutes later, Allon emerged from the bedroom. Avigdor glanced over his shoulder. Her face flushed and her hair matted with sweat. She wore a pair of black leggings and a different top. Blue this time. It was his job to notice details.

"How come you didn't join me, Ez?"

"You were managing just fine on your own."

She kissed him hard on the lips. "I must be going. Duty calls."

Her electric scooter, a silver Apollo, rested against the wall, next to Noiman's pricey Pinarello DogmaX racing bike. She grabbed the scooter and headed for the door. "Bye, lover," speaking to Noiman but looking directly at Avigdor, who felt the bitter bite of bile at the back of his throat.

With a simple wave, she closed the door behind her.

"You gonna be much longer?"

"Be done in just a tick or two," Avigdor said, glancing at his watch and passing the signal to his team. He needed to continue the ruse for another two minutes, give or take, and giving H and T enough time to round the corner. He set about rewiring the perfectly good wiring, making a show of checking the resistance.

"You good on your own?" Noiman asked.

"Got that right, mate."

"I'm jumping in the shower."

"Good onya." Avigdor couldn't be sure if Noiman's shower announcement wasn't also an invitation. He wouldn't be surprised.

Just then there was a knock on the door. "Grand Central here," Noiman said.

"Probably, me mates."

Avigdor was on his feet as H and T burst through the door, guns drawn. Avigdor pinned Noiman's arms behind him. The sour stink of his breath reached his nostrils, making him gag. He shackled Noiman's hands behind his back using the plastic restraints.

"What the hell? What do you people think you're doing? Noiman protested, wriggling his hands against the tight restraints.

"Here to serve and protect. Rack on off with him," Avigdor said.

Noiman started to protest, "I have rights, you know. You can't come into a man's home…" then ridiculously he made a dash for the door.

A foolish play on any day. He was subdued almost immediately. H wrestled him to the floor, while Avigdor's elbow "accidentally" made contact with Noiman's nose.

"Resisting arrest. Nawghty, nawghty."

With an assist from H, Noiman stood. "Take him down to the car. Meet you there in a sec."

"Ah the privilege of rank," T said following Avigdor, A1, to the bedroom. They both looked inside, without crossing the threshold. "We'll be needing Hazmat," Avigdor said.

He grabbed the laptop from the desk on the way out of the apartment, sealing the door with crime scene tape until the forensics team arrived. He then sent Davi a message on WhatsApp®. "N in the cooler. JA scootering. *Baderech*," switching over to Hebrew for "on the way."

* * *

Sunday Morning, 10:54, Gan Sacher, Jerusalem

The Jerusalem-SPCA shelter's van driver leaned on the horn, sending the dozen caged puppies in the back of the van into a barking frenzy. The puppies along with half a dozen older dogs would be available for adoption and the requisite photo ops throughout the Jerusalem chapter of the Society for the Prevention of Cruelty to Animals annual event. Guests were already arriving and there were still millions of small details for Executive Director Tani Bennet to attend to. While *Gan Sacher*, Jerusalem's largest public park, was the ideal venue for the event, it was also a logistical nightmare. Located in the valley below the *Knesset* and other Israeli Government buildings, the open space hosted numerous non-profit events, most notably the spring time Jerusalem Winner Marathon's Finish Line.

The permissions from the Municipality allotted them approximately half a football pitch, or forty-two square meters (fifty square yards) in the middle of the park, separated from the winding walking/running path. Access to the path would have simplified setup; instead, they were forced to transfer equipment and food into half a dozen smaller carts for the trek across the grass; later the carts would do double duty helping less-abled guests who might have difficulties maneuvering over the grassy space. The issue was not insignificant, a significant number of attendees had service dogs or were amputees, casualties from Israel's many wars, including the most recent.

The large space was more than sufficient to accommodate a fenced-in dog park area for the Society's patrons and their dogs, a tent with a wide range of vegetarian, vegan, and gluten-free offerings for humans and their four-legged friends, and the J-SPCA's Friends' Adoption Tent, all ringing the periphery of the square. The Friends' Adoption Tent was a focal point, a new initiative after J-SPCA inherited country-wide responsibility for puppy mill rescues and recent raids on the more questionable operations. Joshua Katz, their honoree, had generously offered to underwrite a substantial amount of the construction costs for a puppy-friendly shelter and a badly needed facelift to the current shelter which would continue to house the older dogs. Hopefully, a few of the society's donors would match his donation. Once the event started, she'd be schmoozing the lot of them, working her way through the center of the square where they expected the estimated 352 ticketed guests would spend most of their time. The setup gave people easy access to the drinks bar which would serve both virgin and blood Marys and Mimosas in the food tent, and which also provided a bit of separation from the inevitable barks and yelps. Volunteer waiters would also circulate among the crowd, offering finger foods.

While J-SPCA shelters cared for a variety of animals, today's event was a dog-only affair, despite passionate pleas from several vocal cat owners including two Board members, cat owners themselves. At 10:55 AM, Tani Bennet stood on the raised platform using a variety of hand signals to direct the van's driver to bring the dogs over to the Friends' Adoption Tent, one of the last major hurdles to set in order before more guests arrived. She'd been on the phone with the less-than-responsible driver, already running a half-hour late, frantically monitoring his progress. Late and lazy.

"I got you," shouted the handsome security guard, 6'2" 20-something with a long blonde ponytail. Avner winked as he jumped into one of the golf carts. He signaled the Belgian Malinois with a single hand gesture. The *Oketz*-trained dog vaulted into the seat next to him.

"Good girl, Luna," he said, loosening the dog's muzzle.

"*Todah, todah,*" Tani shouted after him. *Lucky dog*, she thought to herself.

Avner returned five minutes later, cruising past Tani and headed directly to the Friends' Adoption Tent with two dozen puppies yelping in his ear and Luna sitting quietly on the seat next to him. He leaned over the high fence guarding the puppy pen and set each one gently down. A couple of industrial-strength fans kept the tent cool on what promised to be a scorcher of a day. He put the last puppy in the pen, a cute Labrador Retriever, giving her a once-over.

"How'd you like to come with me, girl?" he asked, then looked at Luna. "How'd you feel about that, girl?" The Belgian Malinois looked at him with very non-puppy-dog eyes. "Maybe not today."

He straightened the yellow ribbon tied around the puppy's neck; it read "*Shiri*" which he rightfully assumed was for *Shiri Bibas*, the mother of the two young red-haired boys *Ariel*, age four, and *Kfir*, nine months old, kidnapped on October 7th into Gaza, along with their father *Yarden* from *Kibbutz Nir Oz*.

The hostages were never far from anyone's mind. Held now for almost an entire year, each day that passed was recorded on a torn piece of tape, a digital counter, or in daily headlines lest anyone forget the 101 hostages were still trapped in Gaza's terror dungeons. September 29, 2024. 358 days too long. Reports claimed that less than half of the hostages were still alive. Avner kissed "*Shiri*" on the nose and was rewarded with a couple of enthusiastic face licks, before putting her into the pen with the other puppies. Each puppy had a gender-neutral hostage awareness yellow ribbon loosely tied in a bow around their neck and each ribbon bore the first name of one of the female hostages. Luna followed closely, walking next to Avner, but then paused for a second for an uncharacteristic look behind her.

※ ※ ※

"Well, I think it's fair to say Luna could see us." GA-717.2 stated, sitting astride *Shiri*. He gently petted the puppy on her head before jumping down to the ground. Ostensibly, he was team leader for the J-SPCA event which called for a team of twelve Guardian Angels. GA-717.2 zipped back and forth, the equivalent of pacing, trying to avoid the pups nipping at his wings, considering the implications of Luna's ability to see or at least sense the GAs' presence.

"I don't think her awareness of us will affect our operational plans, though we may have to improvise in case our furry friends freak out all at once when the proverbial dog poop hits the fan," GA-717.2 mused. He knew the operation was destined to turn into a real *balagan*, a royal mess.

The thirteenth member of his team, GA-721.53, was busy chasing after a raven, or an equivalent species of bird, which hopefully would be found in and around *Gan Sacher*. GA-717.2 dispatched GA-721.53 to the Nili and David Jerusalem Bird Observatory, located adjacent to the *Knesset* hopefully shifting the odds of finding a raven in their favor.

As per Uri'el's instructions, GA-721.53 was charged with finding a raven, though a hooded crow would do in a pinch. But Uri'el was adamant about using one or the other kind of bird. "Accept no substitutes," he admonished.

"Okay, then send us one, if it's so important," GA-717.2 snapped, but then quickly and contritely lowered his head. Everything was always heard in the Upper Realms, and today's J-SPCA program was being featured on all twelve screens at the Multiplex.

"Sorry," GA-717.2 said, able to hear GA-721.53 croaking a couple of "come hither" raven bird calls.

He stopped flapping his wings and floated down, landing on *Shiri's* back. All they could do now was wait patiently for the party to get going. Unfortunately, patience was not a particular virtue found among Guardian Angels. Today, would be different in many ways… monumental in others. GA-717.2 took the downtime to ponder the "why" of the raven, while the rest of his team took turns riding on the backs of the puppies for an impromptu polo match.

※ ※ ※

Tani understood the need for security, a *de rigueur* requirement for private gatherings especially those held in public spaces. The MAGSS security firm brought a three-man, one-woman team; their presence conspicuous and welcomes. Two patrolled the perimeter with *Oketz*-trained dogs, and the female security guard stationed herself at the guest registration table checking-in guests, and checking them out in the process. Guests were required to pass through a metal detector and would be "wanded" only if absolutely necessary. Most guests used the automatic check-in, scanning the QR code on their event tickets before passing through the metal detector and collecting their badges, alphabetically ordered on a nearby table. Security was as much for the event as for the notable guests, among them a couple of MKs who came with their own security details.

The fourth MAGSS guard, the Australian Hunk had disappeared for a time until coming to her rescue gathering up the puppies and older dogs from the shelter's van. She was tempted to head over to the Friends' Adoption Tent. Yes to meet him, but also to attend to the puppies. It wasn't rocket science, though. He could clearly figure out that the puppies would go into the smaller pen, and the older dogs into the adjoining larger one.

Another time. The food tent required her immediate attention. The caterers had done a wonderful job with the canapes, except the dog treats looked as tasty as the human ones, creating more than a little confusion even with the staff. She could see the headlines now, "J-SPCA Event Goes to the Dogs in Food Snafu. Guests flood *Hadassah Ein Kerem* and *Shaare Zedek* Hospital Emergency Departments."

Chapter 18

The sound of an unusually loud motorcycle drew Davi's attention as Joshua pulled into an open slot near the catering trucks and service vans, parked on the sidewalk along *Sderot Ben Tzvi*. She waited for him near the running path, holding his phone in her hand. It had been vibrating non-stop for the past fifteen minutes. How he'd managed without it since Friday night was beyond her. On any given day, her phone was attached to her right hip or tucked into the pretty cloth purse by Emanuel. Today, her phone was in the purse, along with .22 Beretta.

Effi had handed her Joshua's cellphone before leaving for school. "I found it in the backpack's side pocket. Joshua must've forgotten it," he said. Then headed for the door, the Hazon Labs' backpack slung proudly over his right shoulder.

"You didn't…" she said, stopping just shy of an accusation, wondering whether Effi had tried to access anything on it.

"And no," he said, drawing out his reply to the length of three words, then added, "I didn't have time."

She laughed, then looked at the screensaver picture of Joshua, Jay, and a young woman, who she assumed was Julia. The three were all smiles, wearing wetsuits, somewhere on the water under clear blue skies. Odds on, the snap was taken the day of the accident. *Crete 2019*.

"Thanks again, Aunt Davi."

"For what?"

He rotated his shoulder so that the Hazon Labs logo faced her.

"Oh, just happened to work out. I'm glad it did."

"Are you seeing Joshua today?"

"Yeah, I'll be sure to get his phone back to him this morning. You still planning on meeting him at Zedekiah's Cave?"

"Well, yeah."

"I might tag along." Effi groaned out a tsk. "It's business Ef," she said, raising her eyebrows.

"Fine," he said, then unexpectedly hugged her.

"See you later, Ef."

Davi finished her coffee, reviewed the overnight intel, before heading out for the 8:00 AM meeting with her team. The plan was already in play, set in motion a few hours after *Shabbat*. If all went well, the two would be in custody today. After learning that the MINI Cooper belonged to Ezra Noiman, and that he and Jackie were linked, Davi set a plan in motion Saturday night that would carry over to the J-SPCA event. That couldn't be avoided. They couldn't afford to let Jackie near Hazon Labs, and physically separating the pair was an ideal takedown scenario.

While her team worked the event, Davi was still tasked with being Joshua's girlfriend for the day, a role she didn't mind playing in the least. With any luck, they could wrap up at least part of the security gig today. Avner's visit to the Noiman-Allon apartment had conclusively linked the pair to the hack, uncovering a file folder full of Miss Piggy heads. The downloads dated back to May. While the pair had tried to mask the laptop's IP address during the hack, bouncing it across servers in Eastern Europe, Noiman had stupidly gone online to rant at Hazon Labs' downed server, giving the cyber team a linked point.

More damning data was pouring in from the co-opted laptop, necessitating adding a few of the *Mishtara's* data analysts, crack cybersleuths, to the task. Since both were consenting adults, their home-made porn was raunchy but technically not illegal. But neither had declared earned income from their "adventurous" lifestyle. The *Mishtara's* forensic accountants were following the money trail for any "beyond their declared means" unusual assets and purchases owned by one or both. The damage to Hazon Labs was a different issue. Unless one was willing to flip on the other, finding out what kind of damage the two had reaped on Joshua's company would be the tougher job to sort out. Davi had been up most of the night, eager to give Joshua a positive report. She glanced at her phone, acknowledging the text from Avigdor/Avner. Allon had just left the apartment. Her destination: *Gan Sacher*.

With any luck Allon and Noiman would be yesterday's problem, though there were still outstanding threats to Hazon Labs and Joshua, which meant putting anything serious between them on hold, at least for the foreseeable future; if then. Still, the possibilities were interesting to consider. She wasn't a big believer in love at first sight, but there was something intangible between them... a promise meant to be fulfilled.

Davi looked up again, happy to see Joshua coming up the running path. There was something different in his movements. Slower, deliberate steps. She took in the sight of him as he approached, GEOX gray dress sneakers, a black T-shirt with steel-gray black jeans; a couple of ticks past business casual. Beneath his loose-fitting T-shirt, Joshua wore *tzitzit*, the only pair he owned; its four corners fringed with two *tekhelet*-colored strings knotted with six white strings peaking out. Interesting, she thought. He definitely hadn't been wearing *tzitzit* Friday night.

Davi wore a steel-gray colored, short-sleeved T-shirt and dark gray Jodhpur pants with padded knees, topped off with a blue and gray patterned scarf to offset the monotone. Beneath her clothes she'd deliberately worn a lacey blue bra and matching panties, perhaps anticipating a celebratory tryst with Joshua at taking down Allon and Noiman. They would look good together, a couple, as planned.

✻ ✻ ✻

Joshua had found the *tzitzit* among his grandfather's belongings, still wrapped in the original tissue paper; part of the *tallit* and *kittel* set he'd purchased for *Yom Kippur*. The simple garment was a little small on him, coming to just below his midriff and not quite meeting Kosher requirements for his height. He'd tucked the strings inside his pants, though a wisp of the strings were visible when he leaned forward to kiss Davi's cheek. Their complementary clothes choice made them look the part of being together, though they hadn't coordinated their outfits or planned for their instant attraction to one another.

"Hey, you," he said, smiling at her, but his red-rimmed eyes contrasted with his smile. She handed him the phone.

"Thanks," he said, slipping it into his back pocket.

They hadn't spoken since he'd left her apartment *Shabbat* morning. "What's going on?" she asked, genuinely concerned.

He looked at the ground then up to her. "Oh G-d," he paused, knowing there were tears to come, but hopefully not now, not here.

"Joshua, talk to me."

"Um, a friend of mine died yesterday."

"Oh, G-d. I'm so sorry," she said, assuming the friend was likely another casualty of the war in Gaza or up north with Lebanon. But then her mind switched tracks; he used the word died, not killed.

"She's been, um," Joshua could hardly bring himself to say Julia's name, but it would be enough. Davi would know, not because of the intimacy they'd shared yesterday, but because she'd done her due diligence on her client Joshua E. Katz. "It's Julia. She died *Shabbat* morning."

"Joshua. I am so sorry." She stared into his eyes for a long moment, then reached out and took him into her arms.

He took a long breath, welcoming the comfort, but then stepped back, away from Davi. There was more he needed to tell her.

"I hadn't seen her for a long time. I just couldn't… wouldn't. No excuses really. No good ones, only now it's too late."

"I'm sure she knew how much you cared about her. Loved her."

"Yeah, but that's a do operation, Davi. Jay *really* loved her. He always did. It was right that he was with her. No one should have to die alone."

"Can I help with anything? Do anything for you?"

"Roll back time?"

"Out of my purview, I'm afraid. When's the funeral?"

"Sometime this evening at the earliest. *Be'er Sheva*. Her last official address. Her brothers have to get here from wherever they are these days."

She sensed there was more, but didn't push. They stood facing one another, oblivious to the arriving J-SPCA guests that gave them a wide berth. A few recognized him, clapping him on the back as they passed. His muted response let them know not to engage him further.

"There's something else too. Julia, G-d bless her, told Jay something about Jackie."

"What, I don't understand. She spoke?" Davi's file on Joshua included information about Julia, the accident, and her comatose/vegetative state.

Joshua chuckled. "No, she fucking blinked out a Morse Code message. Seriously!" Shaking his head in amazement. Their 8200 team used the low-tech code to communicate using pen clicks, finger taps on tables, coughs, and even blinks. "J4, which Jackie never was or ever could be. 911, an emergency. J4 911. Jay asked her if 911 meant danger. He said, she stared at him for a while, then closed her eyes for the last time."

For a long moment, Davi didn't say anything overwhelmed by the purity of their friendship, the love the three shared, and to honor a most remarkable woman. "What an amazing woman. She loved you both."

"Yeah, till her dying breath. Dying blink," Joshua chuckled at the gallows humor which Julia would have appreciated more than anyone. He hoped she was smiling now, finally freed from the netherworld of non-existence, betrayed by her own body. Her mind was at least free, if only for a little while. Long enough to warn them... Joshua rubbed his eyes, clearing the tears then took in a deep breath. He touched Davi's hand, their fingers intertwining naturally.

She squeezed lightly. "Allon's registered for the event," then squeezed tighter to help him contain a decidedly not Ninja-calm moment.

"What the fuck? She hates dogs! They're not too crazy about her either. She bitches about them all the time at work," he said in a whispered shout, but loud enough for a passing couple with a caramel-colored Labradoodle to hear.

He stared at her bug-eyed. "I don't think I can take her today, or any day ever again."

"I can't get into all of it but..."

"What?" he asked, cutting her off sharply.

Davi looked at him, willing him to calm down. "She's on her way here. I know this is an almost impossible ask, but I need you Ninja calm. We've gotten enough off their laptop to hang *them* for a very long time. The when and how don't matter, except in court. My data guys have been combing through the hard drive. We've got them dead to rights on lots of stuff. The *Mishtara's* C4I division, the cyber guys, have enough to arrest them. Today."

"For real?"

"Yeah. Both of them."

"You didn't say anything?"

"We hit paydirt in the wee hours of the morning. We've been working at it all night. Noiman's already in custody."

"Honest?"

She nodded. His smile said it all as he drew her closer. "I could kiss you."

"By all means."

Instead, he hugged her tightly to him. "I told Jay about them last night."

"Of course, he's your right hand."

"And my left."

"That's what love... friendship is all about."

"Jay was against hiring her from the get-go."

With the benefit of 20/20 hindsight, neither Jay nor Joshua was surprised by Jackie's betrayal. There was something always off about her, and if Davi was right, she'd be history soon enough. For the moment there were other more pressing matters, funeral arrangements to be made, letting 8200's alumni network know about Julia, eulogies to be written. Jay asked if Joshua wanted to give a *hesped* too? Nothing too heavy, just great memories of a life lived, but cut all too short. The last thing on either of their minds was HaMikdash, though they would soon have to deal with the fallout. Noiman may have fallen from grace, but he was every bit the genius as the rest of them… albeit an evil fuck. The damage he could inflict on HaMikdash could be immeasurable… potentially irreparable especially with Jackie working for him, with him, on the inside.

"This is all on me. I felt sorry for her, brought her into Hazon."

"Don't even go there, Joshua. These are very bad people. Really sick. Noiman would have found a way to get to you, with or without Jackie."

"Small comfort at the moment."

"I was trying to help."

"I know. And thanks, to you and your team."

"I promise you, Joshua. They'll get theirs. Karma's a bitch."

"The gift that keeps on giving."

"We all have past sins to reconcile. *Ashamnu, bagadnu, gazalnu…*" she said, referring to the *Vidui* confession prayer recited on *Yom Kippur*, recounting past sins.

Written in the plural, the alphabetical acrostic emphasizes a collective responsibility, atoning not only for individual sins, one's own, but also asking forgiveness as a community, a collective responsibility both to and for one another… the Gestalt of Forgiveness. But in the context of Karma and Karmic debt, Joshua wondered if the plural might not actually refer to our own individual *we*, the *we* of our past lives. *We* have transgressed across all of our incarnations, our *gilgulim*, coming forward to apply a continuous improvement business model to continue the rectifications. The bedtime *Shema* prayer said before going to sleep spoke clearly of forgiveness, of forgiving others in this *gilgul* or any other incarnation.

"Past sins. Past lives. Apparently, I have more than my share of both," Joshua said, wondering where the hell that came from, but at the same time somehow knowing.

He'd never felt like he belonged here. A dream to be woken up from or an alien from another place and time as if this world was part of a dream state where every day he woke up intuitively aware of a shift in time and space. Sunrise was to his left one day, then a quadrant away the next. Some called them glitches in the Matrix, where the movie version reflected "real" life, though in that context none of it was actually real. All he knew was that the world had shifted while he slept most nights. There were times he welcomed the confusion, wishing it was all a dream instead of waking to the nightmare of his parents dying. He rarely remembered his dreams past the five-seconds of knowing after waking up only to have the images vanish in the blink of an eye. The twenty-eight-year-old who'd achieved great success, couldn't help but wonder, what he'd done that was so terrible in this life, or another, to deserve Noiman and Allon's venomous hate? To lose everyone he loved. When would his debt finally be paid? How horrible could his sins have been for G-d to be so angry with him?

"If it's okay with you, I really don't want to hang around here too long," Joshua said, applying pressure to the bridge of his nose hoping to ward off a monster migraine looming behind his eyes.

"Just long enough," she said, offering him a warm generous smile. "Promise me you'll stay cool, today. Don't let on that you know anything. I mean it."

"Yes, ma'am. Ninja calm, ninja cool."

"Good," she said, then tapped her earpiece. "Jezebel on approach. Motorized scooter. Light blue top, black leggings."

Joshua resisted the urge to turn around or glance over his shoulder. Instead, he found a better alternative. "Kiss me," he said.

"Change your mind?"

He swept her into his arms. Davi effortlessly put her arms around his neck as Joshua lifted her a couple of inches off the ground and kissed her. Unrushed, unhurried, until slowly releasing her. The moment seamlessly ended in a smile and warm embrace as he set her back on the ground. He wasn't acting. Neither was she.

"Get a room," Jackie sniped, zipping past them on her scooter.

He ignored her, his eyes intently focused on Davi. "Let's do this," he said.

"With pleasure."

※ ※ ※

They stood in line with the rest of the J-SPCA guests without a QR code, which would have otherwise sped their entry to the event. Jackie was four people behind them, close enough to watch, but not hear them. They made the most of her proximity to them, canoodling to beat the band, but tastefully restrained.

"By the way, Jay's obviously a no-show today. He sent Arik in his place. He's not on the guest list."

"No problem," she winked, gently taking Joshua's hand as the line moved forward. Genia, the MAGSS operative behind the registration desk, didn't blink as Davi approached.

"Hi, welcome to the event. Your name?"

"Joshua E. Katz and guest," infusing his words with an uber-happy lilt. Davi smiled at him.

"You're already on the computer," Genia said, stepping over to the table with the pre-made badges and finding one with Joshua's name. His VIP lanyard was royal blue while the regular guests had white ones.

"Here you go, Joshua," she said, passing him a lanyard before sitting. Each badge had a picture of one of the shelter dogs available for adoption and a yellow ribbon in the upper right corner for the hostages. By chance, maybe, Joshua's badge showed a Labrador Retriever. The back of the badge described the breed.

Joshua smiled as he read the back of the card, which described Boomer to a tee: outgoing, even-tempered, kind, intelligent, friendly, agile, gentle, and trusting.

"And your name, miss?"

Davi leaned forward as if she were passing nuclear secrets and told Genia about Arik Anders. Genia printed Davi's badge with the picture of a tan-coated Canaan dog, and her name printed in the white space above. Genia passed her the badge along with a VIP-colored lanyard.

"Thank you. And good choices," Davi said, referring to the lanyard color and the dog breed. Reading the back of the card, "The Canaan dog breed is known for being vigilant, intelligent, cautious, alert, quick, and devoted."

"Fits you to a tee," Joshua said with a wink.

"Joshua, I believe Tani's looking for you."

"Thanks."

Avner had positioned himself next to the metal detector, eyeing guests as they passed through. Luna remained vigilant by his side. She was trained to identify drugs and explosives, and, more importantly, was acutely sensitive to subtle changes in Avner's body language. While ostensibly working the J-SPCA event, Avner was doing double duty, backup for Davi's team in protecting Joshua Katz and as the *Mishtara* to make an arrest, which seemed all but certain. Both tasks were equally important but were weighted differently in terms of outcome. With all the green cover around the park and open space, a rando loon taking a potshot at Katz was their primary concern. Katz's protestor fan club might foolishly make a move at the event. Foolishly, since it would be self-defeating, coming across as protesting J-SPCA and the helpless shelter animals.

Arresting Allon would be a pleasure. The forensics team had found the equivalent of a smoking gun in Allon/Noiman's computer, making a takedown inevitable. By prior arrangement, the man of the hour was due to arrive by 11:10 AM, fifteen minutes after the event's 11:00 AM official start time. He glanced at the line of guests approaching his station, saw Davi, and imperceptibly nodded to her.

He shifted his gaze back to the registration desk, scanning the line of guests there when his mind screamed, "Skank," at seeing Jackie Allon. He composed himself, fully expecting something lewdly suggestive to come out of her mouth when she saw him.

"Easy, girl," he said, feeling a slight tug on the leash as Luna sensed the change in his posture and breathing.

Neither Avner nor Avigdor informed Davi of the last-minute switch. It wasn't necessary. Both were equally capable of handling either assignment. Avner braced himself for a not-so-close encounter with Allon.

* * *

"This is ridiculous. I registered on Friday. How hard can it be to find me?"

"Did you get a confirmation email from us?"

"I paid the damn 500 *shekels* to get in!"

Davi's instructions were clear: put Allon on edge, mess up her registration, misspell her name, and print her up with an appropriate dog breed.

"Well, *if* you paid, then you should have a receipt," Genia said, sounding equally annoyed.

"I told you I paid!"

"As I said, the receipt should be in your email."

Jackie was used to expensing everything on her company card and rarely checked her personal email which she'd used to register.

Assaulting her phone with angry taps and swipes, she turned it to the dumb bitch, "Here," she sneered.

"Okay, then," Genia said, loading a badge with the picture of a Chihuahua dog breed which she'd saved especially for Allon. Breed Description: capable of biting, territorially aggressive, easily provoked, and very vocal. For good measure, Genia misspelled Jackie's name using a *y* instead of an *ie* then clipped the badge onto a white lanyard.

Jackie looked at the misspelling and groaned out a long sigh. "Forget it," she barked. She wasn't going to waste another minute with this dolt; a "dolt" with an IQ in the high 150s, a first degree in Behavioral Psychology, and a PhD in Forensics.

* * *

Jackie grabbed her badge and got in the security line. She spied Joshua and that woman chatting casually, making the rounds among the other blue lanyards. The girl had given her a white one. By default, as a Hazon employee she should have merited a blue lanyard.

"Twit," she sneered, then looked up to see the hunky Australian. This day might be looking up, after all. Strange though, she wondered how he managed to get here before her? She'd left him in the apartment with Ez. He's certainly big enough to moonlight in security. Let's hope so, she thought, thinking what else might be big enough, already planning her assault.

"Hey there, you," suggestively lowering her voice.

"Please move on, ma'am," Avner said, affecting his best Texas drawl. "There's a line piling up behind you."

"What happened to your accent?"

"Please, ma'am. I asked you nicely as a guest of this here soirée. Move along."

She followed his instructions, still trying to make sense of the odd encounter. Granted, she'd taken a couple of hits off Ez's bong earlier, but his stuff was never good enough to make her hallucinate. Though there was always a first time.

Jackie watched the J-SPCA photographer trail after Joshua and his date before turning his attention to the rest of the guests, snapping candid shots of the crowd. Jackie tried catching his eye, but the photographer had already disappeared into the Friends' Adoption Tent. "Now there's a picture-perfect moment if there ever was one."

* * *

"Heads up, angels. Harpy at 12 o'clock," GA-717.2 said, sounding the alarm.

Unfortunately, the impromptu polo match had tired out the GAs and the pups, who were dreaming of pup cups from Starbucks. His puppy, the one honoring *Shiri Bibas*, was the only one up and about, making them the designated hitter. GA-717.2 hoped GA-721.53 had found the requisite bird, hoping to hear a squawk or two. Without said bird, the plan could easily fall apart.

Jackie sauntered over to the Adoption Desk, but rather than filling out the adoption forms insisted on giving the puppy a test drive first. "Just once around the block. Promise."

She bypassed the older dogs and made her way to the puppy pen. When she bent down, her shirt fell forward, giving GA-717.2 an eyeful. He shielded his eyes. Generally, "people" didn't run around naked in Heaven, only those in the Garden. He also didn't think breasts were supposed to have writing or pictures on them.

"Wish me luck, boys," he shouted, offering a wing-tipped salute as Jackie picked up the *Shiri* pup. GA-717.2 held fast as Jackie roughly handled the pup, bringing her face close to his nose. "You'll do," she grinned, a misleading signal for the young pup who thought she might be friendly. Happy to oblige, *Shiri* attempted to lick her face which Jackie withdrew immediately. "Ichsa!" she sneered, holding *Shiri* at arm's length. But as she stepped out of the tent, Jackie cradled the puppy in her arms in case the photographer happened to snap her picture.

"Good, girl," GA-717.2 whispered into *Shiri's* floppy ear. "If you can pee on her, that would be great too."

The official program was just getting underway as ear-splitting feedback from the sound system prompted an equally ear-splitting round of barking from the Friends' Adoption Tent, and even a howl or two. *Shiri* joined in with a howl, metered down to puppy-level vocals.

Joshua stepped onto the small podium. Tani smiled for the photographer, edging herself as close to him as possible. Davi positioned herself near the podium and watched Allon leave the Friends' Adoption Tent, carrying a labrador puppy in her arms and crossed the grass to join the crowd near the stage. *Poor puppy*, Davi thought.

"Thank you all for coming today, and for supporting the Jerusalem Society for the Prevention of Cruelty to Animals. Prevention certainly, but also protection for all our furry and feathered friends. We're proud to be there for them when they need us most. We've brought some of our dog pals here today, and just a reminder, they are available for immediate adoption."

She paused for the attendees to clap. "We're starting a new era at the shelter, opening our doors to younger animals, puppies and kittens. No cats here today, except for our honoree, Joshua Katz," pausing again, expecting tittering laughter at her witty joke. The applause for Joshua was genuine; the joke didn't go over so well. "Our plans to upgrade the existing shelter are well underway and I'm pleased to announce we've broken ground on an adjacent lot of land for the Boomer Memorial Shelter for our young animals. That wouldn't have been possible without the generous support of our honoree." Tani led the guests in the round of applause, then stepped away from the mic.

Joshua waited an extra beat for the applause to die down. "Thanks, Tani, and thanks to all of you for supporting J-SPCA throughout the years. I'm new to your group, but I've been a longtime lover of animals, dogs especially." His comment immediately drew a couple of "Boos" from the guests, led by technology entrepreneur Gil Gelfand, a diehard cat lover. "Thank you, Gil," Joshua said, pointing a finger at the Cat2See founder.

"I'm hoping that when people consider getting a pet, they will come to J-SPCA as a first choice, rather than going to a puppy mill. But to make the most of that all-important first impression, we want that meeting to happen in a more welcoming atmosphere."

The current facilities were frighteningly industrial and not always family-friendly for people looking for a first-time pet.

"My best friend growing up was my dog, Boomer. I miss him to this day. I believe wholeheartedly in the Society's mission and am pleased to announce that I am increasing my donation to further develop the shelter's puppy and kitten adoption space."

The announcement was met with the expected round of applause. "Thank you, Joshua. Your gift to the J-SPCA is very much needed and appreciated."

As expected, an oversized check appeared onstage, and more photographs were taken as Joshua added a zero to the donated amount. The check was set aside as the Society's Board of Directors rushed to the podium to congratulate Tani and thank Joshua. All qualms about Tani's choice of honoree were long-forgotten with his generous six-figure donation.

Davi watched as Allon made her way to the podium, puppy prop in hand. She began moving to intercept when a large black bird commonly seen throughout Israel dive-bombed toward the crowd, prompting a few screeches and gasps, then veered slightly to land a direct guano hit on Jackie Allon's head. What Davi, and the other two-legged guests, couldn't see was GA-721.53 riding on the back of the Hooded Crow like *Game of Thrones* character Daenerys Targaryen on the back of her beloved dragon, Drogon. The bird gladly complied, cawing with glee as its outstanding *tikkun* was finally rectified in dropping the guano bomb on Allon's head.

As quickly as the bird appeared, it disappeared into the trees along with its Guardian Angel rider who ascended to Heaven carrying the bird's spark.

General mayhem followed in due course as Jackie screamed, flung the puppy out of her arms, and shoved her fellow guests out of the way as she ran to the food tent. The puppy ran between a dozen giant legs, making sudden course changes as GA-717.2 guided *Shiri* to Joshua. Finally arriving at their destination, the puppy jumped up and down, scratching at Joshua's bare ankles to get his attention. It worked.

Joshua picked up the puppy, looking into the labrador's sweet, amber-colored eyes... Boomer's eyes. "Hello there, girl," he said.

The photographer snapped the only picture of Joshua with his new puppy. "What do you say... should we give it a go, Boomerang?" He was rewarded with a dozen sandpaper-rough licks on his face.

"I think we have our first successful adoption," Tani announced, which prompted a round of enthusiastic cheers. Davi moved in next to Joshua as people crowded around him, too close for her liking. She signaled Avner to take Allon.

Jackie was all but forgotten as she ran into the food tent and poured a liter of bottled water over her head, ranting throughout. A steady stream of hate-filled spew at the bird and the world who'd wronged her at every turn. The front of her shirt was soaked as she stood up, using square cocktail napkins, the recycled shit kind, to dry her curls. It was hopeless, she must look like a drowned rat.

But then the blonde Australian/Texan hunk walked into the tent. "Just look at what that damn bird did to me!"

The food tent was too perfect. He could whisk her away, mostly unseen, through a flap at the back of the tent. "Looks like you're one messed up looking, Shiela." Gone were all traces of the twang and the Aussie was back. "No need to wig out. I gotchu." And so, he did, spinning her around, slapping the FlexiCuffs on her wrist, and leading her out the back of the tent to a waiting golf cart driven by brother, Avigdor. She looked at the two of them, her eyes narrowing, realizing how she'd been duped by the pair.

A1 and A2 rightly figured Allon would lose here mind if brother Aaron were in the mix. With any luck, the Triple A team would be back together at the end of the year.

Avner texted Davi on WhatsApp®, "Allon in custody."

"Good onya," she responded using a bit of Australian slang.

"See ya la."

* * *

Joshua said his goodbyes, which took another seven minutes. Boomerang blissfully asleep in his arms. Davi sidled up next to him, delivering the good news with a simple, "Done and done."

"I like the way you work. I'd kiss you, except I fear this little one might get jealous."

"I'm up for a little friendly competition. Might as well get started." She winked and reached for Boomerang.

Just then Joshua's phone in his back pocket started to vibrate.

They started walking away from the crowd, toward *Sderot Ben Tzvi*. The Caller ID read, J2. "Hey, I've got some good news," mouthing to her, Jay was on the line. It would have been *great* news, but they were burying Julia later in the day.

Davi carefully watched Joshua in the brief one-sided conversation as he listened to Jay. His furrowed brow said it all. Hazon Labs was facing yet another crisis.

"What? I don't understand. Since Friday? Hang on, I'm putting you on speaker. Davi's with me."

"What's going on," she asked, aware that Boomerang sensed the sudden rise in tension, perking up her ears.

"One of our guys hasn't been seen since Friday…" Joshua held the phone between them as they continued walking, their pace quickening.

"Missing how?" Davi asked. They'd been so focused on Allon and Noiman, Davi worried that she'd missed a far more dangerous threat.

"He had a family event over the weekend and didn't show," Jay responded.

"Oh man, I gave him a hard time too. Stupid stuff."

"Joshua, please," Davi interrupted, "are we talking about Tzion Mengistu?"

"Yeah, but how'd you know?"

She didn't answer. "You said, since Friday?"

"Yeah, and no way was he going to miss his brother's *Bar Mitzvah*."

"Since Friday," she repeated. It was more of a statement than a question. "Give me a sec. I think my nephew ran into him in the afternoon." She said nephew instead of Effi for Jay's benefit.

"What?" Jay and Joshua said at the same time.

"Tsk," she said, holding her hand up to silence him/them. She'd already started running scenarios and possible responses, quickly scrolling to Effi's number. "Pick up, pick up."

She and Joshua were now half-walking, half-running away from the J-SPCA event toward the cluster of rental vans and catering trucks. Boomerang yelped a couple of times but remained relatively calm… more so than either Joshua or Davi.

"Come on Effi." Still no answer. She shot off an SMS, "911." He knew better than to ignore it.

Effi immediately called her back. "What's wrong?"

She knew better than to ask a leading question but needed him to be focused. She put him on speaker. "Ef, did you run into someone from Hazon Labs? Friday, in the Old City?" He didn't answer immediately. "You're not any trouble, just tell me."

"Yeah, Tzion Mengistu. His name stuck with me because…"

Confirmation. She cut him off. "Where?" again sensing his hesitation. "Effi, it's important."

"We bumped into one another, just inside the Arab Quarter."

"Where exactly?"

"What's going on?"

"Effi, please."

"It was near *Beit Elchanan*. You know, near the turnoff to the *Kotel HaKatan*."

She knew exactly where that was. The *Mishtara* had offices near that corner. "Did he say anything to you? Maybe where he was going, or someone he was meeting?"

"Just that he was headed to Zedekiah's Cave."

"Thanks, Ef. I gotta go I'll talk to you later. Okay?" She disconnected the call before waiting for his response.

"I'll head over to the cave," Joshua stated, as they picked up the pace, practically running. "Jay, you get that?"

"Yeah, I'll meet you there."

"Does Tzion drive?" Davi asked.

"On it, I'm at the office. I'll check the lot."

"I need his phone number. My people can try pinging his phone. Maybe get us a better fix on its current location. I'll sit with the *Mishtara*. Go over their security camera footage, with any luck we can track his movements in the Old City. Hopefully, he didn't get waylaid somewhere in the Arab Quarter."

"G-d, I hope you're wrong," Joshua said, though the alternative wasn't much better; trapped inside Zedekiah's Cave all weekend, likely injured, or worse.

"Joshua, don't. Don't go there," Jay chimed in, knowing that his best friend was already blaming himself. "His mom's been trying to reach him. No calls to or from him since Friday morning. Nothing Saturday night. Today either. Listen, I need to update them."

Davi looked at the bars on her phone. "Pinging his phone may get us nowhere. Probably out of juice."

"Still worth a try." Joshua's phone vibrated. Davi's rang as well. Caller ID on both showed Jay as the caller.

"I just set up a WhatsApp® group for us."

Good man, Davi thought.

"I'm in the parking lot now," Jay said, already on task.

"Is his car there?" Davi asked.

"Looking. Hold on. Yeah, found it."

Davi heard the defeat in Jay's response. "Look, we have some leads, let's run them down. I'll catch up with you guys after the *Mishtara*." She didn't specify the Ministry of Public Security across from the *Givat HaTachmoshet* light rail stop. They'd have the requisite technology she needed. "A couple of pictures of Tzion would help. Headshots for tracking."

"We've all been pixelized, I'll send over a couple," Jay said, then: "Joshua, I need to check in with Tzion's parents. Get them squared away. They're driving in from *Beit Shemesh* to check his apartment. I'll meet you as soon as I can."

"*Yalla.*"

Joshua and Davi veered left toward the back of the staging area where a dozen motorcycles were parked. They'd both ridden to the event that morning. Her sleek Kawasaki was parked beside Joshua's vintage Royal Enfield; the bike had belonged to his dad.

Davi passed Boomerang to Joshua. "Hold her for a sec," she said, grabbing a leather jacket and helmet from the storage lock under the seat. She rewrapped the scarf into a sling before climbing on, holding her arms out. She put the pup in the sling, securely tucking Boomerang inside her jacket; the puppy's head poked out from behind the zipper. "Snug as a bug," she said, then turned to Joshua. "We'll find him. I promise."

Chapter 19

As instructed, *Barak* called his mother and told her he was spending the weekend in *Ramallah* with a friend. She didn't ask who the friend was, where he was staying, or why he was going to the *de facto* capital of Palestine. Nothing. No one cared about him. But he would be remembered and his sacrifice rewarded. Every month, they'd praise him, thanking him for the money from the Palestinian Authority for his chosen path of *Jihad*. They'd accept the neighbors' congratulations, maybe even shed a tear with pride. *Barak Abadi* would live on forever. A school named after him would be nice. He smiled at the irony.

Barak was glad to be finally free of *Ahmed*. He'd been cooped up with him the entire weekend in the four-room *Beit Hanina* apartment in northern Jerusalem. *Ahmed* warned him about going outside, or even sitting on the balcony, which would draw the attention of the old lady across the way. *Barak* understood. Old people were always getting into everyone else's business. *Ahmed's* apartment was nice, so staying there wasn't so bad, and he had a giant television and satellite cable with hundreds of channels. Too bad there wasn't more time to watch them all. His neck still hurt him from watching the giant television screen which was placed off-center from the couch. *Ahmed* needed it that way because of his neck problem. He told everyone the Jews had beaten him, had nearly broke his neck which was why he was deformed. But everyone knew Arafat's thugs had beaten him, had hung him upside down too, suspecting him of being an Israeli informer. *Barak* liked *Ahmed*, doubting if the "Fixer" as he was known would ever betray his people.

That morning, *Ahmed* dropped him off at the bus terminal on *Sultan Suleiman Street*. A woman with short brown hair was leaning over the Garden Tomb railing, taking pictures of the rock face the Christians called, *Golgotha*, the Place of the Skull. It looked a little like a skull, if you squinted.

She kept waving her hands animatedly, her face twisted sourly, silently screaming at him to move. He didn't. She was as bad as the Jew colonizers, telling him what to do, where to go. He would've stayed there all day if only to annoy her, but then one of the blue and white Arab buses started backing into him. *Barak* jumped onto the small sidewalk in front of the Place of the Skull, nearly tripping over his feet.

That was not how he planned for this day, his day, to end.

He waited patiently at the crosswalk, then casually headed East on *Sultan Suleiman Street* toward Zedekiah's Cave and destiny. *Ahmed* assured him the side door emergency exit would be left unlocked. It was generally only used for moving equipment and supplies in and out of the cave for private events, but he'd taken care of it. *Ahmed* told him how he and his cousin *Jibril* had brought the tanks in right under the noses of the Israeli Police and Border Guards and filled them with the explosive contents. They both laughed. *Ahmed* a little so, telling *Barak* how his dear cousin had already sacrificed his life for the cause. *Jibril's* lore would include how he had outsmarted the enemy… *Ahmed* would see to that.

As promised, the side door to Zedekiah's Cave was propped open by a rock. Considering the gravity of his mission, it seemed like a funny thing to leave to chance… or a rock. Anyone could come along and knock the stone out of place. Then what?

Barak quickened his step, eager to start, and even more ready for this day to be over when he would join his brothers-in-arms in Paradise.

Aunt Davi ended the call before Effi could tell her he was down the street from Zedekiah's Cave. Something was up; he knew that much for sure. While tempted to call her back, he didn't. Hopefully, it wasn't serious enough for Joshua to cancel their meeting. Not that it really mattered since Joshua had already offered him the prized internship. Meetings got canceled all the time; they'd just reschedule. Effi shook away the selfish thoughts that mingled seamlessly with worse-case scenarios. In Israel, everything was fine until it wasn't. It was a fact of life and a reality check — you lived as if each day might be your last because, sometimes, it was.

Effi absently waved at the Border Police outpost at *Sha'ar Shechem* out of habit, before continuing down *Sultan Suleiman Street*. Whether Joshua showed up today or not, he still wanted to check out the cave. The last thing he wanted was to sound like a dolt when Joshua gave him the HaMikdash insider tour. But when he arrived, several tall barriers blocked the main gate. The posted signs said the cave was closed for maintenance. Effi tried to peer around them to see inside, but only a few stray lights were on inside the cave, and he couldn't make out much of anything. Hopefully, "closed" didn't apply to Hazon Labs.

Intent on making the most of his time, Effi walked the short distance down the block to his "Archie" stone. He snapped several pictures of the unusual stone with a relief sculpture of seven columns carved into the stone block. Placed well above ground level, in the Old City's north-facing wall, the stone presented Effi with a classic "outlier" classification problem, prompting the question, "Which of these stone blocks is not like the others?" When he'd discovered it, the bigger questions and the storyline scenario built itself… who placed *it*; why was *it* here; what did the carving mean; was *it* unique; and, where did *it* belong? He'd already identified at least three other locations where the same stone columns were carved into a stone block; a fact that only deepened the mystery. He'd noticed "Archie" because it was so different from the others, strikingly bright against the surrounding, gray-colored stones. In his other finds, the carved columns appeared much older, degraded badly over time and were much larger than the "Archie" stone stuck in the wall above his head. The others he'd found were mostly supporting bases for one or more pillars/columns measuring at least 7.3 meters tall (over twenty-four feet) and weighing at least a ton.

By pure chance, he discovered the others though the "how" of it still mystified him. On *Yom Yerushalayim*, the day commemorating the liberation of Jerusalem from nineteen years of Jordanian Occupation, on the third day of the 1967 Six-Day War, a four-second video clip popped into his feed. The black and white film showed paratroopers rushing through the pedestrian door within the Chain Gate, *Sha'ar HaShalshelet*, leading out from *Har Habayit*. It was a blink of an eye moment he might have easily missed, but there he saw another "Archie" stone set into the base of a pillar immediately adjacent to the Chain Gate. It was all too crazy.

Effi could hardly believe the fortuitous confluence of events when later in the week his 9th-grade teacher surprised their rowdy class of twenty-seven boys with a visit to the edge of *Har HaBayit* for a closer look beyond the massive wooden doors into the Temple Mount. To Effi's surprise, the "Archie" lookalike stone was set into the base of two columns, to the left and right of the massive wooden Chain Gate… the same as in the video clip. The stone bases were badly weathered, worn by time, and larger than the individual stone block set into the Old City's north-facing wall. But the relief pattern, the carving, repeated on both the front and a bit on the side, was essentially the same as the one he'd discovered. After accepting his good fortune at finding these alt-versions, Effi then noticed the unusual shaft designs of the columns. One in particular began as two thick cords of stone twisted around one another, but which appeared to have been chiseled from a single block of stone, a large stone block that would have measured at least 7.3 meters (24 feet) in height.

Clearly, there were more mysteries to discover about the "Archie" stone. His next step would be to investigate *Har HaBayit*. He wouldn't go it alone, however. Maybe he could ask Joshua to take him. With his thoughts still on "Archie," Effi wandered into a fenced-in stone garden next to Zedekiah's Cave. When he looked up again, he saw a double-wide door with a gate. The gate was slightly ajar, and the door propped open with a stone. Its proximity to Zedekiah's Cave meant it could only lead to one place. There, or the Gates of Hell, he smiled to himself. Accidentally locking himself inside would not go over well with Aunt Davi, or Joshua. Effi prided himself on being adventurous, but only to a point. Technically, he wasn't breaking any laws, rules maybe, but no laws since the gate was unlocked. If caught, he'd probably find himself in a world of trouble. *If,* being the operative word.

"*Carpe diem*," Effi whispered and tentatively stepped through the side entrance. The cave was dark. Very dark. He turned on his cellphone's flashlight, waiting for his eyes to adjust and his courage to catch up.

Years ago, *Barak's* grade school class took a field trip to the cave. Much had changed since then. The cave was dimly lit with green and red lights placed on the wall, even though it was closed. Emergency lights, he figured. The lighted stairs cast weird shadows across the stone, making him dizzy. The gaps between the steps were wide enough for him to take two, maybe three steps within each one. The whole lower area was new too. A door labeled, office, and the bathrooms next to it. One was large without a privacy door and had multiple stalls inside; a mixed-gender bathroom. The other had a door labeled, for women only. They'd left everything for him in the women's bathroom, adding another layer of insult to having to wear the enemy's uniform.

Over the weekend, he'd practiced putting on a fake suicide vest a dozen times. *Ahmed* seemed pleased; except, they hadn't counted on the cave's humidity. He was already sweating terribly. Disgusted at the shame of having to use the women's bathroom, *Barak* reluctantly opened the door, pulling the soaked sweatshirt, the new one, over his head. What a waste, *Barak* thought. Before they'd told him what he'd be wearing, he'd bought the nice sweatshirt with a Nike logo, shoes too, special for this mission.

Hanging on the back of the door was the suicide vest, wrapped in a protective black garment bag. He held the vest over his head and carefully slipped his arm through the left armhole first, then the right, the one with the trigger device, making sure the Deadman's switch didn't get tangled. He tugged at the bottom of the vest, admiring himself in the mirror. He'd brought his phone with him and snapped a selfie. Despite the uniform he'd be forced to wear, there would be no question as to his allegiance.

He'd found the uniform behind the toilet tank; crisp, clean, and ugly for all it stood for. The beret fell to the floor as he removed the clothes from the bag. The *kumta* could stay there as far as he was concerned. No way was he going to *All-ah* looking like a fruitcake.

Now came the tricky part. *Barak* began his transformation, changing into the vile clothes. He sneered at the grey-blue shirt and matching pants emblazoned with the Border Police arm patch; an elongated watchtower with the words, *Mishteret Israel* above it, and at the base the name of the Border Police in Hebrew, *Mishmar HaGvul*. He still didn't fully understand what a "false flag" operation was, or why it called for him to dress like the enemy. Lost in thought, he'd almost tripped walking down the stairs to the bathroom area, catching himself just in time before taking a serious tumble. Thankfully, he wasn't wearing the suicide vest at the time since he might have accidentally blown himself up before setting the tank timers running.

He unbuttoned the grey-blue shirt, careful to keep the detonator out of the way, then slipped the detonator into the right-hand sleeve, leading the way for his arm The detonator barely dangled three inches beyond his wrist, hardly enough slack for the quick-draw maneuver he'd practiced over the weekend. Once the trigger was in his hand, the length of the cord didn't much matter, except he was looking forward to using his quick-draw skill.

Did *Ahmed* expect him to walk around the whole time holding it in his hand? Stupid. *Barak* let go of the detonator to button up the oversized shirt that hid the suicide vest well. The trimline suicide vest was hardly visible under the uniform. Good enough for him to walk past the guard post, no one knowing his secret, except maybe a police dog who'd sniff out the explosives.

Maybe he should wait for sundown and walk over to the *Al-Buraq Wall*, the Western Wall as the Jews called it. The place was always crowded, and he could blow himself up there. Now that would be a real triumph, instead of dying in this empty cave. But *Al-Masri* would probably kill him with his bare hands if he deviated from the plan. He was a strange one; maybe his grandfather was right after all.

Ahmed insisted he didn't need to look perfect, but just needed to look the part. *Barak* slipped the pants on, gingerly tucking the shirt inside the pants, ever mindful of the dangling detonator. He yanked open the paper towel dispenser and removed the regulation boots, which were a size too big. As instructed, *Barak* stuffed his clothes and sports shoes into the toilet.

"No need to flush," *Ahmed* joked.

Ha, ha. Not that it mattered, except he'd spent a lot of money on the shoes. He closed the lid, sat on the toilet — stoically enduring the indignity — and began lacing up the boots.

※ ※ ※

The El Paso Christian Church tour group, led by Pastor Jim Hillman and his wife Jeanie, assembled on *Conrad Schick Street*, just outside the Garden Tomb, waiting for stragglers in their group to join them. The rock-cut tomb, located to the north of the Old City walls, was one of two places where Jesus was believed to have been crucified, buried, and risen from the dead; the other location was the Church of the Holy Sepulcher in the Christian Quarter as their tour guide Simon explained. Their next stop, more or less.

"We'll walk the Stations of the Cross first, my friends. Then end our tour at the Church of the Holy Sepulcher," he announced. The schedule was tight and the area was usually crowded, especially on Sundays. Tourism had picked up around the holidays, despite the ongoing war for which Simon Ben-Bar was grateful. "Perhaps, we might hurry your group along, Pastor?"

"I'll see what I can do." This was their last day in Israel, and they still needed to check out of the Dan Panorama Hotel on *Keren HaYesod Street*. If he were to do this again, which he hoped to, his choice of hotels would be smarter. Perhaps, even a bit more adventurous next time.

STRANGE FIRE

"I'll go," Jeannie Hillman offered, knowing her husband would be less forceful in communicating their need to keep to the schedule. Overall, the petite brown-haired woman was pleased with the trip. They had come a long way from their simple Tuesday night Bible Study classes in the basement of the local El Paso community center to the streets of Jerusalem… filthy as they were.

Her husband was a wonderful speaker, passionate, sincere, and generous with his time, sometimes answering questions till late into the night. People from all around Texas began taking notice and joined them online. Pastor Jim had a nice following, but far from the celebrity dreams Jeannie envisioned for them. Her husband liked the idea of being an internet star until his wife explained that having 107 followers didn't exactly make him a viral sensation. But that was in 2018 when he'd first started videotaping his classes. His still-short-of-viral popularity, however, took off during the pandemic when in-person meetings could be hazardous to one's health. He'd been approached by Pastor Jeremiah Vines to join a consortium of good ole' boys ready to storm the Heavens, a Peoples' Church.

Pastor Jeremiah insisted that by working together, they'd be a force multiplier. Saving more souls through their combined internet Ministries. Pastor Jim couldn't argue the point, but Vines was a little too slick for his liking, though apparently not for the millions of followers he quickly found online.

Jeannie had encouraged her husband to join up with Vines, which he was adamantly against and one of the few times he'd stood up to her. Pastor Jim's instincts were spot on. While Vines' sermons and teachings had initially resonated with people, his message was soon lost in the non-Divine revelations of sexual scandals and embezzled church funds. He'd redeemed himself in recent years, sweating and praying up a storm on the internet, begging the good L-rd's mercy. That message didn't quite resonate with his flock who still needed saving and Pastor Jim's boy-next-door good looks and integrity became their salvation.

The El Paso Texas preacher's following, and YouTube "likes" quickly grew into the tens of thousands at the beginning of COVID. Two years later, he enjoyed a following in the tens of millions. Thanks to Jeannie's business acumen, they'd even monetized the channel which paid for their Holy Land trip. Jeanie handled the technical part of Pastor Jim's Ministry, reading the trends and keeping their numbers up with regular posts and specials. Pastor Jim became a magnet for like-minded Christians, looking for salvation in troubled times, while others hoped to understand G-d's ways. Midway through the pandemic, chat topics and questions turned to the Book of Revelations. Was the pandemic disease a punishment in our midst, G-d's wrath on the wicked? Hillman didn't shy away from the challenging questions. When it came to understanding G-d's will, he took the bold stand that while the world was indeed filled with wickedness as prophesied in the End Times, the pandemic had affected the most vulnerable among them… the elderly, the sick, cancer patients and others with compromised immune systems, and of course the poor. He asked a simple question, why would G-d reap a punishment on those without access to medical care or vaccines, on those who were already suffering? No, this pandemic could not be G-d's judgment since the evil and the wicked still carried on… while the simple man, the innocent, suffered from this terrible scourge. He expanded his YouTube channel, was "upward trending across a wide demographic" as Jeannie described it, and which surprised even Pastor Jim since he never considered himself particularly charismatic. His following even included several large congregations of Jewish believers, over which he still scratched his head trying to understand.

The trip to the Holy Land was a special reward for his homegrown faithful, his original congregation. Their pilgrimage was originally scheduled for October 2023, but by L-rd's guiding hand, the High Holidays/Feast of Tabernacles trip had been canceled in late August after a snafu with the travel agency. Something about their hotel being overbooked and no rooms were available anywhere in the country. Despite the obvious disappointment of his El Paso congregation, and Jeannie who railed about the cancellation for a week, Pastor Jim assured them that, "G-d works in mysterious ways. It is not theirs to reason why, but to graciously accept His Will."

Indeed. Their original 2023 itinerary placed them down south on October 7, 2023, a Saturday meeting with peace activists in one of the farming collectives, *Kibbutz Be'eri*, not far from the Gaza Border. The cancelled plans had likely saved their lives, though many, including Jeannie, wondered why the good L-rd didn't just cancel that part of their itinerary rather than the whole trip.

For the re-scheduled 2024 Holy Holyland mission Jeannie decided that videotaping their trip might even be parlayed into a television special with a film crew following them around most days. Jerusalem was to be the highlight of the special she envisioned, but the film crew begged off citing the war as an excuse. Instead, Pastor Jim shared his thoughts using a GoPro setup, focusing less on production values and more on raw emotion, his and those of his flock. Hopefully, Jeannie would find a way to shed a tear or two as well. They'd already captured amazing footage. Their group went south, only this time on a Solidarity Mission to the devastated *Kibbutz Be'eri*, crawling through destroyed homes and bloody scenes as one of the survivors re-told the harrowing story of her miraculous survival. They helped farmers in the *Ramat Eshkol* region harvest vegetables after many of the foreign workers were recalled to their home countries, and they even did a bit of gardening in one of the *Kibbutzim* that had been spared the horrors of October 7th, but whose residents had nonetheless been evacuated for their own safety.

In preparation for their 2024 Holy Holyland trip, Pastor Jim focused on the Book of Revelations, which became even more relevant with the October 7 attack and with Israel facing enemies on multiple fronts, the apocalyptic visions all too real. The shameful attacks on Israel in the United Nations brought prophecy to the fore. Hillman's fiery sermons garnered over 12 million views on YouTube as he defended Israel against the haters. Jeannie turned off the Comments section on their channel when the rhetoric moved from vile to threatening after Jim's Armageddon speech.

"We stand on the frontlines of Armageddon as witnesses to the coming of the L-rd," he was fond of saying. Today's tour through the Old City was the highlight of their time in Jerusalem. It was also the group's last day in Israel. She'd thrown a bit of a hissy fit when their tour guide explained he wasn't comfortable taking them to the foot of *Golgotha*, the site of the crucifixion, citing security concerns.

The reality was that this Christian Holy site was at the back of a bus depot. "Mighty disrespectful to the good L-rd," Jeannie Hillman said, stretching over the guardrail for a better look at the "Place of the Skull," only to be confronted by the idling buses belching their filthy exhaust. Jeannie wasn't sure if she was more annoyed by the buses or the nearby Muslim minarets blasting out the pre-recorded muezzin's call from their loudspeakers five times a day, seven days a week, including in the middle of the night, waking her. "No respect," she repeated often enough, tossing and turning trying to go back to sleep.

Between bathroom breaks and gift shopping done to everyone's liking, it was finally time to get this show moving again. The stragglers proudly showed off their great finds. The collection of colorful Garden Tomb bookmarks and the Anointing Oil were especially popular. Jeannie thought of contacting the manufacturers and offering the oils as a premium through Pastor Jim's Ministry. The little card in the four-pack listed the essences as Rose of Sharon, Myrrh, Oil of Joy, and Spikenard artisan oils, claiming that the oils were made by believers in Bethlehem. Jeanie didn't want to dampen their enthusiasm, but it was likely Bethlehem, Texas. She was pleased to see the last of their group finally rounding the corner. The Garden Tomb was an interesting site as far as these tourist traps went. They sat on wood benches facing the site of the crucifixion, pausing for just a moment to consider the events of 2,024 years ago. Unfortunately, she'd been unable to get a clear shot of the Place of the Skull for Pastor Jim's website. Everyone in their group wanted a picture of the rockface, and their heads kept getting in the way. Not to mention that stupid Arab boy standing there like he owned the place. No respect.

With everyone accounted for, Simon Ben-Bar routed them through the street market on *Nablus Road*. "Well, isn't this special," Jeannie said, as she quickened her pace, passing the swarm of Arabs searching the vendor stalls for bargains on cheap household goods on display. A few in their group stopped to look at some of the trinkets. She wasn't sure what their guide was thinking, taking them through the market which offered them nothing except the wretched smell of unwashed bodies and nary a holy Holyland souvenir in sight, at least none she would be willing to show friends back home.

"Nothing here, that's for sure," she mumbled, clutching her purse close to her body and glad to see several others in the group taking their personal safety seriously as well.

Overall the two-week trip was productive, touring the "safer" parts of the country, such as it was. On Saturday they enjoyed a walking tour of the Old City, visiting the Western Wall, and the *Valley of Hinnom*. She didn't like the Valley, which was popularly known as the Valley of *Gehinnom*, as in Hell, a reputation earned through child sacrifices, Divine punishment, and cursed by the prophet Jeremiah. Sunday couldn't come fast enough for Jeannie Hillman.

It was at least, a picture-perfect Sunday. Sunny, but not too hot. 79 blessed degrees of sunshine to end their Holy Land trip. The rest of the day promised to be special, a perfect capstone for the TV special she envisioned. Jim would lead the faithful, walking the Stations of the Cross, humble as always, and reaching a pinnacle at the Church of the Holy Sepulcher. While she wasn't particularly fond of the Catholic and Orthodox faiths who laid claim to the Church, she planned on grabbing another money shot of Pastor Jim kneeling at the Anointing Slab at the entrance to the Church.

She'd captured a wonderful still shot of her husband emerging from the Garden Tomb, his hands raised to the Heavens, tears streaming down his face. Jeannie was convinced the Garden Tomb was the correct site for the L-rd's burial and resurrection, though many of their newer followers, lapsed Catholics, were partial to the Church of Holy Sepulcher. She was sure her husband would be equally emotional there.

Before the planned trip last year, and this year, she'd searched through images of pilgrims at the Church, identifying critical locations, including the Anointing Slab where petitioners knelt at the purported site where Jesus' body had lain. The lighting in the Church wasn't ideal, though a scene with their group surrounded by warm candle lighting would be inspiring.

The only thing that would have made this day more special would be for them to witness Jesus' Second Coming. Praise the L-rd!

* * *

For nearly forty-five hours, GA-697.4 and GA-696.0 had stayed with Tzion. Once every six hours, they lifted his eyelids, checking to see if his pupils were equal and reactive. It roused Tzion long enough for him to groggily moan, and long enough for them to check for signs of a concussion as recommended by "First-Aid for Newbie Angels," written by the Archangel Gabri'el. Thankfully, the bleeding from Tzion's head wound had stopped a few hours into *Shabbat*. A little over an hour ago, the Word came down from on high… their mission was almost over. Both were disappointed since they hadn't done much more than babysit Tzion, which didn't make much sense since they'd been chosen because of their traceurs' skills. No high-flying antics or great excitement, though they did help Tzion… a good thing.

"Make sure we 'leave no trace behind,'" GA-697.4 said.

"What are we supposed to do about him," GA-696.0 said, casting his eyes at *Jibril's* body.

"Good question."

"Not our mess after all."

"Heavy too. Too heavy to move."

Suddenly, a bright stream of light filled the cavern. They shielded their eyes and when they opened them again the entire Olympic weightlifting team of fourteen Guardian Angels, GAs-698.11 through 698.24 stood before them flexing their muscled wings.

"We understand you have a cleanup here in aisle five," GA-698.11 stated in a testosterone-heavy voice.

GA-696.0 pointed to *Jibril*. His body blocked easy entry to and exit from the Templar Cavern through the hole above. GA-696.0 wondered if they were also tasked with moving the stone blocking the opening.

"We'll get right on it. Word is, time is short. Exciting times ahead, no doubt."

It took the team less than a minute to heave *Jibril's* body to the side of the stepping stone, clearing the way for someone to make their way out… or in.

"You guys sticking around?"

"That's the other word. Here to lend a helping hand, or wing, as needed."

Curious, GA-697.4 thought, since they made no effort to move the large stone boulder covering the opening. Maybe, Tzion's rescue was coming from above.

With *THE* word coming down from on high, GA-697.4 and GA-696.0 encouraged Tzion to wake up, gently fluttering their wings in front of his face, then gently poking him in the ribs, and whispering in his ear.

Slowly, Tzion stirred, coming fully awake after a few sharp jabs. He rubbed his face, assessing the stubble. His facial hair didn't grow fast, but there was at least a day's growth, maybe more. That would make today either late Saturday or maybe even Sunday.

"Consciousness achieved," GA-696.0 and GA-697.4 shouted, slapping their wings in high-five cheer. "Welcome back, buddy!" Though he couldn't hear them.

Tzion eased himself up into a sitting position and touched his hand to his head. He had a headache, but everything seemed to be in working order, no broken bones either. Carefully, he rose to a kneeling position, then stood using the stepping stone rock for leverage. While his legs felt like Jell-O, he stayed upright (with a little help). GA-696.0 and seven of the weightlifting team stood on his left; while GA-697.4 and the other seven GAs stood at his right side ready to catch him, just in case.

"Slow and steady, Tzion. Slow and steady," GA-696.0 whispered in his ear. They prayed he had sense enough to not climb on the stepping stone.

Their prayers were answered as Tzion stood below the sealed opening, using the flashlight function on his phone. His battery was low, the light was dim, but strong enough for him to see the smidgen of a crack above.

Tzion sat on the stone to have a better look at the opening. The phone battery showed only a single tick. The flashlight feature would drain it even faster the longer he kept it on. The Hazon Labs image cube bracelet was equipped with a USB self-charger, designed for emergencies like this. Unfortunately, he hadn't recharged the unit in quite a while. Nonetheless, he removed the cubes' bracelet from his wrist and plugged the USB into the base of his cellphone. The light brightened a bit, but not enough to pass through the opening, or for anyone to see.

Come on, Tzion. Think, he said to himself. The light wasn't going to get any stronger on its own. If anything, the drain on the battery would happen soon enough. If he could reflect the light somehow, it might boost the illumination. Something metal, or maybe plastic. He pulled the package of *tekhelet* strings he'd bought for his brother from his back pocket, amazing that he hadn't lost it. He shined the light on the box's plastic window. Inside, the blue-purple threads brightened under the light. He squeezed the box, tenting the plastic window into a "v" and which allowed Tzion to focus the split beams of indigo-tinged light and move them around with purpose.

GA-697.4 and GA-696.0 looked at one another for the last time. Their mission below was at its end, but part of a new beginning. The sparks had been there the whole time. They'd thought helping Tzion was their primary mission, but no. Their true purpose was to gather the *tekhelet* sparks, the lost frequency of the dyed threads finding resonance in them, with them, for their ultimate return… a most fitting end to their journey.

The GA weightlifters stood at attention as GA-697.4 and GA-696.0 stepped into the reflected light, immediately releasing the *tekhelet* sparks and which sent two streams of light up into the cave above and then beyond… back to the Source.

* * *

Effi had only ventured a few steps into the Hall of the Freemasons when he saw the burst of light to his left, but which then faded out almost immediately. The light had been coming from a corner of the cave, a hollowed-out section with not one, but two skull-and-crossbones symbols drawn on the wall.

Using the light from his cellphone, he drew nearer to where he thought the source of the light had been. "Hello," he whispered. "Is someone there?"

Tzion's throat was parched, but he cried out, "Help." A shouted whisper. He took his cellphone and banged it against the rock, trying to make more noise. "I'm here," he tried again, at last finding his voice.

"I hear you," Effi called down then tried to move the heavy stone covering the opening, pushing against it with his hands. "There's a stone over the opening. I can't move it."

"Help me. Please."

Effi think, he commanded himself. Leverage, he needed to move the stone. He dropped to the ground, clearing any loose rocks around the stone then braced his back against the wall behind him. He put his feet against the stone and pushed hard, with all his might. But the stone moved only a few inches. His legs just weren't long enough to move it any farther. He scrambled back over to the small opening he'd made and peered down into the hole.

The man was covered in chalk dust, the side of his face smeared with blood. He should have been afraid but wasn't as the man looked up at him. He could hardly believe his eyes. "Tzion?" he said, staring at the man who had helped him on Friday.

The bright flashlight from Effi's cellphone hurt Tzion's eyes. "*Yeled*?" he whispered.

"Are you okay? Dumb question," Effi said, his eyes drifting to the body lying on the ground behind the rock, which made him freeze.

Tzion followed Effi's gaze to the dead body. "With me, *yeled*," he said, trying to draw the boy's attention back.

"Sorry. He's…"

"Yes, dead. I need to get out of here."

"I'll go get help."

Just then, Zedekiah's Cave echoed with the sounds of a heavy door, slamming closed.

"Oh no!" Effi said, realizing it was probably the side entrance door closing shut… their only way out. The only question was if someone had left, or if someone else was now inside Zedekiah's Cave with them?

* * *

Joshua gave his eyes a moment to adjust to the dimly lit cave. The door had slammed closed loudly behind him, realizing he must have kicked the small rock that had wedged the door open out of place. Getting out was a second priority; finding Tzion his first. Davi knew where he was headed; she could call in the troops and also smooth out the near-miss he'd had with a group of tourists who'd stubbornly refused to move out of his way.

He'd driven onto the sidewalk, trying to maneuver around them, shouting, "Out of the way!" One woman flatly refused to move, crossing her arms. He revved the motorcycle's engines ready to run her over if need be, when a tall man physically picked up the brunette and moved her himself. Joshua was surprised that their yelps didn't draw the attention of the *Mishtara* or Border Guards, which might not be such a bad thing. As he swerved past the group, he saw a workman's barricade blocking the main entrance gate to the cave. The sign, written in Hebrew, Arabic, and English, read, "Closed for Maintenance."

"Damn it," Joshua shouted, revving the engine again and circled around the corner. The side entrance was his only option. He set his dad's motorcycle against the wall and vaulted over the railing. He'd be lucky if the bike was still there later. *Be open, be open*, his mind screamed. He jumped over a few low bushes and made a beeline for the side entrance.

"Yes. Thank you, G-d," he said, lifting his eyes to the Heavens then grabbed the heavy door, swinging it wide open, and rushed inside. He was a second too slow to catch the door before it slammed closed behind him. He tried the doors, but they wouldn't open. Strange… weren't emergency doors supposed to open from the inside? Hopefully, help was on the way.

Out of the corner of his eye, he saw a light in the distance, but in the next instant, it was gone. He wanted to call out Tzion's name, but every instinct in his body told him to move quietly. Quickly. Something didn't feel right. With nothing else to go on, he headed towards where he thought he'd seen the light, using only the cave's emergency lights to guide him forward.

* * *

Ministry of Public Security, Bar Lev Video Surveillance Center

Davi, and by extension MAGSS, enjoyed a special relationship with the *Mishtara* and other Israeli security services, giving her unprecedented access when she needed their help. It took her a couple of minutes to explain the situation, using the word, *dachoof,* meaning urgent, with the new reception desk clerk who was more taken with Boomerang, than with doing her job. She texted Noam that she was in the building and needed his help.

Less than a minute later, the Director of Operations, Noam Z., still devastatingly handsome and dressed as if he had just walked in from a photo shoot, waved her forward. A two-fingered come hither.

"Come," he said, placing his identification card on the reader. She waited for the plastic fins to open, then joined him on the other side of the security turnstile, a go/no-go stop for anyone entering, or leaving, the secure area.

"I'm not sure your *Oketz* friend is authorized," he joked, adding a wink for her and a scratch to Boomerang's head.

"Careful, she bites."

"Like you, darling," he smirked, then kissed her on both cheeks.

"I appreciate this, Noam."

"This morning's work is thanks enough," he said, staring at her knowingly. "Cyber division is with them now."

"Make sure, they lose the keys."

"They were into a good many things. It will take time to process everything."

"I have a situation."

"As always."

She smiled. He liked giving her a hard time, but always helped.

He placed his left thumb on the fingerprint reader, unlocking the door to Jerusalem's nerve center, the security video monitoring center. Wall-to-wall monitors filled the cavernous space, capturing the tens of thousands of live-streamed video feeds from security cameras throughout the city, tracking, monitoring, and recording the movements of its citizens… *all* its citizens. This had been her home for five years. She sensed a heightened level of activity in the room and which matched her own anxiety.

Then, as if he could read her mind, "A bit of a situation of our own."

"Dare I ask?"

He hesitated an extra moment before responding. "I hope you are TAMA 38-compliant by now." He raised his neatly trimmed eyebrows, opening his amber-colored eyes, silently transmitting the earthquake alert they'd received that morning from the Geological Survey of Israel folks.

Davi understood the cryptic message all too well. TAMA 38 was the Government's incentivized program to upgrade buildings, built before 1980, and which failed to meet safety standards for a country located on the Great Rift Valley and where earthquakes have been known to happen. While her building was built before 1980, it squeaked by meeting the lowest safety threshold, allowing them to avoid the lengthy and noisy TAMA 38 upgrades.

"Anomalous readings for now," he added. "We're running our protocols."

"Good idea," she said, knowing that the printed protocols had been gathering dust in a binder in one of the storage rooms in the basement. Hopefully, they'd at least been digitized in the past five years.

Noam set her up in a cubicle as she explained what video footage she needed, the location, and the approximate time frame. She'd narrowed down the time frame based on when Effi texted her that he was heading home from the Old City and wouldn't need a ride. He'd seen Tzion Mengistu somewhere within a ninety-minute window from when she'd dropped him off.

Davi loaded Tzion's image into FARS, the *Mishtara's* advanced Facial Recognition Search program, as Noam pulled up Friday's video footage into a desktop screening room on the widescreen monitor. He sped through the footage using a trackball, starting her at a 13:00:00 timecode.

She put in the additional parameters, what Tzion was wearing, that he was Ethiopian, and his height and weight from his Driver's license. The computer would run the search in the background, while she manually scanned the footage at 1.5x speed. Even so, it was a lot of data to cover, and potentially more if Tzion had turned off, or been forced off, into one of the side streets in the Arab Quarter.

"You have quite a bit to cover," Noam stated as if reading her mind. "With the war, we've doubled coverage in the Old City. A good and bad thing. I'm sorry I can't spare anyone to help you."

Davi would have been surprised if the *Mishtara* hadn't upped the coverage. "I understand," she said without shifting her concentration from the screen. She continued scrolling then stopped, glimpsing a familiar face in the crowd and rewound the footage. It was Arik Anders.

That's odd, she thought. Anders' file indicated he was in the process of converting to Judaism, so then why the hell was he going into *Ecce Homo* Pilgrim's House on a Friday. That particular mystery, however, would have to wait for another day.

She needed to rethink her strategy, occamizing the problem to the simplest solution. If Tzion was headed to Zedekiah's Cave, then she should be able to pick him up closer to his destination and confirm his moves beginning at the end, rather than at the beginning. If not, then she would have to use the more tedious and time-consuming approach, though the advanced AI facial recognition system would hopefully speed the process along.

"Make it *Sha'ar Shechem*. Friday. 13:00 hours."

Noam called up the *Sha'ar Shechem* master files and entered the date and time. "I'll leave you to it then. Terminals open, if you need anything else."

"Thanks, Noam."

"Always." He winked then turned his attention back to the rest of Jerusalem and the nightmare prospects of an earthquake hitting *his* city. They always knew it was only a matter of time. He'd only hoped it would be *after* his tenure.

Jerusalem wasn't just the center of *his* world, but of the world. Hanging on the wall in his office was a lithograph of the well-known *circa* 1581 World map showing the continents of Europe, Africa, and Asia as an open three-petaled flower with Jerusalem at its center. Jerusalem's centric status dated to the 4th or 5th century as the *Midrash Tanchuma, Kedoshim 10:1* described the land of Israel as the navel of the world with Jerusalem at the center of the land of Israel, and G-d's Sanctuary on the Temple Mount in the center of Jerusalem where the *Beit HaMikdash* had once stood. The artist he'd commissioned to create the verse in calligraphic script, grumbled non-stop about its length and how it ruined the map's aesthetics. In the end, it was done to his specifications, including the passage that the *Kodesh HaKodashim* was at the center of the Sanctuary, and the Ark of Covenant at its center, set atop the Foundation Stone from which the World was founded. Admittedly, it was a long quote, but spot on to his view of *his* city.

Noam knew Davi well enough to know she wouldn't be here unless it was important. The arrest of Allon and Noiman that morning should have been her priority. She'd be right in the thick of things, seeing it through to the end, unless something else more pressing needed her attention. He crossed to one of the Observer techs, quickly scribbling a note. *Sha'ar Shechem*, 600 meters, left and right. "Let me know if you find anything. Anything."

"*B'seder.*" The observer nodded, welcoming the new assignment. He'd been tasked with re-positioning camera angles on secondary targets. If the phantom earthquake ever decided to show, all hell could easily break loose with looters and other criminals targeting supermarkets, pharmacies, and electronics stores. If, and when, they would be ready.

Chapter 20

Blame his Spidey sense, but Joshua's gut told him something wasn't right. Maybe it was the light that winked out quickly; the whiff of a chemical odor he couldn't place; or, the simple fact that he'd nearly jumped out of his skin as the door slammed shut behind him. Despite his best efforts to keep his footsteps as quiet as possible, the loose stones and soil crunched noisily under his feet. He hopped over the railing, following the stairs into the Hall of the Freemasons. Tzion had done an amazing job capturing the essence of the cave that pre-dated the garish mold-fighting green and red lights and the slick 3D-like audio-visual presentation that intruded on the limestone cave's natural beauty. Joshua only hoped he'd have the chance to tell Tzion what a good job he'd done.

From the Hall of the Freemasons, Joshua took the path to his right, the more direct route to Zedekiah's Tears, where he thought he'd seen the light.

Effi pressed his body into the back wall, a recessed corner hoping it would be a blind spot to whoever was coming their way. He tried to slow his heart rate and breathing, but which wasn't happening fast enough. In another minute, he'd hyperventilate himself into unconsciousness. The rock in his hand was hardly a weapon, but it would have to do. He did have the element of surprise on his side, except that would only get him so far. OMG, what was he thinking? This wasn't one of his stupid video games… he was in a load of very deep caca.

Joshua realized he could spend hours trying to find Tzion, even walk right past him, and not know it. Despite his concerns, he had to take the chance. "Tzion," he whispered, then louder with greater urgency, "Tzion."

He scanned the hewn rock spaces on either side of the stairs, then hopped over the railing to have a closer check at a recessed area in the corner. The deeply carved-out section connected to another area of the cave that dead-ended at a wall marked with a skull and crossbones. He was about to turn around when a testosterone-deprived whisper reached his ears. "Joshua?"

"Effi?"

The boy sprang out of the shadows and threw his arms around Joshua. "Oh boy, am I ever glad to see you. Tzion's stuck down below." The words tumbled out of him in a rush of relief, laced with a healthy dose of panic. Effi grabbed Joshua's arm and pulled him over to the hole. "I couldn't move it any farther."

Joshua only half-heard Effi as he turned on his flashlight and peered into the small opening, and felt like crying. "You, my friend, are a sight for sore eyes."

Tzion managed a weak smile, swaying in the process. Looking up made him dizzy.

"Let's see about getting you out of there. Okay?"

Joshua immediately understood how Effi had managed to move the heavy stone. Thankfully, his legs were longer and should finish the job. He pressed his back into the wall and pushed the stone forward using the full force of his legs. It wasn't enough though. He needed another foot and a half to move the stone covering the hole. He repositioned himself, turning over onto his stomach, planting his feet on the edge of the stone, then pushed his arms against the wall gaining the extra reach he needed to move the stone.

Tzion stood unsteadily, propping himself up against the wall to clear the way for Joshua to climb down onto the stepping stone. The GA bodybuilder team lent their collective wings to keep Tzion upright. The chatter about Joshua E. Katz was positive, and they looked forward to working with him.

"Eyes on the job, boys," said GA-698.24, who had taken over as foreman.

Joshua handed his cellphone to Effi. "Keep the light on us. Okay?" But didn't wait for Effi to respond and dropped into the hole. He caught sight of the dead man, the body already bloated and foul-smelling. The questions could wait.

"Tzion, *achi*. I'm so glad you're okay," gently taking him into his arms.

"Me too. *Ha-Shem Yishmor*," he said with pure gratitude.

"Amein," Joshua said, slinging his arm over Tzion's shoulder, helping him to stand on the stepping stone. "I got you, Tzion. Right behind you," Joshua said, bracing himself against the wall since there wasn't enough room for both of them to easily, or safely, stand on the stepping stone. He crouched down, planning to use a leveraged squat and bringing himself up to full height to give Tzion a boost out of the cavern. He grabbed Tzion around his legs and hoisted him up through the hole, giving Tzion enough purchase above to crawl out, with a welcome assist from Effi.

Joshua came up right behind him. Resting on his haunches, Tzion hugged Effi, then Joshua.

"Let's get out of here," Joshua said, hoping he sounded confident since he wasn't exactly sure how they would manage that.

Just then a whisper of light reached them as the sound of a door slamming closed echoed through the cave.

Joshua swiftly brought his finger to his mouth as the three huddled together.

Barak finished adjusting the shirt and pants for the umpteenth time and stepped out of the bathroom into several inches of water. Strange, the area had been dry when he'd first entered the bathroom. Where was all the water coming from? He listened for a moment but didn't hear anything. The large tanks were set deeper inside the cave, except for the first one near the emergency escape; none would be affected by water. The last tank though was different. He remembered *Ahmed* saying something about humidity, but that wasn't water… was it?

The water kept pouring in, quickly covering the bottom of his boots. He tried closing the bathroom door but had to force it against the rising water. No one mentioned anything about water. After some effort, he was finally able to slam it shut; the sound echoing through the empty cavern. The water sloshed against his boots as he carefully climbed the stairs, mindful to keep the detonator switch dry. He tucked the dangling cord into his shirt sleeve, grabbing onto the railing to keep from slipping or falling. He wasn't sure if the vest could detonate because of a fall and didn't want to find out either.

Ahmed had given him a map, detailing the location of each of the tanks. *Barak* wondered what would happen if the water kept rising, could it flood the entire cavern? There was only a one or two-minute preset delay on three of the timers. The tanks would explode in quick succession. The last tank was the bad one. *Ahmed* made sure he understood to get clear of the tank once he'd set the five-minute timer. Then, he could blow himself up.

Barak still wished for an audience, an opportunity to shout *Alla-hu Akbar* and see the fear in his victims' eyes. So much for that…

Ahmed told him to use the map and keep a lookout for a fluorescent orange "X" painted on the side of each of the three black tanks. He said they looked like the ones visible on rooftops throughout Palestinian-controlled areas or where Palestinian Arabs refused to pay the Israeli government for services. Except, the water still came from the Jews. Stupid.

The first tank was located next to the cave's emergency exit. *Ahmed* said, it would trap first responders. *Barak* smirked to himself. *Ahmed* promised him that each of the tanks would create a wall of flames. What a glorious sight, especially if the Jew-responders rushed into the fire. If only he could wait for them to show and blow himself up then. That would be special, only those weren't his instructions and dealing with the fallout from *al-Masri* would be worse than dying if something went wrong.

No, *Barak* would activate the pre-set timers and do as he was told. He only needed to turn the screw cap a half turn to the right. Done. Ninety seconds. He needed to hurry. According to the map, the second tank was placed deeper in the cave. *Ahmed's* instructions were clear, "Boom, boom, boom. One right after the other before the final tank, and then his big boom."

Besides, he didn't want to be near any of the tanks when they exploded. He scrabbled his way across the loose rock to the stairs and climbed over the railing. His foot immediately slipped on the slick stone as a steady stream of water poured over the steps from the bathroom area and onto the main staircase. *All-ah be praised*, he managed to catch himself before landing on his backside. *Barak* might not be able to read well, but he did have a working brain. It didn't make sense that the water could have already flooded the bathroom area, which was located a good four-plus meters, fifteen feet, below the cave's entrance. *And so fast?* He didn't know how limestone reacted with water or the heat from the fire, but this turn of events couldn't be good.

What if the water put out the fires? Ahmed would not be pleased. But how could they blame him… he'd tried. No one, not even *al-Masri*, could blame him for what was clearly an act of G-d.

To find the other tanks, *Barak* needed to go deeper into the cave, except making progress without falling and breaking his neck heading down the stairs meant holding onto the railing for dear life. He re-positioned the

Deadman's switch over the top of his wrist so it wouldn't get caught on the railing. He continued down the stairs making good progress and finally reached the bottom and entered the Hall of the Freemasons. The limestone floor of the large cavern was wet, slippery, but the water wasn't deep here.

Barak's confidence soared, more sure of completing his mission. Here, the water was only a minor concern. It would take days to fill this space, if then, and would require a flood of truly Biblical proportions. He could follow the tiny rivulets, coursing through the Hall and running deeper into the cave. The map told him to go to the left and set the timers on the other two firebombs before handling the tank with the chemicals near Zedekiah's Tears.

He braced himself, anticipating the blast from the first tank, and was duly rewarded. "*Alla-hu Akbar*," he shouted as a thick plume of smoke filled the cave as the small explosive charge set off a chain reaction as the nitrogen-based fertilizer mixed with the petrol/oil mixture, igniting it into a flaming fireball. Boom!

There was no time to waste or to worry about water. The first blast would likely draw an audience, which was apparently always part of the plan. The rush of first responders, the fire and police, would fall victim to the deadly gas in the fourth tank, a yellow cylinder. Emboldened, he quickly activated the preset timer on the second tank and hurried over to set the timer on tank number three. The blasts would create a cascading firestorm of diesel oil and thick smoke. Even so, he still wasn't sure how any of the explosions would be strong enough to weaken the cave's roof to cause it to collapse… just hopefully not on his head.

After congratulating him on his *shahid* video, *al-Masri* clapped him on the back, nearly knocking him over and gleefully explained, "*Barak* your glory will send the mice scurrying in the streets above." Al-Masri's words sounded good at the time, now he wasn't sure. *Who exactly would be the mice scurrying in the streets above? By his calculations, the cave was under the Muslim Quarter, maybe some of the Christian Quarter, but nowhere near the Jews. Strange. Very strange.*

* * *

Joshua kept a protective arm over Effi and Tzion and watched as the light approached their position before its owner veered to the left. He was on the roundabout route, taking the long way around to get to Zedekiah's Tears. A brief reprieve, since the path would eventually lead him straight to them. This was their chance. He'd do his best to buy Effi and Tzion as much time as he could. He got them over to the stairs, wondering where all the water had come from. Just then an explosion shook the ground, a concussive blast of superheated air, sending a salvo of rock shrapnel, limestone dust, particulates, and dense smoke through the cave. The area beyond the Hall of the Freemasons, up the stairs, glowed orange and yellow.

How could he send them there, but what other choice was there? Up, was their only way out. Then again, maybe they could wait it out in the Templar Cavern below? Maybe… maybe not. There were too many unknowns.

Joshua scooped up a handful of water and wet down his T-shirt before pulling it up over his nose, indicating Effi and Tzion should do the same. They were still huddled together when the second blast shook the ground beneath them, knocking Effi off his feet. Joshua helped him back up. The path to the right curved away from them, yellow and orange flames licking the limestone walls. The second blast had followed less than a minute after the first. There was no time left.

The shouted war cry of *Alla-hu Akbar* left no doubt in Joshua's mind, eventually the terrorist would make his way around to them. What he couldn't figure out was what the *mechabel* hoped to accomplish… Zedekiah's Cave had stood for 3,000 years despite having its innards gutted as its high-grade limestone was quarried. What was the point?

While Joshua's words were slightly muffled by the makeshift mask, his words were still understood. "Head to the entrance."

"But smoke rises," Effi said.

"Point taken, but staying here isn't an option. Now, go."

But Effi didn't let go of Joshua and tried to pull him along. "Go on, Effi. I'll follow behind you. Tzion needs your help. You need to hurry."

✳ ✳ ✳

Barak covered his ears as the concussive force from the second blast nearly knocked him off his feet. A powerful blast of superheated air and the smell of burning oil made him gag, but the fiery glow from the burning oil-petrol mixture lighting up the cave spurred him on. He braced himself, knowing the third tank would explode in less than a minute. One more boom and then he too would blow. *al-Masri's* instructions were clear, "Get as close to Zedekiah's Tears, and as far away from the chemical tank," he said, referring to the fourth tank, the yellow metal cylinder.

He didn't have time to consider how much time he had left. He'd already secured his place in history. He offered another *Alla-hu Akbar* to the cave's winds that carried swirls of heated dust but could only manage part of the *Jihadist's* call as the rest was swallowed in a cough. A *keffiyeh* would have helped him, but that wasn't part of the dishonorable uniform *they* insisted he wear.

The floor of the cave shook again as he reached his destination. Zedekiah's Tears would indeed flow, filling the streets with the cries of the Jews, their blood running through the streets of the Old City. The man known as *al-Masri* assured him the main blast would be centered at the Western Wall, sending the Jew devils straight to *Jahannam*. They'd taken him into their confidence, though he wondered why they didn't just send him to the Western Wall. Why bother with the cave at all? Its limestone was said to be of the finest quality, the kind their King Solomon supposedly used to build their false Temple. Lies all of it, that much he'd learned in the UNRWA school.

Barak tried not to think about the many questions he had. Except for one that still bothered him. Wasn't the cave below the Arab Quarter — its busy streets just a few feet above his head? It had to be. He hadn't walked long enough, far enough or even deep enough into the cave to be anywhere near the Jewish Quarter. Even walking fast, it was a fifteen-minute walk along *Haja'y Street* to get out of the Arab Quarter. The Jews called it, *Haggai*, named for one of their prophets. *Haja'y*. *Haggai*. Strange, the names weren't so different. Why name a main street in the Arab Quarter after a Jewish prophet? Something wasn't right… So many questions. Too many questions.

He felt a headache coming on. The foul-smelling smoke didn't help. He pulled his shirt over his nose. It helped make breathing a little easier. He was almost done and hurried over to the last tank. Everything was moving quickly now as he approached his final destination. Zedekiah's Tears and the fourth and final tank… the bad one.

* * *

Effi and Tzion rested for a moment before tackling the next set of stairs. Breathing was getting more difficult but thankfully the smoke had risen towards the ceiling of the cavernous Freemasons Hall, giving them a taste of cleaner air near the stairs He remembered his emergency training from school. "Stop, drop and roll" was one and the other, "stay low and go." Effi looked up the long staircase and saw the raging yellow-orange flames to their right, and heard the sound of crackling or cracking.

Strange, there wasn't anything to burn in the cave. No wood, paper, or the like. Just limestone.

Just limestone. In an instant, the inorganic chemistry formulas raced through Effi's mind. If hot limestone made contact with water, superheated steam would be released. But there was more about limestone's chemical reactivity Effi wished he didn't know. If limestone got hot enough it could start to decompose. With enough thermal cracking, the whole cave could come down on their heads. He was tempted to race back and warn Joshua, but Tzion urged him on. The only way out was forward and up toward the raging inferno ahead. As they made their way to the main entrance, a plume of dense smoke and debris raced through the Freemason's Hall. They crouched low, hoping to avoid the worst of it but to no avail.

Barak made his way to the fourth and final tank. He found it lying on its side, down a flight of stairs. The fluorescent orange signature called to him. The water had found the cave's lowest point… here, with the final tank. The water was already sloshing around his ankles too. The timer was located under the dome-shaped gas cap; protection against accidentally hitting the valve and prematurely releasing the tank's deadly contents. Like the others, the cap had been modified with a timer and fitted with a small explosive charge. This one would blow the valve and release the deadly gas. A simple twist to the left. No, wait. A twist to the right. His fingers could barely squeeze through the opening. He tapped the pre-set timer.

Done. He couldn't actually see the digital numbers, only their flickering red reflection as the numbers raced down to zero. A five-minute timer. *Barak* hurried back up the stairs, remembering how *Ahmed* and *al-Masri* laughed that if he wasn't careful, the chemical could burn off his face when it reacted with water in the air. Burn off his face, blow off his head – what did it matter? They laughed. He didn't find it so funny, but he laughed too.

Ahmed reassured him, "They will all know of your selfless martyrdom. They will bless the name of *Barak*."

He would meet *All-ah* before the timer ran out on the final tank. He was grateful to be spared from a most painful end. His death was a given, but enduring the kind of agonizing end *Ahmed* described was unnecessary. Long suffering was the way of his enemies, both the Jewish and Christian infidels. Now, they would know true suffering.

Barak braced himself, crouching low to the ground as the third blast spewed sharp pieces of stone and splintered rock shrapnel into his back, knocking him flat on his face… an appropriate show of submission before meeting *All-ah*.

Joshua watched the young man, just a boy, maybe sixteen or seventeen years old, fall to the ground. He was wearing the familiar uniform of the Border Police, but he was definitely not one of theirs. The boy's shirt had become untucked, revealing the lower portion of a suicide vest as he rose from the ground. His shouts of *Alla-hu Akbar* were enough; the vest only defined the rest of his intentions. Joshua moved closer, intending to surprise the *shahid* and hopefully buy Effi and Tzion more time to escape. Though, whether he would escape the day remained a critical unknown.

The Deadman's switch, a simple plunger trigger, hung just below the *shahid's* right sleeve at the ready for his "most proper" right hand to detonate the explosive vest. Press the plunger, then release it, Boom! Given enough explosives plus the heat from the fires, the entire cave complex might just collapse on itself… the outcome not only here, but also above ground and all too devastating to consider.

Right hand, my ass, Joshua thought. In Islam, the right hand was considered to be honored and noble. By all means, go to *All-ah* with your most proper right hand, the one reserved for proper intentions even for mundane daily rituals like putting on pants and shoes, entering a mosque, clipping nails, trimming a mustache, combing hair, exiting the bathroom, eating, drinking, or shaking hands — all actions suitable for the right hand. The opposite was true of the left, reversing the actions… when entering the bathroom, exiting a mosque, blowing one's nose, cleaning oneself, and undressing. Joshua couldn't see how blowing up the Arab Quarter qualified as a Holy mission worthy of anyone's right hand. *Shahidom* most definitely came from the very dark left, the more sinister side of things.

Judaism had similar left-hand bugaboos. As an ambidextrous *Kohen*, with a bit of left-hand dominance, some Rabbinic authorities held that he, and his kind, wouldn't be allowed to offer sacrifices in the Holy Temple. A moot point, since there wasn't a Third Jewish Temple. HaMikdash3.0 operated under a different set of rules and didn't discriminate against the left-handed world, though whether 3.0 would ever get a chance to buck the trend remained an open question. Assessing the full extent of the damage Jackie and Noiman had done to the system would take weeks, months, maybe forever. Joshua still couldn't figure out what he could've done to Jackie for her to want to destroy him. Another moot point. If Davi was right, both she and Noiman would be seeing the inside of a jail cell for a very long time. Justice served, though their victim HaMikdash3.0 might not survive.

And from the looks of things, there was a good chance neither would he.

Fortuitously, Joshua had left Jay a handwritten missive outlining his thoughts on HaMikdash with a just in case, "if something happens to me" clause. By handwriting the note, he automatically authenticated the document against any legal challenge to his last wishes. For whatever reason, he'd felt the need to write it, to properly put it to pen and paper. Who knew it might actually be his Last Will and Testament? Between the suicide belt and the unknown device ticking away behind the *shahid*, the writing was on the wall. By Joshua's reckoning, he was northwest of the Temple Mount, deep under the Arab Quarter but which also had a sprinkling of Christian Holy sites. That the *shahid* was dressed in a *Magav* uniform had initially confused him as to "who." No longer. Though, he was still confused about the "why."

Why on Earth would a *shahid*, an Islamic good ole' boy, want to blow up the Arab Quarter? One plus one generally equals two, and by following Occam's Razor the simplest explanation should be the correct one. In a moment of absolute clarity, Joshua recognized the scenario for what it was: a false-flag play. The cleverly devised ruse would spark absolute outrage around the world, uniting all in their condemnation of Israel even before the dust settled. False flag operations were favored by hackers, soldiers, and spies and which shifted blame away from the real perpetrators and onto the doorstep of an unsuspecting, but all-too-plausible scapegoat. The ploy worked best when the planted seeds seemed logical and counterclaims absurd; as in, why on Earth would an Arab want to blow up the Arab Quarter? For what reason, would he willingly sacrifice his own people?

Sickeningly perfect and which made it unlikely that this boy had dreamed up the scheme, the bombs, the entire plot, on his own. Some unseen hand had manipulated him into believing his *Jihad* demanded a high body count. The higher, the better. Facts didn't matter. If preliminary evidence pointed to a Jew, an Israeli, or better yet, an IDF soldier or police officer, that would enough to pronounce sentence. And even if incontrovertible proof later exposed the real perpetrators, no amount of media retractions or evidence to the contrary could undo the knee-jerk vilifications and finger-pointing at Israel. The outcome? All too predictable and predicted. The religious war to end all wars, wrapped in eternal hellfire and damnation. Israel, canceled by the world and the final nail hammered in the coffin to justify wiping her off the map once and for all. Welcome to the Apocalypse!

Joshua knew he had to stop him. But disarming a suicide bomber isn't as easy as one might think and this one appeared dead set on dying. Despite the high stakes, his life being chief among them, Joshua approached the problem like any other… systematically. Unfortunately, no matter how many scenarios he ran, differentially factoring each with Boolean operators — AND, OR, and NOT — he was left with only one approach.

Amuse. Confuse. Diffuse.

One of Joshua's favorite -isms, though seeming at odds given that "defusing" the *shahid* wasn't really an option. But maybe he could defuse the situation, stalling long enough at least for Tzion and Effi to escape. As long as the Deadman's switch dangled free from the *shahid's* wrist, there was still time before reaching a point-of-no-return.

But first, Joshua knew what he needed to do… had to do. He placed his right hand over his eyes, then closed them tightly. He took a deep breath, inhaling through his nose, and began recited the words of the *Shema* — the ultimate expression of faith, trust; a declaration to willingly sacrifice his life to sanctify G-d's name. Today could only end in one of two ways… he'd die or he wouldn't. Either way, he'd go to G-d with a clear conscience, giving thanks for sparing his life or for finally setting him free.

* * *

Uri'el listened to the heart of the man. Joshua would soon realize he'd overlooked another option — one he'd experienced long ago. Dead? Not dead? Other.

> And He said: 'Go forth and stand upon the mount before the LORD.' And behold, the LORD passed by, and a great and strong wind rend the mountains, and broke in pieces the rocks before the LORD; but the LORD was not in the wind; and after the wind an earthquake; but the LORD was not in the earthquake. And after the earthquake a fire; but the LORD was not in the fire; and after the fire a still small voice.
>
> 1 Kings 19:11-13

CHAPTER 21

*B*arak checked the Deadman's switch, making sure it would be ready when the time came. He wondered what it would feel like when he pressed on the plunger. Maybe a surge of pride before releasing it? Or, sheer terror? Would he feel it? Or, what if it didn't kill him, and instead he was left crippled stuck in a wheelchair for the rest of his life?

His life had always been a comedy of errors, a Murphy's Law of Things that could go wrong and invariably did. Murphy was probably still shadowing him today. Just in case, Barak decided to inspect the detonator's connection to the explosive vest. It could have easily become disconnected, or dislodged from one of the detonation wires. He started unbuttoning his shirt, twisting around to inspect the connection, near his ribs. Thankfully, he was still connected and was at once relieved that he wouldn't have to handle the vest any more than was absolutely necessary.

"You must wear the uniform," *al-Masri* insisted. *Barak* couldn't see how it could've mattered. Who was here to see him? Carefully working around the Deadman's switch, he began rebuttoning the shirt eager to make his ascent to Zedekiah's Tears.

Joshua made his move while the *shahid* was distracted, checking the buttons on his right sleeve and stepped directly into his path.

"Hey, how's it going?" Joshua casually said as if greeting an old friend. Without a moment's pause, he launched himself at the *shahid*, leading with his right foot, careful to keep one eye on the Deadman's switch. They tumbled backwards, rolling down the stairs on a deadeye drop for the chemical tank, clearly labeled Chlorine and stamped with a skull and crossbones danger symbol for good measure. Whether in gas or liquid form didn't much matter… both were deadly.

Barak scrambled up the stairs, desperate to get away from the tank and the crazy person who'd attacked him. Time was running out. But he still had time to finish his final mission, to die with honor, despite the intruder.

Joshua caught a glimpse of the flickering digital timer inside the chlorine tank's gas cap, but the numbers were unreadable. How much time he had left… a critical unknown. He vaulted himself over the low guardrail, stepping again into *Barak's* path.

Barak dropped to his knees, facing Joshua, hopefully, he was also facing *Mecca*. With practiced ease, he swung the detonator cord up in a quick draw, intending to close his hand around the Deadman's switch, press his thumb on the spring-loaded trigger in one smooth motion, then release it without any further delay. Boom.

"Oh shit," Joshua thought, then said the words out loud, but then tried not to laugh as the *shahid's* attempted grabs at the plunger failed again and again, turning his master plan, Act One, into a spastic comedy. The detonator cord was too short to execute the move.

But then as if reading Joshua's mind, the *shahid's* frenetic movements slowed. He lowered his arm, allowing the cord to naturally fall into the palm of his hand. Barak wrapped fingers around the Deadman's switch but didn't depress the plunger. With an evil smirk, he held the trigger switch out in front of his face, proving himself capable, his thumb poised just above the plunger.

"Oh shit," Joshua repeated, but then saw the opportunity. *Baruch Ha-Shem*, his mind whispered. They weren't dead men… at least not yet.

Joshua stared down the *shahid*. He still had one advantage; the terrorist hadn't planned on anyone interrupting his blown smithereens' party. His adrenaline "fight or flight" response, an internal binary decision-making dilemma switch, might be failing him, falling on the flight side of the equation despite the death stare and the taunt, gripping the Deadman's switch, his thumb teasingly poised above plunger. Joshua's sudden appearance had ruined his original plan.

The *shahid's* eyes shifted between Joshua and the chlorine tank below, likely calculating how much time remained on the timer. This move,

Barak knew well. He'd learn it from birth. With practiced ease, he rose from his kneeling position to stand in front of Joshua. The Deadman's switch at the ready.

Now was as good a time as any. Joshua made his Amuse, Confuse, but hopefully not Kaboom move. "By the way, my name's Joshua. I don't think we've been properly introduced. Didn't catch your name, though. You have one, yes?"

"What?"

"I asked, what is your name," Joshua said, pedantically enunciating each word.

"What's it to you, Jew?" the *shahid* said, spitting out the words.

"That rhymes. You, Jew. Very clever. But seriously, I'd like to know your name. This way, when I'm interviewed and the news people ask me the name of the moron who tried to blow himself up, I'll have a good answer."

"Everyone will know my name," *Barak* said, puffing out his chest and adding an arrogant sneer for good measure.

Something was wrong. The timer must not have been set right. It was taking too long. At least, he'd have his audience.

"It's not a hard question. You won't be graded if that's what you're worried about."

"What's wrong with you?"

"Me, nothing. Just tell me. Don't you want to make sure your family gets their blood money? You know, the money's less if you don't complete the job and you only end up in prison. I mean you still get a lifetime of payments, but less thanks to your friendly alphabet soup of governments and agencies, UN, US, EU," Joshua said, speaking very quickly and seriously. Confuse, took on many forms and Joshua did his best to contain the smirk as the *shahid* tried to follow his verbal convolutions.

"Shut up! Shut up! You make too much noise."

"I've been told as much," Joshua laughed.

"You think you're so funny. A real funny Jew-ape."

"I see that UNRWA education is really paying off."

"Laugh now. You will die today. I, will be in Paradise, you in *Jahannam*."

"Huh?" Joshua said, then waited an extra beat before continuing. "Oh, I get it. You mean, *Gehinnom*. That's how we Jews pronounce it," Joshua said, putting on his best poker face.

Without taking his eyes off Joshua, the *shahid* leaned back again, trying to get a closer look at the tank cylinder. The cap was almost completely submerged by water, but the timer was still running, at least he thought so since the red light's reflection on the limestone walls flickered in sync with the changing numbers.

Clearly, *Mr. Shahid* was keeping to a schedule.

"Look man, no one has to die today," Joshua said, lame but effective in trying to move this along.

The *shahid* smiled. "I am prepared to die. Are you?" *Barak* said, surprised at the strength in his voice and conviction of his words.

Without waiting for the requisite "*Alla-hu Akbar*" proclamation, which preceded all such offerings, Joshua again launched himself at the *shahid*, feet first. He landed awkwardly on the ground but, nonetheless, managed to knock the *shahid* down and the detonator out of his hand. The detonator lay only a few inches out of the *shahid's* reach. Joshua scrambled to his feet, doing a kip-up from the prone position. He landed hard, one foot on the cavern's uneven limestone floor, the other smashing into the *shahid's* wrist.

They locked eyes, a world of hateful emotions filling the moment, when suddenly the floor beneath them shuddered as a jagged gash running the length of the limestone cavern opened up. Weaving and swaying, Joshua tried to maintain his footing. He needed to keep the *shahid's* wrist restrained under his shoe. He wished he'd worn his riding boots instead of the soft-soled loafers. The harder he willed his body into place, the more the ground resisted. Deep fissures opened up all around him, spewing tremendous blasts of steam from deep within the earth, or more likely from the raging fires of Hell.

Joshua watched the water pour over the chlorine cylinder tank, completely submerging it in a maelstrom of rushing water. And then time stopped, as the flickering red numbers on the timer blinked out as a deep fissure opened beneath the cylinder and swallowed it whole. Between the timer shorting out and the tank disappearing, Joshua recognized the moment for what it was — a miracle. *Baruch Ha-Shem*, the chlorine tank was gone, but they had reached another impasse and the danger wasn't over as Joshua desperately tried to restrain the *shahid's* wrist.

A low rumble, followed by a roar filled Zedekiah's Cave. The trembling walls tore into the restraining nets covering the walls freeing tons of splintered rock and chiseled stone from their confines, exploding and imploding all at once. The earth continued to rumble beneath Joshua, a tortuous groan reverberating within the closed space. Joshua felt the cave's floor shift again under his feet, tipping him sideways in a fall he was helpless to stop. Unable to regain his balance in time, he watched in horror as his boot lifted off the *shahid's* wrist as he hit the ground.

Finally freed, the *shahid* gritted his teeth as he reached for the detonator. *Barak* couldn't resist shoving his triumph in the *yahud's* face. But then his victory moment lasted a second too long as the cave's ceiling collapsed, raining tons of limestone on *Barak*.

Joshua scrambled backwards across the cavern floor as pieces of the ceiling continued to fall all around him. He got to his feet and began making his way to the lighted stairs. He waded into the warm waters which filled the shallow grooves and chiseled steps, slowing his movements into staccato of freeze-frames. His footing was unsure as he slogged on across the slippery wet limestone toward the main stairs.

And then he heard it; a still small voice, a *bat kol*, calling his name.

Chapter 22

The stairs were slick as the water continued to stream down towards them from above. They moved to opposite sides of the railing, using a hand-over-hand motion to climb the long staircase up to the entrance. The smoke grew heavier, the temperature rising the higher they climbed, each step straining their lungs with each breath. All around him, hot steam exploded from loose piles of limestone rocks next to the staircase. Tzion bent down, scooping up handfuls of water to wet his shirt again, pulling it up as a mask across his mouth and nose. He signaled Effi to do the same. The smell of burning diesel oil triggered a long-ago memory from his misspent youth. He and his gang of miscreants would warm themselves over a burning fire in a metal drum, eagerly planning their next misadventure.

He and Effi reached the second landing and saw the wall of flames off to their right. Tzion sat down on the steps, while Effi leaned over the railing to get a better view of the inferno. Raging orange and yellow flames, mixed with thick black smoke engulfed the side entrance. With the main entrance gates locked, Effi had hoped the side entrance could be their way out. He didn't say anything to Tzion, who'd dragged himself to his feet and came up behind him.

Tzion knew everything about the cave, including about the emergency side exit, which was now behind a wall of flames.

"Yalla, we have to climb," Tzion said.

Effi helped Tzion up the rest of the way, staying closer to the left railing, before veering over to the stairs leading down to the bathrooms. The main entrance was engulfed in a tempest of smoke, coursing through the cross-hatched metal gate. The side staircase at least kept them out of the worst of the smoke. The bathroom area was almost completely submerged, though the stairs had begun to dry. Strange and stranger still. The smell wasn't as bad, so hopefully the water wasn't some toxic brew of sewage. Not that it mattered much... they'd been sucking it in through their shirt masks.

"Sit," Effi said.

"You too, *yeled*."

They both dropped to the ground, sitting on the stairs to catch their breaths. Tzion rested his head against the railing. Despite the makeshift face mask, the acrid smoke burned the back of his throat.

"I'll be right back," Effi said, as he started to rise when Tzion grabbed his shirt.

"What, where are you going?"

Both had to shout to be heard as suddenly the sound of the rushing water grew louder. Tzion glanced over his shoulder isolating the source to a quarried pit next to the stairs. A swirling whirlpool of small rocks and dirt skittered across the water's surface, percolating with bubbles of hot steam rising from the deep and releasing its fury into the cave.

Effi tapped Tzion's hand. "I just want to look at the side exit again." He then raced up the stairs, slipping on the slick surface. Maybe, there was still a way around the burning tank. If so, they had to try. Staying here wasn't an option.

He carefully climbed over the railing but didn't get very far as hot steam exploded from the loose piles of limestone rocks scattered across the sloping ground. The wet shirt covering his mouth and nose only made it harder to breathe. The heat from the fire was more intense than he expected. Effi shielded his eyes, but knew trying to get any closer to the side entrance was pointless… there was no way they could get out that way. He started to climb up the steep slope, but the worn soles of his boots made it almost impossible to gain any traction over the slick rocks as Effi found himself skittering down the rocky slope toward the wall of flames. He dug in his heels, trying to stop himself, grabbing for anything solid to hold onto when a hand reached out and grabbed hold of his arm.

Tzion had stretched himself under the railing, holding on to it by the fingertips of one hand and reaching out to Effi with the other.

"Climb over me," he ordered, "do it," knowing what little strength he had left was fading fast.

Effi scrabbled over him, then helped pull Tzion back in. They lay on the stairs, sprawled on their backs. Neither spoke for another moment.

"Thanks, Tzion. I thought for sure… I was…"

"*Baruch Ha-Shem.*"

Effi smiled. "Amen. We can't get out that way."

"I thought we'd covered that before?"

Effi shrugged. "I'm sorry."

"No worries. How 'bout we try the gate, together?" While Tzion doubted the effort would work, hope was important to hold onto… as was doing something. Anything.

They climbed the last flight of stairs, stone this time, and shook the metal gate back and forth. It was double padlocked from the outside with an industrial strength U-lock. Effi managed to squeeze his hand through the gate and checked to see if, by some miracle, it had been left open. He shook his head, no.

Unfortunately, the barricade in front of the gate kept them from seeing out, and also anyone from looking in. Still…

"Help, help," Effi shouted and was quickly joined by Tzion when the smoke suddenly rose up, engulfing them and choking their words.

"Help, help!" Effi shouted again, inhaling more of the heavy smoke that stung his throat.

"We can't stay here," Tzion shouted, dragging Effi away from the gate. The stairs leading down to the bathroom was still relatively clear.

"The smoke isn't as heavy down there," Tzion said, pointing toward the bathrooms. "The water should protect us from the worst of the smoke and the fire."

"I'm not such a great swimmer," Effi admitted.

"Neither am I, *yeled*."

Tzion debated whether to tell Effi that water wouldn't stop this kind of fire, it would only help spread it. But he decided less is more, and kept the information to himself. His old street crew thought it funny to light up the neighborhood's garbage cans and the occasional stray cat. Gasoline and diesel oil were their weapons of choice. That's when he'd finally gotten his head on straight. He also knew too much about limestone and its reactions with heat.

Before leaving the office, he reviewed a bit of basic chemistry, acid-base reactions, and the various pitfalls they might include in the revised HaMikdash3.0 gaming scenario for Zedekiah's Cave. Ironically, a potential gaming storyline was playing out in real time… "Escape from Zedekiah's Cave."

He looked again at the entry gate. *Sultan Suleiman Street* was one of the busiest commercial areas in East Jerusalem. Where was everyone?

Why didn't anyone hear them? Or, see the smoke? Someone must have noticed.

Someone did.

※ ※ ※

Davi tried texting Effi another "911" message, but again she got no reply. Hopefully, they would all survive the day. She'd try him again in a bit. She picked up Boomer from the floor and tried to catch Noam's eye, but couldn't. Clearly, he had his hands full. A damn earthquake… could this day get any crazier? She'd send Noam a note later, thanking him. Hopefully, she would clear security without any problems.

Joshua was no doubt searching Zedekiah's Cave by now, Jay too, and that was exactly where she needed to be. She'd confirmed what she needed to know. Tzion had made it out of the Muslim Quarter.

"Davs," Noam shouted and signaled her over to the main screens. He'd pooled seven live camera feeds in and around *Sha'ar Shechem* including *Sultan Suleiman Street*.

"You might want to see this?" referring to the distinct haze and smoke trailing into the sky. Stranger still, the area was mostly deserted.

"Where's all that smoke coming from?" she asked, panicking.

"I've got search and rescue squads on the way," Noam said, his voice calm as always.

"I have to go," she said, panic infusing her voice.

"There's more." He barely looked at the observer technician, who rewound the footage. She caught the time code change. Thirty minutes.

The camera feed was from the Arab Bank on *Sultan Suleiman Street*, across from Zedekiah's Cave. In a horrifying instant replay, the feed showed Effi climbing over the fence around the corner from the cave's blocked entrance.

"We've also detected some seismic jumps, getting stronger too."

She checked her panic. "Where's the live feed?"

"On twenty. We can't get a clear shot of the entrance. But there's your smoke source." Rising from behind the barricade, smoke poured out of Zedekiah's Cave.

"I have to go." There was no time to waste.

"Be careful," he said. "Not a lot of people around. Suspicious to say the least."

"Forewarned."

Noam nodded. Davi filled in the rest on that particular blank. "An action," a riff on the familiar Nazi term, *Aktion*. The word had gone out, "Stay away."

She took one last look at the live feed and grabbed the side of the desk as she watched Jay break through the barricade, tossing the metal and plastic guts to the side. His shirt was already up around his face and nose, and in the next instant he was swallowed by darkness as black smoke poured over him.

Davi texted Jay that help was on the way, then tucked Boomerang into her jacket and raced for the door.

Out of the corner of his eye, Noam saw her leave, then turned his attention back to Zedekiah's Cave. The scene was all wrong. He continued scanning the *Sultan Suleiman Street* feeds. A slight movement caught his eye. "There," he shouted, pointing to a lone Arab, scurrying back and forth between the arched vertical supports in front of the Arab Bank. Male, 5'6", thick around the middle, an awkward tilt of his head to the left, a permanent disability that made him appear to be always looking to the side. Even with his face hidden behind the *keffiyeh*, Noam recognized him, *Ahmed* "The Fixer" *Tamimi*. The little man was a little too interested in the goings on at Zedekiah's Cave.

* * *

Jay saw the smoke spilling out of the entrance to Zedekiah's Cave from half a block away. There was no time to waste. He had driven the SUV onto the sidewalk, jumped out of the car and tore down the barricade. His shirt was already up and around his face and nose when he was swallowed by the darkness, a rush of smoke and heated air made him dizzy. The back of his throat felt like he'd swallowed a lit cigar.

But none of that mattered. He almost didn't recognize his own voice as he shouted Tzion's name, then called out for Joshua.

The roar of the fire almost drowned out the testosterone-iffy voice. "We're in here."

"Tzion?"

"He's here with me."

"Joshua?"

Tzion marshaled all of his strength to call out to Jay as he and Effi worked their way back up to the entry gate.

"You are a sight for sore eyes," Jay exclaimed, reaching his arm through the open metal gate and slapping the back of Tzion's neck.

Effi rushed over to Tzion's side.

"Joshua's not with you?"

Tzion shook his head. "We got separated. *Mechabel*," he said, using the Hebrew word for terrorist.

"He'll be okay, I'm sure," Jay said, trying to convince himself that his best friend would make it out of this one alive. "There's got to be another way out of here." A statement rather than a question.

"The side entrance is blocked too," Effi said.

"Try to stay out of the smoke. Me too. I'll be back."

He studied the metal gate; the top and bottom were drilled into the stone. Nothing short of a bulldozer or towline with a chain would be able to tear it down. There wasn't much in the SUV that would be of any use, except maybe his climbing gear. He stepped back from the gate and looked around for any smoke signals. Any opening would do. He could work with that before help arrived.

Jay circled around to the right side of the entrance, looking for any breaches, then over to the left side. He first saw the wisps of smoke, rising from behind a pile of pipes and garbage. He kicked the debris out of the way. A plume of smoke rose out of a ventilation shaft, a plastic pipe. The opening measured no more than a meter across, a tight fit, but a possible way in, and out.

"I think I've got something here," he shouted, clearing the rest of the debris from around the opening. He dropped his leg into the hole and kicked out the mesh lining at the other end, then peered inside. His reward: a clear view of the raging fire.

He turned on the flashlight function and stuck his hand through the hole, waggling it back and forth. "Can you see my light? I'm to the right of the gate on your side." The flashlight function on his phone was at its highest intensity.

Tzion and Effi leaned over the railing. Neither was sure exactly where they should be looking. The cave was lit by the fire in all directions.

"Towards the top, to the right of the gate," Jay shouted again, getting his bearings straight relative to the view inside the cave. "Beyond those portable toilets."

Tzion knew exactly where Jay was. He dared to venture inside one during the shoot last summer. "I see it," Tzion shouted, pointing to a steeply sloping area, under a low-hanging rock shelf, about 4.5 meters (15 feet) beyond the ticket booth. "We got you, Jay."

"*Baruch Ha-Shem*," Jay said. Now to get them out.

He raced back to the car, popping the liftback on the go. He dropped behind the wheel, backing up to within two feet of the ventilation hole, then jumped out of the car and grabbed the gear. Two rope coils, gloves, belt, and carabiners. He tied off one end of a coil of rope to the SUV's tow hook, setting the anchor line with a simple figure-eight follow through, then tested the tension against his weight. The gloves and the belt with half a dozen carabiners went on next. Jay yanked on the rope, looping himself in and checked his knot skills. Joshua's knots were always better; his own would hold.

"On my way," he shouted, contorting his body into the hole, feet first on his belly. A tub of Crisco® came to mind when he found himself stuck three-quarter of the way through. It wasn't a graceful entry or an ideal one. Descents were meant to be vertical, not horizontal.

Jay came through the hole, belaying out some of the line, getting into a tight tuck position to get his feet under him, then came up to a standing position... such as it was — sharply angled on the rock ledge, the heat from the fire sniping at his back. He looked over to his left at Tzion and the boy; both were eagerly leaning over the railing. They looked more confident than he felt. The next part of his plan had more than a few tricky points.

He tied off one end of the rope coil, linking it with a carabiner to the tow line, then tossed the coil to them. The angle was off, as was the throw, landing just short of the railing. Effi dropped down immediately and reached through the railing, pulling the rope toward him.

"Tzion, you need to anchor the line to something strong on your end," Jay shouted, concern wrapping his words. He hoped Tzion remembered how to tie off a clove hitch or even figure eight from their spring team-building adventure.

As if Jay had asked the question aloud, Tzion shouted back, "Will a clove hitch work?"

Jay nodded and smiled.

Tzion's stomach did a flip-flop at the memory of him hanging off of Dalton Cliffs up in the *Galil*, swinging back and forth with nothing but air under him when his feet slipped out from under him. The loose rock here would make their crossing every bit as dangerous. Incongruently, he smiled to himself, adding a "slip towards a fiery doom hazard" to his "Escape from Zedekiah's Cave" scenario for HaMikdsh3.1; he only hoped he'd live long enough to pitch it to the team.

Tzion tested the railing, but already knew it wouldn't be strong enough. The entry gate was a good option. but he'd have to angle the line around the ticket booth. Parts of the gate were anchored into the surrounding stone wall so at least it wouldn't give out. A good choice.

"I'll tie it off on the gate," Tzion called out.

Jay offered him a thumbs up and fed out enough rope to lower the tension on the line, but not too much. He figured, they could use a hand-over-hand movement and walk the line over to him. He was glad to see Tzion help the boy over the railing, letting him go first. They could make any adjustments on the fly but without Tzion's heavier weight to consider.

Effi held onto the rope, slipping more than he liked on the loose stones. It snapped taut as he dropped down a few feet but held. About halfway to Jay, he wiped off his hands and reset his grip. He looped one arm around the rope and wiped the other on his pants.

"You're doing great, *yeled*. What's your name?" Jay shouted.

"Effi. Effi Davidson."

The mystery of the *yeled* now made sense. Joshua had told him about Effi when they spoke briefly over WhatsApp® Saturday night. "Just a little farther."

Effi paused again to catch his breath, his feet slipped out from under him, landing hard on his side. "I'm okay," he shouted, pulling himself up again.

"Damn near gave me a heart attack, Effi," Jay laughed.

"Me too," Effi replied, smiling as he crossed the last few feet and fell into Jay's arm, hugging him.

"Nice to meet you too, kid. Now get out of here."

Effi maneuvered himself in front of Jay, then crawled into the ventilation hole. In the distance, Jay thought he heard sirens... at least he hoped so.

"I'm through," Effi shouted.

"Your turn, Tzion. Just hold the line tight. You'll be okay." Jay could see how unsteady Tzion was, even thinner than usual. His weekly 24-kilometer mountain biking kept him fit but left him with little, if anything, in reserve. "Just take it slow," he said. If need be, he'd risk a pendulum swing to reach Tzion and guide him across.

Effi leaned into the hole and shouted, "Come on, Tzion. It's easy."

As he backed out of the hole, Effi felt strong arms sweep him up. "Aunt Davi," he shouted and hugged her tightly.

She looked at him, not sure if she wanted to kiss him or kill him. He was covered from head to toe in dust and soot. "Are you okay, Ef?"

"Mostly."

"Good cause, I'm going to kill you," she said, breaking down in tears. "Later." Noam and everyone at the *Mishtara* were probably watching her. "Did you find Tzion?"

"Yeah, and then Joshua found us. You won't believe everything that's happening in there." He started coughing and couldn't stop.

"Take it easy. I've got water on my bike."

He started to go, then turned. "What's with the dog?"

"Go. Water. Rinse and spit."

She dropped down to the ventilation hole. "Jay, it's Davi. Are you okay?"

"Tzion's on his way over *Hatzalah*, if you've got a signal."

"On their way," she said, silently adding supposedly. Help should've been here by now.

From across the street, *Ahmed* watched and waited for the sound of *Barak* blowing himself up. What was taking him so long? He was sure he heard the sound of approaching sirens. *al-Masri* would not be pleased. As it was, he'd have to answer for spreading the word, a warning to people to avoid the marketplace near *Sha'ar Shechem*. No doubt, the abrupt change in the flow of Arabs coming and going through the gate hadn't escaped the Border Police's notice or their ever-watchful eyes in the sky.

As one of the few Arabs still about, *Ahmed* couldn't risk hanging around much longer. They were sure to take notice of him. Besides, he needed to get to work. *Ahmed* turned the corner onto *Nablus Road* and walked directly into the waiting arms of two Border Guards, previously alerted to "The Fixer's" presence and his interest in Zedekiah's Cave.

✻ ✻ ✻

"Okay, Tzion. Slow and steady. No hanging off ledges this time," Jay joked.

"Let's hope not," he replied.

Jay couldn't help but notice how tentative his friend's steps were; he also kept looking down at the fire.

"Eyes on me, Tzion. You almost got it." Jay wanted to reach out and bring him in the rest of the way. He could only imagine what he'd been through over the last couple of days. Jay kept one hand on the rope and reached out with the other breaking every rule of climbing.

Tzion was breathing hard "No rush, but…" Jay said.

"But hurry up," Tzion smiled and closed the last few feet. He held onto the line, then dropped to the ground, using Jay's legs to support his back.

"It's a short crawl and you're home free," Jay said, hoping to hide the urgency in his voice. His feet were slipping on the loose rock, even more so with Tzion's extra weight leaning into him.

Tzion's movements weren't as nimble as Effi's but he managed to maneuver himself over to the opening and crawl through.

"Got him," Davi shouted. Effi helped Tzion to his feet and over to the SUV.

"Okay, Jay you're up. Jay?" she shouted. Davi unzipped her jacket, forgetting her jacket was the only thing restraining Boomerang. The puppy broke free. Effi jumped after him, but he was too late as the puppy squeezed through the gate's lattice and ran into the cave.

"Jay, talk to me?" Still no answer. The rope line remained taut; at least, she knew he was on the other end. Davi considered crawling into the shaft, but didn't want to leave Effi and Tzion.

Unfortunately, Jay couldn't answer her. He was lying face-down, hugging the line, his feet only a few meters from the fire. A noise from deeper in the cave had startled him, twisting to see if it might be Joshua, only to knock himself off balance. Everything that could go wrong did as the belay line slipped, and he began sliding down the slope on a deadeye drop toward the burning fuel. He managed to grab hold of the ATC, stopping his descent. He took a moment to catch his breath, then started the treacherous climb, or rather crawl, back up. Chatting with Davi would have to wait.

The ventilation shaft opening was still a few feet beyond his reach. No point trying to stand now, and which would probably earn him a one-way ticket down again. He closed the distance, finally slapping his hand into the opening just as another hand grabbed his and helped haul him through. The assist was most welcome.

His face and abs were scraped, cut, or blistering in a few places, but otherwise, he was fine. Davi used her jacket sleeve to wipe the soot and dirt from his eyes. "Thanks," he said.

"No, thank you," she replied, nodding toward Effi perched on the SUV's runner near Tzion. "What about Joshua?"

"I don't know," Jay said, his voice barely above whisper.

Sirens blared in a cacophony of competing emergency vehicles which seemed to converge on the cave, the sound bouncing off the Old City walls. Then just as suddenly, faded off.

"What the hell," they said at the same time.

* * *

It was another ten minutes before two fire trucks, three police cars, one Magen David Adom ambulance, and two *United Hatzalah* Ambucycles converged on the cave. They were all more than a little late to the party, Davi thought. Jay had been tempted to drive Tzion to the hospital himself when his parents showed up and took him themselves. Truth be told, Jay didn't want to go anywhere, not without Joshua.

The search and rescue teams easily breached the entrance gate using heavy bolt cutters and quickly doused the fire near the emergency exit with foam. They sent more suited units farther into the cave to fight the other fires, and to look for Joshua. They started where he'd last been seen, near the Templar's Cavern. The first report came in an agonizing five minutes later.

"There's been a cave-in near Zedekiah's Tears. We've got two bodies. They're bringing them out now." Effi listened carefully.

Despite Davi's protests, he'd refused to go to the hospital, insisting he'd inhaled more smoke at *Lag b'omer* bonfires. She'd take him to Urgent Care later and have him checked out. Effi told the search and rescue team about the body in the Templar's cavern. A recovery. *Only* two bodies. The terrorist could be the other one. Joshua might still be alive.

The first of the bodies came out. A young man, early 20s; his body bloated and already decomposing. The medical emergency response teams from *United Hatzalah*, now joined by *Magen David Adom*, concurred… based on a preliminary examination of the body, the man had been dead for at least a day, maybe two. Despite the condition of the body, a photo ID from the Waldorf Astoria Hotel confirmed his identity. *Jibril Hassan*.

The second body took longer to retrieve as the team began digging it out from beneath the rubble. They managed to free an arm to check for a pulse. There wasn't one.

Suddenly, everything came to a terrifying stop when the words, "*Mechabel*," crackled over the radio.

The team of eight responders rushed out of the cave as a bomb disposal unit charged in. A late straggler from the team of emergency responders emerged, carrying Boomerang in his arms. He flipped up the visor on his helmet, taking a deep breath of fresh air. "Any takers?" he asked.

Davi rushed forward, "Boomerang!"

"He yours?"

"She, and sort of."

"Well, this girl is one brave little pup. She started barking and led us to the rock pile and the *mechabel*."

She looked at the future *Oketz* trainee. "You did that, girl?" Davi asked, wondering if the puppy had tried to find Joshua.

"You didn't find anyone else?" Jay asked, coming alongside Davi.

"No, and the *chablanim* still have to clear the area before we can continue the search."

"I sense a but…" Jay said.

"What is it?" Davi demanded.

"Nothing, best to have a Vet check him, her, out," the firefighter said, scratching Boomerang's head. He decided against telling the pair that they'd found the puppy sniffing the cave's floor in a tight circle pattern, at a spot *next* to the rubble, and she'd only started barking once they arrived. "If he's in there, we'll bring your friend out."

"Thanks," Davi said, but she had to ask. "What the hell took you guys so long getting here?"

"We got diverted at the last minute. There was a major cave-in near *Sha'ar HaArayot*, Lion's Gate."

"At the gate?" she asked, finding that hard to believe.

"Nah, below one of the churches along the Via Dolorosa."

Bombs going off here. Cave-in there. What were the odds? Jay and Davi thought at almost the exact same moment and looked at one another knowingly.

"Mostly structural damage. We rescued one guy. Sort of. A tour group was visiting the ruins below. They were right there. Their priest or whatever you want to call him, got him out. The guy got it all on his GoPro."

"Thanks again. Glad you guys made it here," Jay said.

"*Achi*, you did a helluva job getting your people out."

Not *all* my people, Jay wanted to say. Davi took his hand and squeezed it, knowingly.

Then she remembered seeing Anders entering one of the buildings along the Via Dolorosa. The name was written above the door on the lintel; and, near the doorframe there was a medallion denoting it as one the Stations of the Cross. She closed her eyes, trying to recall the number on the medallion. Number 2, the Second Station of the Cross.

"You wouldn't happen to know the name of the Church."

"Not sure. Something in Latin, Greek, maybe. It's all over the news," he said, then left to join the rest of his squad.

"What?" Jay asked as Davi handed Boomerang to him.

She pulled up the *Keshet 12* newsfeed on her phone, and they watched it together.

The video wall behind the news anchor showed a freeze-framed photo… the "money shot" of a man's hand reaching out from the rubble like the mythical Excalibur sword. Only the hilt of this "sword" was the man's index finger wearing a silver ring bearing the iconic battle standard of the medieval Knights Templar, an iconic red cross on white enamel.

The lore of the Knights Templar includes a mystery about the Temple treasures and untold wealth, fodder for writers and historians alike. Charged with protecting Christian pilgrims to Jerusalem beginning in 1119, their iconic Cross patée can be found on buildings throughout the Christian and Arab Quarters. Their mission ended in 1187 when the armies of *Saladin*,

Sultan of Syria and Egypt routed them. Jerusalem remained under near-continuous Muslim rule for 730 years, as her "ownership" passed from one Arab clan to another... *Saladin's Ayyubid* dynasty was conquered in 1260 by the *Mamluks*, which lasted until the beginning of Ottoman Rule in 1517 for the next four hundred years.

During World War I, on December 9, 1917, British forces took control of Jerusalem, marking the start of Colonial rule that lasted for the next thirty-one years. In a *quid pro quo* agreement, the *Hashemite* family, long-serving members of the ruling class in *Mecca*, was recognized for their support of the Arab Revolt in helping Britain's fight against the Ottoman Empire. Their reward? In 1921, Britain ceded control of the area east of the Jordan River, birthing the country of Transjordan, later renamed the *Hashemite Kingdom of Jordan*. During Israel's War of Independence in 1948, Jordan laid siege to Jerusalem, destroying the Jewish Quarter and much of the *Har HaZei'tim* cemetery, before annexing East Jerusalem, including the Jewish Quarter.

That status quo remained in place until Jerusalem was once again returned to Jewish sovereignty after nearly 1,897 years, liberating the Holy City on June 7, 1967, Day 3 of the Six-Day War. Jerusalem remains unified, a place for all peoples, and with but a few exceptions, peoples of all faiths and beliefs have unfettered access to Holy sites.

Some see the reunification of Jerusalem as the end of a long exile... the beginning of Redemption, *Geula*, as the footsteps of the Anointed One draw ever closer...

> On that day his feet shall stand on the Mount of Olives, which lies before Jerusalem on the east; and the Mount of Olives shall be split in two from east to west by a very wide valley, so that one half of the Mount shall move northward, and the other half southward.
>
> – Zechariah 14:4

Epilogue

For Joshua, the next few moments carried an eerie sense of *déjà vu*, but which were also strangely comforting. A host of unanswered questions ran through his mind. Dead? Not dead? Did he stop the *shahid* or not? How had he gotten onto Temple Mount from Zedekiah's Cave? And who were all the others, "standing" to either side of him?

Strangest of all was the feeling in his body, such as it was or rather wasn't. He certainly couldn't perceive one in himself or the others, but he was "standing" on the Temple Mount's ramparts. Here, wherever *here* was. He had no reliable ground truth that adequately covered *shahid* encounters, or the "after" moments.

Joshua ventured a better look at those around him. While he didn't perceive them as having heads or eyes, their focus was nonetheless trained on a figure in the distance, near the top of *Har HaZei'tim*.

"I don't understand," he said, directing the comment more to himself than to the "others."

"It's all for one and one for all here, son."

"What?"

"You know, the three musketeers. Don't you remember?"

"Yeah, it's one of my favorite movies. But what does that have to do with anything? I just want to know what's going on?"

"Don't we all?"

"And?"

"Well, that's hard to say. You three are the last to arrive. Guess there's no more room at the inn, so to speak."

"What are you talking about?" No, not talking. The conversation was happening in his head. He needed to get some answers and decided to play along. "You said three, who else?"

"The first was Red over there. Bet she was a real looker back in the day. Not so long ago. Can't tell so much now, but you get a feel for these kinds of things."

"Julia," Joshua said, sensing a warmth, a smile radiating from her center.

"She'd come and gone before. Not really here or there for a time, but here now."

"You said, the three of us. Who else?"

"Well, him," directing Joshua's attention to his right. "Can't quite figure him out though. Readings are all messed up."

Joshua could "read" him alright. He'd spent the last minutes of his life with the *shahid*, though the dark energy he'd vibed from him was gone, replaced by light, dimmer than the others around him, but light, nonetheless.

Looking to his left, then to his right, there were no other empty spaces, just a line of "others" as far as his "eyes" could see. *Oh, god, this had to be a bad dream, or more likely Hell,* Joshua thought. He couldn't imagine spending eternity in this nebulous ambiguity, especially with this guy. He'd damn well demand a refund on life. Maybe, ask for do-over. Still, he couldn't shake the feeling there was something oddly familiar about the old man. The way he "spoke" struck a chord with him, answering but not really answering a question, a lot like his *Opa Jacob*.

Since the old man seemed to be the only one speaking with him, Joshua decided to give it another go. "So, here, being where?" he asked, hoping to extract a bit more information.

"Well, not there. You know, here. Look enough with the questions, already. You'll find out soon enough. It's been a long wait," the old guy sighed.

"Waiting for what?"

The old guy laughed, then added a heavy sigh of resignation. "What indeed, my young friend. What indeed?"

Another Opa-ism. "Don't you have any actual answers?"

"Definitely more questions than answers, I'm afraid."

"I don't understand."

"Such is the nature of things."

"So how long are we supposed to be like… this?"

"Now, that's a good question."

"And…"

"Hard to say."

"Oy…"

"There's the spirit."

This line of questioning was getting him nowhere fast. "Look, I'm just asking for your opinion, that's all. What do you think?"

"What was the question?"

"How long will we be here?" If he could shake this guy, then maybe *here* wouldn't be so bad. He could talk to Julia, apologize to her for everything. Funny, how she didn't seem angry, upset, or anything when she "smiled" acknowledging him. She was just here, and a helluva lot better adjusted than he was at the moment.

"Now, Time with a capital T is an interesting metric."

"I'm sorry, what?"

"Time, it's a reference point or not. Doesn't carry much meaning here. But to answer your question, it's fair to say as long as it takes…"

"Again, not exactly an answer."

"You haven't been here long enough to complain, kid."

"I'm not complaining, just wondering is all."

"Most of us have been waiting a very long time. A very long Time, relatively speaking of course."

"Waiting for what?"

"You really don't know, do you?"

"By all means, please enlighten me."

The old man paused before speaking again. As instructed, he'd held his peace since his grandson, the soul he'd known and loved in this past life, had only just arrived. "Why, Joshie, we've been waiting for you."

✻ ✻ ✻

The Celestial trumpets sounded in Heaven, a call to gather and mark an ending and a beginning. The Heavenly Hosts lined the shimmering walls to bid one of their own goodbye; round-robin wishes for a safe journey. *Archangels, Seraphim, Chayot HaKodesh, Ofanim*, and the *Chashmalim* stood side-by-side with the *Kedoshim*, the Holy Ones, who would remain above but were forever linked to those standing guard on the walls of Jerusalem. Together, they breathed as one *neshama*, a single *neshima*, a breath.

The 1.7 million Guardian Angels, called into being by the blasts from HaMikdash3.0's *tekiot* stood solemnly filling the in-between spaces across Heaven's ten dimensions, its ten directions — Beginning and End; Good and Evil; Up and Down; East and West; North and South — the pairings twinned to the *Sefirot*, ready to complete their final task of fire.

Uri'el stood in the wide aisle between them, spreading his wings across all the Heavens and released the *Cherub* he'd guarded for over 2,500 Earth-years. The Time had come for the *Cherubs* to once again spread their wings over the Seat of Glory covering the Ark of the Covenant. The other *Cherub* had remained with the Holy Ark in its hiding place, ever-present on the Earthly plane but dimensionally shifted beyond Space and Time. Hidden and fully protected from the dark forces who sought to ensnare its power.

In an instant, Uri'el and the HaMikdash3.0 Guardian Angels entered the Earthly plane, breaching the last *rakiah*, the separation between the waters above and the waters below. As Uri'el passed through the *mechitza* separating the spaces, the *Cherub* freed itself while Uri'el and the GAs remained in the upper reaches of the Lower World watching as the *Cherub* flew above those assembled at the foot of *Har HaZei'tim*. Like a seamstress weaving a golden cloth, it pierced their line, crafting a ribbon of light, gathering the sparks, spinning the soul parts onto the glistening thread.

Pulling from the left, then right, and then left again the *Cherub* drew the soul parts closer, stopping on either side of Joshua, before once again taking leave to gather more sparks, until all that could be gathered had been joined as one. The *Cherub* circled above the *Kidron Valley*, above the *Mount of Olives*, spinning and revealing each of its faces in a glorious dance of praise and anticipation. The wait was finally over as one *Cherub* was joined by a second, spinning together in a dance of long-lost friends, separated by Time. They circled the valley once more, before completing the dance, the golden thread held between them. They released the gathered sparks, setting the shining thread spinning like a top, a whirlwind of fiery light gaining strength with each turn and drawing down Light from Above to nourish the assembled souls. *Nefesh* from the world of *Asiya*, the lower worlds, joined with *Ruach* from the plane of *Yetzira* in creation, joining with *Neshama* from the consciousness of *Beriya*. At long last, *Chaya* from that far place known as *Atzilt* stepped closer to *Yechida*, the transcendent G-d consciousness beyond the known and unknown, THE Spark of Sparks.

STRANGE FIRE

Chaya took comfort in knowing that perhaps one day *all* the sparks would be joined into an even greater soul consciousness, a unity with the Upper *Sefirot* of Wisdom (*Chochmah*) and Understanding (*Binah*) together bringing Knowledge in approaching the *Sefira* of *Keter*, in true and trusted communion with the Divine. That day was now one moment closer when they too would know her. The *Cherubim* paused in front of Joshua, showing him each of their faces, dipping their heads in gratitude and making an offering of the spinning whirlwind of light and fire.

With the dance completed they disappeared into the Old City walls.

"That was different," Joshua said. Then in what might be perceived as his eyes opening wide, added, "And so's that." His gaze fell on the human face of the Archangel Uri'el in full-winged glory appearing before him.

"It's time," Uri'el said.

"Wait, I know you."

"As I know you, Eliyahu…" Uri'el paused, allowing the name to resonate with the man once known as Joshua Eli Katz in whom the *gilgul* of generations of scholars, prophets, and priests was found. Incarnations of *gilgulim* and *iburim*… *Elisha the Prophet. Shmuel HaNavi. Chizkiyahu, King of Judah. Matisyahu ben Yochanan HaChashmonai. Rabbi Akiva. Rabbi Yochanan ben Zakai*… and more.

Eliyahu, not Eli. A secret hidden in plain sight.

The comfort of finally knowing himself, past and present filled the man once known as Joshua with a sense of calm, of being that he'd never known in life. Time passed in the blink of an eye as the Wheel of his Life continued to turn, arriving at *Pinchas*, the son of *Elazar*, the son of *Aharon HaKohen*. He'd been joined with *Pinchas* in life as an *ibur*, a higher soul, an add-on to assist *Pinchas* in his rectification. But there was more yet to know, of yet another past linked to the brothers *Nadav* and *Abihu*, the sons of *Aharon HaKohen*.

The brothers had brought strange fire to the altar and were consumed by fire. They had been brought forth from the highest soul level from *Adam Kadmon*, the very first. And while their earthly actions were judged harshly, their sin of bringing strange fire became a warning, repeated throughout the generations and in their sacrifice saving others from a similar fate. Their intentions had always been pure, seeking the Divine, and so their souls lived on through the generations of Man, until *this* Time was at its end.

The man *Yehoshua Eliyahu ben David HaKohen* had also brought strange fire, but his intentions had also been pure, and the reward of generations past was now his to give to the world.

Uri'el shifted his wings to reveal Elijah's fiery *merkava*, his chariot, the flames burning with the love of the 1.7 million Guardian Angels for the man they knew as Joshua, captured with each *tekiah* blast that drew them out from the Spirit.

"The world waits," Uri'el said. "The Anointed One can wait no longer. It is time for you to announce his arrival to the people and families of the Book."

Elijah the Prophet, *Eliyahu HaNavi* climbed on board the fiery *merkava* as the sound of 600,000 *tekiah* blasts, one for each of the reassembled souls, completed soul roots. The call reverberated across the Heavens, shaking the foundations of the world and reaching the hearing hearts of people from one end of the Earth to the other, proclaiming the Oneness of G-d.

※ ※ ※

Jay re-read Joshua's letter for the umpteenth time, wondering how his friend had known. Maybe that Spidey sense of his was working overtime, or maybe he just knew. In theory, he was the only "J" left from their band of three musketeers. In theory, since Joshua's body had never been found in the rubble, despite searching for days, then weeks. Nothing. It was as if he'd just disappeared, taken away like *Eliyahu HaNavi* in a whirlwind of fire. Joshua left him in charge of everything, the foundation, his trust fund, the patents, the company, his Rehavia and Netanya apartments, and Davi.

> *I know you loved Julia more than I ever did, but Jay you need to open your heart again. Julia would have wanted that for you. I know, I do.*
>
> *I don't want to hear any arguments either, it's about time you moved to Jerusalem. It's long overdue. On that front, I think you and Davi would really get along. You might have to pries Boomerang out of her arms or maybe you can look at it as a package deal.*
>
> *In the interest of full disclosure, my gut tells me I may have left something behind. A final bit of unfinished business. I leave him or her in your care as well. If you can, throw my family name in there somehow.*

I love you, achi. I couldn't have asked for a better brother or friend in this world... or any other.

Joshua Eli Katz

Yehoshua Eliyahu Katz

Him or her, Jay laughed. "You chose the wrong Boolean operator, *achi*. Not "or" but an "and" function. One of each, *achi*. One of each."

He folded the letter, slipping it back into the envelope, then picked up the *Dimensional Torah Codes* printout. Joshua's last search for answers beyond this world. The timestamp, read shortly after midnight, 00:52, early Sunday morning. The printout was sitting in the tray when Jay opened the apartment a few weeks later. The file was named *miani*. The file name took him an extra second to realize *miani* was: *mi ani*, who am I?

He scanned the printout, immediately recognizing the text from his own *Bar Mitzvah parsha*, *Shemini*; Joshua's *Bar Mitzvah parsha* too. The story of *Aharon's* sons, *Nadav* and *Abihu*. Jay wasn't surprised the encoded answers were in Joshua's birth *parsha*. There were numerous color-coded, highlighted letters throughout the text forming words across horizontal, vertical, and diagonal axes that could be read forwards and backwards in a discontinuous crossword-like pattern. One string of overlapping letters stood out from the others. Two words. *Eliyahu HaNavi*, Elijah the Prophet.

"Jay, can you grab the coffee carafe from the counter," Davi called out from the balcony.

"On it," he shouted, slipping the printout into a larger envelope for safekeeping.

Jay joined Davi on the balcony, leaning over to kiss her. He held her in his arms, her head resting naturally against his chest. She grabbed his hand and put it against the right side of her belly.

"Kicking up a storm." Jay smiled.

"A tandem drum set between the two of them."

They stood there for a long moment, looking at the magnificent structure hovering over the Old City, over the Temple Mount. The reports were still pouring in reaffirming a simple truth that no matter where people were in the world, by some miraculous, hocus-pocus folding of space, the *Third Beit HaMikdash* could be seen from one end of the Earth to the other.

"I can't imagine ever getting tired of this view."

"Something else, I have Joshua to thank for."

"That *we* have Joshua to thank for…"

"Do you think he knows how everything turned out?"

"I'm guessing, yes." Davi smiled. "Oooh," then yelping, "ow. Ow. Ow. Hmmm."

Boomerang no longer a lap dog, now weighed in at a healthy sixty-plus pounds. She dropped her chew toy, sensitive to her mom's condition and immediately ran to Davi's side.

"Kids, mom needs to get to the hospital," Jay called.

"Finally," the six-year-old blonde-haired boy said to his twin sister as they raced out to the balcony.

"I hope it's a girl," Cate said.

"Boys town all the way. Three to one," Katz said.

"We'll see," Jay said, then smiled at Davi knowingly.

* * *

Eliyahu HaNavi stood next to Uri'el and smiled too.

"Everything in its time. *B'sha'ah Tovah.*"

Acknowledgements

Many thanks to my early supporters who were "allowed" to read only excerpts from *Strange Fire* when I wanted to share meaningful scenes, but without giving away critical plot points. I still kept quite a few to myself, especially Joshua's *gilgul/ibur* (reincarnation) lineage. Thank you to my family and friends: Tehila Goldberg, Penny Kaganoff, Aviva Kashuk, Rabbi Aaron Dovid & Bina Sujanani Poston, Rav Zev Shandalov, Koppel Shvueli, Leya Shvueli, Aver & Edna Zussman, and Rayna Zussman… each of you not only championed the work in your own way, and encouraged me along the way, whether directly and indirectly (and whether you know it or not). I appreciate the special permissions from: Rina Ariel, Jamie Geller, Matisyahu, Rabbi Yakov Nagen, Matan Raz, YONINA (Yoni & Nina Tokayer), and Rabbi Moshe Zeldman. My sincerest apologies to anyone I missed. Thank you to all the people who helped me grow through their insights, lending libraries and welcoming resources as I ventured into new areas of study. Most of all, thank you to many others, past and present, who continue to be a source of inspiration.

The *Strange Fire* story includes significant details from my life. My birth *parsha* is *Shemini*. An interesting *Torah* portion which includes the story of *Nadav* and *Abihu*, the sons of Aaron the High Priest, who brought strange fire. The second notable fact and influence in the story is that my mother's family Priestly line, the Robert Katzenstein/Katz line, has ended so no possibilities here for us filling any future High Priest roles should a position open up. While I began writing *Strange Fire* in the summer of 2019, I stopped abruptly during COVID-19 and did not pick up the story again until the tragedies of October 7, 2023. Like many, I renewed my soul-searching mission trying to understand the "why" of it all or at least move with the missing pieces in my heart, mind, and soul.

Strange Fire became my lifeline, immersing myself in the stories of the heroes and the victims, the dead and the kidnapped; the ongoing war and the pain of the families surviving day-by-day under the constant fears for their loved ones; and, the ongoing loss of life, of young people killed in the prime of their lives, and the darkness that seemed to overtake the light on a daily basis. *Strange Fire* was written during this time, in real time, and captured the heart-wrenching truth of people I know and people I've never met, but whose stories and lives touched mine. I took certain liberties with their lives but only hope that I honored them by telling parts of their life stories. If I have failed, it was not intentional. The *Strange Fire* story ends officially six days before *Rosh Hashanah 2024*. Though the story of this time continues.

While preparing the manuscript for publication in the months that followed many more IDF soldiers were injured and killed in the south and north; Yahya Sinwar was killed; hostage bodies were recovered from Gaza; a "deal" beginning in January 2025 saw the release of hostages; and the body of First Sergeant Oron Shaul (HY"D) was finally brought home after ten long years. A final note, one of the "characters" in the story, "Ari of Judah" is the avatar ambassador for HaMikdash3.0. I named him after Ari Fuld (HY"D), a person I greatly admired and who helped me find my voice… a voice I hope you, my readers, will appreciate.

I'll close with a very special thank you to all those who let me share some of the most beautiful and painful parts of your lives and put them on the pages of *Strange Fire*. Most especially, thank you *Ha-Shem* for giving me the heart and wisdom to write *Strange Fire*.

Tami "T/R" Ellison is a visual storyteller; a scientist/inventor with six image-based technology patents; and a photographer with an extensive fine art photography portfolio with numerous solo and group exhibitions. Her writing reflects these diverse interests and skills, conveying rich visual textures and an easy confidence when exploring bold concepts in medicine and technology. A dominant theme in her work is the examination of ethical and philosophical issues while exploring the Human experience – a narrative Gestalt where the story transcends the sum of its parts. With roots in Chicago, she moved to Colorado after 9/11 to be closer to family, and in 2014 she fulfilled a lifelong dream, moving to Israel where her heart, soul, and mindful pursuits became confluent. Tami began writing her initials as T/R long before it became fashionable, signing her photography using her Hebrew middle name, Rishona. She holds a thesis research Master of Science degree from UIC, with extensive research in developmental model systems, expression patterns, and systems-level regulatory control mechanisms.

Author Q & A with T/R Ellison

1. **Throughout the story, you hint to Joshua's true identity, emphasizing his middle initial. Are there other clues?**

   Yes, but if I told you what would be the fun in that?

2. **Do you believe that a hovering Temple is possible?**

   Taking the view that the Temple is a possibility, then a hovering structure is certainly within the realm of possibilities, both in the physical and metaphysical sense. In Judaism, there is a view which holds that the Temple is in Heaven, waiting to descend to Earth, but which doesn't necessarily mean it has to touch ground.

   If you think about it, in many ways we've been primed for years to look to the skies, to see unusual hovering crafts whether you call these UFOs or now known more as UAP – Unidentified Aerial Phenomenon.

3. **You choose to include semi/autobiographical information in *Strange Fire*, why?**

   I think honesty is important and writing *Strange Fire* became a way for me to channel my energies and emotions in the aftermath of October 7, 2023. As such, I tried to be authentic and true to myself by weaving some of my family's history into the story, and addressing questions I've had in life.

   The family name of Katz/Katzenstein is on my mother's side. My mother's family are *Kohanim* and our line, through my grandfather Robert/Reuven Katzenstein, has ended. Joshua's middle name is the same as my great grandfather on my father's side.

   My Hebrew birthday is *Nisan* 27 and my birth *Parsha* in the *Torah* is *Shemini* from the book of *Vayikra*/Leviticus. This particular *Torah* portion describes the eight-day preparations taken by the *Kohanim*/

Priests in order to bring sacrifices, which is the translation of the word, *Shemini*. The *parsha* mentions the deaths of *Nadav* and *Abihu* (Aaron's sons) for having brought **strange fire** before the altar; hence the name of the book. *Nisan* 27 corresponds to *Yom HaShoah*, Holocaust Remembrance Day, and while it may sound irrational I've always felt that I'm driven to fulfill unfinished business for people who were killed in the Holocaust. In Judaism, there are different types reincarnated souls and different reasons for reincarnation. Lastly, I've always had an interest in the *Beit HaMikdash*, the Temple, probably dating back to before I was born.

The rest of the story integrates my worldview, the philosophical questions of why we're here, where's all this/we are all heading from a *Kabbalistic* standpoint, as well as a utopian perspective in the hopes for a better world. Most importantly, *Strange Fire* was my way of coping with life in the wake of October 7, 2023. The pontificating and moralizing are all me, as is the hope for a better future for all working from this side of sanity, and which pre-dated October 7.

4. **Where did the idea for *Strange Fire* come from?**

You can glean part of the answer from my response above, but I think of myself as a spiritual person and a big believer in providence and confluence. Providence of what will be and the confluence of events, people, and circumstances that lead to an outcome or path. In Judaism the term *Hashgacha Pratis* (individual supervision) and *Hashgacha Klali* (Divine communal oversight) would describe how these elements come together.

5. **You chose to mirror the lives of actual people and stories – living and dead, why?**

I'm only sorry I couldn't include more people and their stories. True heroes. People whose lives moved me and which I hope will be remembered in a slightly different way through *Strange Fire*. Many of these stories were simply part of living during this time.

For example, I attended the program organized by Tzvi Steve Zussman, father of Sgt. Major (res.) Ben Zussman (z"l) held in the Great Synagogue Plaza. During the program, a photo of Aner Shapira, Ben Zussman, and Hersh Goldberg-Polin as 7th graders at the Himmelfarb school was presented. That picture was juxtaposed with the images of the three as young men. The story of that image is an integral part of *Strange Fire*. In many ways, I became a reporter of what I experienced, but in this case, I told much of their story from the perspective of a thirteen-year-old boy.

6. **Is there a sequel to *Strange Fire*?**

    Without giving away the open-ended questions that remain, there is a time gap to be filled in. So, the short answer would be, yes. But as creative as I may be in storytelling, prophecy is not part of my skillset so we may just have to wait and see how things shake out.

7. **You incorporated humor into the story, most uniquely delivered by the Guardian Angels, why?**

    It's certainly a coping mechanism for me to get through heavy content, and I imagine also for the reader. I also imagine that Celestials have got to have a sense of humor as they have a front-row seat to the machinations of we Earth-dwellers.

8. **Both *Strange Fire* and *The Chladni Progression: The Power to Heal* deal in metaphysical and spiritual concepts, is that your "happy-place" genre?**

    I'm not sure it can be considered a genre, but I believe there is more to heaven and earth than what we can see or perceive with our five senses, and that our understanding of Space, Time, and Dimensions is still in its infancy. These are topics that have always interested me.

    In Book One of *The Chladni Progression*, the protagonist Blaise Manning notes that, "he knows what he knows, and knows enough to know he doesn't know shit which keeps him always wanting to know more." That's a great message that hopefully keeps my ego in check and always on a quest to learn more.

9. **Any strange things you can share that happened when you were writing *Strange Fire*?**

    Where should I start? As I mentioned, I took writing cues from people, places and things around me. The dream that Joshua has, I had. For the story, however, I added a fourth panel/storyboard; my dream only had three panels. But one of the strangest was during the final copyediting and proofing of *Strange Fire*.

    There's always a missing word, an italics that should or shouldn't be, and/or a sentence to be restructured, but this particular missing piece was a page number. One page without a page number. It's something you notice, which I did.

    Considering the nature of the book, I take nothing for granted, and I had to wonder. Did it mean anything? Since you're probably wondering it was page 379. The pages before it had numbers, and the pages after it were numbered as well, so it didn't make much sense. Why this particular page? My fantastic book designer, Benjie Herskowitz, asked if I wanted to fix it. I said, no, feeling like I was at the Blackjack table, saying "let it ride."

    In the days before in finalizing the back cover text, I began re-framing the book as less of a thriller and more of a mystery, asking the question: "Who is Joshua E. Katz?" Page 379 was in fact the answer to that very question in the big reveal. Strange…

10. **Could you go into a bit more detail about the *Torah Codes*?**

    That's a great question, but I'll limit my response to what I know and understand. The continuous wraparound analysis method and CT-styled reconstructions using cross-section of a rolled scroll were ideas I came up with, but which are in fact active areas in *Torah Codes* research. In the story, the Archangel Uri'el describes the fidelity with which each of the 304,805 letters and 79,980 words has been maintained down through the ages, thousands of years, and how it has been analyzed by scholars and mystics without the benefit of AI or supercomputers.

Today, we're able to "crunch" the text in new and amazing ways. From a mathematical standpoint, we can appreciate the elegant probabilities of finding words and ideas are clustered together to tell a story within a story – many life stories hidden within the *Torah*.

Printed in Dunstable, United Kingdom